Reaching 40

The Richard Stockton College of New Jersey

Edited by Ken Tompkins and Rob Gregg

Editors
Ken Tompkins and Rob Gregg

Copy Editor
Lisa Honaker

Designer
Margot Alten

Cover Photo
Margot Alten

Endpaper Art
David Ahlsted, 'Seasons'

Published and distributed by:
The Richard Stockton College of New Jersey
101 Vera King Farris Drive
Galloway, NJ 08205-9441

ISBN: 978-0-615-48940-7
Library of Congress Control Number:
2011929983

http://www.stockton.edu/reaching40

Contents

Preface: Gordon K. Davies   VII

Prologue: Ken Tompkins and Rob Gregg   1

The Stockton Idea

Elite Education for State College Students   5
William Daly

Getting Started

What Have I Done?—Elizabeth Alton   16
Ken Tompkins

Choosing a Solution—David Taylor   17
Ken Tompkins

No Mere Substitute—Magda Leuchter   19
Ken Tompkins

Shakespeare Had it Wrong   20
Ken Tompkins and Rob Gregg

Breaking Eggs—Richard Bjork   22
Rob Gregg

Children of the Sixties   25
Daniel N. Moury

In a Heart Beat   28
Ken Tompkins

Observations   30
Richard Gajewski

Stockton Campus Planning, 1969-1974   32
Richard N. Schwartz

Different from the Beginning—NAMS   35
Daniel N. Moury

Why Go East?   43
Richard E. Pesqueira

Policing the Academy   45
James A. Williams

Dealing with Unexpected Change   47
Joseph A. Tosh

The Sinking of the Mayflower   49
Lew Steiner

Settling In

"Stockton Changed Me, More than I Changed Stockton"—Peter Mitchell   52
Rob Gregg

Building An Environnemt For Excellence—Vera King Farris   55
Harvey Kesselman

Shared Governance?   57
Robert Helsabeck

The Union Made Us Strong   62
John W. Searight

Life Sports—Beginning and End   66
Joseph Rubenstein

The Mighty Burner—G. Larry James   69
Rob Gregg

When Lower K-Wing Rocked the World   70
Melaku Lakew and Patricia Reid-Merritt

Providing Funds   72
Jeanne Sparacino Lewis

Reflections   74
Nancy M. Messina

Nurturing Community   76
Elaine Ingulli

Voices and Experiences that Echo Across Time   77
Franklin Ojeda Smith

In Good Faith   79
Nancy W. Hicks

Stockton's Impact on the Community   81
Israel Posner

The Organizational Paradox   83
William C. Lubenow

The Primacy of Teaching

What Then Of a Legacy?   87
Joseph L. Walsh

Designing the Self—Creating General Studies at Stockton   90
Ken Tompkins

Joyous Serendipidity   94
G. Jan Colijn

The Tsardeana of Stockdons—Ingie LaFleur   96
Penelope Dugan

Not Left Behind   98
Gordon William Sensiba

Dancing in Chains   101
Leonard Solo

The Origins of Teacher Education   104
Ronald J. Moss

A Brief History of NAMS   106
Roger Wood

A History of the Psychology Program   108
David Lester

Recent Trends in Teaching

Cheerleader or Dreamer?—Stockton's Teaching Excellence   112
Alan F. Arcuri

Assessment—Good Teaching Practice   114
Sonia V. Gonsalves

The Quantitative Reasoning Across the Disciplines (QUAD) Program   116
Frank A. Cerreto

Planting a Program with Deep Roots and Good Growth—Writing at Stockton   119
Penelope Dugan

Born (and Reborn) within the Currents of Academia—The Shifting Literature Curriculum   122
Thomas Kinsella

Changing Lives—The Interdisciplinary Minors   124
Linda Williamson Nelson

The Information Age at Stockton   126
James McCarthy

advising@stockton.edu   129
Peter L. Hagen

The Most "Transfer-friendly" Institution in the State   131
Thomas J. Grites

The Spaces We Occupy

Environmental Studies at Stockton   135
Claude Epstein

Sustainability at Stockton   138
Tait Chirenje and Patrick Hossay

The Natural Environment   145
Jamie Cromartie

Promoting the Professions

Professional Studies—Competing Perspectives   149
Marc Lowenstein

Health Science Education at Stockton   152
Nancy Taggart Davis

Embracing Graduate Education   155
Bess Kathrins

Growth and Change—Graduate Study   156
Deborah M. Figart

Looking Forward

Toward the Environmentally Responsible Learning Community—Herman J. Saatkamp, Jr.   160
Rob Gregg

20/20 Vision   162
Claudine Keenan

Changes at the Turn of the Century   163
Claudine Keenan and Rob Gregg (with assistance from David Carr and Marc Lowenstein)

A Tribute to Stephen Dunn   165
BJ Ward

Poems by Stephen Dunn   166
Stephen Dunn

Not Taken for Granted—Grants and Grants-seeking   168
Beth Olsen

Stockton's Regional Economic Contribution   172
Oliver Cooke

Impacting the Region—SRI & ETTC   175
Harvey Kesselman and Patricia Weeks

Enhancing Public Child Welfare   177
Diane S. Falk

Tales from an Argonaut   179
Emily Heerema

More than the Sum of it's Parts

Epilogue   182
Ken Tompkins and Rob Gregg

The Contributors   184

Preface

The organization and content of *Reaching 40* come as no surprise. This is not a college faculty and staff that would produce a six-chapter book organized chronologically or around themes, with an introduction and conclusion.

No, it is entirely fitting that the book contains sixty essays (at my last counting) that are reports, reflections, judgments, and commendations. It also is fitting that there is some disagreement among authors, occasionally about what happened and more often about what it meant. But I am surprised that the disagreements are so mild and that there are so few of them.

While the essays are eclectic and nominally about a variety of topics, a single theme seems to run through almost all of them: how to be useful. Primarily, the challenge is to be useful to the students, many of whom have been the first in their families to attend college. But the essays also discuss being useful to local communities, the state, and to people in general.

Being useful to students was the key goal of Stockton's founders, and it seems to remain the goal today. This challenges everyone—faculty, administrators, and the students themselves—to find the right balance and pedagogies to combine general education and practical skills in undergraduate education. Essay after essay touches upon combining these two elements in the best possible ways.

The undergraduate experience should help students learn the best that has been thought and said over thousands of years and, at the same time, help them acquire the tools to do what they think needs to be done in this world. It should teach the skills of critical and quantitative thinking, writing, and speaking, while at the same time teaching the everyday skills needed for work, family, and community engagement.

This was the commitment of Stockton's founders; it was what we argued about constantly during the time I was there (1971-1973); and it seems still to be what the community cares—and argues—about. There is no final answer, no solution to the challenge of combining these two elements. Our lives keep changing; so do what we need to know and how we come to know it and what we do and how we do it. Richard Stockton College has struggled creatively and courageously with this question for four decades now. It has not been alone among colleges and universities, but the College is distinguished by its continued emphasis upon General Studies, the persistence of its effort, and its results.

Stockton was founded at a time when American higher education still was increasing its capacity to handle growing numbers of students. The capacity-building continued, probably for too long. At the same time, the reward system for institutions of higher education placed more and more value on selectivity in admissions. The more applicants rejected, the better the college or university. This is a kind of elitism to which Stockton did not originally aspire.

The decision to become more selective in its admissions seems to be important in Stockton's history. The College may have been faced with a difficult choice: change its curriculum and maintain its commitment to students of average ability and those who were often unprepared, or keep its curriculum and admit better-prepared students.

Stockton originally proposed, in Bill Daly's words, "to make available to state college students at state college prices the kind of interdisciplinary and individualized liberal arts instruction . . . usually reserved for students at the most selective and expensive private liberal arts colleges." It would do so while recognizing that the "best and most expensive undergraduate education in the country was to be delivered to the students who most needed it, but who also could least afford it and (as a number of early critics argued) might also be the least prepared for it and the least interested in it." Here again there is a struggle that will not have a final resolution. We want to offer excellent general education to average students, but there are people with poor or average preparation who are neither ready for this kind of education nor interested in it.

The discussion that began with Stockton's founders and has continued at the College during the past forty years is still going on across our nation. Advocates of increasing the numbers of Americans, especially those between ages twenty-five and thirty-four, who hold college degrees or certificates can become dangerously utilitarian in their assumptions about the value of higher education: jobs for individuals and global competitiveness for the nation. They can ignore the broader purposes of baccalaureate education.

It is easy to forget that college education is not simply preparation for a job or a profession. But higher education has often been seen in very practical terms in the most prestigious universities, and it still is. In 1871, exactly a century before Stockton opened at the Mayflower Hotel, a Harvard student told Henry Adams that the "degree of Harvard College is worth money to me in Chicago." Only a few years after Stockton was founded, a professor glumly wrote to me that "there now are only two majors at Yale: pre-med and pre-law."

Colleges and universities should not be just places for career or professional training. But it has become critically important to help students acquire (I quote Bill Daly again) the "knowledge and practical skills that . . . permit them to transform themselves and their futures into what they decided that they should be." Even if General Studies at Stockton has become less spontaneous and creative, the fact that it remains a key part of the curriculum after all these years, and that a workable balance between higher order and practical skills is still sought, is a singular achievement for the women and men who have taught and administered at the College.

Still, the past forty years are history, and the next forty will play out differently. The massive recession that began in 2008 is global. It still hampers economic growth and the financial security of millions of Americans, as well as people in most other nations. It won't be over soon. This fiscal calamity will influence our lives for decades.

Higher education is called for now, not to create more capacity, but to use what we have more effectively. This could require more streamlined curricula, different schedules for the academic year, the use of more online instruction (sometimes in cooperative arrangements with other institutions), and much greater emphasis upon student retention and completion of programs of study. Given the financial condition of many states, it probably also will require doing more with the same or less funding.

Higher education also will have to come to grips with a changing student body. According to a recent study, nearly half of students at four-year colleges work more than twenty hours a week. At community colleges, sixty percent work more than twenty hours a week and many more than thirty-five hours. Large numbers of college students can attend only part-time. Many are caring for and supporting children of their own. Many are from backgrounds that do not include good preparation for college.

In a new century, with a different body of potential students, perhaps the model has to change. Perhaps the high level of choice and the absence of time pressure, once so commendable, now inhibit completion of degrees by the average, non-affluent students of the kind Stockton chose to engage in its first years. These students may want, and need, a more directed and structured learning experience. Perhaps they will have fewer choices and less autonomy to design their own programs of study. A more structured curriculum may be compatible with the other demands of their lives.

Can Stockton maintain its balance between General Studies, the majors, and the minors? With remarkable loyalty to the vision of those who helped to shape the college in its early days, faculty and staff have persevered when times were tough.

It may be that Stockton has made its choice: keep the model and change the kind of students served. Less than a fifth of its students are part-time, it accepts only about one half of its applicants, and it has good retention and graduation rates. It now may offer an elite educational experience to a fairly elite student body.

I am sure that the College will continue to consider whether its philosophy of education meets the needs of a new generation of potential students. This next one is the fourth college-going generation since the massive growth made possible by the GI Bill. Expectations have changed. So have circumstances.

Welcome to the twenty-first century. Congratulations and best wishes.

Gordon K. Davies
March 2011

Prologue

Ken Tompkins and Rob Gregg

The idea for a book on Stockton has a number of sources. The first person to think about recording the history of the College's beginnings was Trustee Elizabeth Alton, who did indeed publish an autobiographical work describing what she contributed to the process of bringing a college to Atlantic County. After her, Ingie LaFleur, a Dean of General Studies in the early 1980s who became fascinated by the Stockton experiment, began to pull together materials for a book before she died tragically in 1993. La Fleur was followed by William Gilmore-Lehne, who undertook a good deal of research in the archives and had indicated an intention to move forward with a publication in this area; unfortunately he died suddenly in 1999 before he had moved far along with the project. Paul Lyons then took up the mantle, and, as the fortieth anniversary of the College approached, he became increasingly preoccupied with the idea of pulling together a volume, spending a great deal of time wandering the halls drumming up support among faculty and administrators.

In Lyons' mind, what was needed was a response to David Riesman's *The Perpetual Dream* (co-authored with Gerald Grant). One of the leading sociologists of his time, Riesman had undertaken a study of many of the new colleges founded in the 1960s and 1970s. One chapter, entitled "Two New Jersey Experimental Public Colleges," compared the two colleges established in New Jersey in 1969—Ramapo and Stockton. Riesman's view of Stockton was not especially flattering. He had visited the College, met with administrators and faculty, and come away with grudging but critical respect for the college. He didn't take to Stockton's founding president, Richard Bjork, whom he described as "forceful and energetic" but also as someone who "showed no interest in faculty personally," and about whom "the faculty felt their relation . . . was simply that of employee to employer." (By contrast, Riesman seemed very much taken with George Potter, the more urbane and donnish president of Ramapo.) Moreover, while being supportive of much of the thrust of General Studies, he seemed to find its more innovative elements, embodied in Experimental Studies, too radical. Lyons hoped to bring Stockton's faculty together, from the founders to more recent employees, to reconsider *The Perpetual Dream*. He felt that a symposium should be held and that a published volume would emerge from there.

With the assistance of Jan Colijn, Lyons managed to convince the administration that the time was ripe for such a volume. Unfortunately, he never got the opportunity to commit himself to this project, owing to his untimely death in January 2009. For many months after his death the project remained in mothballs

until the president, Herman J. Saatkamp, Jr., determined that it should move forward, asked one of the current editors, Rob Gregg, to assist in this. Gregg then sought the assistance of the other editor, Ken Tompkins. Tompkins had been the founding Dean of General Studies, and he had been keeping records of the College's history for many years. Since he had frequently complained that the College had not done enough to commemorate those who had founded the institution, he seemed the logical choice to become lead editor of the volume. Indeed, in 1999, he had assigned a student, Heather Martin, to undertake an oral history of the college's Mayflower faculty, and this document ("The Oral History of The Richard Stockton College of New Jersey") remains in the College's archives. In short, he too had been promoting the idea of a book to commemorate the history of Stockton.

* * * * * * *

When President Saatkamp approached us to write this book he gave us a difficult charge: the book should be attractive and should be something that we could share with anyone who has had a connection with the college, or whom we may want to come to us in the future—as an administrator, faculty or staff member, student, or potential donor. It should also be scholarly in nature and ask the important questions about what the College has undertaken and accomplished over the years. It should also—and here the President was emphatic—be willing to incorporate differences of opinion about the College and its history. This ought not to be a rubber stamp of the College or a puff piece. The editors believe that we have met this charge. In this volume the college is studied with a seriousness of purpose that we believe matches the seriousness with which it saw itself at the time of its founding and at present. There is also considerable difference of opinion, as Gordon Davies has noted in his Preface, and this has been true to the spirit of the place, with its lively debate echoing down the halls or along email chains throughout its history. We also hope that we have met the charge in terms of the design of the book. With the presence of images from some of the artists at the college over the years, the poems of Stephen Dunn, and the photographs of former provost, David Carr, we are confident that the reader will find the volume an attractive one.

One possible plan for the project would have been to research all aspects of Stockton's history and provide a linear narrative for the reader to quickly absorb. We avoided this approach for several reasons, the most important being that it would not do justice to the complexity of the college we are describing. There is no singular story for Stockton—even if there may be a Stockton Idea, as Bill Daly calls it. The College was established to teach students to interrogate and question simple narratives, and while certain themes and outlines emerge from the interwoven testimonies, to simplify them into one story would have meant drowning out many voices, losing many aspects of the history. Far better, we felt, would be to try to capture more stories and, if we still came up short, we could fall back upon the legitimate claim that the stories we are telling represent only a point of departure. Each student, faculty, and staff member has his or her own sense of what Stockton means or meant, and these images and ideas of the College do not all fit together neatly into one package. Rather than the Rubik's cube that requires a single solution, our book more resembles the early classroom at the College that incorporated hexagonal furniture, which could be reconfigured in multiple ways, according to the needs of the teacher or the students.

Further, by simplifying the story we might easily have beautified it, but this beauty would only have been skin deep. It would have been like the landscaped garden that seems attractive, but which, owing to all kinds of chemicals used to make the plants grow in unnatural environments, soon appears ugly and offensive. An institution of higher learning should not resort to such measures, and it needs continually to interrogate itself, to determine whether what appears beautiful, correct, and true today will seem so tomorrow. If it doesn't do this, it will indeed become complacent and will become—to borrow from Santayana (an inspiration for President Saatkamp)—an "intellectual slum." In simplifying Stockton's story, our book would become as ugly as the one-dimensional institution it reflected.

In contrast to this, we quickly decided that the book should make a contribution to analysis of the College, that in its layout it should reflect the quirky, quixotic, and sometimes querulous aspects of Stockton. We believed we should include multiple contributors from the different areas of the College; we felt we ought to let them say their piece, as much as possible, endeavoring to edit factual problems more than opinions; and even though we could not incorporate all the perspectives that are out there, and we will inevitably be criticized in numerous areas, we wanted to be expansive in our approach, knowing full well that to be expansive is to reveal, rather than cover up, omissions. And at the end of the process, we would be able to say that we hope this is not the end of the journey, that in ten years time, when the College reaches its half century, another volume could be attempted that would draw in more and different voices.

So we are pleased that there are disagreements among the authors and that the authors of the different essays have brought their passion for the College and for their views of it into this volume. Stockton inspires passion, and even when people have disagreed vehemently—and the history of such disagreements has been a long one—there always seem to be feelings of love for and commitment to the institution. Even the losers in some of the battles that occur do not leave the field believing that all is lost;

they stick around to fight the next battle. They seem to recognize that the College is an organism that undergoes change and can therefore be changed. They also come to the view that their own positions are not the only legitimate ones. If they are senior faculty, they understand that their views may differ from their junior colleagues. If they are from a particular background, they understand that their experience may differ markedly from those of other backgrounds—along the lines of race, gender, ethnicity, religion, sexual orientation, and so forth. If they are students, they understand that they are also part of a changing body, changing in terms of styles and opinions, sometimes collectively and sometimes not, so that the majority opinion today may be found among a minority tomorrow. If they find themselves in conflict with an administration, they understand that the latter undergoes sea changes and that its members (frequently rising out of the faculty and often finding their way back there) may be persuaded and cajoled into adopting new policies that they prefer. Any book about Stockton, therefore, has to be intimately aware of its own incompleteness in its attempt to reflect this changing landscape.

* * * * * * *

This book is being written and produced at a time when some of the principles on which the Richard Stockton College of New Jersey was founded are being challenged daily. The liberal arts are now frequently considered a luxury, and many assert that education should be more about the vocational training of individuals in particular fields and disciplines. Indeed, some would comment that we need less arguing about what we consider important and more effort in simply making ourselves competitive. The well-rounded individual, aspired to in the 1960s and realized to some degree at Stockton, is no longer considered a primary aspiration.

But if we glance briefly at a 1964 study of the importance of the humanities, the backbone of a liberal arts education offered at Stockton, we can see that there is still a great need for what Stockton offered at its founding. *The Report of the Commission on the Humanities* (ACLS, 1964) suggested that the humanities could provide national ideals towards which Americans could strive: they could teach wisdom on which democracy depended, they could remind Americans that they were not simply a nation of materialists, they could teach Americans to recognize that world leadership could not merely be about superior force, vast wealth, or dominating technologies but must be about leadership based on elements of the spirit, and, finally, they could make the enormous amounts of leisure time that members of modern society had more meaningful.

We would like to believe that these ideas are still embedded at Stockton and can be seen in the humanities-based curriculum, in our assumptions about students, in the mission of the College, and even in the design of many of the buildings. While we do more at Stockton than teach courses in the humanities, these ideas still inform and help shape the college as a whole.

The humanities, after all, are only secondarily about democracy, the nation, and the world. The humanities are also about us—individual humans trying to understand who we are, what we are capable of, and why we are here. Endeavoring to appreciate these things is a laudable and critical goal. From its inception the College was meant to respond to such impulses and to train its students not just for particular professions but for life in all its messiness.

For many professors at Stockton, therefore, teaching is a kind of religion, with only one commandment: strive to find out what it means to be human. We devoutly believe that humans and, therefore, human life have meaning. It is our task to convince students of this and to help them pull the meaning of life from literature, from history, or from whatever field we study and, by extension, to expose the meaning of students' lives to them as well. We do not, therefore, study the humanities just to learn, we study them for pleasure, for us.

We live at Stockton in a physical and intellectual environment steeped in humanistic values. These are terribly practical here and, we submit, essential to a meaningful life. It is hard to imagine Stockton without them.

For example, the original college was constructed out of metal panels; those panels can be changed at any time. Every wall throughout the older buildings can be taken down and raised again in a different configuration. While this made the original construction easier, it also made it possible for the building to match human needs (in ways that traditional buildings with immovable walls could not). If we decided that we needed smaller classrooms, we could partition off a larger room into smaller rooms. Simple. Human needs should change buildings.

Those who created the College were also convinced that privilege was a detriment to learning; inequalities caused class resentments, and students could not learn if they felt suppressed and unheard. As a result, there are no faculty parking lots, no faculty dining rooms or faculty lounges. Students often call faculty and administrators by their first names; doctor and professor are seldom heard. When we were undergraduates, we seldom saw the president of our colleges, and it wouldn't be possible to meet with him. The Stockton president, by contrast, can be seen everywhere on campus and will chat with you if his advice is needed.

Perhaps the most important of the humanistic values here at Stockton is choice. Stockton students have always had an enormous range of choices compared to other institutions. They can choose from a wider array of classes, can choose which days of the week to be on campus, can choose preceptors, where to eat, where to park, and even what to wear. Not too many years before Stockton was established, all men wore sports coats and ties, women wore dresses, students had almost no choices of classes, when they would be on campus, where they would park or where they would eat. Stockton students had these choices from the beginning, and while many of them may strike one as insignificant today, they are not—and were not. Choice was a fundamental value when the college was founded; the early documents are full of discussions about the need for choice and how having choices will better prepare students for their lives after college.

The point is that humanistic values are practical and democratic, and they allow us all to learn about ourselves in powerful ways. As such, what follows in the pages of this book are descriptions of the efforts made by visionary administrators, faculty, staff, and students to fashion a college that would promote these values. It is important, therefore, to commemorate the forty years of this college's existence not merely to celebrate the passage of a number of years and the growth of an institution, though both may be significant in their own right, but because to do so provides both an opportunity to reflect on what it was that was attempted and a forum for recommitting ourselves to the humanistic values to which educational institutions should be dedicated.

At a time when state funding is being cut and the public commitment to education is on the wane, we present Stockton College as a beacon of the values we hold. To paraphrase President Herman Saatkamp, education is a promise we make to the generations we will never see. What will that promise be worth if we do not maintain our commitment to the kind of humanistic values on which Stockton College was founded?

The Stockton Idea

Osprey Alighting On Nest **by David Carr**

Elite Education for State College Students

William T. Daly

The 1960s was a time of high idealism in higher education. There was much talk, particularly among younger academics, about college education being a "transformational" experience. Our job as academics was to introduce students to what Matthew Arnold had called "the best that has been thought and said" by all previous generations, in order to expand our students' understanding of the full range of things that they, as human beings, *could* be. Then, we would try to give them the knowledge and the practical skills that would permit them to transform themselves and their futures into what they had decided that they *should* be.

Stockton State College set out to approach this universal educational task in a very different and, arguably, better way.

So at least it seemed to this idealistic young pilgrim when I first read the planning papers constructed by Stockton's founding administrative team and then came across the country to join their effort. And, frankly, so it still seems to me now, forty years down an exhausting but exhilarating road. Stockton has been one of those few instances in life where most of what one hoped would happen, after many twists and turns, actually happened. In my judgment, we approach the fortieth birthday celebration of this lovely little college with a good deal to celebrate.

This essay is one attempt to tell the story of the Stockton Idea— of its origins in the tumult of the 1960s, of its evolution in the first ten years of the College, and (much more briefly) of its continuing advantages in the contemporary world of American higher education.

Two important caveats before beginning the story. First, there was a good deal of planning for this new college that occurred before the arrival of the faculty in the fall of 1971—by President Richard Bjork and his staff two years before the opening of the College and by Ken Tompkins (the co-editor of this volume) and his academic colleagues in the year immediately before the faculty and students arrived. While I was involved in many of the discussions and decisions that shaped the direction of the College after fall 1971—as a faculty member, as an occasional administrator, and as the author of the self-study that led to the initial accreditation of the College—I had no part in those two earlier and critical planning stages. I was, rather, a "convert" to many of the ideas that emerged from them—subject to all the legitimate questions about historical accuracy and objectivity that attach to that status.

Second, the opportunity to build a college from scratch, to write on a blank slate, predictably produced sharp disagreements over what should be written on that slate. My repeated references to what "Stockton" or "we" decided to do in the first ten years refer only to the *results* of the struggles over the direction and soul of this new college that must have occurred among the members of the administrative planning team before the faculty arrived and that certainly did occur among the rest of us in the years that followed our arrival. These two caveats noted, now on to the story.

THE SIXTIES

Stockton is a post-Sixties college and was shaped by the ideas that emerged from that decade. But the 1960s were, in fact, convulsed by two very different kinds of reform movements, which were, to some degree, mutually contradictory.

The first reform movement was grounded in the civil rights movement and expanded by Lyndon Johnson's more general "War on Poverty." This movement spoke on behalf of the portion of the population near the bottom of the economic ladder, and its goal was that the economically disadvantaged be allowed *into* American society as full and equal participants in its prosperity. In higher education, this reform movement built on and strengthened the long-standing notion that education should be one of the primary mechanisms by which Americans could make themselves better than they had been born. The impact of this movement on Stockton can be seen in the degree to which it viewed itself as a social mission institution, which would open its doors to a portion of the population that had not previously had access to quality collegiate education and hence would admit, through those doors, a portion of the population that sought education primarily as a method of economic and career advancement.

The second reform movement of the Sixties grew initially out of the protest against the Vietnam War and morphed into the broader critique of American society often dubbed the "counter culture" or "hippie" movement. This movement arose from and spoke to the concerns of comparatively wealthy, predominantly white college students who wanted *out*-of American society, at least as it was currently constituted. Ultimately they came to object to almost all societal constraints on their spontaneity and, in particular, to the constraints imposed by the materialistic emphasis of American society. In higher education, this often translated into criticism both of the very career-oriented education that the less affluent students prized and of the constraints on educational freedom imposed by the traditional academic disciplines, which, in their view, prepared and certified students for particular careers. The impact of the second movement on Stockton, and on some other like-minded colleges of the period, can be seen in their tendency to value broad-based liberal arts, or general, education (terms often used interchangeably in this essay) over career-oriented education; in their desire to blur or break down the boundaries that separated the traditional, more specialized disciplines; and in their desire to give students the freedom to structure their own individual educational packages across those disciplinary lines.

What was most striking to me about the Stockton Idea, when I first encountered it, was that Stockton seemed committed to adopting and reconciling *both* of these seemingly contradictory educational reform thrusts from the 1960s.

THE STOCKTON IDEA

Stockton proposed to make available to state college students at state college prices the kind of interdisciplinary and individualized liberal arts instruction initially developed in America for the children of the ruling elite and, in the contemporary world, usually reserved for students at the most exclusive and expensive private liberal arts colleges.

In other words, what was arguably the best and most expensive undergraduate education in the country was to be delivered to the students who most needed it but who also could least afford it and (as a number of early critics argued) might also be the least prepared for it and the least interested in it. State college students were known to range from very well-prepared to very poorly prepared, but the average level of academic preparation was likely to be a good deal lower than that which could be assured by rigorous admissions standards for entering students at exclusive liberal arts colleges. And the economic situation of many state college students and their parents was likely to place them generally in the career-oriented camp. They were unlikely to be attracted to a college that preached the civilizing impact of liberal arts education unless it could be demonstrated that such an education would also contribute directly to career success and economic gain.

This attempt to combine what was in the early days virtually open admission access with high-powered education once admitted, to combine working-class career education with upper-class liberal arts education, was exquisite 1960s stuff—noble to the core in concept but also audacious and likely to prove difficult in the implementation phase—as we and a few other like-minded colleges of the Sixties were soon to discover.

It was my distinct impression, as the first-year faculty assembled in fall 1971, that those of us who had packed our bags and come running to serve the Stockton Idea were attracted both by the nobility of Stockton's educational goals and by the near impossibility of achieving them. We were overwhelmingly young. It was the end of the Sixties. And we could still hear the ringing words of John Kennedy, speaking of the quest to put men on the moon: "We choose to do these things, not because they are easy but because they are ha-a-a-ard" (New England for "hard").

We arrived at the College (temporarily housed in the collapsing boardwalk Mayflower Hotel) to discover that the administrative planning team , which had spent the previous year constructing an initial plan for Stockton, had anticipated many of the difficulties associated with Stockton's declared and very ambitious mission and had built distinctive structures into the College plan designed to give us a fighting chance of actually making elite liberal arts education work for a career-oriented state college student body. All of those distinctive structures were compelled by hard realities to evolve during the first ten years of the College. But they are all still here and are all still central to what makes Stockton different, and arguably better, than most other undergraduate institutions. I have focused on four of these pillars of the Stockton Idea.

1. The General Studies program and the traditional degree programs
2. The Skills program
3. The Preceptorial Advising program
4. College-wide faculty involvement in all of the above

What follows is a summary of the early thinking (as I understood it) behind each of these structures, of their evolution during the first ten years of the College, and (much more briefly) of their current status both at Stockton and in contemporary American higher education—as this lovely little college approaches its fortieth birthday.

GENERAL STUDIES: INITIAL STRUCTURE

From the beginning of American higher education, there has been a struggle between those who wanted to emphasize broad general/liberal arts education and those who favored more specialized career-oriented education. The former has usually been defined as a *common core* of what *all* college graduates, as future citizens and leaders, should know—usually with a focus on the core values of Western European civilization from the time of Greek and Roman antiquity, together with the intellectual discipline and skills necessary to evaluate and then selectively pursue those values rationally and effectively.

The other school of thought prefers to focus on what Benjamin Franklin and Thomas Jefferson called the "practical arts"— the development and teaching to the future workforce of the burgeoning scientific and technical knowledge in agriculture and industry necessary to develop the American economy and to secure a prosperous place for college graduates within it. The curricular reflection of this philosophy was centered in the specialized "disciplines" or "majors" in which that knowledge was generated and through which it was to be passed on to each new generation.

The advocates of general education and the liberal arts had the

Entrance to the Mayflower Hotel (Fall, 1971) - Courtesy of *The Press of Atlantic City*

early edge and later, as they lost ground, successfully launched periodic counteroffensives to restore the centrality of Western Civilization, its great books and central modes of thought in special curricular programs, and even in entire experimental colleges within large universities. But the more specialized academic disciplines, with their more direct relationship to economic growth and career opportunities, steadily gained ascendance in American higher education. Perhaps the clearest indication of that ascendancy is that all that remains of general education programs at most colleges and universities is a set of required introductory courses in the major specialized disciplines. The initial structure of the curriculum at Stockton seemed to reflect the understanding on the part of the first-year planning team that, in attempting to make elite liberal arts education work for career-oriented state college students, the liberal arts/ general education component of the curriculum would need more protection than the traditional disciplinary majors. As a result, the planners built no fewer than five philosophical and structural protections for it into their scheme—most of which are still clearly visible at Stockton.

1. A Separate Curriculum. Their most interesting and prescient innovation was to argue that, under emerging economic conditions of accelerating and unpredictable change, the breadth of education traditionally provided by the liberal arts might actually constitute the best possible career education. It would provide students with a clear understanding of what there was to choose from in selecting a major and a career path, leading to wiser choices in both those areas. And, that same broad background would permit students to move with greater facility from one entire specialty and career path to another if the shifting demands of the job market required it.

To promote that kind of breadth and adaptability, general education at Stockton would *not* be composed of a scattering of mandated introductions to the traditional disciplines, as it was at most colleges and universities. It would be composed, rather, of an entirely separate curriculum of "G" courses, *each* of which would be broadly interdisciplinary, with a great deal of student freedom to choose among those courses in such a way as to construct their individual educations around their own interests, abilities, and estimates of the job market they would confront.

Finally, Stockton would offer to *all* its students as many as they chose to take of the even more highly individualized modes of instruction that are often limited by number and student qualifications even at private liberal arts colleges—independent study projects, internships, opportunities to study abroad, and even a Bachelor in Liberal Arts, in which students could construct an entirely individualized baccalaureate degree free from virtually all college-wide degree requirements.

2. A Separate Dean and Division. To provide general education with an institutional power base and advocate, General Studies was given a separate division and dean, organizationally equivalent to the divisions and deans of the traditional disciplines in the natural sciences, arts and humanities, and social and behavioral sciences. And most of the cross-disciplinary academic activities (e.g., academic skills, academic advising, various topical concentrations, etc.) were gradually and logically assembled under the control of the Dean of General Studies.

3. A Faculty Mandate. All faculty were contractually obliged to provide two of their six annual course offerings to General Studies. Stockton faculty were, therefore, hired for their likely interest in, and capabilities in, general education as well as in their disciplinary specialties.

4. A Student Mandate. All students were required to pursue breadth of education by taking fully one quarter of all their courses for the BA in broad, interdisciplinary G-courses and (a little later) an additional one quarter either in additional G-courses or in disciplinary courses that were clearly "distant" from their major. Thus, for the Bachelor of Arts, fully one half of a Stockton student's entire education was to be dedicated to breadth of education.

5. Interdisciplinary Disciplines. Even the traditional disciplines/majors at Stockton were to lean in an interdisciplinary direction. Traditionally powerful department chairmen were replaced by organizationally weak "coordinators"—an essentially clerical position. Personnel and budgetary powers were vested not in the individual disciplines but in interdisciplinary divisional faculty committees and divisional deans. And faculty offices were intentionally scrambled, with long walks through Stockton's broad galleries for individual faculty members to get

to their mailboxes and secretarial services—explicitly to avoid disciplinary clusters of faculty offices and to encourage regular encounters in those galleries with students and faculty members from other disciplines.

GENERAL STUDIES: PROBLEMS AND MODIFICATIONS
The early difficulties encountered by this very broad and very individualized approach to general education (also quickly encountered, as we shall see, in the other three central components of the Stockton Idea) did not seem to result from any fundamental flaw in the basic goal of developing in students a capacity for intelligent choice among college and career options. It seemed to result, instead, from the fact that the College had probably overestimated our students' capacity for making such choices without some specification of at least the spectrum of choices available to them. Most of the modifications of the original set of ideas on general education took the form of just such a specification.

In the early years, the General Studies curriculum was generated one course at a time by individual faculty members, operating under very few collective and institutional constraints. It was hoped that this approach would generate innovation, faculty enthusiasm, the ability to communicate that enthusiasm for learning to students, and an environment in which faculty and students would explore new areas together. And it did. It generated a number of fascinating courses (including a few that the more conservative members of the faculty and administration saw as downright bizarre). But it also generated concern that, under this venturesome system, the College lacked a mechanism for ensuring that all students would be exposed to the full range of curricular and career options necessary to provide them with a basis for intelligent choice among those options.

As a result, effective in the College's fifth year, a movement toward more structure in the General Studies curriculum developed. First, General Studies courses were grouped according to their educational purposes. And later, in the College's seventh year, an even more traditional restructuring required students to take some coursework in all of the major bodies of human knowledge (the arts and humanities, the natural sciences/ mathematics, and the social sciences) and in the interrelationships among those broad areas of knowledge. This last restructuring also had the additional purpose of giving each of the divisional disciplinary faculties their own piece of General Studies turf and hence a vested interest in monitoring its quality and keeping General Studies itself alive and well. Thus, the current distribution requirements among GAH, GNM, GSS, GEN, and GIS courses. While this new set of requirements did restrict student freedom to some degree, it did *not* abandon the initial goal of helping students to develop the capacity for intelligent choice inside the College and the capacity to adapt to changing circumstances after graduation. Great care was taken not to reinvent the elaborate set of specific course-by-course requirements found at many institutions, which would have obliterated the opportunity for student choice. Rather the new General Studies distribution requirements were only designed to make it clear to students what the broad areas of human knowledge were—from which they might sample. A wide range of choices among and within those areas of knowledge were left to the individual students and their individual advisors.

GENERAL STUDIES: RESULTANT STRUCTURE

Thus had Stockton attempted to make good, by the end of its first decade, on its promise to provide to state college students a liberal arts education, which would also be the best form of career education in an economy increasingly dominated by accelerating rate of change.

By the end of its tenth year the General Studies curriculum, while considerably more structured than at its inception, could still be defended as offering students much of the breadth of education valued by elite liberal arts colleges for its civilizing impact. But Stockton's version of a liberal arts curriculum was also structured in such a way as to provide career-oriented state college students simultaneously with a needed understanding of what there was to choose from in courses of study and in subsequent careers, and with a broad educational base along which they could move after graduation as the economy and the available jobs shifted beneath their feet.

Finally, the General Studies edifice itself had survived the inevitable battles with the traditional disciplines for scarce resources, which had destroyed or eviscerated ambitious general education initiatives at many other colleges. This fact seemed to validate the wisdom of the College planners in creating something of a General Studies bastion—with its own dean, its own separate curriculum, mandated course contributions to that curriculum from the entire faculty, and an even wider general education curricular preserve, which controlled fully one half of the courses required for a Stockton BA.

That General Studies bastion naturally shows considerable signs of wear and tear after forty years. Not all of the courses in the General Studies curriculum may be as general as the original idea intended them to be, and some students, by careful planning, may still manage to avoid the benefits of the breadth of education that the College seeks to impose upon them. But forty years down the road from the act of creation, Stockton still has a sweeping, institution-wide structure for the support of general education, available for refreshing and remodeling as needed, which most other institutions cannot match and which they have next to no chance of creating now in the current educational and political environment.

The remaining three structures built into the Stockton Idea show a similar pattern of early inspiration, reality-driven modification, and eventual survival.

THE SKILLS PROGRAM: INITIAL STRUCTURE

As already indicated, the first intellectual ability usually valued by traditional liberal arts education was a grounding in the basic values and value issues of Western civilization. The second was training in the intellectual discipline and habits of mind necessary to address those issues and to pursue the values that survived that analytical scrutiny.

In its early planning, Stockton repeatedly honored this second goal of liberal arts education with statements that the College hoped to build in our students the capacity for "independent decision-making," "self direction," or "continuous learning."

The College recognized from the beginning, however, that adapting this second elevated goal to the needs of the least well-prepared portion of an entering state college student class might have to begin with an effort to raise their basic verbal and quantitative skills to a level where they could academically survive in college and eventually do well in the high-powered curriculum that Stockton intended to offer them.

As was the case in General Studies, our first attempt to address this issue proved to be based on an unduly optimistic estimate of student skill levels. Help with skills development was to be provided by a voluntary, drop-in Skills Center. And some of our more motivated students took advantage of that opportunity. But a special task force on skills, carried out in the College's fourth year, revealed skills-deficient students in numbers much larger than those using the center.

This raised the possibility that precisely those students who were most in need of skills training might be the least motivated to take advantage of the Skills Center and that many students might therefore derive less benefit from their courses than they would have with a better basis in academic skills. Of equal concern was the possibility that those poorly prepared students might drag down the general quality of instruction even for those students who arrived at college well-prepared in basic academic skills.

As was the case with General Studies, this early brush of idealistic hope with hard realities lead to a substantial tightening of requirements.

THE SKILLS PROGRAM: PROBLEMS AND MODIFICATIONS

1. In the College's fifth year, Stockton established a Basic Studies program (BASK). All students entering the College were required to take skills placement tests in college-level writing, critical thinking, and quantitative reasoning. Those who lacked these essential skills were then compelled to acquire them—by passing mandated skills courses or an exit test by the end of their first year at the College —or face dismissal for academic reasons.

This reasonably draconian requirement was intended to provide poorly prepared students with a maximum incentive to make the major effort necessary to overcome their educational deficiencies. Even more draconian was the belief that the

William Daly talking with a student (1976)

practical effect of such standards would be to retain those poorly prepared students who were willing to make such a maximum effort and dismiss those who were not. This selection among poorly prepared students according to their level of effort was intended to be both the most just criterion morally and the most accurate predictive criterion of academic success—to the degree that level of effort is the single best predictor of future success both in college and after graduation. Finally, the insistence that all students must meet these standards before moving on to the next stage of their education was designed to protect the general quality of instruction, and hence the quality of instruction that would be available to the portion of the student body that was well-prepared academically upon admission.

1. The standards that skills-deficient students must meet in order to demonstrate competence were to be set by the faculty who taught in the Basic Studies program. And, as was the case in General Studies, instructional responsibility for that program was to be assumed by the faculty as a whole. Basic Studies courses were to be offered not only by a "core" faculty of skills specialists but also by a "rotating" faculty drawn, on a voluntary basis, from all of the College's regular degree programs and trained by the core faculty. For the most part, these rotating faculty were to be recruited selectively from among those instructors who already had reputations as effective classroom teachers. Thus, contrary to the all too frequent practice of foisting skills instruction off onto inexperienced adjuncts and hostile junior faculty, who

would rather be doing something else, this social mission college intended to give those students who most needed help the best teaching talent we had.

2. This idea of collective, college-wide faculty responsibility for setting standards and providing skills instruction has suffered from a decline in the number of regular faculty who teach BASK courses but, at the same time, has been steadily extended in scope—by the establishment of a Freshman Seminar program (which assures initial training in reasoning skills for all Stockton freshmen) and the establishment of the requirements that all Stockton students must take a minimum of four writing courses, and three quantitative reasoning courses before graduation. This emphasis on basic skills development and reinforcement throughout a student's entire education at Stockton contrasts sharply with the practice at many other colleges and universities of confining skills instruction courses to a few quickly forgotten freshman-year experiences. In all of these courses, regular faculty from the major disciplines voluntarily assume the responsibility for emphasizing critical thinking, writing, and quantitative skills, in addition to content mastery, in a number of their regular classes.

THE SKILLS PROGRAM: RESULTANT STRUCTURE

Thus has Stockton reconfigured the traditional liberal arts goal of an educated elite, capable of rational analysis and lifelong learning, into a four-year screening and instructional program, involving a significant portion of the entire Stockton faculty, which seeks to carry even skills-deficient state college freshmen to that exalted level of intellectual skills.

PRECEPTORIAL ADVISING: INITIAL STRUCTURE

The advising system, which the College planners of the first year constructed to help state college students make choices among the glittering array of courses, majors, and career paths that Stockton hoped to lay before them, had the same central characteristics as the General Studies curriculum, which was to lay out those options, and the Skills program, which was to give students the intellectual tools to explore those options successfully.

1. The advising program, like the General Studies and Skills programs, sought to incorporate and reconcile both of the potentially contradictory educational reform thrusts of the 1960s—the belief in the value of broad multidisciplinary education, on the one hand, and the desire to meet the educational needs of working-class students seeking career-relevant education, on the other. The reflection of this dual concern in the initial advising system was that Stockton was to provide each student with two preceptors—one to help shape the student's general education (and to protect it from intrusion by courses directly related to the more specialized majors) and the other to monitor the student's progress toward graduation in that more specialized and career-oriented major.

2. The advising system also reflected the recognition that state college students, confronting the wide range of choices allowed them in Stockton's curriculum, would require much more than a simple monitoring of their progress toward meeting the detailed graduation requirements characteristic of most other colleges and universities. Hence, each faculty member was to be assigned a maximum of sixteen preceptees, and a full week of advising was built into the schedule for each semester. Beyond that, these sixteen-student preceptorial groups and their preceptors were then grouped into larger "Collegia," which, beyond their advising function, were also to serve as the basis for student participation in shaping co-curricular activities and for student participation in college governance. At Stockton, in short, a student's entire collegiate life was to be enveloped and shaped by "preceptorial teaching."

3. Finally, like the General Studies curriculum and the Skills program, the burden of this labor-intensive approach to academic advising was not to be shunted off to lower-level student services personnel. It was to be the collective (and contractual) responsibility of the entire Stockton faculty and most of the upper-level administrative staff.

PRECEPTORIAL ADVISING: PROBLEMS AND MODIFICATIONS

To an even greater degree than had been the case with the General Studies curriculum and the Skills program, some of the more optimistic aspects of this elaborate advising system were trimmed back as we confronted the realities of a state college student culture. But, as had also been the case in those two other areas, the Stockton approach to advising was significantly modified but not abandoned completely.

1. The idea that the College's co-curricular and governance system could bubble up from the Collegia was crippled by student indifference in the very first semester of the College's existence and died a slow and agonizing death shortly thereafter. State college students were interested in good advice about their courses of study and their career prospects. They were apparently very much less interested in building the co-curricular and governance structures of a new college.

2. The weeklong advising period of the College's first year was gradually reduced to two days. And the College's initial attempt to assert the equal importance of General Studies and the major by assigning each student both a General Studies preceptor and a major advisor, was dropped at the beginning of the College's third year, largely because it took too much of everyone's time. It was replaced by an advising system in which each student had only one advisor at a time—a general education preceptor before declaring a major and a program preceptor after declaration.

3. The College regrouped after these two substantial setbacks by organizing a special core of freshman preceptors. As was the case with the Skills program and in General Studies, these freshman preceptors were drawn from among our best faculty advisors on a voluntary basis. We were attempting, once again, to give freshmen, as the group most in need of good advice, the best advisors we had. And, as was the case with the faculty participants in the Skills program and in the General Studies curriculum, these advisors were to meet in annual workshops to review the College's graduation requirements and to discuss the relative effectiveness of various advising techniques.

PRECEPTORIAL ADVISING: RESULTANT STRUCTURE

1. Once again the College did *not* respond to initial difficulties by abandoning its central commitment to developing in students the capacity for making intelligent choices on basic value issues, courses of study, and career options. And it did not impose in their place a detailed set of course-by-course graduation requirements such as those found at many other colleges and universities. The education of the Stockton student was, indeed, in need of structure. But it was to be an individualized structure built, course by course, around the interests, abilities, and career plans of each student—as developed in conversations with their individual advisors.

2. And, once again, the labor-intensive burden of providing that kind of individualized advice was to be borne by the faculty and much of the upper-level administrative staff—with freshmen, as those most in need of advice, to be served by the best and most committed advisors, in the form of a volunteer core of freshman preceptors.

Thus, Stockton, once again, responded to the endangerment of one of the central wagers it had made on its ability to build a different and better kind of undergraduate education by counting on its ability to mobilize additional faculty effort to rescue the bet.

This brings us to the fourth and final pillar of the Stockton Idea.

It is, in many ways, the most remarkable of the four, and certainly the one most often slated for early extinction by outside analysts who came, in the early years, to study this new and different approach to undergraduate education. That fourth element is the ability of Stockton to mobilize collective, college-wide faculty effort to sustain all of the above, very labor-intensive, elements of the Stockton Idea.

THE MOBILIZATION OF COLLEGE-WIDE FACULTY EFFORT

1. The Challenge. To understand how remarkable this final element of Stockton's approach to undergraduate education is, we need to recall that each year's new batch of both faculty and upper-level academic administrators have arrived at the gates of the College having been systematically mistrained for the efforts required to sustain the Stockton Idea.

The requisite credential for almost all of Stockton's faculty and upper-level positions in academic administration is a PhD. Those degrees are earned at major research universities, the central purpose of which is to generate new knowledge. And, save for occasional paradigm-shifting general discoveries, the generation of new knowledge requires specialized research in relatively narrow disciplinary areas.

Most new Stockton faculty and academic administrators have therefore arrived at the College with a deep investment in their particular disciplines, in an even more specialized personal research agenda, and in demonstrating intellectual excellence to a sophisticated audience of specialists.

Upon their arrival at Stockton, however, they are told that they must now stretch beyond the boundaries of their specialized graduate school disciplinary training, shift some of their research efforts from their personal scholarly agenda to the research necessary to prepare broad interdisciplinary General Studies courses, perhaps spend the enormous amounts of time necessary to effectively teach skills-deficient students basic verbal, quantitative, and thinking skills, and allocate additional blocks of time to advising entering students who often have very little initial idea what either college or Stockton is all about.

1. The Response. The fact that so many Stockton faculty have successfully made this difficult transition is probably attributable to both good planning and good luck, at levels that most educational institutions have not been able to match.
• First, Stockton had the institutional good luck to be born at the right time—at the end of the 1960s and beginning of the 1970s when there was a buyer's market for new faculty, many more newly minted PhDs entering the market looking for positions in higher education than there were positions for them. Specifically, in the year when Stockton hired its first fifty-five faculty members, the College had over 5,000 applications for those positions. And a similar situation has prevailed in many areas of the curriculum throughout the life of the College. As a result, Stockton, to a degree not typical of state colleges, has

regularly been able to recruit high-powered faculty from the very best graduate schools in the country. Smart isn't everything, but smart helps with almost everything—particularly if the new recruits are being asked to learn quickly to do things that they have not been trained to do.
• Second, the first-year planning team had the good sense to make full participation in two of the three central elements of the Stockton Idea, (teaching in the General Studies curriculum and preceptorial advising) contractually mandatory for all faculty. Faculty seeking employment at Stockton in the tough job market of the early 1970s understood that they had no choice but to make the difficult transition required to meet Stockton standards.
• Third, the Stockton ideal of providing elite education to state college students was an inherently noble and attractive mission at the end of the Sixties, with drawing power of its own, and has remained so for many prospective Stockton faculty members even to this day.
• Fourth, Stockton's early faculty, particularly because of the strength of their ideological commitment to the College's ideals, tended to replicate themselves in their subsequent hiring decisions.
• Finally, even those who entered the College without a strong commitment to those ideals have often been converted to them—particularly in the case of the General Studies curriculum, because of the opportunity it offers faculty members to explore new and interesting areas as a part of their regular teaching load. This opportunity would not have been available to them if a more traditional general education distribution requirement among introductory disciplinary courses had forced them to teach endless sections of "Introduction to" courses in their own disciplines.

THE LEGACY OF THE STOCKTON IDEA

By the end of its first decade, Stockton had been compelled to absorb a number of disappointments and necessary modifications in its founding philosophy but had managed to do so without abandoning its initial goal of providing a kind of liberal arts education that would work for state college students. And, with those modifications in place, Stockton confronted entering students with a tough but thin line of requirements designed to give them *something very close to what many of us had hoped to give students at the beginning of our journey ten years earlier—* the intellectual basis for taking charge of their own educations, followed by the freedom to do precisely that.

The intellectual basis necessary for students to take charge of their own educations was to be built upon, and thirty years later is still being built upon:
• A required set of General Studies courses designed to give entering students an understanding of what there is to choose from in basic values, academic courses of study, and career opportunities.
• A required set of skills courses designed to give students the basic reasoning, writing, and quantitative skills necessary to

explore successfully that range of courses and career options.
• An individualized advising system to help guide students through all of the above choices.
• The assurance that those who would be providing students with their general education courses, their instruction in essential academic skills, and their advice in charting their academic and career futures would not be graduate student teaching assistants, adjunct faculty, or lower-level administrative staff, as they were at many colleges and universities, but virtually the entire regular faculty and senior administrative staff of the College—the best we had to offer.

The freedom for students, once that basis had been built, to take charge of their own educations and to build them around their own interests, abilities, and estimates of their best career opportunities, was to be maintained by, and thirty years later is still maintained by:
• The care that was taken to see that the required General Studies and skills courses never developed into the kind of course-by-course graduation requirements that largely obliterate individualized education for students at many other institutions.
• The continuing commitment in the advising system to structuring students' educations around their individual interests, abilities, and career plans.
• The continuing availability to all Stockton students of such highly individualized instructional opportunities as independent study, internships, study abroad, and individually constructed degree programs.

Nothing is forever. And there is no point in arguing that Stockton is or should be the same institution that it was in the first decade of its existence. But the mark of that first decade can still be seen clearly in much of the basic academic structure of this lovely little college and in many of the several things that it still does uncommonly well.

It may, therefore, be important to retell the Stockton story: to prospective students who need to understand what makes Stockton a genuinely different kind of option for them; to current students and recent alumni, who need to set their aspirations and self-confidence at the elevated level commensurate with the real quality of the education they have received here; and to newly arriving faculty and staff whose level understanding of, and enthusiasm for, the educational enterprise undertaken here forty years ago may determine if the Stockton Idea and its continuing advantages can be maintained into the future.

Therein lies perhaps the central justification for troubling to construct this little essay and the larger historical collection of which it is a part.

Don't let it be forgot
That once there was a spot
For one brief shining moment …

Canoes on Lake Fred (1971). See page 178.

Getting Started

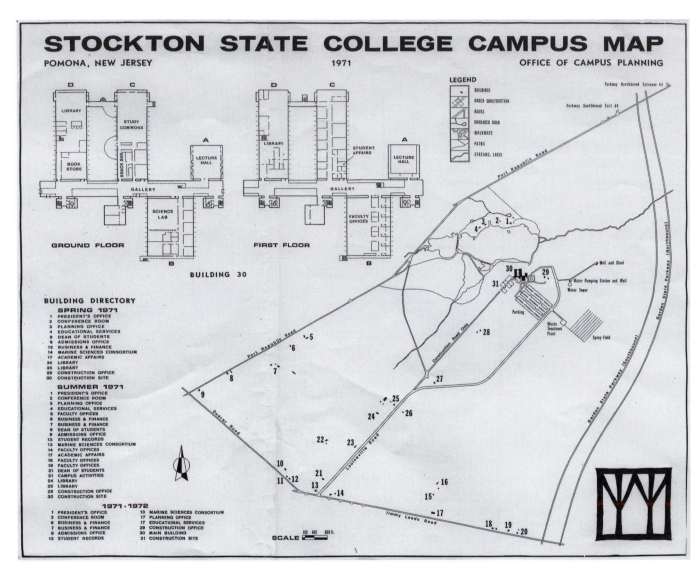

First campus map (1971)

This section of the volume focuses on the earliest days of the College, from the planning undertaken by President Bjork, the board members, and the newly appointed deans, to the College's first classes at the Mayflower Hotel in Atlantic City.

We begin with three different views of the early years. Based upon Elizabeth Alton's autobiography, and two interviews undertaken with David Taylor and Magda Leuchter, Ken Tompkins provides insights into what they believed they were endeavoring to accomplish, and how they perceived the College that they helped to found.

What name the new institution would adopt was a very important issue, as for many at the time it seemed to signify what kind of college it would become. Would it be a local college with locally recruited students, or would it reach for state and regional influence? We endeavor to highlight the conflicts revolving around the name selection, show what alternatives were offered, bring into question several of the narratives associated with the naming, and consider briefly some of the reasons that the name has not always been considered a blessing.

The next essays provide insight into what several of the administrators at Stockton were doing and what they accomplished. Rob Gregg provides a glimpse into the mindset of the founding president, Richard Bjork, about whom so many have had strong feelings. Gregg finds much to praise about what Bjork did, and certainly finds no lack of vision in this activist president, but notes that many of his problems were those of his own making—stemming from his belief that to be good he needed to be unpopular. Ken Tompkins then describes all the early deans who worked alongside him when the doors of the college opened, and Dan Moury gives an intimate view of what it was like to be a new dean at Stockton.

The essays that follow then drill a bit deeper into the Stockton foundation, revealing what was established at other levels. Richard Gajewski describes his experiences as the founding Vice President of Administration and Finance, responsible for overseeing the securing of land, budgets, and even undertaking some precepting. Richard Schwartz provides a very detailed and informative piece about what was going on behind the scenes in the planning and the building of the Pomona campus, showing what a remarkable feat of engineering and construction the main campus was, and why it would become such an important asset for the college over the years. Dan Moury follows with an in-depth view of the earliest days in the Division of Natural Science and Mathematics, giving a clear sense of why it was that that division (now school) developed such a strong sense of community and identity.

Richard Pesqueira provides a strong sense of the idealism affecting many like himself who arrived at the college. He had been comfortably established at a college in California, only to feel the urge to contribute to this experiment in southern New Jersey. He came east to take charge of Student Affairs at Stockton, which he found to be very rewarding, though sometimes difficult owing to Bjork's position on the role of Student Affairs at his college. James Williams also had a difficult job in endeavoring to establish a police force at the college. As his essay shows, he needed to provide security in such a way that he would not alienate students and faculty, who were very much influenced by 1960s culture, while also appearing to be professional to the other forces in the region. His work was not made easier by the fact that he was the only African American chief in the region, and he needed to work hard to earn the respect of some insensitive colleagues who initially referred to him as "the boy out there at Stockton."

The section ends with two pieces about the Mayflower period. Joe Tosh provides the perspective of a student in those heady days, while Lew Steiner focuses on the "sinking" of the Mayflower. Lew was the photographer for the *Argo*, and when the college moved to the main campus he fabricated a picture that made it seem as if the hotel was sinking into the ocean. The Mayflower had been a temporary vessel for the college, so this apparent demise seemed only fitting.

Throughout the section one gets a clear sense that hope was in the air. For all of those present at the founding, Stockton was supposed to be a different college. Indeed it was intended to be unlike all the colleges that the founders had experienced in their own educations. But could it fulfill this promise? Could it reach for the highest ideals and meet the expectations of all those who arrived in Pomona to become a part of the Stockton experiment?

What Have I Done—Elizabeth Alton

Ken Tompkins

On February 10, 1966 Elizabeth Alton spoke at the Atlantic City Kiwanis Club. Her subject was to be the bicentennial of Rutgers University. She wanted to include remarks on the possibility of having a state college in South Jersey but was advised to stick to the topic. At the end of her remarks on Rutgers, she announced that she hoped the state would build a college in the Atlantic City area. Mrs. Alton knew that many of the most important men in Atlantic City were in her audience, and she couldn't pass up the opportunity to plant the idea of a local state college in their heads.

She was immediately interviewed by the *Atlantic City Press* on the idea of a state college here. As she writes in her book, *The Stockton Story*, "That article was to change the course of my life for some time to come."

The road to a new college was not easy, of course. Mrs. Alton continued to speak publically whenever asked, but strong forces were gathering in the northern part of the state to assure that the "seventh college" be built there. In April 1966 she spoke at length to the state Board of Education about our need for a college, but, by May, politicians in the north had written a bill—Senate Bill S434—that would have guaranteed a new college in the north. At the same time, those same northern politicians passed a law requiring that a state Board of Higher Education be formed and tasked to choose a site for the seventh college. Senate Bill S434 was passed in November 1966.

The new Chancellor of Higher Education took office in August 1967, and at the first meeting in September he presented the request for the seventh college to be located in Bergen County.

Throughout 1967 and 1968, Mrs. Alton was indefatigable in her efforts to meet with any official at any time. Indeed, she had intended to make her case for building the college in Atlantic County at the September meeting of the Board of Higher Education, but, strangely, she was called for jury duty three days before. She was not released from that obligation until days after the September meeting.

Still Elizabeth Alton spoke, argued, wrote hundreds of letters and formed a local entity named Citizens Committee for a State College-University. Largely as a result of her work, in May 1968, the state Board of Higher Education sent a recommendation to the legislature for two colleges. Mrs. Alton then turned her attention to passing a $990 million bond issue, which passed in November 1968. A college in Atlantic County was assured, and members of the board were chosen in January 1969.

Elizabeth Alton is rightfully revered as a founder of the College. Her tireless efforts to bring the College here are remarkable, especially if you happened to know her. She was tough in her pursuit of a dream and deserves honor and appreciation for her efforts. She is reported to have said, when she first visited the College at the derelict Mayflower Hotel in Atlantic City, "My God, what have I done?" It is certainly a remark she could easily have uttered.

A Confrontation of Biblical Proportions

When The Rev Carl McIntire (d. 2002) of the Bible Presbyterian Church (& the Christian Admiral Hotel in Cape May) was picketing Bill Daly's Revolution & Revolutionaries on the Boardwalk at Atlantic City (when Stockton was still at the Mayflower Hotel), a number of people, including President Richard Bjork, attempted to introduce some logic and perspective into his world view. I talked to one of McIntire's junior clergy and asked what he knew about the nature of the lectures. Of course, he knew only that they were about revolution. I suggested he should find out whether Bill was for or against revolution and that attending a lecture might make that clear. He reluctantly agreed. But a more interesting interaction was between another minister and Demetrios Constantelos. Now the funniest part of all this is that, if you were to identify the three most conservative members of Stockton's faculty, they would have been Daly, Mench and Constantelos.

Constantelos had a PhD in History but also was a priest of the Greek Orthodox Church (and later founder of Holy Trinity Church in Egg Harbor Township). When he was accosted by a belligerent minister demanding to know if Demetrios knew John 3:16, Demetrios said he would be glad to answer, providing the minister told him whether he wanted him to quote it in Greek, Latin or English. The conversation was not a long one.

Fred Mench

Breaking ground, December 9, 1970. Frank Farley speaking with Magda
Leuchter, Richard Bjork and David Taylor to his right,
and Ralph Dungan, Elizabeth Alton and Franklin Berry to his left.
Courtesy of *The Press of Atlantic City*

Choosing A Solution—David Taylor

Ken Tompkins

In 1965, the Citizens Committee for Higher Education in New Jersey issued a report on the "crisis" in public higher education in the state. Reviewing every aspect of the state colleges, it made many recommendations, among which was the following: "Active planning should go forward for the establishment of new state colleges, enrolling no less than 8,000 by 1975." This simple statement is the reason Richard Stockton College exists.

One of the members of the Citizens Committee was Dave Taylor. Taylor was the president of Taylor, Wiseman, Taylor and Sleeper—civil engineering consultants—in Moorestown, New Jersey. He had been a member of the local school board and had been on the boards of local banks. At this time he was also a member of the Board of Trustees of Trenton State College (now the College of New Jersey). Thus, Dave Taylor brought

17

considerable experience guiding higher education efforts in New Jersey. This is important because, once a college was approved for South Jersey, the board of that new institution was going to need considerable experience to start a new college.

Ralph Dungan, the Chancellor of Higher Education, asked Dave Taylor to leave the Trenton State board and take up the duties of Chairman *Pro Tem* at Stockton. Stockton's Board of Trustees consisted of nine members selected from the four southern counties. They met for the first time at the local community college on February 4, 1969.

The board, under Taylor's leadership, saw its role clearly and very quickly went about its work. The first issue was the selection of a president; the board announced the position, interviewed candidates, and from a large group chose Richard Bjork. At the time, Richard Bjork worked for the Department of Higher Education and was Interim President of Glassboro State (now Rowan University).

In an interview, Dave Taylor said that there were no significant dissensions in the early years of the board and that it was the best board he had ever served on.

The board, he remembered, did not get involved in any personnel decisions, though it reviewed recommendations. It was, he insists, in charge, however, and was very clear about its power and its responsibilities as defined by state law. When challenged—as it frequently was by faculty in the early struggles for power—it simply would not be moved.

At the same time that the board was interviewing candidates for president, it was also deeply involved in selecting a site. Taylor remembers that site selection was hard work. First there were many competing demands—urban or rural, near or far from Atlantic City, isolated or near transportation, empty site or one already established—to weigh and balance. At the end, the board actually took helicopter flights over all of the sites being considered. The present site was approved on September 15, 1969.

Dave Taylor is a tall, stately, no-nonsense person. He is rightly proud of his service to the College. He is friendly and outgoing, but you sense that his strength comes from knowing what the problem is, what the issues are, and what the possible solutions might be. Once all of those factors are known, choosing a solution is a predictable result.

Mayflower Memories

• *A significant number of courses were invented during registration. One was a proposal to hitchhike from Atlantic City to Ypsilanti, Michigan, keeping a journal on the way. Len Solo was the teacher. Approved.*

• *Then there was a proposal to hitchhike back. Disapproved.*

• *Bill Lubenow was the College Examiner, which involved his judging when to grant credit for life experience and how much. He had no tools but his own good judgment and I don't recall that he awarded much credit.*

• *A women's band came from Michigan for a gig at Stockton. No men were allowed. The band agreed to stay at our home, but only if our 5-year-old son and I went elsewhere. We stayed with Marty Miller and his son.*

• *The evening of Bill Daly's first lecture on "Revolution and Revolutionaries" at the Mayflower, two state police officers who were Stockton students and members of my preceptorial group assured me that there were several plain clothes troopers in the audience. They were prepared to handle any insurrections.*

• *A number of us were unhappy about the public schools. We met one Friday evening to discuss our concerns and agreed to start an alternative school. It opened in the next week. Planning? Who needs planning?*

• *A 35 year old woman, studying part-time to finish a degree, came to complain about the instructor in one of her classes. The instructor was very popular among the traditional-age students but she was not into adulation. "Goddammit!" she exploded, "I don't need a friggin' guru! All I need is a teacher!" She finished the course and, as I recall, earned her degree.*

So it went.

Gordon Davies

No Mere Substitute—Magda Leuchter

Ken Tompkins

Magda Leuchter was forty-one when she was appointed to the first Stockton Board of Trustees. Actually, then-Governor Richard Hughes had decided to appoint her husband, Ben Leuchter. Ben and Magda owned the *Vineland Times Journal*, and either of them would have been a good choice: both were liberal Democrats—just the sort of trustees needed for an innovative college. But Ben Leuchter declined, suggesting Magda. Hughes agreed, and she received a call from Ralph Dungan—then Chancellor of Higher Education—asking her to accept appointment. She served from 1969–1980, and was elected once to be the board chairperson.

Magda Leuchter had had plenty of experience on various boards; she had served on the Vineland Hospital Board and had been the President of the Vineland Hadassah. In addition, she had served as Secretary of the Board of the Vineland Public Library and was a very active member of the League of Women Voters.

Her appointment was also a logical choice because there was strong interest in the eventual location of the College: the "Committee of 50" from Vineland had been a powerful advocate for locating the College in western Atlantic County. So, that part of the county needed representation.

When asked in an interview about choosing the site, Mrs. Leuchter said that, as she remembered it, the best site would be near the Atlantic City Expressway, would not be in Atlantic City, and it would be one that could be expanded.

She also said that the Stockton Board of Trustees was never personal in its disagreements. While her point of view—like those of others—was sometimes rejected, it was not a rejection of her. She attributed this to the leadership of Dave Taylor. Other board members have noted the same reason for the early board's success.

Concurring with Dave Taylor and Elizabeth Alton, Mrs. Leuchter said that the board was not involved in personnel decisions, was not involved in curricular design, and was not involved in the daily operations of the College, or in the design of the first buildings.

Mrs. Leuchter related a story about choosing the name of the College. She said in an interview that naming the College after Richard Stockton occurred at one of her family dinners when the issue came up.

Magda Leuchter was one of the central members of Stockton's first Board of Trustees. She was knowledgeable, informed, patient, and clear about her role and that of the board.

Board of Trustees Meeting: Left to Right: Richard Chait, Richard Bjork, Elizabeth Alton, Franklin Berry, Magda Leuchter, James Hayward, Robert Brooks and Charles Reynolds. (1976)

Shakespeare Had it Wrong

Ken Tompkins and Rob Gregg

Shakespeare had it wrong; names mean everything: acceptance, financial success, loyalty or rejection, satire, failure, and abandonment. A quick computer search turns up the five rules for naming a company or an organization. A name

• has to be memorable,
• should have a visual element,
• has to have a positive connotation,
• needs to include a hint about what the company does, and
• has to be fairly short.

Colleges, today, will name anything for a specific contribution. In a *Los Angeles Times* article (November 30, 1999) about the practice of naming objects on a campus, the following list of examples is compiled:

• Your name on an elevator—$50,000
• Your name on a scholarship to put a quarterback through school—$350,000
• Your name on a street light—$15,000
• Your name on a bench—$12,000
• Your name on a school—$45,000,000

Naming provides proof of generosity, a kind of immortality, family recognition, and evidence of being high in the cultural pecking order.

So it should come as no surprise that the naming of Stockton has become a legendary event. There are, for example, at least three publically told stories about how Stockton got its name.

One First Cohort faculty tells the story of the Stockton board meeting at one of the service areas on the New Jersey Turnpike. Not yet having a name for the College, board members decided to name it after the person for whom the service area was named—Richard Stockton.

Both Richard Bjork, the first president, and his wife Joan have told the story about having a small boy in their Lawrenceville, New Jersey neighborhood come to their house. He had heard that the College was looking for a name, and he told the president that he had a couple to suggest. Neither the president nor his wife remembered all of the names; the one they did remember was Richard Stockton State College—thus naming the college after one of the five signers of the Declaration of Independence from New Jersey.

Another First Cohort faculty member says that he heard that there had been a disagreement from the beginning of the College as to whether it was going to be a distinctive liberal arts college, which would draw from all over the state and perhaps beyond, or whether it would be a college that would cater primarily to the needs of South Jersey. Ralph Dungan and Bjork favored the former position, and some of the trustees, supported by many in the outside community, favored the latter. These trustees were putting pressure on Bjork to name the college in a way that would identify it with South Jersey, and so he asked Dungan to preempt that discussion by imposing a name that would not do so. Dungan had to do this in a hurry in order to close off the discussion before the next meeting of the Stockton Board of Trustees. He and the folks at the Department of Higher Education grabbed Stockton's name, as a signer of the Declaration of Independence from New Jersey, to meet the deadline without undertaking a thorough investigation of Richard Stockton's credentials.

The Board of Trustees had previously requested suggestions from the pubic in the spring of 1969. By August they had received sixty-four names, which fell into three general categories: places, things, and people.

For places, there are the expected South Jersey shore areas:
• Atlantic Highlands College
• College by the Sea
• Garden State College
• New Jersey East College
• Ocean Sands State College
• Southeast College of New Jersey

For things, there are some unusual suggestions:
• Berry Bottom Bog State
• Blueberry State College
• Boardwalk College
• College of the Sand
• Gull College
• Sand Piper State College
• Jersey Tomato College

For people, there are also some strange possibilities:
• Einstein State College
• Farley State College
• Pinky's Corner College
• Virgil I. Grissom State College
• Woodrow Wilson State College

Some brief explanation seems warranted. Berry Bottom Bog State or Jersey Tomato College cannot be considered as serious suggestions. Einstein was living in Princeton, New Jersey at the time, and, though Woodrow Wilson was long deceased, he, too, was connected to Princeton. Pinky's Corner is a long-running interview show on radio and tv in Atlantic City. Farley State would have named the College for an incredibly powerful state senator who was instrumental in getting the legislation establishing the college passed in Trenton. Finally, Virgil Grissom (an early astronaut) had no connection to New Jersey and is a strange suggestion, perhaps based on the fact that his death was in 1967—two years before this list was collected.

The process following the public request for names was this:
- In June 1969 the Board of Trustees had received thirty names from its public request.
- In July 1969 Jim Judy (secretary to the board) reported that forty names had been received.
- In August 1969 there were sixty-four names included in the Board of Trustees' minutes.
- By the September 1969 meeting, the board had winnowed the list to twelve names, and the trustees chose five to vote on.
- By October 1, 1969 the Board of Trustees had decided officially on Richard Stockton State College.

The name Richard Stockton State College is in the original list of June 1969, so it seems to have been a contender early in the process. However, in the initial vote by the Board of Trustees it came in bottom of five names, behind Southern New Jersey State College, South Jersey State College, Atlantic State College and Jersey Shore State College.

Given this fact, the question of who came up with the name is perhaps less significant (since the name was offered up early in the process) than why it was that the name progressed from being ranked at the bottom of the major contenders to being picked. This certainly lends credence to the story about Dungan making the decision. The other question is why none of the other four signers of the Declaration of Independence—Abraham Clark, John Hart, Francis Hopkinson, and John Witherspoon—were ever contenders as possible names for the college. Each one of these men might have been appropriate for different reasons, bringing something different to the college. Francis Hopkinson, for example, was a musician, composer, and a man of letters; John Witherspoon, for another, was President of New Jersey College (later Princeton).

What was clear, however, was that no investigation was undertaken about any of the names offered and certainly not of Richard Stockton. He, after all, was the one signer who had signed an oath of loyalty to the Crown after he had signed the Declaration of Independence. There were extenuating circumstances for this act. Nonetheless, this might well have given the college founders pause had they known about it. Moreover, the fact that the college was being established in the immediate aftermath of the civil rights movement and at a time of growing awareness about the history of slavery in the United States would perhaps have led the board to shy away from Stockton had they known that he had been an unrepentant slave owner.

SUGGESTED NAMES FOR NEW COLLEGE—ADDENDUM
(presented to the Board of Trustees, August 1969)

A-1 College
All Wars Memorial College
Atlantic Beautiful College
Atlantic City College
Atlantic Highlands College
Atlantic Lighthouse College
Atlantic Seaboard College
Barren Pines College
Beach College of South Jersey
Berry Bottom Bog State
Blueberry State College or Blueberry College New Jersey State
Blueberry College
South Jersey Blueberry State
Boardwalk College
Cape Security
Coastal Plain State
College by the Sea
College in the Pines
College of the Sand
Convention City College
Delanta State College (Delaware and Atlantic)
Eastern College
Edge State College
Edison State College
Einstein State College
Excelsior State College
Farley State College
Garden State Source
Garden State Southern College
Great Egg Harbor Bay College
Gull College
Jersey Tomato College
Jonathan Pitney State College
Leeds College
Lenape State College
Lower Jersey Liberal Arts College
McKee State College
Neptune Shore College
New Air College
New Jersey Bayside State College
New Jersey Colonial College
New Jersey East College
New Jersey Southern College
New Jersey State Bell College
Ocean Sands State College
Ocean State College
Pinky's Corner College
Resort College
Richard Stockton State College
Sand Piper State College
Sandy Harbor State College
Sea Breeze College
Seashell College
Sea Spray State College
South Atlantic Delaware College
Southeast College of New Jersey
South Jersey College
South Jersey College-by-the-Sea
Southern Pines of Knowledge
Star of the Sea College
Triangle College
Tri-County College
University of South Jersey
Virgil I. Grissom State College
White Cap State College
Woodrow Wilson State College

Richard Bjork and Joan Bjork at a Stockton basketball game (1975) - Courtesy of *The Press of Atlantic City*

Breaking Eggs—Richard Bjork

Rob Gregg

Being the founding president of an organization is, by any measure, a difficult task. If you have been responsible for the creation of that organization, then, perhaps, you will be given a little more license to bring your vision for the organization to fruition, and, like a George Washington, you will end up being revered. But if you are creating a college, where you will need to bring together and lead many different and contending forces—trustees, administrators, faculty, students, and the surrounding community—it is most likely that you will remain a person beloved by few, even if you do earn the grudging respect of many.

This was certainly the case for Richard E. Bjork who served as Stockton's founding president from 1969 to 1978. Many members of the college community were affected directly by decisions that he made, and those who had a different vision of what Stockton might be, or a different sense of how to achieve a shared vision, would complain bitterly about him. Much of this was fair criticism, derived from honest disagreements over the direction in which Stockton should move, but some of it devolved into *ad hominem* attacks, so that the name Bjork became a receptacle for everything at the College about which people wanted to complain.

Creating a college at a time when idealism was very much in the air meant considerable conflict from the different visions held by individuals or groups. Different constituencies clung strongly to beliefs about what made the College special and often shared overlapping (and at the same time varying) commitments to student independence, to shared governance, to interdisciplinarity and General Studies, or to the precepting system. Like revolutionaries in the aftermath of a revolution, each group judged others in terms of their purity—the extent to which they conformed to those beliefs in a manner similar to themselves. Trying to lead the college under these conditions, confronted by these competing forms of idealism, was always going to be difficult as every administrative decision had its detractors. Once you are aware of this, then it is possible to view Bjork's presidency in a reasonably detached manner and recognize his accomplishment.

Richard Bjork came to Stockton at age thirty-eight, after briefly holding the positions of Vice Chancellor for Higher Education in New Jersey and Acting President of Glassboro College. He was involved in the planning of the College from the very beginning, taking part in all the discussions about what kind of institution it should be and whom it should serve. Bjork's own vision in this regard was an expansive one. While three of the first trustees of the college, Elizabeth Alton, Charles Reynolds, and James Hayward, had a more regional view, wanting to bring a college to South Jersey to serve local communities, Bjork's view was that the new college, while located in South Jersey, should reach for a statewide and even national reputation.

This idea was reflected in the naming of the institution. While many in the area and among the trustees were happy when it looked like the school would be called the College of South Jersey (or some other name denoting its location), Bjork indicated that he wanted a name that would not simply tie the College to the region. He and Dave Taylor, Chairman of the Board of Trustees, prevailed upon Ralph A. Dungan, Chancellor of Higher Education for New Jersey, to reject naming the College for its location. Stockton was, instead, selected, after a signer of the Declaration of Independence who had been strongly identified with the premier private university in the state (named the College of New Jersey until 1896 when it became Princeton University). Bjork thought Stockton was a better choice for a name, giving the College some cachet and promoting its position as a statewide institution.

At the same time that he held this more elitist sense of the College, he was very much aware that its mission lay in admitting average students and improving their performance. He had no expectation that Stockton would draw the most elite students from around the state. Instead, he believed that the College would recruit students from other state colleges because of the kind of education it offered. Stockton would treat these students as adults, giving them choices and flexibility, and providing them with an excellent faculty from which to learn. Average students would benefit by receiving a strong liberal arts education, he believed, and the college experience could be a transformative one for them.

Right from the outset, however, this vision would run into problems. Treating students as adults in some ways went against the grain of American education at this time as it moved towards greater provision of services for students; acting *in loco parentis* provided a cushion that many students (and their parents) welcomed; treating students as adults who might participate in governance meant they might oppose some of the things you wished to accomplish. And of the many "petty tyrannies and fiefdoms" that he believed he was confronted by at the College, Bjork maintained that the worst were found in the student groups. Initially, he began without establishing a separate Division of Student Affairs, believing that this was unnecessary. He soon learned that this was not the right decision, but, in some ways, the damage had been done. As Student Affairs grew over the years, it would be seen by those in Academic Affairs, not as one of the cornerstones of the College, as it was at other schools, but as something that was both siphoning off resources from the academic realm and departing from the original vision. Bjork's vision had been strongly grounded in the idea that students are and should be treated as adults, but the landscape of higher education was changing so dramatically that there seemed little likelihood of Stockton competing with other colleges with this as a guiding principle.

Providing choices and flexibility meant that the College required greater commitment from faculty members, who had to cater to the needs and interests of students. This would soon lead to friction over questions of their workload. The problem was exacerbated by Bjork's unsympathetic view of the faculty. "It would be pretty hard to convince me," he proclaimed, "that many people in higher education, and even at Stockton, are that overworked, that they're worn down and ground down." Whether or not he was accurate in his general assessment of higher education, Bjork missed the fact that faculty compared themselves to faculty members at other educational institutions, not to industrial or other laborers, and, by that measure, they saw, what he recognized as well, that they were working harder than their peers. Early Stockton faculty members got the impression that he was the state college president least open and responsive to faculty concerns.

Lastly, hiring and retaining an excellent faculty would necessarily lead to questions about who should make decisions over reappointment and tenure, who would decide whether or not a faculty member was good enough. In many situations a new college would want to hold on to whatever faculty it could secure, but Bjork recognized that it was a "buyer's market," with plenty of faculty looking for jobs, so he believed he could be a little freer to replace faculty he felt were not performing at the necessary level. Thus he imposed high standards, and he became very much involved in tenure decisions, often determining their outcome against the recommendations of the faculty. This led to widespread consternation and even outrage among faculty, which only intensified when he promoted the idea of a tenure quota, arguing its necessity for the health of the College. By placing himself at the forefront of discussions about tenure quotas in New Jersey and pushing for its adoption at Stockton, Bjork provided the Stockton Federation of Teachers with a very strong issue to unite around.

A great deal of the opposition he engendered, however, resulted from his style as an administrator, which rested on his belief that to be good was to be unpopular. As president, he felt he needed to make the unpopular decision if this was required for the good of the institution. "The biggest problem internally," he claimed, "is to maintain a dynamic institution." In order to accomplish this, top administrators, he felt, needed to be willing to "open the window to new ideas." Almost everyone would agree that this is a good goal, especially at a new college wishing to foster a reputation for innovation and experimentation. But the corollary to this, for Bjork, was that the College needed "to have an administration that is decisive because someone [had] better make the choice. And the business of choosing is between good and bad. If you don't have top administration willing to be very unpopular, you are going to have difficulty achieving what [you hope to achieve]." The difficulty, for administrators who served Bjork, was that he often saw their disagreements with him as a lack of resolve, an unwillingness to make "determinative decisions that really stick," rather than as alternative and valid viewpoints. The turnover of administrators under Bjork, which was very high, is thus suggestive of a problem that arose directly from Bjork's style, rather than from his failure of vision or his adoption of ideas that were fundamentally out of tune with the College.

Bjork's achievements were certainly great. He placed the College on a secure footing financially and made the College a power with a very strong reputation in the state. He oversaw the construction of buildings that, with their adaptability, could serve the institution throughout its formative years exceedingly well. He expanded the institution from an enrollment of 900 in the first year of teaching at the Mayflower, to 4,914 in 1978, when he resigned. He presided over a college with a very different approach to general education, bolstered by its own institutional structure—something that he felt was important to establish if General Studies was to thrive at Stockton. He also achieved the goal of hiring an excellent faculty (and Stockton has indeed always boasted a faculty that compares favorably to many elite private colleges). And this faculty was fiercely loyal to the Stockton experiment, a feeling that may have grown stronger,

ironically, as they engaged in conflict with the administration (as reflected in the simultaneous intensity of the union's opposition to Bjork and its loyalty to the ideals on which the college was founded). While Stockton College might have been considered another backwater college in the state system, under Bjork it was able to establish the kind of reputation he had wanted for it.

There is an old saying among revolutionaries that you can't make an omelet without breaking a few eggs. Bjork would probably have agreed, seeing each of his own "determinative decisions" as ones that would likely crack some shells. But those who believe such things sometimes forget that it is still important what kind of omelet you cook and how tasty it ends up being. When eggs are being broken and the concoction leaves a bitter taste in the mouth, then the feeling sometimes grows that the eggs should have been left untouched. Certainly many who dealt with Bjork ended up feeling this way. However much they admired and respected him for being forceful and decisive, they saw that his actions often created animosity towards him personally and distrust of the administration generally. Certainly this distrust (of *any* administration) remained one of the defining features of the College for much of its first forty years, and it has only recently been displaced as new administrators and faculty have been hired who no longer bear the scars of the early years.

Richard Bjork's achievements were remarkable, and by the time he resigned in 1978 to move on to the position of Chancellor of the Vermont State Colleges, he had helped to create a unique college in Pomona, New Jersey. But it has to be said that the omelet could have been more palatable.

Children of the Sixties

Daniel N. Moury

Left to right: Dan Moury, Philip Klukoff, and John Rickert (1970 and 1971)

Stockton and its Division of Natural Science and Mathematics (NAMS) were children born of the 1960s.

Higher education in the 1960s faced a time it was not prepared to meet. The students of the late 1940s and 1950s were children of the Great Depression. Many of the men had traveled all over the world at war. Women had taken their places in the factories, as well as serving many noncombat roles in the military. They came out of the war serious about getting educations and building better lives for themselves and their families. And their children were to become our students of the 1960s and 1970s. Even though the military was still largely segregated, travel had given many southern Blacks a taste of integration. The environmental movement was aborning. So the seeds for change on many fronts were quietly germinating.

By the 1960s we were embroiled in an unpopular war in Vietnam. The civil rights battle under the leadership of Martin Luther King and many others against discrimination and for equal rights for Blacks was building to a climax. And the first Earth Day was held in 1970. College students, rebelling against conservative parents who were children of the Great Depression, became activists as tv put the pictures of war and racism in front of them daily. They also rebelled against the traditional *in loco parentis* nanny role embraced by most colleges and universities. And the FDA approval of the first birth control pill for sale

was about to introduce the first generation of young people to the sexual revolution. It was a period of radicalization for both students and faculty. Stockton was, in many ways, a response to much of this environment.

YEAR MINUS TWO (NOVEMBER,1968-JUNE 1971)

This was a planning period of more than a year that was set in motion by the passing, in November 1968, of the authorizing legislation for Stockton and Ramapo Colleges. This was a major step for New Jersey. For years it had been known as the "Cuckoo State" since it sent the majority of its young off to colleges in other states. Because the state had so few public or private institutions relative to its population, many small southern private colleges recruited twenty to fifty percent of their enrollment from New Jersey.

The process started with the appointment of a Board of Trustees, the naming of Richard Bjork as president, the hiring of assistants, and the establishment of Stockton's first administrative office next to an abandoned pet store on the Black Horse Pike. During this period, the president and staff met with a number of groups from South Jersey (e.g., public school administrators, public health professionals, and business leaders) to determine their expectations for and perceived needs from Stockton. Information from these sources along with consultant reports and position papers from the president and staff were folded into

Left to right: Ralph Bean, Elizabeth Marsh, Dan Moury and Alan Steinberg at the Wildlife Sanctuary (1972)

a document for consideration, in April 1970, by the Education Policies Committee of the board. This was, in many ways, a radical document that already included the proposed modular clock, the three-two-three calendar as one of three options under consideration, and the "unit" four-credit course. The academic program was already divided into General Studies, Liberal Studies, and major. And Stockton was to be a community in which students were treated as adults and would work collegially with faculty and administrative staff on policy and all other matters affecting the life of the college. In the early years, the trustees were generally supportive of, if sometimes puzzled by, the unruly creature they had had a role in creating.

YEAR MINUS ONE (1970-1971)

During this year there were seventeen professional staff plus clerical support. There was a lot of day-to-day contact among the six in Academic Affairs but not much interaction on a regular basis with colleagues outside Academic Affairs. And all of the deans were primarily focused on putting their divisions together. Staff meetings were used to work on policy and administrative issues that were the responsibility of Academic Affairs. Any approvals by or interaction with President Bjork were taken care of by Wes Tilley, the Vice President for Academic Affairs. Other staff were being hired and were working with the state to acquire the land and with the architects to develop the construction plans, building a library collection, setting up an admissions apparatus and recruiting students, and a myriad of other issues. The coordination of all relations with the state Department of Higher Education rested with President Bjork. And the deans seldom heard from the president unless there was something he didn't understand or didn't like.

ACADEMIC AFFAIRS

On or about July 1, 1970 all of the academic staff, including myself, the Dean of NAMS, gathered in the Scott house on Jimmie Leeds Road. The group included:

- Wes Tilley, Vice President for Academic Affairs, who had hired all of the rest. Wes had the look and manner of a traditional academic in the humanities, but he talked a soft revolution.
- Ken Tompkins, Dean of Experimental Studies (EXPT), who was the colleague with whom I felt most comfortable personally and philosophically. Ken was talking about a new approach to teacher education that made sense, a physical education program that was to be built on life and club sports, and an approach to the history and philosophy of science and technology that was understandable. There was also Methods of Inquiry, another interesting concept. Several of the NAMS faculty, forty years later, credit Ken with being one of the reasons Stockton looked attractive to them.
- Phil Klukoff, Dean of Arts and Humanities (ARHU), who was the youngest of the group at thirty-two. As the group began to work together, he was clearly working from a different philosophical base. He seemed to be much more impressed with past scholarly achievements in the candidates he reviewed than with their potential as teachers of undergraduates.
- Woody Thrombley, Dean of Social and Behavioral Studies (SOBL), who was, at fifty, the oldest of the deans. He was the only one to come from a major university (Indiana University), and his views were a product of that background. Woody was an old-line liberal, but it was not immediately clear that he was "one of us." However, as the group began to work together, they learned to accept Woody's more educationally conservative perspective and came to value his political savvy and skill. As things began to unravel in the second year, his perceptions were valuable to us all.
- John Rickert, Dean of Management Sciences, who was hired later than the rest. (Another candidate for this position had been offered and had accepted the position during the fall

of 1970, but he was diagnosed with terminal brain cancer soon after and never arrived.) The other deans participated in recruiting for this position. Management Sciences differed from the other divisions in that it offered career-oriented programs such as Management, Accounting, and Criminal Justice. The desirability of having such disciplines, in addition to the arts and sciences, as a part of Stockton was probably viewed differently by the various deans. In addition, John came after his interview some months after the May 4, 1970 Ohio National Guard shooting on the Kent State campus. That day, in a period of thirteen seconds, members of the National Guard shot thirteen Kent State students in and around an anti-war rally on campus, killing four and permanently paralyzing one more. It was one of the worst atrocities of the Vietnam debate, and John did not seem to be as concerned about it as we were. Not all of us thought he was a good choice for Stockton.

- Gordon Davies, Dean of Academic Development (ADEV), who was a very energetic and enthusiastic member of the group. He pretty much had to define his division, which was very different from the other academic divisions. He probably had the best analytical skills in the group and was a strong colleague.

THE DEAN OF NAMS

I most likely saw an announcement of the position available at Stockton in the *Chronicle of Higher Education*, or another publication, during the winter of 1969-1970. I was in a tight spot. With a wife and two children to support, I was about to be without a job for the 1970-1971 academic year.

The previous year, as president of the local American Association of University Professors (AAUP) chapter at Tusculum College, I had challenged the president's nonrenewal of an instructor in the Music department without giving her adequate notice. The move had been made to allow the Music department chairman to elevate his wife from half- to full-time. The instructor and I were both given terminal one-year contracts.

So I had been searching in a very crowded job market for almost a year and had had no luck. I was negotiating to buy a neighborhood Phillips 66 station and was about to get out of higher education when I got the call to come to New Jersey for an interview. The invitation to join in the birthing of Stockton as the Dean of the Division of Natural Science and Mathematics (the deans were actually hired as chairmen since the state formulas couldn't accommodate five deans at an institution with zero students) followed soon after.

I was thirty-five years old, a graduate of Wake Forest (College) University (1960), and I had completed my PhD in molecular biology (biochemistry) at Purdue University (1963). I served as a postdoctoral fellow and Instructor in Biochemistry at Bowman Gray School of Medicine of Wake Forest (1963-66). And I came to Stockton after four years (1966-1970) with the unmerited title of Professor of Chemistry and as the chair of a 1.5-member

department at Tusculum College, a small Presbyterian college in east Tennessee. The other half-time member was a retired chemist who had worked on the project that created the first sustained nuclear chain reaction under Soldiers Field in Chicago. And given my situation with my current employer, I did not bring much in the way of references.

Given my lack of both time in grade and quality of experience, it is something of a mystery as to why I was chosen. I had never hired anyone in any capacity. With the exception of running a crew selling magazines door-to-door in the summer of 1955, I had no supervisory experience. And I had never built a working birdhouse, much less an expensive science lab facility. I was not, it would seem, an obvious choice in a time when at least a hundred academics were scrambling for almost every job available. I did bring to the interview and the job a fairly radical view of what I thought undergraduate education should be and an overweening self-confidence, with which I had always been blessed. I assumed I could do anything if given the chance.

Before coming to Stockton, I had worked with my students to overcome the authoritarian nature of the teacher/student relationship. It was replaced with a junior/senior scholar model, adapted from St. John's College of Annapolis. But while St. John's used Mr. (or Ms.) in addressing both faculty and students, I adopted first names. And I had discarded the coat and tie as a badge of authority and dressed casually. Students were required to become partners in their own education. At Tusculum, I had four students who had entered as freshmen the year I arrived and graduated as I left four years later. Two of them have now served for many years on the Tusculum Board of Trustees and one chairs the board. I had also attended the Danforth Summer Workshop on the Liberal Arts in Colorado Springs and spent a summer at Antioch College of Ohio learning about cooperative education. The image presented by Stockton was most attractive. In short, nothing in my life had really prepared me to be the founding Dean of NAMS, but I was ready to create a new educational model.

I was given a copy of a sixty-page document prepared for the 1970 trustee planning seminar. It said that, among other things, Stockton would:

- Be "an alternative to the traditional."
- Be "strong in the liberal arts as well as professional education."
- Take advantage of its "own and neighboring physical and human environments giving special attention to environmental studies."
- "Acknowledge and respect the maturity of students" and build "a community of mutual respect" among students, faculty, and staff.
- Have "an acceptance of and responsiveness to change."

While there was no detailed plan describing how all of this was to be accomplished, it seemed to respond to the malaise in higher education and the nation and was more than appealing to me.

In a Heart Beat

Ken Tompkins

Inventing a college isn't exactly something that the academic experiences of the founding deans had prepared us for. In a strange way, we had to invent the process of inventing a college while we were inventing it. It took us time to learn what to give priority to and what to shove down the list. It took time to imagine what our particular division might look like, what policies it would follow, what college-wide policies needed to be set, how recruitment of faculty would happen, what the students might be like, as well as what it might be like living in the physical college. There were—for each of the four of us—literally hundreds of decisions to be made in each month of the fifteen months we had before we opened.

We met for the first time in 1970 at a Fourth of July picnic (though I can't remember exactly where, perhaps at the president's home on Shore Road in Linwood). It's strange that we didn't mark the event with photos; if we did, I haven't found them.

On the next day, we gathered to begin the fifteen-month process of starting a new college. Again, I'm not sure where we met. All of the land for the college had not been purchased yet, so I don't think it was in any of the buildings on campus. Eventually, we were located in the Scott House (named for the people who sold it to the state) on Jimmie Leeds Road. My office was in the back, northern corner of that building.

There were originally four of us: Philip Klukoff as Dean of Arts and Humanities, Woodworth (Woody) Thrombley as Dean of Social and Behavioral Sciences, Dan Moury as Dean of the Natural Sciences and Math and myself as Dean of General Studies. While we were different in many ways, we had all come through the undergraduate and graduate training of the 1960s, we had all taught undergraduates, and we all had PhDs, so we had completed major research projects. All of us had also navigated the academic chaos and revolutions then occurring.

Woody Thrombley had been at Indiana University in the Political Science department. He was the oldest—and in some ways the most academically experienced—dean. I used to refer to him privately as the "Gray Fox," partly because he had graying hair. He was an expert on Southeast Asia, which made him a supporter of the Vietnam war. As a matter of fact, I had actually seen him at Indiana University in a famous debate on Cuba. Woody was appointed as Academic Vice President after Wes Tilley was fired. Though conservative, he worked well as vice president. We remained friends even though he was responsible for firing me in 1973.

Philip Klukoff was appointed Dean of Arts and Humanities. Klukoff had come from the University of Michigan and was a typical research-oriented academician. Unfortunately, we never agreed on much. He was much more of a traditional academic than the rest of us, and, therefore, created a traditional division. For example, he hired the most and oldest full professors of any of the deans. This made Arts and Humanities very different from the other divisions, all of which had hired young faculty.

Dan Moury was the Dean of Natural Sciences and Mathematics. He was a southerner coming from small colleges, where he had taught chemistry. He appeared, in both his interviews and when we gathered, with a peace symbol around his neck. In some ways, he was the biggest risk-taker among the deans. The division he created had an incredibly strong sense of community absent from the other divisions, and the lab facilities he designed were the most radical in the country.

It should be noted that a Dean of Management Sciences had not been appointed in March as the other deans had been. Indeed, we did not interview and hire that dean until very late in 1970. Wes Tilley did not especially like business academics and, by waiting until the rest of the deans were in place, wanted to assure that the professional dean had a liberal arts background. We found and appointed a person in the late fall of 1970, but before he could take up his duties he died suddenly of a brain tumor, and we had to initiate another search, which resulted in John Rickert being appointed in early 1971.

As for me, it was a cold Iowa night in March when I got the call. My former English department chairman—Wes Tilley—was on the phone. Wes had been my chairman at Millikin University in Decatur, Illinois; when I went there in 1965, he quickly became a close friend and academic mentor. Indeed, I went to Millikin in large part because of Wes Tilley. I had other offers but because of an instant connection wanted to teach with him.

By 1967 we both had left Millikin, he to go to St. John's College on Staten Island and I to go to Central College in Iowa to take up a chairman's position. It was in my office at Central that I got the call. As I remember it, after pleasant greetings, Wes asked me, "How would you like to start a college?" That certainly is a sentence most of us never hear. He had just been appointed Vice President for Academic Affairs and was rounding up candidates for dean positions. He explained to me that he wanted me to consider two positions: General Studies and Arts and Humanities. I later chose General Studies because it was a

Left to right: Ken Tompkins, Woodworth Thrombley, and Wesley Tilley (1970)

totally undefined role and because we had—when we were both at Millikin—spent hours discussing general education.

Like the other candidates, I came to Atlantic City to interview in March. The interviews were held in the college offices located in One Williams Plaza—a strip mall of six stores on the Black Horse Pike outside of Atlantic City. The store next to the college offices was a pet store, and all during my interviews puppies could be heard yapping.

I moved to Pleasantville, New Jersey in June. A local realtor found a clean, empty apartment near the bus station for me and a staff member. The other deans were moving their families into homes they had bought; my family in Iowa could not come with me then, though they came in early July.

As Dan Moury points out in his essay on his experiences as a founding dean, we had little contact with the other sections of the college except through the president, vice presidents and directors. I have always wondered how different Stockton might have been had we had constant and engendering contacts with everyone else at the College. For example, President Bjork was totally against an *in loco parentis* policy, and he would not allow any of the Student Affairs staff to consider such support systems as counseling or any other health services. Because we had little contact with other College offices, we were never brought into any discussions (that I remember anyway) about these issues and how they might affect our pedagogies or student performance.

I have a file of minutes of the deans' meetings; there are thirty-nine pages recording our discussions from July 23, 1970 to August 4, 1971. The issues that we discussed are, in a way, predictable:

1. July 23, 1970—Recruitment, General and Liberal Studies, and the grading system.

2. July 31, 1970—The two phases of the campus buildings.
3. August 28, 1970—Library issues: subscriptions, book requests, and services.
4. August 31, 1970—Preceptorial advising, transcripts, lectures, grades.
5. September 14, 1970—Role of the chairmen. (We were originally not called deans.)
6. September 23, 1970—Phase II and Phase III buildings and facilities.
7. October 1, 1970—Among others: what furniture we needed in the Scott House.
8. February 24, 1971—Budgets, institutional governance.
9. March 24, 1971—General Studies and Teacher Development (the program for preparing high school teachers).
10. August 4, 1971—Second round of recruitment, chairmen's role in promotion and tenure.

It is my considered opinion that while the founding deans were good at inventing a college, we were not very good at—or interested in—administering it. Indeed, not one of the founding deans survived—for various reasons—after five years. All of us were either fired or shifted to other responsibilities or moved on to other institutions. Klukoff and I were both fired and returned to full-time teaching in Literature. Moury was first moved to the deanship of Academic Services and, later, left for a position in the New Jersey Department of Higher Education. Thrombley, after serving as Vice President of Academic Affairs, left for an administrative position in Alaska.

It was a heady time. I have never been so busy, so stimulated, so gratified, so frustrated, so cooperative and, finally, so rejected as I was as the Dean of General Studies. I'd do it again in a heartbeat.

Observations

Richard Gajewski

Before coming to Stockton, I spent six years with a large national CPA firm in New York City, followed by five years as Controller of Rochester Institute of Technology in Rochester, New York. I was probably not the best qualified person for the position at Stockton since my experience was somewhat narrow as controller at RIT. However, while I was at RIT, the Institute constructed an entirely new campus on a 1,300-acre site just south of Rochester. As a result, I learned a great deal about construction and moving an entire institution into a new facility.

While at RIT I got to know Dick Bjork, who served as Assistant to the President there. Dick decided to leave RIT in 1968 after being there for two years. On the way to his new position in the higher education system of the state of Wisconsin, he received a phone call from New Jersey's Chancellor of Higher Education offering him an appointment to the position of Vice Chancellor. Dick decided to take the offer and cancelled his trip to Wisconsin and drove to Trenton, New Jersey instead. Dick was appointed President of what would be Richard Stockton State College in June 1969. Shortly after Dick was appointed to the position, he contacted me and asked if I might be interested in applying for the position of Vice President for Administration and Finance. I traveled to Trenton and spent the better part of the day with Dick discussing his and my expectations for the position. I was really intrigued with the prospect of helping to build a brand new college. After discussing the idea with my wife, I decided to accept the offer.

So there I was, leaving my job in a 140-year-old institution to take a position at this brand new college. When folks asked me the name of the college, I had to tell them that I did not know. When they asked where the college was located, I also had to tell them that I did not know—somewhere in Atlantic County. Some thought that I had taken leave of my senses.

I began my employment at Stockton in early September 1969. My first day on the job was spent with other staff and trustees taking helicopter rides to look over the several sites that had been identified for the location of the college. The Board of Trustees then decided on the Galloway Township site and a name— Richard Stockton State College.

Our first office was in Williams Plaza on the Black Horse Pike, a former veterinarian's office next to a pet shop. We remained there until the college offices could be moved to the newly acquired residential buildings on the Pomona campus. Faculty offices and some administrative offices were moved to the Mayflower Hotel in Atlantic City in August 1971. Some of us even had two offices, one on campus plus an office in the Mayflower Hotel.

I had a rather rude awakening when I realized that just about everything we wanted to do had to be done through the bureaucracies in Trenton. Purchases had to be done by the state purchasing department, all disbursements went through the state treasury, and most service staff had to be hired through the state civil service system. While this procedure did slow things down somewhat, I did find the staff of the central bureaucracies to be helpful and cooperative and willing to help us, given the tight deadline we had to have our facilities ready to go in less than two years.

My responsibilities at Stockton included the typical business and finance functions, such as billing and collection of student tuition and fees, purchasing and accounts payable, budget development and management, security and safety, physical plant maintenance, personnel services, bookstore, food services, and mail and telephone services. Management of the construction project was the responsibility of an agency in Trenton and the Director of Campus Planning.

This was a significant increase in my responsibilities compared to the narrower scope at RIT. I had a lot to learn and a very short time to learn it, but that is what made the job interesting and challenging. Thanks to the help I received from the offices in Trenton, the chief financial officers of the six existing state colleges, and the competent staff that I was able to hire, I succeeded.

The first thing that had to be done after the Board of Trustees selected the site was to identify the property owners and negotiate the purchase of their properties. The actual negotiations were done by personnel from Trenton based on appraisals of the value of the properties. After acquisition, it was my responsibility to determine the moving cost allowance each property owner would receive. This allowance, also, was based on guidelines provided by the state.

Planning, design, and construction of the campus buildings began as soon as was practicable, but I will leave that description to the Director of Campus Planning since he was the person on staff who had the responsibility of monitoring construction. Suffice it to say that the construction processes we used broke new ground for the state of New Jersey. Good construction management and fast-track construction techniques were the only way to complete the project for occupancy by September 1971.

In May 1971 it became obvious that the new buildings would not be ready for occupancy by September and we would have to find a location to accommodate the entering class of 900 students expected in September. We considered several alternatives but finally settled on using the Mayflower Hotel located at the boardwalk and Tennessee Avenue in Atlantic City. This was just one more challenge, but with the cooperation of the hotel management, we were able to convert the hotel into classrooms and faculty and administrative offices. College offices were moved into the Mayflower Hotel on August 25, 1971. On September 7, 1971 the college opened its first semester with students in the Mayflower Hotel. An adjacent motel was used for student housing.

Construction of the first phase of the academic buildings was completed in time for classes and offices to be transferred to the Pomona Campus at the end of the fall semester. The first phase of student housing (apartments) was opened in September 1972. The development of the balance of the campus buildings, E-wing through M-wing, by October 1976 seemed almost routine after the anxiety and frustration of getting the first phase, wings A through D, ready for occupancy.

CONCLUSIONS

An important part of my position was to serve as liaison between the college and the various agencies in Trenton that set the financial policies for the college. I am sure that faculty were often frustrated by the bureaucratic process for obtaining equipment and supplies, but my staff and I attempted to smooth the way. I found the faculty always cooperative, and I believe that I had a good relationship with the faculty in general.

I was delighted that I was able to serve as a preceptor for students. As a result, I developed a good understanding of the college's programs and got to know a number of students personally. Usually the only contact a person in my position has with students is with those who have difficulty paying their bill or those who have come to my attention through our Security Office. After I left Stockton, I served as an advisor to freshmen at two colleges where I was employed. My experience as a preceptor helped me in those roles.

My experience at Stockton was a huge learning experience for me. The experience I gained at Stockton served me well at the three institutions I served after Stockton. As I look back, I believe that my experience at Stockton was the most interesting and most exciting in my career in higher education administration. Very few people in recent years have had the opportunity to participate in the building of a new college from the ground up.

Stockton has certainly come a long way from the simple beginnings in a former veterinarian's office next to a pet shop in Williams Plaza in Hamilton Township to the present significant academic campus in Pomona. That entering class of 900 students at the Mayflower Hotel in Atlantic City has grown to a student body of almost 8,000 today.

The Stockton story is an amazing story, one that will long be remembered by those of us who were there from the very beginning.

Reappointment Travails

For tenure, contract renewal and promotion, the college required professors to submit self-evaluations of their work, teaching, writings, and critical evaluation of colleagues. The dean of our department, the V.P. of Academic Affairs and the president of the college would make their own judgments and statements to the school dean. In my yearly performance evaluation, Wesley Tilley, the Vice President of Academic Affairs, praised my teaching as well as my devotion to research and writing. He ended an otherwise good evaluation with the statement: "Demetri is very conservative, perhaps the most conservative person in the school." I did not understand what he meant by that, so I called Dr. Tilley to ask what he meant by his observation and ask whether I had any future at Stockton. With a family of six, I did not want to move again. After I told him of my uncertainties he smiled and said, "Demetri, don't worry, it was just a personal, spontaneous observation. Go and get back to work without fear." I received similar encouragement the following year from both the Vice President for Academic Affairs and the President of the College, Richard Bjork, who said to me that they "consider it an honor to have me at Stockton and that I was not somewhere else." In my third year, I was officially given tenure and have been devoted to Stockton ever since, having turned down offers from other, bigger schools. In 1986, the College promoted me to the rank of distinguished professor and rewarded me with the Charles Cooper Townsend Sr. endowed professorship.

Demetrios Constantelos

Connecting bridge between Phase I and Phase II buildings (1976)

Stockton Campus Planning, 1969-1974

Richard N. Schwartz

While working in Cleveland, a colleague informed me about a totally new college being formed near Atlantic City. I was intrigued because my campus-planning experiences at existing colleges had been limited by numerous factors. Existing institutions are usually hemmed in by the surrounding communities, projects are usually single buildings, and entrenched fiefdoms limit options. I contacted Dr. Richard Bjork about my interest, and he invited me for an interview in Trenton, where he was finishing his duties as Vice Chancellor for Higher Education. When

we met, in the summer of 1969, he explained the concept for the College, which included an innovative educational plan, a sizable non-urban setting, and the need for a physical plant that would reflect the College's educational mission—based on the interrelatedness of knowledge. With the concept and the funds in place, this opportunity to create a totally new type of college was real. It was unlike any other. When offered, I immediately accepted the position.

When I arrived in November, I met Dick Gajewski and Jim Judy who were already on board. Other early founders soon joined the team. We worked together to rapidly develop the college, with wide-ranging discussions where everyone's input was welcome. We had daily if not hourly brainstorming sessions, working with the college president to transform the educational concepts into reality. Time was critical as our goal to open in fall 1971 was just two years away.

The Board of Trustees was a group of dedicated individuals who supported and guided our efforts. David Taylor, an engineer with his own firm, chaired the subcommittee overseeing construction. He insisted that Dr. Bjork spend his time on major educational issues and leave the physical development details to his campus planning staff. Elizabeth Alton was an early voice for the creation of a college in South Jersey. She gained the key support of Senator Hap Farley. Mrs. Alton was excited about the cultural and educational advantage, for the students and the community, represented by the college. Her forcefulness was a key factor in the high quality of the 540-seat theater in phase III. Chuck Reynolds, as editor of the *Atlantic City Press*, was instrumental in keeping the public supportive of the College's progress.

Dr. Bjork's influence on the design of the College's physical plant was extensive. His vision was to hire a design firm capable of creating a master plan, as well as designing the buildings and infrastructure, to save time. He made sure the educational philosophy was properly reflected in the physical plant. In addition he allocated enough dollars to land purchase so that the college would not be landlocked.

The Educational Facilities Authority was used to acquire the 1,585 acres. It purchased over one hundred separate parcels. Once that was accomplished, we recommended to the trustees, and with their concurrence, to the Department of Building and Construction (DBC) in Trenton, that the architectural firm of Geddes, Brecher, Qualls, Cunningham (GBQC) of Princeton, be appointed as our single source design consultants. DBC made it official in January 1970. This choice was obvious because of the firm's extensive experience, convenient location, and familiarity with DBC. As a plus, the head of the firm was Robert Geddes, who was also Princeton's Dean of Architecture. He totally understood the educational mission of the College.

The first GBQC effort was to produce a master plan based on anticipated student body sizes over time and the available dollars from the 1968 bond issue for the beginning phases. Phase I (wings A, B, C, and D) was planned for 1,000 students, with Phase II planned for 3,000 students, and Phase III for a future goal of 7,500.

Secondly, the physical plant had to meet the educational criteria, in both site and building development. Stockton's educational plan was based on academic divisions rather than traditional departments. Therefore individual buildings for departments were not considered, and all of the building units were designed to be part of one continuous facility, with each multi-use wing or pod connected to a central spine or gallery. The Gallery would facilitate formal and informal interaction between students and faculty of various disciplines and interests. The multi-use wings running off the Gallery would encourage the same interaction by mixing users and uses.

Of equal importance was the goal of causing the least possible damage to the environment. Building pieces were kept at two stories to stay under the tree line, and full-length windows were spaced along the Gallery so the Pine Barrens landscape could be observed and appreciated. Because of the metal exterior panels, trees very close to the wings were saved, and views of Lake Fred were intermittent where tree cover permitted.

At the same time GBQC's plan also had to integrate the fast-track approach we adopted. Normally a new college building takes three years or more, and we had twenty months. The approach used was to convince DBC to allow the bidding of building systems before the working drawings were completed. These systems were structural steel, ceiling and lighting, interior partitions, HVAC systems, and the exterior skin. Although never before allowed by the state of New Jersey, DBC agreed because of the College's pressure and GBQC's competence. Additionally, a five-foot open module was adopted, so that the wings could be readily changed as needed.

Once the working drawings were finished, four prime contracts were bid and awarded by DBC to the lowest bidders. Costanza Construction of Pennsauken was the low bidder for general construction. In addition to their own work, they were also required to coordinate the work of the other prime bidders. It would have been much better if DBC had been able to award one contract for everything. Then the mechanical, electrical, and plumbing work would have been financially controlled by the general contractor, i.e., Costanza, and coordination problems would not have occurred. Delays did happen, and the planned campus opening date was pushed to January 1972, with the first-semester classes held in the old Mayflower Hotel.

On a parallel track, the site work development had to be designed and built simultaneously. This included the tertiary sewerage treatment plant, two 175-foot deep wells for the water supply, College Drive, exterior lighting, parking lots, and sidewalks. Much of this work was completed by PHA Contractors of Cologne, New Jersey. As a time-saving function, College Drive and the parking lots were built and graveled only. Since the opening had been moved to January, we were able to obtain the help of the New Jersey Department of Transportation to pave College Drive in November. Director John Kohl was instrumental in making that happen, due in part to the fact that he was once my professor at Michigan. The College reimbursed the department for the materials.

One of the most critical concerns raised by the community related to the sewer plan. The three-stage plant was the most ecologically advanced. The third stage produced pure drinkable water to be sprayed on the land. People in Port Republic became concerned that Moss Mill Stream might be contaminated. Dr. Bjork and I attended a public hearing in Port Republic. We were able to explain the concept and point out that the disastrous alternative would be to run a long interconnector to the Atlantic City treatment facility. At that time, this facility was only primary, which allowed raw sewerage to flow into the Atlantic Ocean when the facility was overtaxed in the summer. As the result of this hearing, no local or state governmental agency stopped our tertiary plant.

Obstacles occurred, and we overcame most of them. Good relations in Trenton were the key. One obstacle that had a long-lasting and continuing impact on the college was the intervention of the New Jersey Wetlands Commission. The commission ruled that a number of acres were too close to sea level to support building development. This impacted the area beyond phase III, and major changes later resulted.

Many people contributed to the successful construction of the College's physical plant. It was an educational, political, and architectural feat completed and opened in twenty-four months, four short of the original goal but still incredibly fast for such a monumental undertaking. When I moved on, I could feel we truly had accomplished our mission impossible. One change the early work brought to subsequent phases was the employment of a construction manager to overcome the state's slow four prime contractor approach.

Another subsequent change was adding accreditation planning to the Campus Planning workload. Tom Boyd was promoted to Director of Campus Planning, and we added staff for institutional planning. My job became Vice President for Institutional Planning. I left the College in 1974 and returned to Michigan with a much broader range of responsibilities as Vice Chancellor for Business at Dearborn. Yet nothing in my subsequent career proved to be as exciting and rewarding as being one of, and interacting with, the founders of The Richard Stockton College of New Jersey.

A Student of Life

Having been hired, shorn and shaved, by Ken Tompkins in the Division of Experimental Studies, I immediately attempted to blend in with my new surroundings and allowed my hair to grow. And, well, it just grew…and no one seemed to mind.

Least of all the students. So why not be a student. I was, technically, still one anyway…writing my dissertation at the New School while teaching at Stockton. And in New York City there were still half-price student admissions to movies and museums to be had.

Things were a little looser at Stockton then. A friend lined me up with the students and my picture was snapped. No one called me "sir" then, or "Professor Rubenstein." I passed, and MOMA was none the wiser. Could it have been the hair?

Then that first curl of grey, followed by many more, and my "student" days were over. Full price for years, until one day at the checkout line in G-Wing cafeteria, without my asking…a senior disount on my sushi! Ah, life at Stockton had come full circle. Could it have been the hair?

Joseph Rubenstein

34

Different from the Beginning—NAMS

Daniel N. Moury

THE BEGINNING OF NAMS

In July 1970, on arriving at Stockton, I wrote a five-page document that described the Division of Natural Science and Mathematics (NAMS) in the present tense—as if it really existed. This document was created to explain to the community and to prospective faculty what, at least in my view, NAMS was seeking to become. It was a bit pompous in style, but it was, after all, describing a Dream to come. It was divided into five sections: General Philosophy, Reflections in Staffing, Reflections in Program, Reflections in Facilities, and Summary. Forty years later I would only make one significant change. The imposition of the single very large interdisciplinary lab at Stockton was a bad idea.

To bring the document to reality, I had four broad tasks (in order of time pressure) for the year. The order of importance was the reverse:

- Provide the architects with rough plans for building temporary lab facilities in Phase I.
- Provide the architects with a detailed concept document for the design of the permanent lab facilities to be built in Phase II.
- Prepare descriptions, to be submitted for approval by the state Board of Higher Education, for all of the academic courses and programs to be offered by the division.
- Hire the first thirteen faculty.

FACULTY

For someone who had never hired anyone, hiring the faculty was the most challenging task. First, the number of faculty needed in each discipline and specialty had to be guessed, with no way to accurately project student demand. And I had to learn how best to advertise for and evaluate faculty candidates in areas with which I had no experience. Because the job market was so bad, the number of applications was very large - about 1,500 for the thirteen positions. Still, selling a college with no campus, no students, and no colleagues was an interesting experience. The only images that most candidates got were those of the Deans of NAMS and EXPT (and sometimes the other deans), the Vice President for Academic Affairs, and the president. So, in an effort to present an image that would be comfortable to the types of people I wished to attract, I kept my casual style of dress and wore a very nice peace medal I had found in Atlantic City.

I began trying to identify individuals who appeared to be in tune with the "new" student and the advertised mission of the college. I wanted to build a faculty that valued undergraduate teaching in a collegial mode. The mantra of too many faculty at too many colleges had become "we could do wonderful things if we just had better students." So it was also important that faculty be comfortable with the level of student most likely to be attracted to Stockton. The faculty should also have research interests they wanted to continue, but their research could not require specialized labs or other facilities that the state was not likely to furnish. And the research should be of a character that would permit meaningful involvement by undergraduates. Although publishable research was not discouraged, research projects with students did not necessarily have to be original or publishable. The ultimate goal was to bring in individuals who:

- Presented strong academic backgrounds from reputable schools and graduate programs.
- Had a stated interest in primarily teaching undergraduates and the type of outgoing personality that promised to support their interests.
- Had interdisciplinary interests and did not seem to be boxed into a narrow field.
- Had an identifiable and strong OBQ (Odd Ball Quotient).

All of these were important and were balanced in different ways for each candidate. The OBQ—some remember it as Odd Ball Coefficient (OBC)—is the most interesting. The idea was to factor unusual personal life experiences or interests into the mix. Since there was no objective way to evaluate the OBQ or to defend it traditionally, it was only significant, as viewed by me. It included, for example:

- Two biologists who had met when they were both arrested at the first Free Speech Movement sit-in at Sproul Hall, UC-Berkeley led by Joan Baez. One had served as treasurer of the FSM.
- An environmentalist with an interest in folk dance and folklore who had taught at a very experimental (radical) college.
- A chemist who had a pony tail and motorcycle and was clearly a philosopher at heart—and was lost in a Southern Baptist college in North Carolina.
- A biologist living with his family in a 1960s commune.
- An environmentalist who at fifty, and after raising four children, had earned her doctorate and was seeking to set out on a new life adventure.
- A biologist who had an MBA from Harvard and some years experience in the corporate world and who wanted to become an ethnologist.
- A mathematician who had been jailed as a civil rights activist in Knoxville, Tennessee.
- A chemist with a PhD from the California Institute of Technology who had taught in an Historically Black College in South Carolina.

Students working in F-wing lab (1976)

Faculty candidates, after showing the required academic tickets for admission, were hired primarily for who they were as people. Over the first ten years, the OBQ usually served NAMS well as a parameter in hiring, but there were a few times it didn't work. Of the thirteen hired in the first year, all either had their PhDs or were ABD (had completed everything but their dissertations). All degrees had been awarded by the end of the first year. All but two of the faculty hired were younger than I, which led the president to refer to the NAMS faculty as the Dean's Children's Crusade.

But the bottom line was that the thirteen individuals who chose to come to Stockton were all my first choice. And at the end of the process, after reviewing all of those hired, I concluded that, had I been a candidate, I would not likely have been good enough to make the cut.

Why did candidates offered positions in NAMS choose to accept and join the enterprise? Good jobs were hard to find, but most of them probably would have been able to find something more conventional, something professionally safer. Usually candidates can evaluate the history and reputation of the institution, the ambiance of the campus, the facilities and resources available for their work, the peers they will be working with, the students they

will be teaching, and the administrators they will be working under. All the NAMS candidates got was the last of these, i.e., three or four administrators. So it is likely that those who bought the Dream and came to Stockton were largely risk takers.

A group of the early NAMS faculty had a chance to revisit these reasons thirty-nine years later, and other factors were common among those present. They wanted to teach undergraduates and were not looking for careers advanced by publication. In one case, a faculty member was attracted by my description of Stockton as "the Antioch for the forgotten American," since he particularly wanted to teach students likely to be attracted to a state college. Many liked the freedom to create General Studies courses out of their interests outside the discipline with no hassles from a curriculum committee. They appreciated that, while research and other activities were valued, teaching was job one.

Most were also excited about getting in at the beginning with the opportunity to design a new institution that would give equal value to the major and to General Studies. The prospect of collegial governance within the programs—without department chairs—was also attractive

PLANNING THE CURRICULUM

While I was comfortable with biology and chemistry curricula, I was not qualified to create curricula for math, environmental studies, marine science, or physics. It was not hard to produce all of the basic course descriptions required for approval by the state Board of Higher Education by pirating from undergraduate catalogs from other colleges. But the final decisions and design had to come from the faculty.

As part of the planning process for the first year, funds had been budgeted for all of the deans to bring in the individuals whom they had selected to be program coordinators for two months during the summer of 1971. They were to determine what courses would be taught and were to write the course descriptions and assign the other faculty their loads for the fall.

I petitioned to use the money set aside for the division's program coordinators to bring in all thirteen faculty for whatever time the funds would support. I proposed that the several program faculties and the division as a whole would work together on these tasks, select their own program coordinators, and develop their General Studies courses. After much resistance, the president relented and the entire first-year NAMS faculty came in for two weeks in August 1970. Since there were no facilities available, on campus or elsewhere, my family headed south and our home was turned into a conference center.

This turned out to be a very creative and exciting time. Faculty built relations across disciplinary lines and formed a very cohesive group that continued to work well together and to translate and refine the plans envisioned for Stockton and the NAMS division into reality. The decision to take this path was probably the best decision I made during this period and was worth the fight. Whatever NAMS was and became in the early years is to the credit of these first faculty and their colleagues who followed.

The faculty reviewing these early days thirty-nine years out agree that, as a result of the two weeks together, they began the year in the Mayflower Hotel with an entirely different frame of reference than the other divisions. The divisional collegiality that started then continued to be a positive force in the division, giving it a commitment to the Dream that persisted for years.

An outside observer from the first year on argues that NAMS was different from the beginning and held to the values of the founding more closely than the other divisions. He suggests that the fact that a core of early faculty from the first year persisted for many years helped later recruits to buy into the Dream. An incident to support the point: on a 2010 visit to Stockton, I was introduced by two chemists I had hired in year two to a recently hired colleague. They were pleased that they had been able to find someone who understood the nature and value of the unique Chemistry I-IV sequence that they had created nearly forty years ago. Now they both could enjoy retirement, content that it would not soon be undone.

THE INNOVATIVE LABORATORY FACILITY

The laboratory design was a colossal mistake. The concept, as a way to promote interdisciplinary interaction, had much to recommend it. At St. Andrews, a small liberal arts college with few science majors where it was first implemented, it has worked well for more than forty years. However, it turned out to be a bad decision and an expensive error in judgment for Stockton. I can only say that in year minus one there were few checks on inexperience.

The laboratory had its roots in a presentation I had heard two or three years before coming to Stockton. It had been built as the focal point of the new science building at St. Andrews Presbyterian College in Laurinburg, North Carolina. Soon after being hired at Stockton, I got a call from the facilities planner asking me to prepare a concept document describing the laboratory needs for Stockton in both Phases I and II. This led me to visit St. Andrews to see exactly what they had done and how it worked. Rather than having separate and specialized labs for various biology and chemistry courses, they had built one very large lab with a couple of seminar rooms, fume hoods, and a storeroom/preparation facility off to one side. The lab floor had a grid of floor wells with all utilities available with quick-connect fittings. Islands (about thirty inches square) with a sink could be placed over them and connected in any arrangement needed. Or tables could be set up in an area without utilities. The Stockton lab in Phase II was very large and was a copy of the St. Andrews lab. All of the present F-wing labs have been carved out of that one lab. The present lab at the north end by the windows retains the original concept.

On the plus side, the Biology faculty worked together to develop student laboratory experiments that fit the facility. As a result, the Biology program has never used published lab manuals in most courses but offers exercises better suited to the programs.

The open lab failed at Stockton for a complex of reasons:

- The first problem was that the lab was put in place without any faculty involvement. And faculty were never given any suggestions or ideas as to how best to use it. When Dick Colby served as Acting Dean of NAMS after my departure, he traveled to St. Andrews College and was convinced that if someone from there had spent some time with the early faculty, the success of the lab might have been very different.
- An early problem developed with optics courses that needed a darker space than could be curtained off in a corner of the lab.
- The number of students in the sciences overwhelmed the space. It had been originally designed to serve St. Andrews, where there was a general education science requirement for one year of a laboratory science for all students. Most took biology, and the few who chose chemistry were not enough to overwhelm the space with noxious fumes. (The fumes are why, in all older conventional science buildings, chemistry is on the top floor.) At Stockton the attractiveness of Environmental Studies (ENVL) and Marine Science (MARS), added to regular Biology (BIOL) and Chemistry (CHEM) enrollments, overwhelmed the facility.

- With several groups of students working in the lab at the same time, it was very disruptive if a faculty member needed to talk to one group.
- As the sciences got more sophisticated, expensive equipment was hard to secure.
- At the time the Stockton labs were built, formaldehyde fumes came along with biology, and many other fumes came from chemistry. There were hoods for working with the really bad stuff, but common solvents were not thought to be of any particular concern. With the advent of OSHA (the Occupational Safety and Health Administration), everything beyond water has become a hazardous substance to be feared. The open lab and OSHA could never peacefully coexist.

So the open lab concept was destined to fail at Stockton, a victim of too many unintended consequences.

TEMPORARY PHASE I LABORATORY

Before Phase II could be completed, NAMS was given a first floor lab space in the B-wing of Phase I. The temporary lab was designed on the same principle as the permanent lab. But since Stockton was built in a modular arrangement, to allow for easy conversion of space from one use to another, the design had to do minimal damage to the structure. Utilities were run over the ceiling and dropped down to several four-foot high partitions that ran across the lab. The lab also had a hood and a stockroom. Almost all of the fixtures were selected to be re-used in the permanent lab.

In fall 1971, the division hired a laboratory manager, even though there would be no labs until at least January 1972. The faculty, teaching in the Mayflower Hotel where there were no labs, worked through the fall to order everything they would need in the lab once it was finished. The College assigned the division a small house on the left side of the entrance drive off Jimmie Leeds Road where the lab manager set up a receiving department—without heat, air, or electricity—for the division. As shipments came in through the fall, they were checked in and stacked in the house from floor to ceiling, starting at the back of the house and working to the front. By the end of December, there was a little space to stand inside the front door.

When the temporary Phase I lab was finished, just days before the beginning of the spring term on campus, the contractor had not had time to seal the bare concrete floors to keep the dust down. The contractor supplied the sealant and several faculty volunteered to help me roll it on. The only problem was that there was no heat or air circulation, and the sealant was in a volatile solvent. By the time the floor was half sealed, all of us were high on the fumes to the point of passing out. So we would roll a few minutes and then go outside into the fresh air for long enough to clear our heads and go back. As soon as the floors dried, the movers emptied the house and brought everything into the lab, where the lab manager unpacked and set the lab up for the spring term.

THE FIRST YEAR

Leading up to the opening of school in fall 1971, there was some anxiety that we might be giving a party to which no one would come. The decade opened in a recession with rising unemployment. If parents were out of work, could they afford to send their kids to college? But it worked in our favor. If the kids couldn't find work, college was a good alternative. The character of the early student body was significantly influenced by the number of returning Vietnam veterans. They saw the world differently than the recent high school graduates. And they were also very different from the veterans who had returned from World War II.

Opening the fall term in the Mayflower was an adventure the likes of which few faculties could ever imagine. And during the first year, 1971-1972, things could not have worked out better. The Dream was new and alive. All of us were building something together. Discussions may have been passionate, but they were open and collegial.

At the end of the first year, it became clear to me that the division faculty needed to consider program evaluations. I asked the faculty in each program to provide me with the names of the best authorities and most outstanding educators in their fields to conduct external evaluations of each of the five academic programs. They were asked to exclude people with whom they had had any significant professional relationship. In most cases it came down to a single academic star. The dean invited each consultant to spend a couple of days on campus reviewing the programs as they had been designed and taught in the first year. The consultants were intrigued with taking a look at this rarity—a new institution in New Jersey—given the state's history of not providing much in the way of funding for higher education.

When I called the consultant selected for Marine Science he was adamant that there was no such thing as undergraduate marine science. Give him a graduate with a strong background in the basic sciences and math, and he would add the graduate degree. He was told that his attitude was just right, and he agreed to come. At the exit interview with me, the consultant conceded that Stockton's graduates would be welcome in his programs. The interaction between the consultants and the faculty on their own turf was stimulating for the programs and the faculty. And all of the consultants gave the programs strong evaluations.

At the end of the first year, the dean and the NAMS faculty sat in a circle and cast the *I Ching*, the ancient Chinese oracle, to see where we were going next. The hexagram generated was number sixty-one, Inner Truth. One of the faculty had tee-shirts made for all the NAMS faculty with the hexagram and "Inner Truth" on the front and the Chinese character on the back. So the year ended looking collegially toward the future. And the shirts continued to be worn for special occasions for, at least, the first ten years.

View of F-wing lab (1976)

YEAR TWO AND BEYOND

In the second year things began to unravel. Stockton had a president with a Student Affairs background and little idea of how to manage faculty. In spite of the near revolutionary innovations he had put in motion before the deans were hired, he was basically a conservative who needed to maintain a high level of control. And he found himself confronted by a very liberal and activist faculty. The planning rhetoric about college-wide committees made up of students, faculty, administrators, and classified employees at all levels that would make effective decisions faded into committees that would make recommendations for the president's decision.

Then came the tenure quota. Whatever the policy (or policies) had been for the original six state colleges, Stockton and Ramapo presented a new challenge. The entire faculty from the first year (1971-1972) had completed one third of their three-year probationary period and were facing a situation under which they would either get tenure or a terminal-year contract in the

second year. I was facing, with a little dilution from second- and third-year hires, the prospect of having everyone tenured, leaving little flexibility for the future. Thus was born the sixty-percent tenure policy. There is some debate as to whether this was imposed by the president, imposed in some form by Trenton independently, or by Trenton at the urging of President Bjork. But a very understandable level of paranoia began to build within the faculty.

Also in the second year, I was managing a faculty of extremely creative and capable teachers—with one exception. One of the faculty proved to be a very poor teacher. His students complained to his colleagues and to me. His Student Evaluations of Teaching were nearly off the bottom of the scale. He was not reappointed. Apparently he had already been involved in union activity, so anti-union bias was alleged. But his contract was not renewed for the third year.

In the meantime, the faculty was looking to organize its muscle.

39

They were apparently not impressed with the Association of New Jersey State Colleges and University Faculty (ANJSCUF). The American Association of University Professors (AAUP), which represented Rutgers, refused to represent them. But the American Federation of Teachers (AFT) was in the wings. Since it was an avowed union, as opposed to the public school-based National Education Association (NEA) affiliate, it was probably more acceptable to the more old-line liberal faculty. Apparently following Stockton leadership and activism, AFT became the bargaining agent for all of the New Jersey state colleges.

The confrontational stage was set between a president who seemed to go out of his way to say outrageous things to the faculty and a very strong faculty that was going to protect its interests to the best of its ability. Along with the other deans, I was in the typical middle-management dilemma. This was the part of deaning that was no fun at all. My sympathies were with the faculty, but this was a position I could not openly take. Most of the faculty had probably come to Stockton with the normal AAUP expectation of a seven-year probationary period (or four years with previous experience) and found themselves trapped in a miserable state system. I had been naive enough to have held the same expectation and had hired the faculty without ever warning them. During hiring for the subsequent years, candidates were told about the shorter probationary period and that tenure would not be likely for many of them. I continued to support faculty needs, and the programs continued to evolve and grow, but a level of trust in me, in hindsight, was understandably lost. I understood what the faculty was doing to try to protect its interests, but collective bargaining took me out of the debate.

There was another event that affected NAMS. Gordon Davies, the Dean of Academic Development, left Stockton at the end of the third year to become Secretary of Higher Education for the State of Virginia. Woody Thrombley, who was then Vice President for Academic Affairs, was having trouble finding a replacement. He asked me to move over to ADEV with the argument that he could find a replacement in NAMS more easily. So the change was made.

I never really explained to the NAMS faculty what was going on. I was perceived, by some, as abandoning NAMS too early in the game. And that was true. At that moment, it was not too hard to make the move. The union-management friction and hostility was hard to deal with. Escaping the annual exhaustive and exhausting evaluation of faculty with the prospect of having to let faculty go to satisfy the tenure quota, regardless of strong evaluations, was appealing. In general, "running" was not as much fun as "creating." ADEV had a smaller group to manage and seemed to offer a creative escape.

The story didn't end until about a year and a half later when the Academic Affairs vice president called me in to say that President Bjork had decided Stockton did not need ADEV. Bjork did recommend me for a position in the New Jersey Department

of Higher Education with Ralph Dungan—who was even more irrational and difficult to work for than Bjork. So after five years I was gone, and the Dream was totally in the hands of the faculty, who nurtured it well.

DREAMS TO REALITY: SOME OF NAMS'S CONTRIBUTIONS TO STOCKTON

So how were my original plans translated into NAMS?

Through an interdisciplinary faculty. The inclusion of faculty in Biology, Environmental Studies, and Marine Science as members of more than one of these program faculties was natural. But one second-year faculty member brought into NAMS for a strong academic background in invertebrate zoology held a PhD in experimental psychology. She was a very early example of a faculty member holding program memberships in two different divisions. A physicist was hired in Experimental Studies in year one and worked with the NAMS faculty. When EXPT was disbanded, he joined NAMS as part of the Physics program.

Through faculty that met the needs of the Stockton students. One of the Math faculty came to Stockton with the concept of a math lab. With a dedicated classroom and a minimum of financial support, he created a place where students with math phobias could find a way to become comfortable with and productive in math. It also helped any student weak in math to build the confidence and the background needed for other courses that used math heavily.

Through a very eclectic and imaginative range of General Studies courses. In addition to many creative discipline-related courses offered in General Studies, the NAMS faculty members also offered some very unique and distinctive courses. These included The American Prison System, The Philosophy and Psychology of Chess, Cooking: Art and Science, Experiential Chemistry, Space Travel and Extraterrestrial Life, Muckraking, Hebrew, Utopian Communities, Tropical Ecology (in Costa Rica), Judaic Studies, Alternative Energy Sources, Gambling, and Town Planning.

Two offerings introduced a unique use of General Studies courses. One of the hopes of the founders was that Stockton would attract students who were primarily interested in the liberal arts. These would be its ideal students, who were just coming for the love of learning and not interested in a career-oriented major. For those students, a NAMS faculty member created two options out of his own background. The first was two courses in waste water treatment management, with which a student could be certified and find a well-paying job. The other was a two-course sequence in surveying that would qualify a student to work in that area.

Through offering college courses for inmates in Bordentown Prison. This practice began in NAMS. During the 1970-1971 planning year, the president received an inquiry from Burlington Community College asking if Stockton would be willing to offer upper-division work to inmates at the state prison at Bordentown, having been turned down by state colleges closer to the prison. The president passed the request on to Academic Affairs, and I volunteered to meet with staff at both Burlington County College and Bordentown to determine the needs.

Burlington County College had been teaching there for several years and students who had earned associate's degrees still had years to serve on their sentences and wanted to work toward their baccalaureates. I agreed that, once the College opened in fall 1971, I would try to identify faculty willing to teach students at a location that required a 120-mile round trip. There were a number of faculty from the several divisions who volunteered, and the students agreed to let their courses be determined, in part, by who was available to teach. Over the first few years, several students were released and came to the campus to study full-time.

The first to be released was a thirty-five-year-old white male serving a sentence for murder during the commission of a robbery. In seventeen years, he had only spent a few months on the street after his first conviction as a juvenile. Through counseling, he had come to understand the roots of his antisocial behavior. Pressure from prison activists had moved the governor to grant him clemency, erasing the many years left on his sentence. With scholarship support from a state rehabilitation program, he took the bus to Atlantic City to enroll in Stockton full-time. I picked him up at the bus station and brought him home for dinner. A NAMS chemist, who was single, invited him to live with him. But before he could finish his degree, he fell in love and married the daughter of an officer from Fort Dix and left Stockton to run the Right to Read program inside Bordentown. Not all were so successful. Another inmate was taken in by a marine scientist who was robbed before the student disappeared.

FACULTY RESEARCH

Faculty interested in and motivated to do research have made many substantial contributions and used their research to extend the educational experiences of their students. Some examples include:
- Studies of the environmental impact of the Stockton waste water management sprayfield.
- A project to study the effect of vitamin C on the common cold. This project led to an invitation from Linus Pauling for the faculty member and three students to present their results at a conference in California. One of those students is now a Professor of Oncology at the Columbia University Medical School.
- Vertebrate paleontology research amenable to student participation on campus and in summer field studies. One of the early students who participated in this research is now a Professor of Paleontology at UCLA.
- The Energy House developed by two NAMS faculty, which served as a base for research on solar and wind energy and other environmental issues.
- Studies on the genetics and ecology of the rare pygmy pines that grow only in areas of the Pine Barrens.

AND WHAT OF THE DREAM—AND OF THE DREAMERS?
Thanks to the generosity and kindness of a large sample of the first-through-third-year faculty, I was given a chance to look for answers when I spent three days on campus in April 2010. Other than a drive through several years before, it was my first time back at Stockton in about thirty-five years.

"What happened to the Dream?" depends to a great degree on whom you ask.

There are some who feel that the original Dream was mostly lost early on. For them, the glass, at first glance, seems to be much less than half full. They feel, with good justification, that I oversold the Dream, overstated what Stockton would become, and left NAMS too soon. In great measure the faculty and I were both a bit naïve in thinking that what Stockton was being allowed to do in its earliest years could long persist in a world of formulas and bureaucracy. But these folks, in spite of the negative changes, have spent long careers here and greatly appreciate the freedom to teach, the fun in General Studies, and the high degree of collegiality.

On the other hand, there are those for whom the glass is still nearly full. They see the changes that have occurred and understand the history and the reasons for changes. But they still feel that they are free and have the support they need to do the things that originally drew them to Stockton. They just try not to let changes that they may perceive as contrary to the Dream get in the way of their life at Stockton.

In the middle, there are those who see the Dream as having been dimmed but not extinguished. One NAMS faculty member felt, from the first semester, that while the Dream was alive in NAMS, the other divisions were very traditionally staffed and not very innovative as a group. His response was to devote his career to his own domain and to maintain the Dream in his own sphere. All credit the absence of a college-wide curriculum committee charged with approving all courses as one of the features that makes life at Stockton worth living.

It is understandable that the departure of early faculty and their replacement by newer folk would dilute the Dream. There is very general agreement that the tendency of the early NAMS faculty to remain at Stockton has provided a continuity for NAMS and its programs that is not present in the other divisions. Also, faculty coming in after the first year were told not to expect certain tenure, and many of them felt a need to excel in areas like research, which carried higher currency value than teaching in the larger academic world. Various NAMS faculty agree that there have been administrative policies that have evolved through the years that have worked against the Dream. For example, evaluating faculty for contributions made only to one main program rather than valuing multiple program memberships devalues interdisciplinary involvement. Management, over the years, has also become more traditional and hierarchical. The union, by its nature, tends to work against innovation. In its efforts to protect faculty workload, the union makes things that are out of the ordinary, like team-teaching, or going the extra mile more difficult.

But there is something else. In the first year, when Stockton was still very small, there were a camaraderie and an openness among students, faculty, and staff on the campus. These were outgrowths of the social revolution and were cultivated to be an integral part of life at Stockton. That openness and camaraderie are still alive at Stockton and are much to be valued.

While visiting Stockton, I wandered around the gallery and other open spaces inside and outside the buildings. The changes in the physical plant were almost overwhelming. The food court and other activities in the gallery and the large numbers of people circulating have brought the campus to life in a way that was not evident in the start-up years. I observed the interactions among students and between students and faculty to be generally friendly and relaxed. Further, I made eye contact with and usually spoke to all I passed. My greetings were usually returned with a smile. Two students I had met in a seminar the day before stopped me to see how my visit was going and if I needed anything. This kind of casual openness and friendliness is not common on campuses today.

Stockton was founded to be a special place. Much is owed to those who brought Stockton to life and nursed her through the early years. Much more is owed to those who came early and stayed late at the party, for it is they who have held the course as best they could. They now have a forty-year-old adult child of whom they can be justly proud. May she live and thrive for many years to come.

Napkin Scribbles

Acronyms seem to be a central part of modern life; there is NBC, OMG, RTFM, TGIF and ASAP. There is even an online searchable database (DB) of over four million of them. Stockton seems to have more than most, though probably not.

The acronyms that we use for disciplinary programs and schools fall off our tongues like so much spittle. They seem about that natural.

I was present when they were created and it was really done out of boredom and almost as a joke. In the fall of 1970—it had to be after courses and curricula had begun to form—there was a Board of Trustees meeting upstairs at the Quail Hill restaurant at Smithville (which was torn down many years ago). Wes Tilley and the deans were at the meeting though not participating. As I remember it, we were quite bored. Tilley picked up a paper napkin and began writing on it. I sat next to him and could see what he was writing: various four-letter acronyms for real and imaginary programs. I remember WOMB and FART among others but ARHU, SOBL, NAMS and the others were written as well. We all seemed to get involved, each with a candidate or two on the list.

A few days later, Tilley suggested an acronym for each of the divisions and for every program. I cannot remember why there were four letters; perhaps to distinguish program courses from the two-letter acronyms of the General Studies courses. There may have been other reasons as well.

It is interesting to note that our lives today are embedded in acronyms that started in boredom forty years ago.

Ken Tompkins

New apartments north of Lake Fred (1976)

Why Go East?

Richard E. Pesqueira

I was very happy in my position as Executive Dean of Students at the University of California, Riverside when I first learned about the creation of a state college in the southern environs of New Jersey. I received my doctorate from UCLA with honors in 1969, worked at UCLA and then UC Riverside in Student Affairs, and assumed my career would remain in the multicampus University of California system. However, I learned about the creation of Richard Stockton State College via ads in the *Chronicle of Higher Education* and further learned that its founding president, Richard Bjork, would be interviewing candidates for the Dean of Students position opening in 1970, two years ahead of the planned opening of the College. I interviewed, along with dozens of other candidates, mostly curious but also intrigued with the idea of being "in on the ground floor" of a new college in the United States. By all accounts this was to be a "new mission" college, blazing new paths in terms of values, aesthetics, curriculum, education, "town-gown" relations, student-centered curricular and co-curricular offerings, even new physical plant! This certainly caught my attention and against all recommendations by mentors, colleagues, and peers (I was already an officer in the National Association of Student Personnel Administrators) who thought "Why go East when all the action is West?" I accepted the offer from President Bjork and brought my family to Linwood, New Jersey to reside. My twins were two-and-a-half years old; I was thirty-three.

I believe I was the fifth professional hired by President Bjork, and our very small, innovative, visionary team of key central administrators began the hard work of building a college, literally and figuratively. We first operated out of a small shopping center, then out of several homes that had been converted to small office buildings. I will never forget the late-afternoon odors emanating from the pet shop next door to our first offices. Whew!

The college was to be special in every way, and we met monthly with architects in Princeton, hired staff (administrative, faculty and classified), and met with local officials, with trustees, with local legislators, educators, etc. It is fair to say it was a "common calling" to get this special, unusual, if not unique, opportunity right so as to serve the southern part of New Jersey and the state in general with a dynamic offering in undergraduate education.

At the outset I did not find anything unattractive about the college's mission and early development. However, soon it became apparent to me that notwithstanding all of the original thought—about mission, values, and curriculum offerings that were to be innovative, thematic, and not discipline-oriented— the structure of the central administrative hierarchy was not in keeping with such ground-breaking orientation. For example, I was concerned about the fact that staff who assumed "line-responsibilities" and who were thus responsible for outcomes had to answer to others in the president's office who had no responsibility for the actions of the administrative divisions. I was disappointed that the president's office was as large as it was and that I did not have direct access to the president. A second disappointment was that I was only able to hire three professional staff and needed to establish my organization for the second year.

However in that second year (I was promoted to Vice President of Student Affairs) I hired more staff to develop such critical operations as Admissions, Student Affairs, Placement Services, Housing, Extracurricular Activities, Veterans Affairs, Relations with Schools, etc. I continued to support the overall mission of the College, of course, and knew that my visibility and leadership, both on campus with colleagues and off campus with civic, legislative, school, and private sector leaders, were appreciated.

High school students, of course, and their teachers and school leaders were most curious about what would make the college a truly competitive offering among choices that had existed before. Many of us in those first two years made ourselves available at every opportunity. This was critically important since we had the wisdom to have faculty members serve as part of this cadre. Faculty made an enormous difference in those first years in establishing credibility among the schools and school systems in the service area by not only interacting with high schools students but with their teachers.

Among our proudest accomplishments those first two years were (1) progress toward the completion of Phase I of the very distinguished and beautiful physical plant/campus, (2) the quality of the publications authored by a relativity small number of campus staff, (3) a very organized and focused student recruitment initiative, and (4) the development of effective relations with many civic, corporate, and legislative leaders in the area, who were a bit confused about the college and why its purpose would be different than that of traditional colleges.

I was pleased to "buy in" to the inverse logic that prevailed at the campus, the idea of NOT wanting to replicate traditional offerings for their own sake or to establish narrowly defined academic departments and also not to perpetuate the value of *in loco parentis*, whereby the institution becomes the surrogate parent for the students. One major reason for my acceptance of the position originally, beyond the exciting prospect of helping to develop a college "from the ground up," was that we were not going to complicate the relationship between college and student by assuming this absentee parental role and that we would treat students as adults, supporting them when necessary but not interfering with their private lives. Few colleges in the US were thinking along those lines in those years.

I think we all underestimated the complexities behind students' values and choices in terms of housing, on and off campus. We had always assumed that a residential college would be the route to follow because we all know that so much of one's college education is beyond the classroom and that learning takes place in many venues, on, near, and even far away from college. How that was sorted out I would not know as I left Richard Stockton State College before the end of its third year of planning and first year of opening at the Mayflower Hotel. I left to become Vice President of Student Affairs at New Mexico State University, and after six years became President of the University of Southern Colorado.

I would enjoy visiting the campus again after these many years. I have very fond memories of this special experience and enjoyed residing in Linwood.

Policing the Academy

James A. Williams

As I remember my days at the Richard Stockton State College, I think about where we actually started—in the old Mayflower Hotel on the boardwalk in Atlantic City. I recall the makeshift classrooms and administrative offices set up in the hotel, which overlooked the boardwalk that was frequented by young men and women, all having fun in the sun. Beyond that was the sand of the beach, and, beyond that, the water, in which some people were swimming in the warmth of the September ocean. That was Richard Stockton State College. The year was 1971, and the College was in the process of purchasing land in Pomona, for the permanent college.

Colleges across the United States had experienced a great need for the students and the educational process as a whole to be protected against the evils of society, and for that reason the position of Director of Public Safety and Security was created, to which seventy-five people applied. President Richard Bjork and Vice President Richard Gajewski, among other college administrators, had a lot of foresight about providing security for the College. They believed that to accomplish this, the one thing that had to be prevented was for the academic community to feel as if the College was in any way establishing something similar to a "police state." There had to be a way, they felt, that the Director of Public Safety could create an active, productive police force committed to service without having the College community feel that the police officers were not part of that community. I was eventually hired from the Burlington Township Police Department, where I had spent a great deal of my service time as a detective and a police trainer.

During this time, many college students and other members of the academic community had had contact with exploratory drugs. One of the concerns of the college was to make sure that appropriate preventative measures were put into effect to protect the college community from the perils of illegal drugs. The first step in this direction was to liaise with area police agencies. This liaison was short lived, however, as the police described Stockton students as "those long-haired druggies." If this was the way that law enforcement officials described both the faculty and students at the new college, I believed better public relations were in order!

My very first step, therefore, was to recruit young men and women who could graduate from the police academy without the sometimes typical police attitude of "us against them." Once these young men and women were selected, we had to create a friendly mode of police dress, one that did not include huge guns and ammunition belts, handcuffs and night sticks, and things of that nature. President Bjork and Vice President Gajewski were totally supportive of my efforts to create such a force. We first elected to have a uniform consisting of a blue blazer with the campus police patch, gray trousers with the blue police striping, white shirt and blue tie, and black shoes.

The initial group of officers was certified after they had completed training with me, including a course on criminal investigation. At the time, the requirement for becoming a police officer was a high school diploma, but these first recruits were required either to hold a college degree or to be committed to graduating during their police tenure. At first, this change in the usual requirement was met with resistance. However, the new policy prevailed.

The initial officers were certified to carry firearms and did so during their twenty-four-hour, seven-day week duty schedules. The side arms that they carried were not visible to the public; they were under the officers' coats. However, all of the students, and I mean all of the students, knew that they were law enforcement officers. They knew that they were armed, and they knew that state and municipal laws were enforced twenty-four hours a day. The campus police force, even in the early days of 1971 and 1972, was involved in investigating, and solving, crimes involving breaking and entering, disorderly persons, larcenies, shoplifting, weapons violations, assaults, narcotics violations, malicious damage, disturbing assemblies, armed robberies, trespassing, attempted suicide, possession of stolen property, loud and offensive language, and malicious mischief. Other police officers were astonished when Stockton officers brought various lawbreakers before local municipal court judges. Indeed, one of the initial training courses we established was how to submit a case with accurate facts and intelligent presentation before a local judge.

The second step (and one of the most important things during these early years) was ascertaining that appropriate emergency services were available. In visiting the emergency services providers and the area police departments, it was noted that they were quite efficient in what they did, they liked what they did, and they were able to provide these services. What mattered to the Stockton community in the early stages of campus development were the attitudes of emergency services and police personnel. At best, the local police and emergency services personnel were somewhat apprehensive about the new police force being thrust upon them.

The third step was to test what services could be expected by the college community. To accomplish this, a mock emergency situation was planned and initiated. What it actually involved was a simulated explosion in the main campus boiler room. We recruited eleven students with different degrees of theatrical ability. In the mock emergency, the students were lying about in pools of blood, some with blood spurting from veins in their arms and legs. In some instances, there were visible broken bones and other injuries. What was most refreshing to the college executives, the municipal police chief, and me was the response of the emergency services and police personnel. Within five minutes emergency response personnel and police personnel were on the scene and responding to the chaotic conditions. It was only after they had gotten involved in what they thought was going on that they began to realize that this was a mock demonstration and that the students were very accomplished actors.

From that point on, the relationship between the Galloway Township police and the campus police department began to improve rapidly. Even the language employed by area police chiefs began to change. Instead of "that new boy they brought in as the Stockton Security director," they would say, "the new chief over there at Stockton." At a municipal police chief's monthly meeting, much to "the new boy's" surprise, I was nominated by all of the "chiefs" to apply for membership in the International Association of Chiefs of Police. The "new boy," with their support, was accepted into the IACP on his first application.

An area newspaper published an article relating to college donations to the area fire company. While the donations were about $250.00, this initiative was a huge step forward in bringing the surrounding communities into a partnership with the college community.

So area police officers began to communicate and work with campus police officers. At this point, the college community could feel comfortable with the more traditional mode of police uniform and uniformed campus patrol officers. The first student aides to the Public Safety and Security department were hired to perform non-law enforcement duties. They were respected and not looked upon as "narcs."

The fourth step was to integrate public safety and security into the regular organizational flow of the college community. As the academic and college community began to accept the campus Public Safety and Security department, there was certainly no longer any question in the minds of campus residents that they were living in a police state.

By the time I was recruited by the United States Department of Justice Drug Enforcement Administration, I had a profound feeling that Stockton had arrived as a community and the police services at the college were among the best in the region.

But I still remember the Security department being housed in a "leftover building," near the side of the road at the entrance of the campus property at Stockton. It was a wide-open property. Sometimes area residents would show their hostility by riding through the open campus exhibiting boisterous and disorderly types of conduct. As these vehicles and persons were stopped by campus patrol officers and issued summonses for municipal court appearances, the word spread that campus police officers were for real. So, as the building process began and a proper building was created to house the force, some of the things that had been there many, many years began to fade away, and what remained in their place was the college, with its efficient police department.

Entrance to Mayflower Hotel (1971) - Courtesy of *The Press of Atlantic City*

Dealing with Unexpected Change

Joseph A. Tosh

The newness of the day, shedding winter's dull gloom and announcing spring's radiant return, was befitting the mission. I had found my way to Exit 44 and was searching for signs of the new college, *my* new college. The entrance on Jimmie Leeds Road was marked by a small sign identifying Stockton. The road was dirt, with a few old, abandoned, dilapidated buildings and a rusted-out, old car. Ruts in the road indicated the forks to follow. The road led to a construction site situated in a large clearing next to a lake. The site, littered with trailers, mountains of building materials, and partially built exterior walls, was void of people. It was a Sunday afternoon, and the air was still but for the sound of birds returning from their winter haunts. The warm breeze wafting through the cool air was alternately scented with fresh pine and concrete dust. But wait! Was this it? Was this all that existed of the new college that would be welcoming its first inhabitants in less than half a year?

The excitement of continuing my college journey turned to anxiety, to wondering if I had made the right choice. For weeks I had been announcing to anyone who would listen the prospects of attending a brand new college. Would *my* new college really open on time or should alternatives be pursued? After reviewing my criteria and decisions in selecting my next college, I resolved to wait for Stockton even if it did not open *this* fall. The anticipation of participating in the opening of an institution that would be around for generations yet unborn would sustain me.

I had spent the past three semesters in a well-established community college with sequential courses dictated by a decades-old lock-step progression. Could Stockton's suggestion of an open educational environment become a reality? The wonderment of true learning through discovery was something that I had only experienced while in Boy Scouts and during a rare lesson in high school. Little did I know then just how dramatically and positively my life would be affected by my educational and personal experiences at Stockton.

My letter arrived in the early summer of 1971 announcing that Stockton would indeed be opening in the fall, albeit at a temporary location. Stockton was to hold its first semester in a hotel on the famous Atlantic City boardwalk. That hotel, the Mayflower, could not have been more appropriately named, for it would carry the first Stockton community to a new, unexplored educational world.

Upon entering the Mayflower, during those first days, one could not help but notice its stately old architecture infused with a musty odor. Once inside, these sensations quickly surrendered to the cacophony of voices and bodies all excitedly seeking different destinations. Classrooms and offices occupied the lower floors of the hotel in rooms of varying shapes and sizes. Hotel rooms in the upper floors were used as dorm rooms as were the rooms in the attached annex called the Motel.

The location of the Mayflower did have some unexpected benefits that fall. Between classes and meetings students and faculty alike could opt to relax in the salt air and sunshine, play football on the beach, or take a "stroll on the boards," activities not typical at most of the world's colleges and universities.

Most students' initial objective, upon first arriving at the Mayflower, was to find their "preceptor." A preceptor was a faculty member who would double as an academic advisor and an intermediary between the student and the institutional framework. All students were assigned a preceptor, and all preceptorial groups (preceptor and about ten to fifteen students) were attached to a Collegium. The full Stockton learning community—student, professor, and administrator—was involved in the collegial process. The roles of the preceptors and preceptorial groups were mostly predefined. The mission of each Collegium, however, was to establish its own identity within the College and develop its own structure and purpose.

Within the first week all Collegium were scheduled to hold their initial meetings. The groups to which I was assigned were Collegium K and preceptorial group 2. The inaugural meeting of Collegium K was scheduled for late one afternoon in a large conference room. As the appointed starting time approached the room filled with students and faculty. Most students, not knowing what to expect, were anxiously waiting for a "collegium leader" to enter the room and facilitate our inaugural efforts.

After fifteen or twenty minutes had passed, no leader had arrived. I noticed my preceptor sitting in the crowd conversing with a few other faculty. When I approached him to ask who would be starting the meeting, he said that there was no assigned leader, but anyone present could begin the meeting. Certainly I did not expect such an answer, but I came to know that this was to be a typical opportunity for the Stockton community to direct its own future. Not wishing to sit idle any longer, I nervously moved to a central location in the room, cleared my voice, and loudly suggested that we discuss establishing a structure by which to operate. To my delight the room exploded with ideas, and numerous others stepping forward to help direct the discussion and record suggestions. Before we collectively agreed to end this first collegium meeting, a loose organizational structure was formed along with a scheduled second meeting and a sense of purpose within the college. My thoughts upon leaving the room were "Wow, did that really happen? Did we actually set into motion a potentially vibrant productive voice for the future development of this new institution?"

The usual rigors of pursuing a college degree were also realized throughout that first semester. There were, of course, classes and evaluations, although many of both were nontraditional. All courses were worth four credits, and the grading system was far different from what was standard in other colleges or secondary schools. There were only three grades, H, S, and N. A grade of H designated high achievement; S was reserved for those students passing with a satisfactory assessment; N simply indicated no credit. Students receiving an N for a final grade had withdrawn, failed to meet minimum criteria for passing, or suspended their coursework.

Throughout the decades since my graduation from Stockton, I have often reflected on my experiences in those first years and how they have shaped so many of my life's decisions. My ease in dealing with unexpected "change" in my work environment and the idea that all solutions must consider the humanistic element have been paramount. As a "Mayflower person" I have the sense of not only belonging to the Stockton community but having a degree of ownership in its future.

The Sinking of the Mayflower

Lew Steiner

When Stockton State College, as it was originally known, first opened its doors, the view was not of Lake Fred but rather of the picturesque Atlantic Ocean and the Atlantic City boardwalk. Stockton was not ready to open its newly appointed Pomona campus as of September 1971. Rather than postpone the first semester, Stockton's administrative plan was to instruct the 1,000-member charter class of Stockton for four months in the rooms of the Mayflower Hotel in Atlantic City.

The Mayflower was positioned on the well-known Atlantic City boardwalk. Faculty and staff members found their offices set up in hotel rooms while students pursued their education in the hotel's quarters, which were converted into makeshift classrooms. A number of students lived in the hotel rooms for the first four months. During the students' time at the Mayflower, one of the local hangouts was the legendary Mickey Finn Room, which was located inside the hotel and adorned with a bar and seating for shows. Here, our charter class had the ability to witness firsthand the grandeur of Atlantic City's past glory days. Our recreation facility was the hotel's indoor swimming pool, and our gym was the sprawling beach, where serious games of flag football were played.

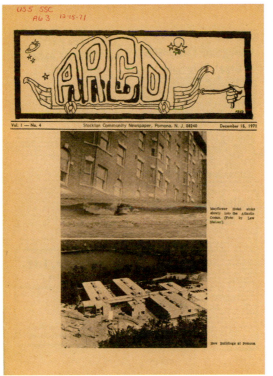

On October 14, 1971, the first meeting of the staff of the Stockton radio station (now known as WLFR) took place in the Mickey Finn Room. It was organized by Steve Kondracki, a junior with several years experience with school stations at Rutgers-Camden and Camden Community College.

During the 1970s at Stockton, the United States maintained its military involvement in Southeast Asia, and there were many anti-war protests during this period. Our charter class was comprised of an eclectic group of students: soldiers home from the Vietnam conflict, transfer students from various colleges, and freshmen straight out of high school.

One of the first projects instituted by the student body was to establish a college newspaper. The founding editor of the Argo (which was temporarily named the *Stockton Community Newspaper*) was Dan McMahon. Dan engaged the services of some of his journalistic colleagues who had transferred from Camden Community College. The synergy of juniors and freshmen working cohesively helped to establish the present-day, independent *Argo*, which has been published regularly at the Pomona campus for four decades.

After the winter break concluded, Stockton's charter class was scheduled to move to the current Pomona campus. Our Campus Activities Director, Paul Jankiewicz, had a great sense of humor and as a farewell celebration he planned a "Sink the Mayflower" splash party on November 22, 1971, for the Stockton community. Admission was a donation of any appropriate food item for Thanksgiving baskets to be distributed to needy families. The celebration included refreshments and cartoons, and it took place prior to winter break at the hotel's pool.

As the first photography editor of the *Argo*, I wanted to create an attention-getting photo that marked the occasion. At that time, there were no laptop computers or Photoshop programs to create this photo. All photographs were processed in a smelly darkroom. Hours were spent in developing the negatives. Next was the tedious process of burning and dodging while printing photographs. To complete the task I took out my 35mm camera and proceeded to take dozens of photos of the ocean and the Mayflower hotel at various angles. The end product was a photo of the Mayflower hotel apparently sinking into the Atlantic Ocean. This photo was published in the December 1, 1971 issue of the *Argo*.

I received many comments about my creation. However the best comment came when I was working in Atlantic City and I showed a customer the December issue of the *Argo* with this photo. The customer looked very closely at the photo and said, "Wow! When did this happen?"

Settling In

Image by Joel Sternfeld

After the first heady months of its existence, the College began to settle down to life as another state college of New Jersey. Some of the idealism remained, and new ideas continued to be brought forward, but a spirit of conflict seemed to predominate. Questions of governance came to the fore, because these were very much contested. Was the college to be led by a powerful executive, in the form of a president and his or her Board of Trustees? Or would a system of shared governance gain hold? And, if it was to be a case of shared governance, what was the power of each constituent element—Faculty Assembly, unions, student body, administration—to be?

In the first two pieces, we are immediately introduced to two presidents whose tenures at Stockton make an interesting contrast. Rob Gregg shows that Peter Mitchell was a man who, to some extent, was a victim of the backlash that occurred against Richard Bjork. He had been chosen to be more open and democratic, but this, in part, led to his downfall, as he had no clear power base upon which to rely. Harvey Kesselman provides a nuanced view of Vera King Farris, whose tenure saw the College grow significantly in a number of ways, but who, like the first president, was not willing to brook much opposition. As a result, feelings were strong about her: many faculty ended up seeing themselves as her adversaries, while there were many others who remained fiercely loyal to her. However, all members of the college community had to respect what she accomplished.

The next two essays view the college from the faculty's perspective. Bob Helsabeck describes in great detail the story of governance at the college, showing how it has changed and describing what he feels it ought to look like. John Searight provides an excellent tribute to the Stockton Federation of Teachers, revealing the many ways in which, by fighting for the rights of its members, it was able to contribute, along with its sister unions, to creating a fair and decent work environment for all Stockton's employees.

Next, we turn to the brief attempt to establish Life Sports at Stockton. Joe Rubenstein (who has since gone on to be the faculty's liaison to the NCAA Division III teams, and who was a great cheerleader for the men's soccer team that won the National Championship in 2001) describes how innovative Stockton tried to be and what his colleague Marty Miller brought to the college community. Based upon the college obituaries for Larry James, Gregg then pays tribute to the importance of "The Mighty Burner," both to the growth of Athletics and to Stockton as a whole.

The next essays provide different perspectives of the college. Jeanne Lewis describes being a young administrator endeavoring to help students afford to come to Stockton, a job that has become increasingly difficult over the years. Nancy Messina reflects on what it was like rising through the ranks of Arts and Humanities, while also pursuing degrees, and witnessing the changes that have occurred all around the college.

The three essays that follow provide different views of the college in its earlier years. Melaku Lakew and Pat Reid-Merritt describe the faculty culture of lower K-wing, the residents of which crossed disciplinary boundaries and worked well together both intellectually and socially. It is a different way of looking at Stockton—and one that continues to have significance as we contemplate moving offices so that people of like disciplines live together—to see it from the perspective of the offices and their almost happenstance arrangement. Clearly, many liked this layout, and, quite possibly, each wing would have had its own story to tell. This is then reaffirmed in Elaine Ingulli's description of her first days at the college, describing how this kind of arrangement led her from her position within Business Studies into interdisciplinary teaching, most notably in Women's Studies. In the third of these essays, Franklin Smith touches on the experiences of being the longest serving African American faculty member at Stockton and the difficulties he faced pushing the college community to recognize its limitations in the area of race.

The next two essays reveal the College's endeavors to align itself, politically and economically, with the world beyond its gates. Nancy Hicks describes how she has endeavored in her position overseeing affirmative action and issues of diversity and equity at the College to keep Stockton in alignment with changing policies in the United States with regard to hiring and equal opportunity. Izzy Posner delineates what the College was endeavoring to do in the surrounding community and what its overall impact was. While the College had difficulties in this area at the beginning, he shows that early on it was committed to helping to transform the region.

Finally, Bill Lubenow, himself a Mayflower faculty member, provides an alternate view of the early years, that echoes, somewhat, the early questioning of the Stockton experiment that Allen Lacy in the Philosophy program had published in the *Chronicle of Higher Education* in 1974. Stockton has always provided space for difference, and there has never been a single way to look at what we are doing. Lubenow's vision certainly differs from many of those among the faculty who taught at the college in the early years.

So, while tensions flared up on numerous occasions, differences of opinion would be many, and a strike would be fought and won by the Stockton Federation of Teachers, the college would continue to grow, both in size and reputation. Perhaps more importantly for the long-term health of the institution, a feeling of camaraderie and solidarity would grow within Stockton's community that would sometimes smooth over the fractiousness.

President Peter Mitchell at a faculty meeting (1980)

"Stockton Changed Me, More than I Changed Stockton"—Peter Mitchell

Rob Gregg

Stockton is a special place. . . . I think it may be one of the most unusual state college institutions in the United States. And I know that some people think that is hyperbole, but I believe it. I think its campus physically is special; I think its faculty is special; I think it's a difficult institution at times to govern; and I think there is a lot of emotionalism on the campus; but I think that the price one pays for this is well worth it, because of the enthusiasm here. . . . Very few places have the kind of feeling for and involvement for higher education, for general education, for what goes on in the classroom [as Stockton]. I judge it almost entirely by the reactions of the students. . . . I have talked literally with hundreds of students here and, with rare exception, and I mean very rare exceptions, I don't meet a student who is disillusioned about his education here. And I don't think there is any more that needs to be said; I don't need to endorse it; I think the students have endorsed it. I don't think they are wrong. I think that students who feel as strongly about their *faculty, about what they learn in their classes; students who come back after three or four years who don't think they were cheated, who think that what they got was demanding, are by and large the best barometer of what we do well here at Stockton. - Peter Mitchell*

There is considerable irony in Peter Mitchell's tenure as president of Stockton. As the second president, between 1979 and 1983, he was welcomed as someone who might bring a more faculty-centered approach to college governance, in contrast to his predecessor, Richard Bjork, whose style many faculty members felt had been too autocratic. And yet, it was to some extent faculty opposition to the very changes that President Mitchell made to achieve this goal that contributed to his early departure.

On the surface Mitchell seemed to be a wise choice to succeed Bjork. His credentials were excellent, having been a vice president of Academic Affairs at Seton Hall University. He was familiar with the New Jersey educational environment, and while he seemed to be open to the Stockton ideals and willing to embrace some of its quirkier aspects, he nonetheless had the reassuring appearance of being very proper in both manner and style. At a time when Stockton had a reputation in the surrounding community for being overrun by hippies and radicals, Mitchell gave the opposite impression.

On the other hand, Mitchell had some obstacles to overcome. He was both an outsider and reform-minded, and this can be a volatile mixture. He needed to fully understand the College that he was coming into while making suggestions for change. Would it be easy, especially at a college that didn't always conform to practices found elsewhere in the academy, to understand what it was that needed changing? Would change be welcomed by those for whom it was being undertaken, when it might be considered an imposition from without, rather than an effort to move towards greater shared governance?

There was much that Mitchell believed needed to be changed when he arrived. He felt that the General Studies program required overhauling, that the personnel procedures needed some tweaking, that the College should be pushing for greater diversity, and that the administrative structure needed streamlining. This was an ambitious program for change, and, because he was likely to disturb some major shibboleths along the way, it was almost inevitable that he would face opposition.

Mitchell felt that Stockton's General Studies constituted a considerable part of the curriculum, and yet it seemed to be comprised largely of a smorgasbord of courses that faculty wanted to teach. It seemed to lack an overarching rationale, and he felt there was little sense of how it contributed to student learning. His initial efforts to articulate these concerns resulted in a very frosty reaction from faculty, who felt that he either didn't comprehend how General Studies had been conceived and instituted or feared that he would be moved to curtail some of the freedom that many faculty believed the General Studies curriculum allowed them. Very quickly, however, he came to value General Studies and began to see that its very uniqueness was a positive rather than a negative aspect of the College.

One aspect of the personnel process that he felt needed altering was the inclusion of students as full voting members on the divisional committees that made decisions over faculty tenure and promotion. His initial feeling was that students had no appreciation of the issues that were raised on these committees and that the process of their selection was problematic; consequently they should be removed. He came around to feeling, however, that the students seldom did any harm and often did some good in providing their input on these committees.

Mitchell was also a great believer in bringing greater diversity to Stockton. He felt that recruiting faculty from diverse regional and racial backgrounds would be healthy for the College. New ideas and perspectives would be brought to the College, and this was especially important for South Jersey students whose experiences were frequently more local and circumscribed. The faculty was certainly a regionally diverse group, but Mitchell felt that there had been insufficient attention paid to recruiting minority academics. This issue would lead to significant consternation among the faculty, as there was some disagreement as to how and in what circumstances affirmative action should be applied.

Mitchell also endeavored to change the administrative structure. He believed that there were too many deans and divisions (there were then five of each) and that this was too costly and inefficient for a college the size of Stockton. His own vision was that the number of divisions and deans should be reduced to three— Arts and Sciences, Professional Studies, and General Studies. True to his own belief that he should not simply impose his own vision, however, he appointed a group of senior faculty to make recommendations. The plan they came forward with, which Mitchell then supported, was far more radical than his own. It called for the continuation of the divisions in the same number, but for the conversion of deans to chairpersons. These chairpersons and their assistants would remain within the Stockton Federation of Teachers, and the appointments would last for four years, before the next faculty members stepped forward to take the positions.

This was a significant departure from the more top-down administration of the early years; it suggested that administration at an educational institution should be more about faculty governing themselves and retaining their faculty status than about developing a cadre of administrators who would take on these roles and remain divorced from the faculty. And yet the president did not receive much positive feedback from the faculty themselves. Some believed that the manner in which the original committee had been selected was insufficiently inclusive; some complained that the rotating chairs were not always going to be good administrators; still others believed that the chairs would not have the same authority as the previous deans so that there would in effect be greater power concentrated in the hands of the president and vice presidents.

This experiment in governance would not continue long into the following presidency. The lack of opposition to reverting back to deans, taking these administrators back out of the bargaining unit (though not the deans' assistants), perhaps highlights the notion that faculty do not necessarily want to govern themselves, or at least do not feel that this is the best way to administer schools or divisions. Perhaps the most significant point was that President Mitchell didn't receive the credit that he deserved for trying to respond to faculty demands and for endeavoring to create institutional structures that might better represent them.

Instead he faced opposition and left the impression that he was just another top-down administrator. This opposition perhaps provides insight into the complexity of Stockton's faculty landscape and the problems that come with endeavoring to be faculty-centered. Because who is that faculty precisely? Do its members constitute a single body? And, who or what represents them?

Mitchell was certainly not undermined by the Stockton Federation of Teachers (SFT). He had heard stories before arriving about how radical the SFT was and how difficult they would be to deal with, but he found them to be cooperative generally, and the faculty was not as radical as on some other campuses where issues seemed to generate a lot more militancy. That he supported the conversion of deans to chairpersons, increasing union membership in the process, suggests that he was not someone who was concerned about union opposition.

More troubling to him were the faculty he called the "Barons." He felt that the College had developed informal fiefdoms and that certain faculty had developed blocks of support, blocks that were easily mobilized to oppose different kinds of initiatives. Indeed, the faculty seldom spoke with a single voice, and the president found himself constantly encroaching on one fiefdom or another. King John could not prosper long under such circumstances, and neither could Peter Mitchell.

Endeavoring to be faculty-centered under such circumstances would be fraught with difficulty, especially when the only thing that could unite the faculty was their opposition to the president. Two issues provoked this unified opposition: the tenure quota and revoking a contract for a new director of the Library.

Under Bjork, Stockton had conformed to a New Jersey state tenure quota, wherein no program could have more than sixty-six percent of its faculty tenured. Stockton faculty found this most troubling. Not only did this potentially undermine new faculty members' efforts to meet the criteria for tenure, particularly those in small programs, but the faculty believed that the College conformed to this when other colleges in the state system were no longer doing so. Some even believed that the idea had originated with Bjork himself and thus represented the administration's general hostility to faculty and their concerns.

Mitchell didn't recognize the vehemence of this opposition and downplayed the issue's importance. Consequently, he did not endeavor to find ways around the problem (perhaps by shifting the focus from the program to the division as a whole, allowing for greater flexibility). Instead, adding fuel to the fire, he suggested that it was not as great an issue as imagined. He believed that anyone who was truly worthy, someone who really was a superstar, would be given tenure—someone like Stephen Dunn who was tenured in Performing Arts because the Literature program was "tenured up." But this was not reassuring to faculty. From their perspective this undermined a sense that there were uniform criteria for all, and it seemed that it would be left to the administration to decide when it would or would not be invoked as a reason for denial of tenure.

Finally, a misstep with regard to a decision to rescind the contract for a new Director of the Library after it had been offered and accepted provoked considerable opposition both within the administration and among the faculty. The Interim Academic Vice President and several of the divisional chairs resigned in protest, and this contributed to Mitchell's departure from the College.

Peter Mitchell decided to leave to take up the position as a Vice Chancellor for Planning and Program Development in the Massachusetts system. While there were some hard feelings associated with his departure, particularly since he had felt that he was trying to improve things for the people who seemed to oppose him most vehemently, Mitchell indicated that he had learned a great deal from his tenure as president at Stockton. He had arrived believing that many things needed to be changed; he left feeling that many of the ways Stockton had been doing things, while unusual, were nonetheless both valuable and effective.

Peter Mitchell's four-year tenure as president was an important one for the College. He required that the College self-consciously evaluate what it was that it was endeavoring to do in all areas of its operation. He believed in debate and dialogue and didn't shy away from provoking opposition when he felt that this was necessary for the College to fully articulate a direction in which to move. He also made significant overtures to the surrounding community, beginning to alter in fundamental ways the perspective that outsiders had of the College. In particular, this effort was focused on his promotion of the Performing Arts Center, which he believed was vital to familiarize people in the area with what the college was like and what its value was to the area. Again, causing opposition in the faculty, he moved the PAC out of the Division of Arts and Humanities, and brought it under the control of the President's Office, making it less tied to the academic mission and more focused on external relations.

While he may have felt that Stockton changed him more than he changed it, there is no question that Peter Mitchell's brief presidency was one that very much helped to shape what Stockton has become since.

Building an Environment for Excellence—
Vera King Farris

Harvey Kesselman

The longest-serving president at the Richard Stockton College of New Jersey placed an indelible stamp on its progress and development. Dr. Vera King Farris' two-decade tenure began when the institution was just twelve years old, lasted for half of the College's lifespan, and paralleled the dynamic change going on in the world during those twenty years.

The Farris era began in 1983 and spanned four US presidential administrations. The dawn of personal computing began a technology revolution that yielded the information age during the Farris years. Two wars in the Middle East, the nation's most prosperous economic period, and shocking terrorist attacks on US soil all occurred while Farris was leading the College. During these turbulent times, the native of Atlantic City —which is also the birthplace of Stockton—led the College through its own metamorphosis. Marked by accomplishments and not without controversy, this was a defining stage of Stockton's history.

Farris inherited an institution that had just gone through a brief yet tumultuous presidential administration. Divisive issues related to affirmative action and tenure quotas had paralyzed the institution, and there was genuine excitement among faculty, staff, and particularly students when Farris first assumed the presidency. Her youthful and exuberant pledge "to make the Stockton degree more valuable each and every year" resonated both internally and externally, and she spent the next twenty years focused on accomplishing just that.

By the time of Farris' arrival in 1983, the "student as adult" philosophy of the College's founding president had proven inconsistent with the times and unacceptable to accrediting agencies and other stakeholders. Farris had to establish a full array of student support services and residential facilities since few existed at the institution.

Farris made certain that the fledgling Division of Student Services took on a heightened priority. When it came to budgets and college policymaking, Student Services was to be considered on an equal level with Academic Affairs and Administration and

Finance. Farris believed that a liberal arts college was responsible for educating the whole student, and that included both the academic and cocurricular aspects of an education. Students were always central in Farris' thinking.

Under Farris, the institution moved from an open to a selective admissions process, resulting in substantial increases in the average SAT scores and high school class ranks of entering freshmen. Student retention and graduation rates consistently improved. Stockton's minority student success rate was the highest among the senior public colleges and universities in New Jersey.

More than a dozen buildings were erected during her tenure, and the world's largest environmentally friendly closed-loop geothermal HVAC system was installed. Stockton established graduate programs, including the nation's first Master of Holocaust and Genocide Studies. The athletics program evolved into a prominent Division III powerhouse, and Stockton hosted national and international tournaments in soccer and basketball.

Farris' approach not only kept pace with a rapidly changing world, it anticipated and stayed ahead. Stockton evolved from a small, experimental state college to an institution of high academic quality, innovation, and "can-do" determination. She termed it "an Environment for Excellence."

The culture of success Dr. Farris forged centered on a simple formula: people deeply committed to the institution, sustained hard work, and outside-the-box thinking. Faculty and staff were at the heart of this formula, an iron-willed determination was its engine, and a sense of family and community its soul. Dr. Farris' summit conferences of her top advisors, faculty, and staff were called "advances" rather than "retreats," because such was her expectation.

In addition to the aforementioned accomplishments, the following represent a few more of the Stockton milestones that took place during Dr. Farris' tenure:

- Housing complexes III and IV opened, as did the Townsend Residential Life Center (1983) and the Lakeside Residential Center (1988).
- Governor Thomas Kean designated Stockton as home to the Governor's School for the Environment (1988), the first of its kind in the United States.
- The Ida E. King Endowed Chair for the Visiting Scholar in Holocaust Studies, named after Farris' mother, was established (1989); the Stockton Holocaust Resource Center opened in 1990.

President Farris congratulates a graduating student (1994)

- The Carnegie Foundation ranked Stockton as one of seven "selective" public liberal arts colleges in the U.S. (1994).
- The expanded and renovated Library opened (1995).
- The Arts and Sciences Building, designed by renowned architect Michael Graves, was constructed (1995).
- The $17 million Sports Center was built (1997).
- The College mission was revised to include graduate degrees; the first master's programs were added (1997); graduate programs in Business, Instructional Technology, Holocaust and Genocide Studies, Nursing, Occupational Therapy, and Physical Therapy were established by 2003.
- The historic Carnegie Library was restored and established as a satellite center in Atlantic City (2002).
- The American Foundation for Greek Language and Culture donated $300,000 to endow an Interdisciplinary Center for Hellenic Studies (2003).

Despite her accomplishments, Farris' personal and administrative style sometimes led to clashes with others, both externally and on campus. Faculty resisted some of her efforts, particularly when they felt excluded from, instead of included in, shared college governance. Farris was also the focus of an Atlantic County prosecutorial investigation, and there were lawsuits filed against her by both faculty and staff members. Insufficient evidence to prosecute was found in the investigation, and the civil actions were settled with neither side claiming victory. A self-described "fighter," Farris never backed away from a challenge. Although critics took issue with some of her methods, few questioned her commitment to advancing the institution.

Born of extremely humble origins, Farris never lost sight of the liberating power of education and was most strongly committed to provide access and opportunity to capable deserving students, irrespective of their financial circumstances. It was as Director of the College's Educational Opportunity Fund (EOF) program that I met Dr. Farris for the first time. I was instantly impressed and never stopped learning from her. My work in an area of great

personal interest to her—educational opportunity—helped create our bond and would strengthen our working relationship through the years. She was the consummate teacher and always had time to share her knowledge and wisdom with those who were interested. She had a very warm, caring, energetic, outgoing personality and her enthusiasm was contagious.

Dr. Farris retired from Stockton in 2004, but she remained active, speaking nationally, teaching, serving on volunteer boards, and attending Stockton events. She appeared comfortable settling into a role as the College's elder stateswoman, until her health began to decline.

Dr. Farris passed away on November 28, 2009. She left a lengthy list of personal and professional accomplishments, including eight honorary doctorate degrees, including one from Tuskegee University, her undergraduate alma mater. She was Chair of the American Association of State Colleges and Universities in 1996 and was reappointed to an unprecedented second consecutive year. She was President of the Middle States Association of Colleges and Schools.

For her work in Holocaust education, Dr. Farris was feted by the Consul General and Ambassador of Israel. Along with such luminaries as former President Jimmy Carter, she was named a "Hero of Public Housing" for her accomplishments following her upbringing in Atlantic City's Stanley Holmes Village public housing project. It would take far more space than this chapter permits to provide a complete listing of Dr. Farris' awards and accolades.

Looking back on the Vera King Farris era at Stockton, one is struck by the very significant gains Stockton made as a result of her efforts and talent. That legacy would have pleased her more than all of her personal and professional accomplishments.

Shared Governance?

Robert Helsabeck

The founding administrators and faculty at Stockton began collegiate political life full of idealism and optimism. We would work together in good spirit without the usual forms of interest politics—faculty, students, administrators, unions and management. In the first year, the faculty rejected the initial invitation of the "mild" association, the New Jersey Education Association (NJEA), to be our representative in contract negotiations: We didn't need a union; we would work it out ourselves. A year later we joined the more radical union, the American Federation of Teachers (AFT). What happened?

This essay endeavors to answer this question by looking at the history of governance at Stockton from the faculty's perspective. It focuses on changes in governance and the reasons for these changes rather than on the substantive matters taken up by the different governance structures.

THE CONTEXT

Stockton began its life at a time of an extraordinary convergence of political factors. It was a time of rich external and internal political culture for a college to begin its efforts to fashion collegiate governance. The larger culture of the late Sixties was marked by the strong anti-authoritarian drive of the student generation and the caution, and even fear, of those "in charge." Many younger members of the culture wished to minimize any hierarchy of authority. Other members of the culture feared the excesses of these egalitarians and were concerned with control and accountability. Stockton had representatives of both subcultures.

At the same time, the American Association of University Professors (AAUP) had just completed a landmark national study of collegiate decision-making in which they suggested that there were times for faculty autonomy in decision-making, times for faculty/administrative partnership, and times when the faculty had lesser roles. This model was at odds with the beginning structure of governance at Stockton and provided some of the fuel for early disputes over governance. The senior administration had put in place (top-down) the governance structure that the faculty inherited. In other words, to the question "Who decides who decides?" the answer was "the administration." The initial model of governance at Stockton made no allowance for a distinctive faculty voice in governance. Still another cultural factor was brought into Stockton—consensus decision-making. Some faculty and administrators had studied its efficacy, and several faculty members were practitioners in this Quaker tradition. Others thought consensus decision-making was inefficient and downright foolish.

Finally, Stockton existed in the state of New Jersey, which was heavily unionized and had statewide coordination. Both of these external units limited the autonomy of Stockton and therefore played a role in internal governance. It was in this political culture that the Stockton founders established Stockton's system of governance.

CORPORATE GOVERNANCE: THE EARLY YEARS

Administrative Working Paper #1 was initially seen by most faculty and administrators as a master stroke of design. It was clear that the early planners thought governance was fundamental to the effective operation of the college. The early planners crafted a design for unitary (corporate) governance centering on the College Council. The College Council was to serve as the principal governing council with Collegia (described below) providing smaller political/social groups. Throughout those early years, the official documents clearly asserted the authority of the president and the Board of Trustees as the legal, accountable authority. Those same documents also resisted the normally constituted authorities of faculty and students as distinct interest groups.

The College Council had broad authority to deal with matters of instruction, co-curriculum, advisement/information, personnel, finance, and campus planning. It met monthly and was made up of ten students, ten faculty, and ten staff (seven from unclassified staff and three from classified staff). The selection of members was a random drawing from among those willing to serve one-year terms and limited to two consecutive terms. The intent was to create a group that felt minimum constituent responsibility but maximum college responsibility. The emphasis throughout was to perform an advisory role to the president and the board and not to presume to have decision-making authority. The College Council was to be a substitute for the traditional interest groups (faculty and students).

The planners resisted the traditional governance groups of faculty and students (senates or assemblies). This lack of special structure discouraged the leadership that normally is represented through these traditional groups. Also, the absence of departments and the chairs normally associated with departments further reduced the natural faculty leadership associated with departments. In most colleges, the "layer" of departmental chairs provides a check on the concentration of power in the senior administration. Stockton's program coordinators, who rotated every year or two, were not the equivalent.

Almost immediately, these "natural" groups began to assert

themselves. By April of the first year the faculty began to call its own meetings with a "moderator" (the Quaker term) to "facilitate" the meetings. (Up to that time the faculty meetings were called and chaired by the Academic Vice President.) For the next three years the faculty met under its own authority, formally constituting itself as the Faculty Assembly during the fourth year of the College. The Assembly was not recognized by the administration for several more years.

During this same half decade, the College Council continued to function but was losing legitimacy as the "representatives" were not elected, and their action was only advisory. The difficulties were well documented in the papers leading up to the first accreditation visit.

On another front, late in the first year, the faculty formed the Stockton Federation of Teachers (SFT), a unit of the larger AFT. Many felt that the "heavy hand" of the president motivated the faculty to join the more radical union. Although the union was not formally a part of the institutional system of governance, it did deal with important issues affecting institutional well being and also unified the faculty during contract negotiations. The union was one place in which the distinctive faculty leadership was identified and developed. Meetings of the SFT were an important setting in which faculty felt some political unity as a faculty. This unity no doubt added to the desire for a more distinct faculty voice in the college through the Faculty Assembly. The students followed the faculty's lead and in the second year formed their own "union." After a few years, the union structure was abandoned by the students and a more traditional student government association was formed.

A couple of additional observations need to be made on the political culture of those earliest years. As regards the curriculum, as distinct from college-wide matters, the individual faculty members had extraordinary autonomy and valued that autonomy. Faculty members engaged in conversations with their colleagues about their courses but resisted any attempts to form a curriculum committee. Put otherwise, the faculty rejected any attempt to place some faculty over others in these individual decisions. So at one level, the faculty had little distinctive collective authority, while at another level they had nearly complete individual autonomy.

Another distinctive feature of Stockton's beginning was the presence of the Preceptorial and the Collegium. The Preceptorial was made up of a preceptor (advisor/teacher) and fifteen students with whom the preceptor worked for four years, helping each student to fashion a good education. The Collegium was made up of six preceptors, five of whom were faculty members from different disciplines and one who was an administrator. The result was ninety-person groups that promised to be foundational to governance. Faculty members were assigned office locations based upon their Collegium, making the sense of "neighborhood" more salient. However, Stockton's initial culture of anti-authoritarianism made the groups resistant to the rise of leadership (in which students dominated), and therefore the Collegia did not emerge as a significant factor in governance. Also the Preceptorial structure collapsed under its own weight, thereby removing the building block for "neighborhood" governance—but that's another story.

Students also played a substantial role in the evaluation of faculty during the college's first decade. They both *reported* on teaching by filling out a teacher evaluation form for all classes and *judged* that teaching by sitting in equal numbers to faculty on the divisional review committees. The review committees were the first group to consider faculty members' retention, tenure, and promotion. With a tenure quota of fifty percent in place for programs during this time, these committees had real power. The votes were cast anonymously, thereby giving the student vote equal standing with the faculty vote. This element of governance was at odds with standard practice in higher education and caused considerable consternation among many faculty members who felt that faculty alone should be making these personnel recommendations. (Egalitarianism had its limits!)

In preparation for the first accreditation visit, a document was written evaluating the success of these early structures. In short, the report was critical of the "centralized authority" of the president and the weakness of the College Council. The 1975 report of the Commission of Higher Education of the Middle States Association was also critical of the functioning of the governance system and suggested a reexamination of it. It was in this context that more traditional forms of governance emerged.

FEDERATED GOVERNANCE: THE FACULTY ASSEMBLY, DEANS TO CHAIRS, AND THE STUDENT UNION TO THE STUDENT GOVERNMENT ASSOCIATION

In June 1975, the faculty ratified a constitution forming the Faculty Assembly. Almost immediately, Ralph Bean, the first union president wrote a memo to Fred Mench, the first Assembly president, outlining the role of the union as distinct from the Faculty Assembly. Because the membership of the union and the Assembly overlapped almost completely, it was relatively easy to come to an understanding of the role of each. Put simply, the union would attend to working conditions, the adherence to the contract, and the fair treatment of faculty. The Assembly would deal with academic policy, programs, General Studies, and issues of institutional well-being and planning. This "division of labor" has worked well over the first forty years, although sometimes administrators have complained that they don't always know to whom they are talking—faculty as Faculty Assembly members or faculty as union members.

By 1980, significant changes were underway in the governance structure of the College. The first president, Richard Bjork, had moved to a position in Vermont, and Peter Mitchell had assumed the position. The internal report on governance evaluated the strengths and weaknesses of the first decade's governance structures and functions and concluded that a move to more recognition of faculty and student structures would improve the genuine sharing of decision-making. The new president seemed attuned to the traditional forms of governance and embraced the efforts underway to make legitimate the distinct voice of the faculty. The Faculty Assembly was recognized in the college's publications, and regular meetings of the faculty leadership and the president occurred.

A notable step, taken by the new president, was to call together a group of senior faculty to work with him in the restructuring of Academic Affairs. The result of these deliberations was to replace deans with faculty-elected and administratively appointed chairs of the academic divisions. This change placed senior faculty in an administrative role, much like the departmental chairs at major universities. This change, as well as the governance process by which the change was decided, further enhanced the perception of the faculty as partners with the administration.

The Faculty Assembly was now operating with full legitimacy. It clearly did not always "win the day" but was taken seriously by the president and the Board of Trustees. The Assembly, made up of the entire faculty and some academic administrators, met monthly. A Steering Committee served as an executive group and provided "steerage" of issues to the appropriate Assembly committees.

Evidence of the "standing" of the Faculty Assembly was found in the role it played in the presidential search resulting in the Peter Mitchell appointment. The Assembly president and one additional faculty member elected by the Assembly were the two faculty members serving on the Board of Trustees' search committee. Additionally, a major change in the structure of the General Studies curriculum was proposed by an Assembly committee and approved by the administration. The faculty had the clear sense that the administration respected the judgment of the collective faculty.

At the same time, costs were already beginning to be apparent in the "town meeting" approach to faculty governance. In the conduct of normal business, the process of governing was slow. A committee had to consider practically all matters and usually met only once or twice a month. Then the entire faculty met to consider the committee's recommendations. Sometimes a quorum was not obtained, and delays occurred. Finally, increasing numbers of committees were generated, resulting in additional costs of time.

Even with the inefficiencies, the faculty preferred the Assembly to the former College Council as the way of giving expression to the faculty's concerns. The Assembly functioned best when the College faced an important institutional concern. At those times, the faculty would come out in full strength, and their decisions had real weight.

Under the third president, Vera Farris, the chairs were replaced by deans so as to produce a "management confidential" layer of administrative officers. The next two decades were marked by a more traditional gap between the administration and the faculty. Many important initiatives happened during these years, but the governing relationship between the faculty and administration was more adversarial than collegial. Despite this relationship, business was conducted with reasonable effectiveness. Two examples give evidence of the mixed effectiveness of the Assembly structure: the Freshman Seminar program and plus-minus grading.

The Chair of the General Studies Committee and the new Dean of General Studies co-sponsored an idea for freshman seminars. The idea was taken to the Assembly, discussed for several meetings, and then approved. The administration was also included in the discussions from the beginning. A distinctive faculty voice coupled with an administrative/faculty partnership prevailed in this adoption.

Another idea, brought forward by a couple of faculty members, was plus-minus grading. The faculty was split on the matter, but after nearly a half year of conversation, the Assembly approved the change. The president resisted the idea, taking it to the Student Senate. She reported that the senate was concerned with a possible deflationary effect of plus-minus grading. She refused to approve the Assembly recommendation until the students also agreed. Faculty felt that grading was the prerogative of faculty and thought it an act of bad faith by the administration.

In the mid-eighties, the Faculty Assembly leadership constituted a task force to revise the constitution with an eye to making it easier for the administration to work cooperatively with the faculty and to realize some efficiencies internal to the assembly. The administration had stated that it often by-passed the Assembly because it wasn't clear to whom proposals should go, and the pace of consideration was too slow.

The constitutional changes created a clear committee to correspond to each of the vice-presidential units with additional committees in Academic Affairs. This structure acknowledged the legitimate concern of the faculty for any issues that affected the welfare of the College, while acknowledging a primary concern for academic matters. The Steering Committee was given more power of substantive review to expedite discussions by the full Assembly. These changes seemed to improve matters.

By the end of the eighties, governance was functioning only modestly well. The Assembly would take action, sometimes finding support and sometimes not. Communication with the administration was conducted frequently after the fact and was often combative. The Assembly seemed to be seen by some key administrators as a hurdle to be avoided on the big issues of planning and the nature of the College. Alternatively, the president used faculty/administrative task forces of her own creation to handle many matters of concern. The Faculty Assembly considered this approach to be a by-pass of the legitimate structure of governance.

The Middle States Report of 1990 ended with a note suggestive of the state of governance at that time:

> One final word of wisdom? Perhaps the key phrase should be "shared vision, shared governance." Stockton has many admirable and unique accomplishments and many excellent and foresighted objectives for its future. At this time, however, the Study Team has missed the sense of an integrated planning process that takes the academic and educational process as its centerpiece. We would close by encouraging the President, who had already made remarkable progress at Stockton; the faculty, which is exceptional for its creativity and loyalty to the institution; and the College's many able administrators to fully integrate its planning process into the ongoing life of the College.

In response to the conditions of that time, acknowledged by the Middle States Report, a group of former moderators/presidents wrote an extended paper on the state of governance and planning at Stockton—"As We See It." It was critical of governance in general and planning in particular as not being at all collaborative and open.

As the College continued to admit more students and hire more faculty, the inefficiencies of the town meeting form of governance was becoming increasingly evident.

REPRESENTATIVE GOVERNANCE: THE FACULTY SENATE

In 2008, the Faculty Assembly approved the creation of a special task force on governance. It was charged with considering alternate forms of governance in an effort to improve the faculty's contribution to the conduct of the College. The charge included the serious consideration of a Faculty Senate. The Assembly, in the past, had considered and rejected the idea of a senate. However, the time seemed right.

The task force, based upon its further deliberation and conversations with colleagues, fleshed out a detailed proposal for a senate in constitutional language. In broad strokes, we proposed a senate larger than the current Steering Committee but smaller than the entire faculty (roughly one tenth of faculty members, about thirty currently). We proposed to preserve the full faculty meeting (Faculty Assembly), which would occur at least once a semester, or more frequently as called by the senate. The faculty would retain the power to override senate decisions and initiate actions not brought up by the senate and could call itself into session with the signatures of a certain percentage of the faculty.

The attempt was to gain the advantages of a smaller group for operational purposes, while retaining the political "weight" of the full faculty when needed. We saw several advantages of a senate over a town meeting of the faculty:

1. Clearly, a smaller body could more effectively deliberate on routine matters that do not warrant the full faculty's attention.

2. By design, a senate would also better ensure the type of constancy and continuity that generally underlie effective shared governance than would a town meeting with inconstant attendance.

3. One's participation in the senate would be clearly recognized in a way not typical in a large town meeting.

4. The demands upon any one faculty member to be heavily involved in governance would be less as one finished a term of service and yielded to colleagues to take their turn. (As one colleague put it years ago, "I would serve a term or two on a senate, but I don't want to waste my time attending these amorphous Assembly meetings."

5. A representative body elected by the whole would be a better representative of the whole than a poorly attended meeting of the whole.

6. By maintaining the sovereignty of the collective faculty (its capacity to override the senate in extraordinary circumstances), the senate would be held accountable to the entire faculty.

7. And finally, although a structural change cannot remove the cultural problem of faculty disengagement or distraction by other demands, it promised to make that disengagement less damaging to the College. A group of faculty dedicated to the notion of shared governance may be adequate.

The effectiveness of the senate is currently being reviewed. It appears to have been a needed change in governance.

LESSONS AND QUESTIONS

What does Stockton's experience in governance teach us and what questions does it raise? Stockton had tried unitary governance with its College Council, federated governance of the whole with the Faculty Assembly and federated governance using a representative body—the Faculty Senate. Stockton had tried consensus decision-making and found it wanting. Stockton has experienced periods of genuine shared governance and times of separations and suspicion. These forms and experiences reflect the efforts of collegiate governance across the country as well as at Stockton.

We have learned some lessons and are left with some questions.

1. We have learned that governance is fundamental to the well being of a college. The question of who is involved with various types of decision is vital to good decisions and good morale. It is also important as to "who decides who decides."

2. Administrators prefer a manageable partner of reasonable size and reliable membership. If the cast of characters is too large and variable over time, a good working partnership is hard to form.

3. "Traditional forms" of any practice, and certainly governance, are usually traditional because they work. When one deviates from standard practice it takes a great deal of human energy to sustain the new practice.

4. Distinct bodies (faculty, students, and administrators) want to have their distinct perspectives given voice. It's not satisfactory to amalgamate the voices into one. Further, choosing representatives by random selection, although appealing in concept, troubles constituents and cripples the development

of constituent leadership.

5. Faculty bodies, like assemblies or senates, can work effectively with faculty unions if the will is present.

6. Similarly, if good people operate with good will, virtually any structure can be made to work. However certain structures are more conducive to good working relations than others. Structure does affect function!

7. Consensus decision-making may require a culture of consensus. A Quaker college, like Earlham College, can make consensus governance work with ease, while a college like Stockton, with its different culture, finds it difficult and even unsatisfactory, except in small councils.

These are some of the lessons we have drawn from our efforts in governance. We are left with some questions as well:

1. Could the unitary governance (the College Council) have worked with a different cast of characters in a different time? With a less authoritarian president, a faculty that was more accepting of the necessity for significant accountability to external audiences, and in a time when faculty and students were less inclined to test limits, perhaps the College Council could have worked. Perhaps, if the council was made up of elected representatives who therefore had political legitimacy, it would have had a better chance.

2. Will the operation of the Faculty Senate, as a subset of the entire faculty, create a further sense of alienation in the rest of the faculty? Can the senate structure gain the efficiencies of a small manageable governing body while creating a sense of involvement and responsibility in the faculty as a whole?

3. Will a senate, with its implication of the involvement of senior faculty, be true to its name? Will long-term faculty step up?

It is my humble opinion that the governance that has evolved at Stockton after forty years will be effective. The current governance structure acknowledges the legitimate interests and perspectives of interest groups through its separate bodies, while moving in the direction of greater collaboration among the bodies. The structure seems right, but its effectiveness will ultimately depend upon the good will of the players.

A Rainbow-colored Sign

From the first of my day-long interviews in WQ 201, I knew this was the right place for me. I felt very much at-home with several of the people who interviewed me that day, noticing the kind of jewelry the women wore (Beth Olsen was wearing some Bakelite, Claire Lopatto and GT Lenard had on earrings like the ones I make), and even enjoying the kinds of questions I was asked (not the usual "Where do you see yourself five years from now?"). By the end of the day, when I was interviewed by my boss-to-be, David Carr, I was exhausted. I made mistakes in my responses and could barely sit up straight. But somehow, I got that "good vibe" from David, thinking he might be a good boss, and that he might think I was the best candidate for the position.

That was in the summer of 2002. That was the summer my mom lay in a coma in an Arizona hospital after suffering a burst brain aneurysm several months earlier. I made three trips to Phoenix that summer: the first to see if there was any brain activity left in her; the second to be with my sister, brother and stepfather at her bedside when they removed her from the ventilator; and the third to come back with my son, Nick, to participate in her memorial service. During the second trip, the morning after my mom died, I got an early morning (Phoenix time) phone call from David Carr offering me the job. I asked if I could have a few days to talk to my husband and make a decision, but David needed an answer within 24 hours for the imminent Board meeting. Jeez, I thought, my mom just died and I have to make a life-changing decision! Then I focused back on the way I felt during my day on campus, and knew at once what my answer would be.

My first day driving to Stockton – we lived in the Trenton area at the time – I found a new route that seemed most direct, rte. 539. I was nervous, starting a new job, and still grieving over my mom's death. As I drove the hour and a half trip, I thought that it was almost magical that I got the job offer just after my mom died, as if she had a hand in making it happen for me. I get mystical in my beliefs during emotional times, but am usually more of a non-believer.

As I got to within about 10 miles of the Garden State Parkway on 539, I saw a large, rainbow-colored sign for a truck company, Phoenix. And then I smiled to myself. My mom was reassuring me that yes, in fact, she was accompanying me on the trip to Stockton, where she knew I would be happy.

Deb Dagavarian

The Union Made Us Strong

John W. Searight

When the first cohort of fifty-five faculty and ninety-seven staff began Stockton's inaugural academic year in September 1971, few had given much thought to the role of unions in higher education, let alone the need for a union at their new place of employment. Energy and effort were focused on organizing academic programs, refining the requirements for majors, and developing the vision, structure, standards, and curriculum that would support a new, innovative, and distinctive undergraduate college in southern New Jersey. Many if not most of the early faculty and staff were attracted to Stockton because they perceived it to be a unique opportunity to be creative, to be free from the traditional academic strictures of their discipline (for example, they would be able to develop and teach two courses in General Studies and were to be assigned offices not by discipline, but by membership in a "Collegium," an interdisciplinary group of preceptors), and to be in on the ground floor of a new college. None of the faculty had tenure, and several had left tenured positions to come to Stockton. Most had visions of a new, flexible, innovative, experimental, and different kind of college.

What happened that caused so many to embrace union membership by the end of the second year? How and why did such a strong local union emerge for faculty and staff?

Stockton was a difficult and demanding place to work in those first few years. The academic calendar consisted of three terms with teaching and advising responsibilities in each of the terms. In the 1972-1973 academic year, the fall term began September 5th and ended December 19th; the winter term began January 3rd and ended March 2nd; and the spring term began March 12th and ended June 1st. In June roundtable discussions

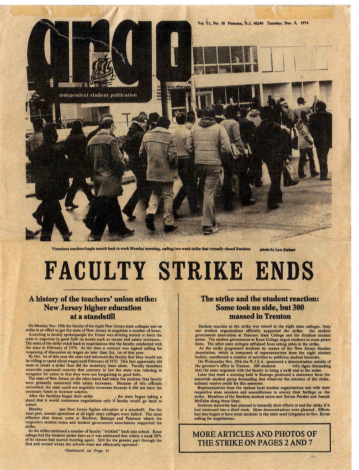

and workshops were organized (and held at Seaview!) by the administration, and participation and attendance by faculty were expected. The College president's position was that faculty were under contract until June 30th and they were to be available to contribute to the planning and development of the college.

Faculty were also facing annual evaluations for reappointment. Everyone was on a one-year contract. The New Jersey statutes governing tenure were undergoing review in the legislature. The tenure statutes were changed in 1973, and the probationary period for faculty went from three to five years. During the public debate about these changes, Stockton's founding president, Richard Bjork, questioned the value and necessity of tenure for college faculty, believing that the public and students would be better served by long term contracts (five to ten years) at the end of the probationary period. President Bjork also articulated his belief that each candidate for reappointment or for tenure should be evaluated against the following standard: "is this the best person available anywhere (in the universe of possible candidates) for this position?" If not, the person should not be reappointed. This principle did not become actual practice at Stockton, but it remained part of the conversation about tenure and reappointment for the next several years.

In these first few years Stockton was developing policies for faculty and staff evaluation and reappointment. Stockton had not been a party to the collective bargaining agreement that covered the original six state colleges, and the administration decided it could and did establish college policies and procedures without having to negotiate. The most contentious of these was Administrative Working Paper #IV (AWP IV), "Faculty and

Staff Evaluation: Policy and Procedure," written by President Bjork over a weekend in February 1972. It was presented to faculty and staff, and for the next four months there were many suggestions for changes and additions. President Bjork then revised his original version of AWP IV, and it was approved by the Board of Trustees in July 1972. The president acknowledged that the revised version was much improved, but negotiated it was not. It became Procedure 6136 in 1978 and continued in effect with only minor technical changes until 2007.

In December 1972, seven members of the founding faculty were not recommended for reappointment by President Bjork. One of the seven was Thomas Wirth, charter member and first president of the Stockton Federation of Teachers (SFT). As these events were unfolding, voting was taking place statewide among college faculty and professional staff to determine whether the New Jersey Education Association (NJEA) or the American Federation of Teachers (AFT) would be our bargaining agent. The NJEA was the incumbent but faced widespread dissatisfaction with the job it had done, including failure to notify the state in 1970 of its intent to negotiate a successor agreement, resulting in an automatic renewal of the old agreement. A challenge was underway by the AFT. Stockton was new to the bargaining unit and became a strong supporter of the AFT, which won in a very close vote. As the 1972-1973 academic year drew to a close, President Bjork was successful in having the Stockton Board of Trustees approve a ten-year staffing plan that set a tenure limit of sixty percent for faculty, by program.

Thus, by the end of the second year a new bargaining agent (AFT) had been selected, seven of the founding faculty had not been recommended for reappointment, the academic year lasted from early September into mid-June, the value of tenure was being questioned by the college president, and an evaluation procedure for staff and faculty and a staffing plan limiting tenure to sixty percent had been implemented without negotiation, and in the case of the staffing plan, without significant consultation.

As the third academic year (1973-1974) began, negotiations were underway for a new collective bargaining agreement to cover terms and conditions for employment in New Jersey's state college system. Representing the college faculty and staff was the Council of New Jersey State College Locals, NJSFT-AFT/AFL-CIO (CNJSCL). Representing the colleges was the Governor's Office of Employee Relations. On the union side each college local had at least one representative at the table (Stockton's chief representative was Ralph Bean, who had succeeded Tom Wirth as SFT president), while the colleges were represented by the Director of the Governor's Office of Employee Relations, assisted by legal staff from the Department of Higher Education, and two college presidents (one of whom was President Bjork). Stockton faculty and staff became very interested in the negotiations for the new contract because they would result in the first master agreement for terms and conditions of employment in which we directly participated in the negotiations. Further, the resulting

agreement would become the contract governing our working lives at Stockton. By this time it had also become quite clear that faculty hopes for shared governance and participation in policy formation at Stockton were not being realized, and the strong and efficient administration of the college president was implementing its vision, establishing its policies and procedures, and shaping the College accordingly. Interest in the activities and work of the SFT was growing rapidly, especially among the faculty, and membership had grown to ninety-nine of the 119 faculty (83.2 percent).

When negotiations stalled in fall 1973, the union set a deadline of February 4th for a new contract. A mediator was appointed, negotiations intensified, and agreement was finally reached February 22, 1974. We had our master agreement. The new agreement was for two and one-half years and contained for faculty and staff of the state colleges many improvements in their terms and conditions of employment. The most significant were:

- A grievance procedure with binding arbitration at the final step;
- protection for academic freedom and nondiscrimination;
- limits for academic teaching assignments to thirty-two weeks of instruction and twenty-four credit hours;
- sabbatical leaves and tuition subsidy;
- agreement to ask the Board of Higher Education to establish concurrent academic rank for librarians (achieved in the next master agreement, July 1, 1977);
- protection for staff against arbitrary nonrenewal of multi-year contracts;
- salary increases, protection of the step increments within each range, and continuation of benefits;
- and a re-opener clause for salaries and fringe benefits for the last year of the agreement, negotiations for which were to begin no later than October 1974.

Shortly after the agreement was ratified, the SFT successfully negotiated local agreements with the administration that protected our practice of having the standard teaching load consist of five class courses and one nonclass course (a combination of tutorials, independent studies, and internships) and provided compensation or a course release for program coordinators.

These local agreements strengthened two distinctive features of Stockton: faculty were to utilize the nonclass course mode as part of their instructional responsibilities, and academic programs would maintain their structure with coordinators rather than departmental chairs.

The sense of accomplishment and the hopes for peace on the labor relations front were quick to fade when the state began to show little interest in scheduling meaningful bargaining sessions for the re-opener clause on salaries and benefits. The newly signed agreement called for these negotiations to begin no later than October 1, 1974 and conclude by February 1, 1975. The issue quickly became framed as lack of respect for

SFT logo designed by Michael McGarvey

the union and a violation of the agreement that had just been signed by the parties. The union believed the state was acting in bad faith when it informed us in the fall of 1973 that it was not prepared to respond to the proposals submitted by the union until after December 1st. Thus, as the next academic year began in September 1974, faculty and staff at Stockton began to hear about the possibility of a strike.

The Council of New Jersey State College Locals had established a central office in Union, New Jersey, elected officers from its statewide membership, and hired a professional staff of two union representatives (Stockton's Tom Wirth and Tony Marino). The council president, Marcoantonio Lacatena, was from Montclair, and the vice president was Ralph Bean from Stockton. Monthly meetings were held at the Labor Education Center at Rutgers, and they were often long, running late into the night. Decisions were made by a vote of the delegates, elected or appointed from each of the college locals, and major policy and negotiation issues were presented by the local officers and delegates to council to local membership for information and instruction. After the master agreement was signed and ratified, Stockton delegates to council were Ralph Bean, SFT president, and John Searight, SFT grievance chair. Both had represented Stockton during the final extended negotiation sessions that resulted in the master agreement.

It was at first difficult to imagine that we would be talking about a strike so soon after the successful conclusion of the statewide negotiations for our first contract, but the CNJSCL leadership believed the credibility of the union and our hard-won contract was on the line. The state also had informed the union that when negotiations did begin they would have limited ability to respond to the salary and benefits re-opener because New Jersey was in financial difficulty and the revenue projections for the next fiscal year were poor. Not only could we not get the state to negotiate seriously, we were being told in advance that a positive outcome was unlikely. Many Stockton faculty were uneasy about using the threat of a strike to force negotiations, but as the state continued to resist serious talks (our modest proposal for a cost-of-living increase received no response), the threat to the union's credibility and our economic well-being became clear.

So strike we did. The strike began November 18, 1974, and ended eight working days later on November 27th, the day before Thanksgiving. Going on strike was a new experience for most of us. When picket assignments were made and 168 of

our colleagues were assigned to six different "crews," it became a reality. We were nervous and unsure of ourselves but also determined to take a stand. There were only two entrances to Stockton that had to be covered. Picket crews were assigned four-hour shifts. Each crew had a "captain" who made the assignments of which entrance you picketed. We used the Pomona Shopping Center parking lot as a staging area. We picketed from 7:00 am to 7:00 pm. We carried signs—"NEGOTIATE, DON'T DICTATE," "BARGAIN NOW," "ON STRIKE," "WE'LL WALK TILL THEY TALK"—and picketing was respectful and orderly. Those coming into work knew they were crossing a picket line, but there was no harassment, very little jeering, and lots of respectful enthusiasm. The strike effectively shut down teaching at Stockton. Very few classes were held, and they were sparsely attended. The student union at Stockton supported the strike. While the administration formally notified faculty that "strikes or job actions" by public employees "were generally illegal" and participation in such actions "may subject employees to disciplinary action and other penalties in accordance with legal action that may be taken," there also was a verbal agreement between administration and union leadership that the strike would have an end, and the administration and the faculty and staff would have to come together to continue to provide a quality education for our students. Leading up to and during the strike, SFT President Ralph Bean urged members not only to leave together but return together as well. For the most part that's what we did.

Six days into the strike, as the holiday weekend approached, Lewis Kaden, Counsel to New Jersey Governor Brendan Byrne, contacted Council President Lacatena to say that he was prepared to seek an injunction to end the strike but then offered an immediate settlement consisting of three days' pay and amnesty for the strikers. This offer was rejected, but talks ensued, and a settlement was reached November 27th. College faculty returned to their classrooms on December 2nd. The settlement included a prompt beginning of negotiations under the direction of a prominent labor relations mediator, with such negotiations to continue until agreement was reached; pay for three days; no reprisals against employees, students, or other persons; a make-up procedure for lost time and pay; and a mutual commitment "to preserve and expand the public higher education system in New Jersey." Early Monday morning, December 2, 1974, forty-five to fifty-five Stockton faculty gathered at the A-wing flagpole and walked back to their offices together. For the most part we felt proud of what had been accomplished and relieved that the strike was over. The SFT emerged as one of the strongest locals of the council, with 130 members and three delegates, one of whom (Ralph Bean) was state vice president.

The SFT soon began to utilize the grievance procedure established in the master agreement to address contractual issues that it believed were being violated by actions of the administration at Stockton. Improvements were made in the evaluation and reappointment process, with reasonable notice required if there were deficiencies in performance and reasons provided in cases of nonreappointment. The process for appointment and reappointment had to be fairly and equitably applied to all candidates. There could be no unilateral appointment of administrators to faculty positions. And the evaluation of tenured faculty at Stockton had to conform to the newly enacted law on tenure. There would be no more annual reviews of tenured faculty and no more annual reaffirmations of tenured faculty by the Board of Trustees (practices unique to Stockton). The new law (A-328) provided for a five-year review of tenured faculty, with provisions for faculty development if any deficiencies were noted. And finally, as the decade of the seventies drew to a close, the SFT won a major case when an arbitrator found that a highly qualified female candidate for tenure had been denied because of the staffing guidelines limiting tenure to sixty percent in spite of the fact that exceptions were permitted for affirmative action candidates. After the ordered reconsideration of her application by Stockton, she was granted tenure.

The SFT engaged in activities to promote community-building among Stockton faculty and staff. An early fall picnic for families, a softball team, and occasional parties were examples. The union also established a good relationship with the Faculty Assembly. The two organizations had an excellent understanding of their respective functions, supported one another for the most part when they shared standing in an issue, and knew when not to intrude upon the other's domain. The union continued to have success at the bargaining table, especially with the traditional issues of compensation and benefits. By the end of Stockton's first decade, a significant majority of faculty and professional staff were SFT members, and the college administration and the union leadership understood their differences and had established an effective working relationship.

Picket line with Joe Rubenstein, John Searight, and Hal Taylor

Diver In L-wing swimming pool (1980)

Life Sports

Joseph Rubenstein

In spring 1972 I took a trip down to Atlantic City from Manhattan to interview for a job in a Life Sports program in the Division of Experimental Studies at a newly formed college no one had heard about, or, if they had, confused with an equally unknown West Coast college located in Stockton, California. (For years our mail crossed.)

I was finishing my degree in anthropology at the New School for Social Research. There, my friends and I prided ourselves that if we ventured out of Manhattan it would be to go to London, Paris, or Berlin in search of the roots of our professors-in-exile from fascist Europe. So it was with some curiosity that I drove down to the old Mayflower Hotel on the Atlantic City boardwalk. Brooklyn's Coney Island was fine with me, but my memories of Atlantic City were as gauzy as the photo of a ten-year-old bundled in a fur-collared winter coat wrapped in the arms of my mother and father. Never mind that Stockton was going to be relocated in the woods. And me without a flannel shirt!

My friend, Marty Miller, ushered me into his hotel-room-cum-office, a place that suited him well; he was a runner, quite a good one, a 4:10 miler in college, and after a long hard run on the beach he would come back to his office and shower. Things were all of a sudden looking quite comfy. Marty was finishing his political science degree and was a serious (and radical) athlete who had been recruited to help start the Life Sports program at Stockton State as an alternative to the conventional NCAA approach (elite athletes, recruiting, highly competitive play, etc.). Marty and I were going to grow sport throughout the campus and make it part of life, just like the kibbutz in Israel where we had met. Plow the fields in the morning, and play the violin at night (or was it the other way around?). Anyway, at Stockton we were going to study during the day and play amongst ourselves after that—all of us. Traditional intercollegiate sports be damned!

My degree was in theoretical anthropology, but I was a decent athlete, and I was sure that Marty and I, with the help of our new boss-to-be, Ken Tompkins, and other fellow academic revolutionaries in the Division of Experimental Studies, could construct a playful socialist utopia in the Pine Barrens of New Jersey (thankfully only two hours from New York City). After all, hadn't I quoted Huizinga's *Homo Ludens* extensively in my dissertation on structured ambivalence in ritual drama?

In its pursuit of Life Studies, Stockton was no different than a number of schools in the country then reacting to the conventional campus. Most of the faculty were educated by professors born in the 1920s and 1930s, and while our respect was enormous, we did not want to be "our fathers." Stockton's campus was the very antithesis of the Ivy League; although designed by Princeton architects, it had no quad, no campus center. Faculty were distributed throughout the campus in no discernible pattern. Like the alphabet, it was built out from A-wing to, at this time, D-wing.

Life Sports mirrored that plan; it was to be everywhere and nowhere: in the classroom (though we might go for a run instead of holding class), out at the beach (where we lived and sometimes held classes), or more conventionally on the tennis court or playing field. More critically, we were all reading radical sports literature, and Marty (with me tagging along) was part of a sports movement that was built "ground-up" by college and professional athletes.

The historian Eric Foner, writing in the *New York Review of Books* (September 29, 1977), rightly castigating Christopher Lasch's attempt to place radical sports (our Life Sports) in the camp

of the "counterculture," perfectly contextualized our goal at Stockton. Paraphrasing sports activist Jack Scott (Marty's mentor from Syracuse), Foner wrote,

> Contrary to Lasch's argument, the sports critics rejected not competition, but the conditions under which competitive athletics take place. They found that the organization of sports stifled the inherent joy of the athletic experience, encouraged violence, hatred for the opposition and sexism, and discouraged intellectual and creative pursuits which were deemed "unmasculine" and antagonistic to the development of athletes.

So there it was. The phoniness of the NCAA's so-called scholar-athletes was laid bare by Scott and others who exposed universities' low graduation rates, mistreatment of athletic injuries, and larger questions of racism and sexism. Life Sports at Stockton simply sought to broaden participation in sports as their counterparts, for example, at Oberlin College, had. Contrary to Lasch's characterization, while competition and excellence prevailed at Oberlin, athletes had a voice in their sports, women and minority coaches were hired, women's sports were expanded, and athletic facilities were built for all, not just the varsity athletes.

Finally, we took life sports also to include hiking, biking, and jogging, the purpose of which was to develop physical fitness, and thus again to provide an alternative to the "virtuosic" athlete who performed before an audience. Jack Scott summed up the credo of Life Sports: "commitment to excellence along with a

Women's basketball in I-wing gym (1978)

desire to achieve that excellence by a process that will humanize rather than dehumanize man."

There we were! But . . . could we pull it off? Somewhere at the New School I had also read Max Weber on the power of bureaucracy. Now looking back at the 1971-1972 *Stockton State College Bulletin*, Marty Miller and Life Sports are not listed. (Marty must have been hired after the book went to print.) By the 1974-1975 *Bulletin* (Ken Tompkins hired me in 1972), all was gone! Missing was any mention of Life Sports, Experimental Studies, and, ominously, Marty's name in the staff register. I was now in the Sociology/Anthropology Program.

What had happened? Well, for one thing the radical critique of society (and sport) clearly had not penetrated the maze of the Pine Barrens. As left-thinking as the faculty might have been, the reverse was true for the president and the Board of Trustees. Sadly, for our playful fantasies, the athletic director, a cigar-smoking, motorcycle riding, good ole pole-vaulting Olympic gold medal winner who could not care less about our Life Sports experiment, was not far behind. We were swallowed whole by the institution, and Marty was spit out in his tenure year. It didn't help that Marty was in Political Science, the program of the president and vice president of Stockton. Colleagues they were not to be.

Now I understood "survivor guilt." Marty wanted many of us to resign in protest or at least to crash the president's office for a sit-in. I was tempted; we had shut down the New School during the Vietnam war, and in my first course at Stockton, In Search of the Primitive (an homage to *my* New School mentor, Stanley Diamond), students finally sat on my desk before a class and said my graduate school pretensions could no longer be tolerated: change it up, or they were leaving! I did, but we didn't, and Marty was fired. He landed a very good history job at a school in New Jersey (he is still there), having finished his dissertation on Irish revolutionaries.

In 1972 faculty and students formed a pretty tight little community. It was not uncommon for us to live together, renting a house from September to May (to be kicked out during the high-rent summer period), only to find another the next fall. We taught classes at the beach in our group houses and thought quite seriously about creating a college that was different from the ones we had attended. Life Sports was just a piece of the whole pie we were cooking up. To repeat and to add some: there was to be no quad, no campus center, no program enclaves, and no program chairs, no faculty senates, no grades, no phony bureaucratic academic specializations; things would be interdisciplinary and we would have General Studies. We invited students to come to Stockton and eat the whole pie, not just a piece here and there. Again, from the 1971-1972 *Bulletin* "statement of purpose" (purposefully in lower case I assume):

> Stockton should not be considered only as a place where students prepare for specific professions or fields of work,

important as these goals may be. . . . It is essential that the college offer programs which greatly increase the students' chances for responsible lives reflecting concern for the quality of life for all.

"Responsible lives reflecting concern for the quality of life for all." Surely a Life Sports program fit that purpose. Looking back, firing Marty, disbanding Experimental Studies and Life Sports, and, I guess, sending me to Sociology/Anthropology added "just another brick in the wall." I'm the NCAA faculty rep now, and I welcome student athletes in the fall, administer surveys to them every now and then, attend games when I can, and if our Sunday faculty tennis match finishes early enough, make it to the Seaview Resort for the yearly awards brunch. I do notice a very lively intramural scene, and Marty would be happy about that. He'd be sad, too, that Larry James, "The Mighty Burner" is gone.

I think Marty might also be happy that we just received a grant to bring junior tennis to Atlantic City and that one of the "tennis girls" on our team patiently and enthusiastically taught the basics to kids, many of whom had never held a racquet. She, this lone volunteer, is the kind of student Marty hoped would flourish throughout the campus.

He'd probably also be happy that we still don't have a football team.

Larry James getting ready for a cross-country race (1977)

The Mighty Burner — G. Larry James

Rob Gregg

An Olympian, educator, and visionary, G. Larry James is considered by many to be the most iconic personality associated with the College. James arrived at Stockton in 1972 and helped spur the College's growth over thirty-six years while serving in such roles as coach, athletic director, and dean. He became the Athletic Director in 1980 and spearheaded the development of Stockton's Athletic program as the driving force behind such projects as construction of the $17 million Sports Center and steady expansion of the Athletic department to its current total of seventeen sports.

James' own track career had reached its pinnacle at the historic 1968 Olympics in Mexico City. Competing on what is widely regarded as the greatest United States track team ever assembled, he won a gold medal in the 4x400 meter relay and a silver medal in the 400 meters. During his distinguished track and field career he earned the nickname, "The Mighty Burner" and was inducted into the National Track & Field Hall of Fame in December 2003.

At Stockton, James shepherded the Ospreys' athletic programs from a largely noncompetitive and club sport model into a perennial national power. The Stockton men's soccer team won the NCAA Division III national championship in 2001, and men's basketball and men's and women's soccer reached the NCAA Final Four. Virtually all Stockton sports programs have been champions and contenders in the New Jersey Athletic Conference and their other respective leagues. Perhaps more importantly, Stockton athletes have accomplished these feats with graduation rates and grade point averages exceeding national averages by a wide margin.

In 2007, Stockton honored James with a special event, G. Larry James: Four Decades of Excellence, which included a reception and tribute that drew 1,000 admirers to the college's Sports Center. Among those in attendance were James' teammates on the world-record-setting gold medalists in the 4x400 meter relay, Vince Matthews, Ron Freeman, and Lee Evans; 1968 Olympic bronze medalist John Carlos; former Villanova teammates; and alumni and numerous representatives of USA Track & Field, the governing body of the sport.

Cancer alone was able to extinguish "the Mighty Burner." Larry James died in November 2008.

John Searight, Ruth Burke, Sherm Labovitz, Pat Reid-Merritt, Paul Lyons and Will Jaynes (1982)

When Lower K-Wing Rocked the World

Melaku Lakew and Patricia Reid-Merritt

It's not that big—fifty by forty feet, roughly 2,000 square feet of space—with a dozen or so faculty offices located in the second half of lower K-wing. But during the formative years of Stockton's existence, the occupants of that space had a profound impact on shaping the identity, direction, and special character of the College. From the very beginning to the early 1990s, lower K-wing was occupied by idealist faculty, those most representative of the socially conscious members of the college community. One can say they were the vanguard of the movement for change.

Diversity was an important key to the success of the lower K-wing cohort. They represented America: blacks and whites, American-born and foreign-born, Protestants and Jews, liberals and radicals, Marxists and nationalists, neophytes and sage elders, and men and women. The faculty in the small space of the lower K-wing represented three of the five divisions (now called schools) but, for the most part, they were members of the Social and Behavioral Sciences. It was a very eclectic group, more like a motley crew, and they were passionate about everything.

It may have started with the hiring of Sherman Labovitz, Professor of Social Work, in 1972. Within a few short years, he would be joined by Betty Elmore, Economics; Don Plank, Mathematics; and John Searight, Social Work. Before the end of the first decade, Patricia Reid-Merritt, Social Work; Kenneth Harrison, Economics; William Jaynes, Social Work; Frank Cerreto, Mathematics; Paul Lyons, Social Work; Melaku Lakew, Economics; David Emmons, Criminal Justice; and a few others would all take up residence in lower K-wing.

The atmosphere in lower K-wing was always intellectually charged. There were constant conversations about students, classes, administrators, the state of the college, and the state of the world. We debated the merits of civil rights, women's liberation, affirmative action, and the Vietnam War. We questioned the leadership abilities of Presidents Bjork, Mitchell, and Farris; and of Ford, Carter, and Reagan. Depending on the season, we argued about the strength of the Phillies, the Eagles, and the 76ers. And we shared, freely, our most personal experiences with one another.

Dave told stories about his harrowing work in Mississippi during the 1960s; Sherm about his trials and tribulations with the Philadelphia Communist Party in the 1940s and 1950s; Melaku about his travels around the world; and, Ken about the success, and failures, of the American economic system. And Pat and Will argued with us and each other about everything, from the best and worst of academic life for Black men and women to the best location for a Philly cheese steak. We invited each other to special events, dined together, experienced different meals in each other's homes, and brought our children to lower K-wing.

Back then, we believed we were raising the next generation of near-perfect young adults. (That didn't quite work out!) And each and every one of us was committed to the creation of an ideal college, a college that reflected diversity in the student, faculty, and staff populations, in economic class and culture, and in the overall curriculum.

However, it was the desire to serve, the willingness to assume leadership, and the ability to "give back" that shaped the personality of lower K-wing. This resulted in a powerful force of influence at Stockton. All of the aforementioned faculty would emerge as program coordinators. Perhaps that was a given. But they also emerged as leaders in other key positions throughout the College as well.

During the early years, four of the lower K-wing community members—John Searight, Kenneth Harrison, Sherman Labovitz and David Emmons—served as presidents for the Stockton Federation of Teachers. They negotiated with the state and local administrators for fair contracts on behalf of the entire faculty and turned Stockton into a strong union shop.

Betty Elmore would assume the role as the first woman to serve as Moderator of the Faculty Assembly. John would also serve as Faculty Moderator, to be followed by Will as President of the Faculty Assembly, the first African American to assume that position. Don Plank emerged as the Chair of the Division of Natural Sciences and Mathematics. John Searight would become Chair of the Division of Social and Behavioral Sciences, later to be followed by Will Jaynes as dean of the division.

Melaku Lakew assumed a leadership role in helping to internationalize the curriculum. He launched the first Study-Tour program to help working and low-income students have an international experience. Previously, most Study-Abroad programs catered to more affluent students with a focus on trips to Europe and Australia. The Study Tour program to South Africa, created by Melaku, permitted students a first-time opportunity to travel outside of the United States and to the African continent.

Pat Reid-Merritt rocked the place with the idea of an inclusive America; she introduced Kwanzaa to students, faculty, and the community at large. The relationship Pat created linked, for the first time, the College to the wider community on an ongoing basis. One might say that she was the queen of African culture. She helped many to accept a new culture and, later, appreciate it fully. As President of the Council of Black Faculty and Staff, Pat created the Annual Awards Dinner and Banquet, which would later become one of the most successful fundraising events at the college and, at the same time, would bring together constituents from all areas of the College and the community for an evening of celebration and civil discourse.

Frank Cerreto became one of the stars of the General Studies division and the Basic Skills and Educational Opportunity Fund (EOF) programs. And Paul was the ultimate renaissance man and grand promoter of progressive causes, serving first as a faculty member in Social Work, then moving to General Studies and the development of G-courses, moving back to Social Work, but still creating courses for the History and Holocaust and Genocide programs, while constantly linking historical and contemporary issues to the needs of the local community.

Each one of us was committed to providing our students with the breadth and depth of a higher education experience truly unique to Stockton. And, for the most part, we succeeded. We were instrumental in bringing to the College the essential ingredients necessary for a liberal arts education.

Unfortunately, the social activist, idealist community of lower K-wing no longer exists. In retrospect, it was the "pull factor," the lure of an office with a window that ultimately destroyed this tight-knit community, which began to disintegrate in the early 1990s. With few exceptions, most of the lower K-wing residents occupied non-window offices. Window offices were reserved for senior faculty, and most of us were not qualified to have one.

Three of the original members of the lower K-wing community—Paul Lyons, David Emmons and Ken Harrison—recently passed away. They all are memorialized for their unique leadership. Sherm was first to retire, and then Don. A few other faculty members are scattered throughout the college. Only Pat and Will remain (in window offices) in lower K-Wing.

The extraordinary contributions and productivity of the original members of lower K-wing is simply a rare historical phenomenon. The leadership, innovations in education, and cultural and intellectual creativity, all came from a small group of faculty members who occupied this unique space. And it was during the early years of the College's existence that the vision and activism of the lower K-Wing cohort helped to rock Stockton's world and contributed to the special character and reputation that Stockton continues to enjoy as it celebrates the fortieth anniversary of its presence in the lower southern portion of the state of New Jersey.

Providing Funds

Jeanne Sparacino Lewis

I was first hired to work at Stockton State College in the fall 1971 term. At that time there were so few staff to serve freshmen and junior students that I was assigned to administer Housing, Career Services, and Financial Aid. My initial impression of the College was that it was very progressive and open to non-traditional standards for the curriculum. This was very different because most colleges and universities of the time had very strict curricula that defined courses to be taken by students for each academic level of enrollment. The College defined the students as being "independent," meaning they were given the responsibility to make their own decisions. They had the freedom and flexibility to choose the courses they desired and to build a curriculum along with a supervisor in order to earn a degree. It appeared to me that this was the single most important factor that drew independent-minded students to the Mayflower campus in Atlantic City, New Jersey. Students felt empowered and in control of their educational destiny. Stockton encouraged students to think, research, and come up with their own conclusions. These were the days when students' grades were H, S, and N, as I recall. The traditional A, B, C, D, and F grades were non-existent at Stockton State College.

My original role, which encompassed several areas of responsibility, eventually morphed into a specialty in financial aid, as this area was in the greatest demand by the students. Within twelve months of my initial employment on October 25, 1971, I was named Director of Financial Aid. So my role at the College was defined by the students themselves. It was their demand for financial aid information and the need for funding to realize their educational dreams that solidified my position as Director of Financial Aid.

Most of the staff in the early years was not much older than the students they served. As a college community of faculty, staff, and students, we collectively defined the college culture. Together we had the flexibility to do so. We were not bound or limited by tradition or history at Stockton because there was none. We formed the foundation, the principles, and the standards that defined Stockton's early years. We also provided the direction that we felt embodied Stockton in particular as one of the newest state colleges.

Like today, I had constant contact with students in the early years. The big attraction was the need for funding in order to attain their degrees. The challenge of applying for financial aid, being determined eligible, and having ample financial aid allocations were all part of the challenges and hurdles to be surmounted before students actually received financial aid. I was in touch with the students throughout this process.

The state and federal governments as well as outside agencies provided the financial aid funding for students as well as the regulations and constraints for those funds. So while I was grateful for financial aid funds in order to assist the students, there were many challenges associated with the regulations. It has always been a challenge to make a difficult, confusing process simpler and less frustrating for the likely recipients of financial aid.

The sheer joy of being able to assist students through financial aid to realize their college dreams has provided me with a great sense of accomplishment. Throughout the years as I participate in each graduation ceremony at Stockton, I have come to realize that my efforts have in part led to the success of each graduating class. Being able to work with young adults who are at the beginning of their career process has provided me with an opportunity to participate in their progress toward a degree. I am filled with a renewed sense of inspiration each fall as we welcome new students to the College.

I believe the wider community sees the staff in a support role for the main mission of the College, which is to educate its constituency. College staff provides the many services necessary to support the students' educational endeavors. In some ways the college staff becomes the surrogate family for many of our students. Students have come to rely on staff for individual consultation, counseling, nurturing, funding, and all the other components that a family unit would provide.

My most memorable and significant accomplishment was actually the creation of the Office of Financial Aid at Stockton. I set the standards for every aspect of the office. In the early days the office was comprised of myself, as director, and one clerical person. This was the beginning of what has grown to a staff of fourteen, including myself. The first Office of Financial Aid was located at the Mayflower Hotel in Atlantic City. This was in the fall 1971 term. The office was a hotel room overlooking the boardwalk. My desk was a collapsible, round banquet table with a tablecloth. In the spring 1972 term, the office was relocated to the main campus and occupied a space in C-wing. This was more like an office setting. As the College grew and there was additional demand for space, the Office of Financial Aid was relocated to a log cabin on Lake Fred. The log cabin consisted of two professional offices, a bathroom, a kitchen, and a living area, which provided space for the clerical staff. On nice days we enjoyed lunch at the picnic table near the lake's edge. Our next move took us to a Student Housing apartment. After some time at this location, Financial Aid was brought back to the main campus where we occupied space in J-wing and eventually moved to F-wing, where we currently reside. Throughout the years not only has the number of staff in the Office of Financial Aid increased but so has the amount of state and federal financial aid funds under my direction. There were three financial aid programs in the early days; today Financial Aid manages hundreds.

Stockton has gone through many management styles that have produced or had an impact on the College's direction. However, the central mission of the College and the most important feature is the education of the students that we serve. Over the years there have been employee strikes, discontentment, disagreement with management. However, in the true style of Stockton, we always reconcile and come together as a family. We support one another in the common goal of assisting our students. Stockton has transformed itself from a virtually unknown institution of higher education to a community leader in the South Jersey sector. Stockton has expanded educational programs and provided opportunities beyond the classroom in order to prepare students for the global economy of today. Stockton has truly made a mark in New Jersey and beyond as a stellar institution of higher learning.

Harvey Kesselman working the numbers (1977)

Reflections

Nancy M. Messina

In June 1974 I entered a world that would change my life. As a person from southern New Jersey just two years out of high school, I had no experience or knowledge of what it meant to work at a college. Much like Stockton in 1974, I was trying to find my own path, so I have always felt a special bond with the College and have always felt that, in many ways, we have grown up together.

Reflecting on the past thirty-seven years is not an easy task. It hardly seems possible that my membership in the Stockton community has spanned that length of time. Sometimes it feels as if only days have passed. One of the most important aspects for me, as a staff member, has been the people who make up this very special community. This aspect of community has always extended beyond the workplace. Many of the faculty and staff's children spent their preschool years at Free To Be, and, as they got older, spent their summers singing the Stockton Day Camp theme song, attending plays each Wednesday at the PAC, or participating in the RSC Soccer Camp. Additionally, for some, the College became the venue for summer job opportunities as junior camp counselors, working with the grounds crew, or stocking shelves at the Bookstore. Though there have been both positive and negatives in terms of being a staff member at the College, the day-to-day community to which we have been connected has helped to make a difference in strengthening our sense of commitment.

Compared with the rest of the college, Academic Affairs (at least from the perspective of someone who has worked for her entire career within the School of Arts and Humanities) seemed initially to have been a neglected step-child. For staff, promotional opportunities seemed very limited, and with the faculty's angst and sense of frustration over tenure quotas, the whole division seemed infused with some degree of resentment. Things have changed considerably, however, over the years.

As a staff member I have had the opportunity to work with people from almost every constituency across the College—faculty, students, administrators, as well as other staff. It has been an interesting and challenging journey. I have held several positions during the past thirty-seven years—all within ARHU—and for part of that time I was both a nontraditional student and a staff member. Working full-time and going to school part-time certainly had its challenges. Along with these challenges came the day-to-day experience of working with many deans over the years—Jaffe, Jones, Burton, Marsh, Mench, Heffernan, Regan, Dollarhide, and Gregg—including two who served as chairperson when the position of dean was eliminated for a brief time. The chance to interact with myriad individuals with diverse working styles has been a learning experience in and of itself. But, in addition to this, Stockton and the Division of Arts and Humanities has always provided a sense of community, and while over the years the landscape has changed, I could not imagine "growing up" in any other environment.

The role of support staff in 1974 was very different from what it is now. Within Academic Affairs promotional opportunities for staff were very limited and the level of your position determined the degree of interaction with the faculty and administration. Unless you worked in an administrative office, there was little interaction with the president or vice president. In the divisional offices, the role of the staff was to support the work of the faculty. There was no flexibility concerning work schedules, no tuition waivers for employees, and initially there was no local union representation for classified staff.

However, there were two significant advantages in being in an academic staff position over the years, and more recently than previously. First, I have been able to establish a rapport with the faculty that is based on a mutual respect and fair-mindedness. Sometimes being the staff member with the longest tenure in the division has its advantages. I have learned and observed much over the years, and gaining the confidence and respect of others is one of the highest honors I have received. Second, I have also been fortunate to have been afforded the opportunity to serve as an academic preceptor for the past twenty plus years and have gained much from the experience of working with our students in this role. These are aspects of my position that I value highly.

In reflecting on my thirty-seven year relationship with Stockton, I find myself comparing our time together to that of watching a child or a younger sibling grow and develop—the one who is trying to decide what she wants to be when she grows up. Since Stockton was always that child who danced to a different tune, it has experienced its share of growing pains. However, much has been accomplished along the way, with the establishment of traditions that may seem foreign to newcomers—H, S, N grades, four-credit courses, preceptorial advising, General Studies requirements, and affording students the opportunity to select courses across the curriculum—some of which have survived the test of time and have become key to Stockton's identity.

The most noteworthy aspect for me has been the education that surrounds me daily. It is the example set by others, the sharing of ideas and passions, the exposure to thoughts and ideas that cannot be discovered in the same way outside of an educational setting. This kind of learning is addictive. To have my curiosity continually engaged is both exciting and satisfying. It is the essence of what it means to live the daily life of Stockton.

Period drama on the Performing Arts Center stage

Nurturing Community

Elaine Ingulli

I came to Stockton in 1986. I wasn't looking for a job—I had already done my syllabus for that Fall—but a colleague leaving Temple said there was an ad for a faculty position at a school that looked like a perfect fit for me.

One look at the Bulletin, and I knew he was right. The peculiarity of its curriculum—General Studies!—caught my attention, and after talking about it at my interview with Marc Lowenstein I was both challenged and hooked. Together with the permeability of Stockton's curriculum—the ability to easily create courses, to wash away disciplinary borders—the interdisciplinarity of General Studies are at the heart of what I continue to value most at the College.

Before Stockton, the chair of my department assigned a teaching schedule along with the books from which I would teach. At Stockton, I not only could request a schedule, and choose my books, but I was asked to develop a course that would stretch me beyond my disciplinary background. My husband, who teaches at a more traditional university, called it "professional dabbling," but I knew then, and continue to believe, that we are, instead, role-modeling the lifelong learning we say we are teaching our students.

I still remember my first Fall Faculty Conference. New faculty were introduced (a wonderful tradition); there was talk at the Faculty Assembly meeting that I didn't fully understand about a Special Prosecutor – but I loved being invited to speak and vote (I didn't) on college issues on my first day. The union president warned that this was a "contract year" and we were gearing up for a possible strike. Clearly there was ferment. More importantly, there was energy and there was community.

I was also overwhelmed: I didn't realize that the week I thought I would have to prepare a syllabus would be filled with orientation, Fall Faculty Conference, and precepting. There was not enough time to do all that I was expected to do, along with whatever I might *want* to do. I could barely understand the curriculum, and found it almost impossible to advise students, although I was expected to do so. I couldn't figure out what to say to any of the students I was expected to "precept". Indeed, while the advising nuts-and-bolts got easier over time, I never got over feeling that I didn't have much to offer as preceptor to business students, having no experience and a relatively unsophisticated understanding of the careers my students seek.

During my first year, I was delighted to find that at Stockton I was no longer confined to a ghetto of business lawyers. Instead, my office hall-mates included a psychologist (Nancy Ashton), a nurse (Mary Ellen Florence), a political scientist (Jackie Pope), a marine biologist (Carol Slocum). Within days, the marine biologist had introduced me to an anthropologist who lived in Philly and I had formed a carpool. Not long after, the psychologist introduced me to a criminal justice professor— Mona Margarita ("You two have a lot in common—and you live near each other!"). And Mona, in turn, introduced me to union payday parties. Mona and I both went to a Friday workshop that trained us to be volunteer mediators for the Community Justice Institute at Stockton. When the workshop ended, she talked me into going to a payday party, with the warning that because it was Halloween, we would have to wear costumes—and she just happened to have two Marx glasses/mustache masks for us to wear. Needless to say, we were the only ones in 'costume'—but we laughed and bonded. My carpool buddy taught in Women's Studies—so she invited me to the end-of-year Women's Studies celebration for certificate-students. It wasn't long before I realized that I really *was* welcome to create a Women's Studies course, and I did.

Indeed, these invitations to join the community kept coming— facilitated by faculty summer workshops, cookie-induced readings of the Junior Writing Test, teaching roundtables, and a commitment on the part of faculty to enculturate newer faculty with Stockton norms. A summer institute ("A Pedagogy of Inclusion") directed by Penny Dugan and Nancy Ashton was pivotal to my teaching, my own intellectual growth, and my career. All were transformed as I more self-consciously thought about 'race, class and gender' in new ways. My re-visioning of business law led to a law review article, that in turn led to my helping to found a 'feminist legal studies' section of my national professional association (the Academy of Legal Studies in Business). Most importantly, it sparked the textbook (now nearly in its 7th edition) that I co-wrote and have taught from for nearly twenty years.

A colleague 'invited me' to run for President of the Assembly (I had never been on the Steering Committee), so I did. My experience as president reinforced my own commitment to faculty governance. Many years later when I moved to a window office in a new wing, I delighted once again to have a hallway of faculty from many disciplines, some of whom I barely knew. We're still creating a community.

So, the two things I most value and cannot imagine Stockton without are General Studies and our welcoming community.

Close study in the Gallery (1977)

Voices and Experiences that Echo Across Time

Franklin Ojeda Smith

Let me establish some things right up front: I've been at Stockton longer than any other Living African American, I've been engaged in many of its struggles, witnessed, and assisted its growth and development; and as to Black Students who came here early on, no one had a more pivotal role in their mentorship than I. So the experiences and impressions offered here are mine- I lived them and I own them.

In my view, 'The Stockton Faculty' I knew back then were not 'A-racial' and certainly not 'Post-racial'; they were products of their times. To pretend otherwise is folly. We lived in parallel universes - Black and White. We all walked the same hallways but lived different realities; negotiated different experiences— "what are you all plotting now?" White folks too often teased when seeing Black folks gathered – this admonition when offered can be funny once, even twice, but not when it becomes

a salutation. I don't think White folks ever had an appreciation of why when we saw each other we gathered, laughed and shared an unspoken empathy. How could they know the loneliness, frustrations and often the despondency that come from being the proverbial unwanted 'fly in the milk?' "But Franklin, how did you know you were unwanted?" some might ask. My answer, I developed acute sensory tools when it came to matters of race, it's a prerequisite to survival. When I arrived at Stockton in 1973 I couldn't help but see that 'The Pomona Mayflower Faculty' was lily white, except for Bill Nettles my colleague in Sociology. When he left, all of the eight Black faculty members who were at "The Atlantic City Mayflower" were gone. Why?

I never accepted the 'convenient rationale' that Black folks left Stockton for bigger and better positions, because the economy at that time didn't support that conclusion, and I'd talk to some of the folks who'd left. Furthermore, it didn't make sense, for faculty who wanted careers in the academy to leave positions where the odds (percentage-wise) of being granted tenure were as good or better than anywhere else in America. No, I believe there were other factors affecting the departure of Blacks from Stockton; factors like: the frustration of knowing that the son of the famous Ralph Bunche, a candidate for a deanship, was not offered an interview, only to have the position filled by an in-house junior faculty member; the feelings of powerlessness from watching the 'musical chairs' being played among positions in the college without any real consideration of affirmative action; or of having to endure the convenient hypocrisy of the Grant v. Sessions dispute over a library appointment, where the so-called reverence for terminal qualifications was turned on its head; the disillusionment of being booed out of a Union meeting because of my views; or the isolation of being a lone voice of dissent when the only female (White) full professor at the college was denied reappointment. Then there was always the first day class experience where inevitability some White students would indignantly strut out of the room the minute I walked in.

There were two other Black faculty members in my cohort, neither survived. From 1970-79, across the spectrum of students, staff and faculty Stockton was a revolving door for Blacks (the highest or among the highest turnover rates in the state).When we talked they reiterated that they couldn't wait to escape the hostile 'Stockton Plantation,' a term I would later use to describe the area outside of the I-Wing Gym where Black students sought refuge after, and too often, instead of classes. Black students generally did not view the student newspaper 'The Argo' as being supportive but instead saw it in an opposite light - as a tool to perpetuate a perception of them as 'other and unprepared.' There were not many black students on campus and if not for the EOF Program that number would have been dramatically reduced. Peter Mercado then the Director of EOF got some White faculty involved with the Program and through their testimony perceptions slowly began to change.

But this shift came some years after Darrilyn Vassar and Claudia Williams, two young Social Work faculty members, had taught me some valuable lessons. "You're a man," Darrilyn cried, "White students won't disrespect you like they do us;" and Claudia added, "they won't follow you after class to intimidate you." Both would soon leave. Back then I often viewed Stockton as a 'White Boys Club' and publicly argued that for some, quality of work performance, penalties and rewards were often measured by one's kinship to such venues as 'The Poker, Union, and Potluck Clubs' or other unseen relationships. Woody Thrombley was Vice President of Academic Affairs and he commissioned Larry Marcus and me to go to The National Institute of Science/Beta Kappa Chi Scientific Honor Society Conference and try to recruit. We interviewed many and brought back 17 resumes of Black faculty in the natural sciences who were PhD's with experience or ABD's. Not one received a follow-up interview. Why? Unfortunately, Thrombley left Stockton shortly thereafter and with him the impetus.

Whatever the causes, by all reasonable measures, Stockton was not very diverse; the situation was so dire, the exclusion so exact by the late 1970's, that the Board of Trustees led by Henry Bass spearheaded an affirmative action effort, that after an horrendous struggle resulted in the appointment of a female African American President - Vera King Farris. She, ironically, had previously been rejected as an Academic Vice Presidential Candidate. During her nearly twenty years at the college more African Americans were tenured than ever; but since there were so few at the start, the increase still amounted to little more than a comparative trickle. Sadly, forty years after its founding, we have not tenured one African American in the Natural Sciences; and with exception of the Social Sciences the numbers are almost as wanting across the college.

As I near retirement and the few who came after me near retirement the picture I saw in 1973 echoes back at me.

In Good Faith

Nancy W. Hicks

Since its early history Stockton College has made a "good faith" effort" to increase the diversity of the workforce and student body. However the results have not always been encouraging.

According to the minutes of the Council of State College Affirmative Action Committee, dated April 1973, the affirmative action efforts of Stockton State College included:

1. Circulation of a general message encouraging affirmative action from President Richard Bjork,
2. Requirement that all employee appointments go through the President's Office, and
3. Submission of reports of recruitment efforts, to include resumes, sex, race, and age identification of all candidates.

In May 1973, the Stockton Board of Trustees passed a resolution in support of affirmative action efforts to "further employment opportunities for women and minorities." This resolution continued throughout the 1970s. As early as 1972, the Minority Recruitment Committee (MRC) of the Faculty Assembly was established. In 1976 the MRC reported that the goals set had not been met and recommended that administrative action be taken. President Bjork appointed a standing Affirmative Action Committee during the 1978-1979 year. The committee developed a number of recommendations, including five-year goals and timetables. Reviewing the work of the Minority Recruitment Committee, the Affirmative Action Committee addressed itself to the specific problem of minority recruitment.

In 1979 the Board of Trustees directed President Peter Mitchell to present a report on affirmative action by its January 1980 meeting. During that January meeting, President Mitchell stated that the college must be more aggressive and creative in advertising positions and recruiting minorities and female candidates. The success of the efforts of the Affirmative Action Committee can be found in the 1980 report, where it is stated that 55.8 percent of the total faculty hired were women and minorities including thirty percent white women and 25.6 percent minority men and women. It is not known if these statistics include only full-time faculty or part-time and full-time.

As a result of the success during the 1980 recruitment of faculty, the Board of Trustees renewed its commitment to affirmative action each year and in 1980 adopted a resolution that "one half of all new appointments for at least the next two academic years should be affirmative action candidates and, at minimum, greater than one quarter should be minority group members." This resolution was renewed each subsequent year. The last year it was passed was 1998. The decision not to renew the commitment through a resolution was based on advice that the legality of setting affirmative action goals was questionable.

In the early 1990s, during the presidency of Dr. Vera King Farris a ten-year plan for faculty diversification was developed by the Office of Academic Affairs. This plan, while not funded, provided ideas on how to become more proactive in the recruitment of minority and women, particularly among the faculty. The diversity among the faculty during Dr. Farris' term in office increased from fifteen percent to twenty percent for minorities and twenty-eight percent to forty-five percent for all women. The diversity of the new hires was among all racial and ethnic groups. During that time, members of the college community expressed concern that the increase among African Americans was insufficient.

As affirmative action became more ingrained in the culture of the college, more emphasis was placed on diversity and then diversity and inclusion. Dr. Herman J. Saatkamp, Jr. reorganized the Affirmative Action Committee and created the College Committee for Diversity, Equity, and Affirmative Action. This college-wide committee includes representation from students, faculty, staff, and administration and is involved in promoting an open exchange of ideas in a setting that recognizes and understands the significance of similarities and differences.

With the support of President Saatkamp and his cabinet, the Diversity Committee engaged a consulting firm to conduct a campus-wide cultural audit. As expected, this was a controversial project, which was challenged by various groups on campus. The purpose of the audit was to examine the current culture as experienced by a wide range of social identity groups. In other words, it asked the members of the college community, "what are you experiencing and what are you perceiving?" Most participants reported that the College is a rewarding learning community. Briefly, more than two thirds of students and employees stated that Stockton is an environment in which people are treated fairly regardless of race and/or ethnicity. This sounds good, but it also means that almost one third of the students and employees do not agree and that more needs to be done to address their concerns.

This emphasis on diversity and inclusion does not lessen the importance and challenges of affirmative action. The College continues to take affirmative steps to increase the diversity of its workforce. From 2003 to 2009 the diversity among the faculty increased from 20 to 22.8 percent for minorities and from 45 to 49.9 percent for women. The progress is slow but steady. Still, despite the progress that the College has made—and it is measureable—we still hear concerns, many of which are the same as those expressed ten, twenty, and thirty years ago.

Yet, the good faith effort is continuing. It continues to transform the campus from one that not only believes in diversity to one that lives that commitment.

The Naked Truth

Two of the legends most frequently mentioned about the early years relate to the Candace Falk trial and the Jack Berense case.

In April 1971, Candy Falk, a young professor in General Studies hired by Ken Tompkins, confronted some Army Reserve Recruiters who were coming onto the campus informing them that they were not welcome. They said that they wouldn't leave unless they were told officially to do so, so Falk went to her office and typed up a letter on official letterhead telling the recruiters to go away. She was then brought before the Campus Hearing Board on the charge that she had misrepresented herself as speaking on behalf of the college in an official capacity. The trial was held and at the end of it the charges were all dropped.

The case hinged on the use of the male pronoun in the college handbook. The defense attorney, David Kairys, who had previously defended the Camden Twenty-eight, argued that since the male pronoun was used throughout the handbook Ms. Falk, a woman, could not be charged with having violated the code. Apparently, when Kairys made this pronouncement a great commotion occurred and Bill Lubenow, the chair(man) of the hearing board, had some difficulty restoring order.

Candy Falk left soon after the trial, went west, and became the editor, perhaps fittingly, of the Emma Goldman papers at Berkeley.

The Barense case was, and is, far more serious and no less legendary. The popular myth has been that Barense held a session of a class he was teaching at his home in the nude. In the spring of 1974, Jack Barense taught two sections of a General Studies course – GS3240 Workshop in Sexism, which "was designed to focus on those elements of sexism as a social problem which seemed to most strongly motivate most of the participants to think critically about sexism; namely, personal examinations of sexism in their own lives."

Barense held nude sessions in each of his courses. He mentioned in a memo to John Rickert—Dean of Management Sciences that his class had visited a local nudist camp in the spring of 1973. Fourteen members of that class disrobed. He did not mention whether or not nude sessions were held in the fall 1973 class; though, given his commitment to the technique, this seems probable.

In both sections of the spring 1974 course, nudity was incorporated into the class. Indeed, in one section, a student's mother participated but the daughter didn't. This group did not disrobe again because "the good feelings of the nude participants were, they reported, spoiled by the non-participants." The other section was so pleased by the experience that they met a number of times in the nude.

These incidents became part of a grievance process, when, responding to outside pressure, President Bjork and Vice President Woody Thrombley ordered Barense to end the nude sessions and bring the class back onto the campus. Barense agreed, but not before filing a grievance about the interference with his academic freedom. During the following semester, Barense applied for reappointment and his application was denied. In the grievance procedure that followed it became clear that Dean Rickert had initially supported Barense's reappointment, but then had been pressured from above to change his recommendation, which he did.

Jack Barense lost his appeal against the decision and moved on. For a time he worked with the ACLU in New Jersey and then went to law school earning a JD so he could practice public defender law. Sadly, Jack Barense died in 2002.

Ken Tompkins and Rob Gregg

Carl McIntire protests against Stockton outside the Mayflower Hotel (1971) - Courtesy of *The Press of Atlantic City*

Stockton's Impact on the Community

Israel Posner

Even before the College opened its doors, President Richard Bjork realized the importance of developing a strong community relations program. He understood what became apparent very quickly, that the College's welcome in South Jersey would require a carefully planned "adjustment period" for the community. The name and location of the new college had not even been decided yet, but the College's commitment to the community had.

The College's commitment to the community was evident from the design of its initial structure. The Division of Continuing Education and Community Service was described by Dr. Bjork in his October 1, 1969 report to the trustees as "being equal in status to the other divisions." This was reinforced at a board retreat on November 25 at which the board stated that the "College should develop strongly in the direction of service to the community." It was clear from the start that Stockton wanted close and supportive community relations and that the College administration saw that need and created an entity to foster it.

Although Stockton has been host to untold numbers of public events, including concerts, seminars, exhibits, symposia, festivals, conferences, and fairs, none would have more dramatic and enduring impact on the community than the one left by our inaugural public lecture series, "Revolution and the Revolutionary" by Bill Daly. Although it was early fall 1971, in South Jersey the clock had not moved forward very much from the era of Berkeley in 1964, the Columbia University riots, the tragic assassinations of 1968, the 1968 Democratic Convention, and, of course, the trial of the Chicago Seven. Would Stockton's young, "hippie"-looking, "rambunctious" (a term Richard Bjork used to describe the faculty in a report to the trustees during that period) bring all that radicalism to what was at the time a very conservative Republican-controlled community?

President Bjork's report to the board on November 3, 1971 was quite straightforward: "The public lecture series . . . continues to play to full houses every week and . . . has done a great deal to bring the college and the community in contact." While the public's perception and feelings about the lecture series were hard to gauge, the *Atlantic City Press* focused on a boardwalk march led by Dr. Carl McIntire, a fundamentalist minister with a considerable following from his radio broadcasts. Dr. Bjork also reported to the board that Reverend McIntire "organized a picket line at the Mayflower Hotel to protest the discussion of revolution and Communism." Dr. Bjork went on to report that "Dr. McIntire and his associates declined either to attend the lecture series or to accept an invitation to speak at the college and distribute their materials." This episode added to the negative view that the college was different and, perhaps, suspect.

While most audiences in 1973 turned on their televisions to watch *All in the Family*, *The Waltons*, or *Hawaii Five-0*, local audiences could also tune into the first tv course offered by Stockton. Again, Stockton's community outreach pioneer was none other than Bill Daly. In the fall of 1973 four local outlets of the state's Public Broadcasting Authority featured his course, America and Her Critics. Students were able to register for the course, which included a toll-free telephone line and locations for live conferences and exams with Professor Daly. While a Nielson rating was not available, the course did receive coverage in the *Atlantic City Press* on July 24, 1973.

Jimmie Leeds Road and the Pine Barrens surrounding the College had only a handful of small business establishments during the college's early days. (Louie's and the Pitney Tavern stand out.) Clearly, the most significant impact on the face of Pomona and the region was a strategic decision made by the trustees on December 2, 1973, approving plans for the construction of an extension of the Atlantic City Medical Center and the construction of the Betty Bacharach Home on a few hundred acres of the campus along Jimmie Leeds Road. While Dr. Bjork reported that "Stockton would benefit from the availability of medical services close by . . . and the anticipated development of baccalaureate programs in the allied health professions would benefit from use of the hospital as a clinical training facility," it is hard to imagine that anyone at the college or in the community could have anticipated the enormous economic and social benefits that this relationship would have on the college or the community. A drive down Jimmie Leeds Road today with a few quick glances to either side reveals numerous nursing homes, medical complexes, and scores of doctor's offices, providing ample evidence of the synergy that higher education and health care created in this area.

Aside from health care, the other large industry in South Jersey that emerged in 1978 was, of course, casino gaming. As is the case with health care, Stockton's influence and support of this industry has been enormous. Indeed, the growth and success of the Hospitality and Tourism Management Program is well known; the program is very highly regarded in the area. Beyond the hundreds of student interns and graduates who have begun their careers in the casino, hospitality, and broader tourism industries, a few student standouts have risen to become CEOs of major casino hotel properties. The Stockton Institute for Gaming Management (SIGMA) has trained over 15,000 casino hotel employees in Atlantic City in addition to the scores of managers who have participated in SIGMA management programs, with approximately thirty having earned Gaming Management Certificates. Its successor organization, the Lloyd D. Levenson Institute of Gaming, Hospitality and Tourism builds on the work begun by SIGMA and has a broader mission that includes research, conferences and strong linkages to academic program in the School of Business.

On October 3, 1990 Stockton opened its Holocaust Resource Center, ironically the same day on which East and West Germany were officially reunited! Over 100,000 members of the community have attended public lectures and seminars, and the center has attracted educators and scholars from throughout the world, resulting in worldwide recognition. Stockton is indebted to the Schoffer Family Foundation for its generous gift to the center, now renamed the Sara and Sam Schoffer Holocaust Resource Center.

When Stockton was born forty years ago, the community was probably anxious and uncertain, much like a first-time parent might be. Through the mid-1970s the community clearly experienced the challenges associated with having a "rambunctious" toddler in the neighborhood. As the college has grown into middle age, it can be proud that it has become a mature, reliable, and engaged citizen, taking on the mantle of leadership to enhance the lives of the people who live and work in southern New Jersey.

The Organizational Paradox

William C. Lubenow

Words are deeply revealing. The spirit of the College, as well as that of others that took life at the same time—Ramapo, Evergreen, Hampshire—was expressed in a particular language. "Innovative," "traditional," "relevant," "experimental"—each word had special and magical meanings. This language contained incantations—various forms of hope—and curses—various forms of fear—often held and expressed by the same people. We who joined the College at the outset were part of an elite that dared not speak its name.

It is important to recollect that those days were at the end of what David Reisman and Christopher Jencks, tellingly, called "the academic revolution." From the end of the Second World War until 1970, the period of the Cold War, had been a period of expansion in American higher education. Great wealth had been poured into colleges and universities. Numbers flooded into these institutions. Faculty shaped disciplines in new ways and developed new forms in such fields as area studies and urban studies. Graduate departments produced graduate students in vast numbers. It was a great age of optimism. People had hoped that the hump of that academic revolution could be feasted on to produce even greater advances. But that period of expansion and wealth had been exceptional in the history of American higher education, and Stockton and other "innovative" colleges were founded in a period that would witness the return to normalcy with limited resources and limited opportunities.

An age that considered itself marked by the end of ideology produced an age marked by ideologies. The optimism that shaped the founding of these colleges, therefore, masked a dark side because the academic revolution had contained within it the seeds of its own destruction. It is another irony that the iconic texts of the new generation—books by Kuhn, de Man, White, Rorty, Geertz, and Fish—emerged from pens (and they probably were pens) from white (male) writers who were a part of the academic revolution. Great wealth and vast numbers sometimes created a spirit of alienation among the very people who benefited from this great expansion. Gender studies, perhaps the most important and powerful impulse of the time, was beginning to reveal the inadequacies of curricular innovations. The authority of departments, the bulwark of the revolution, now became an object of distrust. And then there was the Vietnam War. It is impossible to overestimate the role of the war in shaping attitudes in the 1960s and 1970s. It is fair to say that many students and faculty fled to institutions of higher education precisely to escape Vietnam. As a consequence they did not share the values of those who in the 1940s and 1950s created the academic revolution. Stockton and other colleges were founded by those who distrusted the institutions from which they came and the political system that produced a war they detested.

Our founders, like faculty in other institutions, sometimes carried resentments from their graduate training, and they hoped, therefore, to convert institutions of higher education into agents of criticism. That is why words like "relevant" and "interdisciplinary" took on their magical meanings and had such a powerful hold on those who used them. They were devices to create new systems of loyalty and belonging. They also broke down alternative systems of loyalty: to intellectual disciplines, to other institutions, to other associations, such as the family and community.

It was a period of tremendous creativity. This shift from the academic revolution of the 1940s and 1950s to the "innovative," "interdisciplinary" institutions of the 1970s produced a vacuum that was filled by many good things—in particular a different view of general education and a different view of what disciplines should look like. As the advertisement summoning applications for the first faculty shows, the language of our founding fathers (and they were all men) contained the ambiguities and uncertainties of the time. The humanities, for example, would consist of programs that would "break away from traditional rationales and conventional methods." Notice the distinctly odd positioning of "methods" at the end of this formulation. And the social sciences would develop new "interdisciplinary methods" to produce a "horizontal integration" to "complement" the "customary vertical integration of the departmental major." Notice the placing of the word "customary." There was no anticipation in reticulated language such as this that institutions like Stockton could sustain the emergence of knowledge formations as we now know them, formations that defy flat planes. What we call knowledge does not come together in ninety-degree angles. The natural sciences sought "innovative and experimental individuals" who would, at the same time have "expertise" in one of a list of standard disciplinary fields. The upshot was that this internally conflicted program of action actually produced an amazingly disparate group of intellectual (ad)ventures.

It also created what an historian of the Department of Social Relations at Harvard called an organizational paradox: without some sort of theoretical closure these programs had only a negative ideal—what they were not; however, efforts to achieve some kind of closure were regarded as "traditional" and authoritarian.

Therefore, the vacuum was also filled by structural characteristics of dubious value: innovations often became ossified into new traditions. Students became consumers whose demand had to be met by new markets. With the authority of departments gone, a managerial regime emerged to organize (and control) hitherto more autonomous practices. The advertisement for the humanities noted pretty uneasily that the "faculties would work closely with the Chairman" in the development of their programs. It is a way of speaking that discloses the possibilities of suspicion and distrust. A Middle States official once told me that the organization's proudest achievement was the professionalization of administrators. In an odd way these many good things produced a kind of complacency and self-satisfaction, a kind of isolation, a curious kind of twentieth-century parochialism.

Stockton, Ramapo, Evergreen, and Hampshire are a part of a uniquely twentieth-century phenomenon. I suppose the lesson to be learned from this is to be skeptical, especially about those things one loves the best. Zhou Enlai, the Foreign Minister of China under Chairman Mao, once asked Mao about the significance of the French Revolution. Mao responded that it is too early to tell. So it is.

Mezuzahs

The campus was not ready until January 1972, and we held our first semester in the bankrupt Mayflower Hotel on the Boardwalk by Tennessee Avenue, formerly a Jewish hotel with Mezuzahs on the doorpost of each room. Faculty offices were the hotel bedrooms, with two faculty members to each room.

Suicidal Chipmunks

I had conducted research on rats as a hobby at graduate school (while I did my dissertation on suicide), but I thought it would be fun to have my students work with chipmunks. My Dean bullied the staff to find room for my chipmunks in the hotel. After much protesting, the Dean got a call from Ken Stow who told him that he had finally found a place to house my chimpanzees! Ken was very relieved to find out he had misheard the request. So, my office-mate, Adrian Jaffe, in ARHU had to adjust to a cage of chipmunks in our hotel room. Unfortunately, they escaped one day. One got out of the window and fell several stories to the road below, and the sad news circulated that one of my chipmunks had committed suicide!

Tuneful Grades

There was a great deal of humor in the early days. One plan was to have no Office of Student Records. Students would keep their own transcripts and carry them around. One professor suggested facetiously in a memo that grades be assigned musical notes and tempos. After each course, we would sing the grade to each student, and then students could sing their whole transcript to their advisors. (We had high pass, satisfactory and no credit grades in the early days.)

Registration

In the early days, faculty members were in charge of registration. We sat at tables and handed out IBM cards for the courses directly to students. If there was a demand for a particular course, we cut more cards or added sections. If one instructor's course was not attracting enough students, we would persuade students to sign up for the course (so that the course would not be cancelled) and then drop-add in the first week, and we promised them their preferred course.

Majors

A student could come to Stockton, reject all of our majors and courses and design 32 courses of their own choosing for their own major. One of my preceptees majored in parapsychology. Another student wanted to study exosociology. Exobiology is the study of whether there is life on other planets. He knew that there was, and he wanted to study the social organization of the life forms up there. (His proposal was rejected.)

David Lester

The Primacy of Teaching

Inside Out by Joyce Lawrence

The focus of this chapter is the "primacy" of teaching. All educational institutions teach. The question, however, is whether teaching is the primary activity of the institution. The founding deans and the first Vice President of Academic Affairs came from large research institutions where teaching was, much of the time, left to graduate students and adjuncts. Following Wes Tilley's insistence, research became a clear second-rate activity for faculty at Stockton, and teaching was the heart of all we did.

In a document dated August 1970, Wes Tilley—the Vice President of Academic Affairs of the yet to be built college—described the desiderata for recruitment of faculty. Two—the first two—of the list of seven are about teaching. Tilley writes:

1. Our first consideration must be pedagogical excellence. This would be a simple requirement if it were not so easy to confuse with popularity.
2. It is essential that the candidate show an interest in teaching the kinds of students we shall probably have at Stockton.

Not only was teaching the center of what we did, but Tilley further argued for a special kind of teaching: Socratic and interdisciplinary. At the heart of teaching were questions, and the answers to those questions were comprised of facts from a wide range of traditional disciplines. One way to see this working was in the multiple program memberships of most of the first faculty. Allen Lacy, Associate Professor of Philosophy, for instance, was a member of the Philosophy Program, the Environmental Studies Program, the Methods of Inquiry Program, and the Urban Studies Program. Each of these disciplines could be brought to bear on the others.

This heady mixture provides the context for the essays in this chapter.

Tilley's central postulations were not about the traditional disciplines on the whole; they focused almost exclusively on General Studies. These courses were to start with questions, they were to mix disciplines, and they were to have the most powerful and creative teaching. If we hired faculty who would tirelessly implement General Studies, the disciplinary teaching they did would, perforce, be exemplary.

Thus, the emphasis on the philosophical underpinnings of General Studies in essays by Joe Walsh and, then, by two Deans of General Studies: Ken Tompkins and Jan Colijn. Penny Dugan's reminiscences of a third dean, Ingie La Fleur, also emphasize the philosophy and feelings of possibility General Studies embodied in its early incarnations. Walsh analyses a seventy-five-page document by Tilley (1973), in which Tilley examines the state of General Studies and finds it wanting. Tilley's conclusion was that neither faculty nor students understood General Studies and, therefore, would not adhere to his original vision.

Colijn and Tompkins describe the state of the General Studies

curriculum during their tenure; Dugan also describes it under La Fleur. All three authors discuss the ways that the collection of General Studies courses changed in the face of institutional change while the faculty generally tried to live up to the original ideas. Indeed, balancing change and original vision or intentions is a tension throughout this volume.

The pedagogy of questioning was at the heart of Bill Sensiba's teaching as he suggests in his essay. Bill was well-known for identifying with students' issues, for connecting with their lives, and for challenging them to change themselves and, ultimately, to strive to change the world. Thus he organized protest trips to Washington, protested nuclear power plants and took students to Guatamala to harvest coffee. What he understood was that questioning, though central to teaching inside the classroom, must be lived outside of the classroom. His essay reveals his struggles to confront his students, peers, and community with this central truth.

Originally, Stockton was not going to train teachers. The then-Chancellor of Higher Education in New Jersey was on record as not wanting the two new colleges to become teacher-training institutions. But local demand was so strong for the college to provide teacher training that it was added in 1970.

It was widely understood that Stockton was unlikely to train teachers in traditional ways—or for traditional employment. Therefore, the early Teacher Development Program (TDEV) was created to place teachers in alternative jobs—in alternative schools, homes for the elderly, prisons, and other forgotten environments. Leonard Solo reviews the problems he had with Stockton faculty and administration and, more significantly, with local public school leaders. As it turns out, Solo was unable to gain the confidence of the state to certify that Stockton's model was viable for training teachers. Ronald Moss reviews the process of reconstructing the curriculum so that the state would approve.

Finally, we selected two disciplines—psychology and biology—to examine how actual programs created curricula, offered classes, built labs, hired faculty, and still managed to balance the dream with the actuality of building a college. Both authors—Lester and Wood—are First Cohort faculty members so their history is, in many ways, the history of their individual programs and of the College.

Looking backwards, the tectonic fault lines are clear. It is easy to see where we succeeded and where we failed. It is easy to see which of our original ideas would work and which wouldn't. It is also clear that for forty years, there has been a tension between the dream and the actuality. Much of that dream was valid, significant, and truly unique. That is what this volume asserts is critical to understand and preserve.

What Then Of a Legacy?

Joseph L. Walsh

There is no doubt that the early Stockton had much in common with the spirit of the times in higher education. The General Studies Self-Study of 2001 notes the effect of "the cultural climate of the sixties" in giving to the faculty the freedom to design "courses in areas that tweaked their own intellectual curiosity and excitement. " Of crucial importance also was the National Defense Act of 1968, which funded an enormous expansion of state colleges and universities across the country at that time. Designed to create a populace better able to compete with the Soviets in the Cold War, it sometimes included, in addition to laboratories, dormitories and classrooms, experimental and innovative educational components (David Riesman and Gerald Grant, *The Perpetual Dream: Reform and Experiment in the American College*, Chicago, 1978). In other words, there existed a national climate of reform enabling the then-Chancellor of Higher Education in New Jersey, Ralph Dungan, to decide "to do something different" at the two new state colleges, Stockton and Ramapo, after which we [Stockton] were "pretty much left on our own" (reported in a personal recollection by President Bjork in a 1979 interview available in the college archives).

While Stockton had much in common with this national movement, it was also, in certain ways, highly unusual, if not unique. Many other experimental colleges typically created innovative new curricular structures to meet widely recognized specific problems in contemporary higher education. Thus Evergreen in Washington State and Hampshire in Massachusetts established a contract system, with the student and faculty advisor together formulating an always revisable, but always agreed-upon contract within which student choices were made. SUNY-Old Westbury in New York and Kresge College at the University of California, Santa Cruz functioned as living and learning communities of students and faculty to foster improved sensitivity to human communication, both individual and social, in their students. At Ramapo the curriculum was in large part divided into a number of interdisciplinary schools, e.g., the School of Metropolitan and Community Studies and the School of Human Environment, in the hope of offsetting the excessive specialization much criticized in higher education.

Stockton differed from these and other innovative institutions in not presenting students with new, content-specific curricular structures. Our primary curricular innovation was General Studies, a definite structure to be sure (half the required student courses) but one that lacked specific content. An early planning paper on General Studies described it as "a series of general . . . classroom, studio or laboratory courses with no prerequisites, aiming at the student's general artistic, intellectual or scientific understanding." Another early description defines General Studies at Stockton as aiming "quite directly at the requirements of citizenship—the knowledge, taste, judgment and general wisdom that enable a human being to play a useful and rewarding role in modern and highly complicated societies" (Wes Tilley, "Goals At Stockton," an early critique and evaluation by the founding first Academic Vice President,16).

The same document explicitly contrasted General Studies at Stockton with the model of undergraduate general education then widely in vogue, in which undergraduates were generally required to have a distribution of introductory courses to the various academic disciplines. General Studies at Stockton, on the other hand, aimed at a "general cultural understanding of a discipline or problem," understood as "the ability of students to relate areas of knowledge to one another and . . . to carry out the responsibilities of citizenship" (Tilley 17). In any given General Studies course the method(s) of the various disciplines drawn upon in that course were to be highlighted, a point underscored some years later by the founding Dean of General Studies, Ken Tompkins. "General Studies was really Methods of Inquiry," he said, referring to the early Methods of Inquiry program (META) where "the method" of method-formation was to be the specific object of study.

How did the first faculty measure up to this demanding agenda? For Tilley the General Studies program had "succeeded in a very general way." But he lamented the fact that too few of the offerings appeared to be interdisciplinary and that "significant groups of the faculty find the identification of general courses very hard if not impossible." He doubted "whether most of the faculty and students . . . ever fully grasped its [General Studies] significance" (Tilley 15-16). He also regretted that the first Dean of General Studies (Ken Tompkins) had to "to instruct the faculty" about General Studies and the design of appropriate General Studies courses (Tilley 43, 44). Compounding these difficulties was the failure of the elaborate preceptorial program of advising and informal teaching to engage students "in a serious and comprehensive discussion of their work in General Studies" (44). (The advising dimension of these early years, arguably Stockton's potentially most original pedagogical innovation, is more fully discussed elsewhere in this volume.)

Tilley may have been correct in concluding that the original Stockton faculty was not in general liberally educated enough to lead their students and preceptees to "the general cultural understanding" of academic disciplines and methods, as described above. But it also may have been the case that he failed to discern the distinctive creative energies alive in his generally young new faculty. The process of instruction in General Studies by Tompkins was pivotal for me and, I suspect, for many others in suggesting that the profound upheavals taking place in society and in our own and students' lives at the time could in General Studies be the object of disciplined and existentially vital academic study.

Some years later Tompkins describes this process of individual, one-on-one interaction with prospective faculty as sniffing out whether they were "committed to teaching students," since "teaching is the center of what we do, the absolute essence ("Oral History of the College," Tompkins 7). It was also, as I recall, his way of "sniffing" out the prospect's capacity for General Studies teaching and innovation and experimentation in general. It is likely that the other deans followed a similar pattern, since they were all recruiting faculty for their various divisions, which had been advertised as seeking "*the teaching* (my italics) scientist or scholar," willing to "break away from traditional rationales and conventional methods" (ARHU) and open to "new interdisciplinary methods and approaches" (SOBL). NAMS sought "innovative and experimenting individuals . . . to develop programs centering on ecology and environment" (*Academe*, June, 1970).

Sandra Hartzog (Bierbauer) describes the early exhilarating freedom experienced by her and her NAMS colleagues. There was no department or college curriculum committee to be grappled with; what she as a biologist would teach was for her and her alone to decide, and likewise for her colleagues. On the other hand, she also describes the need for the programs in NAMS as a whole to contribute to the shaping of the interdisciplinary ENVL and MARS programs, which resulted in a very high level of collegiality and mutual respect ("Oral History of the College," Hartzog 28). Rosalind Herlands remembers with pleasure grasping the difference between the Stockton idea of general education and the distribution of introductory courses that had characterized her undergraduate years. She also welcomed being encouraged as a trained scholar to reach outside of her primary field to other areas, which, in her case, led to a teaching and research interest in the then-nascent field of bioethics ("Oral History of the College," Herlands 74).

No one more vividly represents the personal developmental possibilities of the General Studies curriculum, however, than the chemist Shelby Broughton. Coming to Stockton in the first year with a research interest in the chemistry of human consciousness, he recounts with a warm chuckle the gradual dawning on him of the opportunities General Studies offered. Accordingly he applied in the spring of 1971 for a summer institute at Esalen in California, then the center of the burgeoning human potential movement, and found himself accepted as the only natural scientist in a roster of humanist psychologists, artists,

and practitioners of meditative and contemplative techniques. After his return to Stockton a successive series of General Studies courses taught by him emerged: the GT course Hallucinogenic Drugs and Perception, the GIS course Models of Consciousness, and, finally, the GT course Altered States of Consciousness (see page 100), which attracted national attention in the person of playwright and filmmaker Paddy Chayefsky, then working, as I recall, on a subsequent novel and movie of the same name.

General Studies also allowed others to respond to the widespread cultural interest in the human consciousness movement. Gerald Enscoe and Bill Sensiba, along with others, created group sensitivity courses that responded to that area of student interest. The flexibility of General Studies allowed for timely, *ad hoc* responses in this area and others, but when student interest waned, as it did in this case, the college was not left with lingering structural commitments.

Tilley's complaint about the relative lack of appropriate General Studies courses in the first few semesters might at first glance seem somewhat warranted. Judging from titles and course descriptions in the first two or three semesters, a significant proportion of courses very early on could have been well suited to Program Studies or even noncredit adult education programs rather than General Studies of the Stockton genre. Outstanding exceptions to such an observation, however, were immediately evident. Jonathan Griffiths' Experiential Chemistry, for instance, with its emphasis on moving in the laboratory from experiential fact to theory, in contrast to the typical reverse procedure, was immediately and for many years a premier example of responding to the frequent admonition in the early working papers to start wherever the student's knowledge already was. Roger Wood's Scientific Exploration, an interdisciplinary course on the literature and personalities of great explorers, was also present from the very beginning and, with appropriate revisions, became another classic General Studies creation.

One can also observe a developmental pattern in these first years. In Arts and Humanities, for instance, Fred Mench initially taught General Studies courses, which, judging from their titles and descriptions, could well have been part of any good Classics curriculum. Soon, however, his Daily Life in Ancient Rome and Egypt emerged, which dealt with the lived experience of ordinary people in ancient times and which remained perennially popular as a General Studies course. James Hollis moved from surveying Romantic literature in General Studies to Myth, Folklore and Fairy Tales, presciently responding to burgeoning popular interest and contributing to his personal evolution into a Jungian scholar and lecturer of national and international reputation. Similarly Yitzhak Sharon moved in General Studies from at first teaching Space Travel and Extraterrestrial Life to Atom, Man, and Universe, which, by many reports from generations of students, was their single most enlightening General Studies course. I believe one can see in the work of these faculty members and many others who could be cited a timely if gradual grasping of the possibility through General Studies to bring their former experience in the ivy tower into the lives and interests of undergraduate students.

It must also admitted, however, as Tilley also observes, that a certain number of the early faculty found General Studies as it was taking shape distasteful or even irresponsible. Some, particularly among those attracted to Stockton because of its proclaimed emphasis on general education, found the curriculum as it actually developed lacking in coherence and encouraging dilettantism or other kinds of irresponsibility among faculty (the "faculty sand-box" was a quip sometimes heard). Soon the college-wide General Studies Committee of the Faculty Assembly began to formulate proposals, partly in response to these critics but also to a widespread consensus about the lack of breadth in many graduates' transcripts, particularly transfer students.

Generally these proposals required, in varying ways, a minimum distribution of courses among the structured components of the General Studies curriculum (GAH, GNM, GSS, GEN). A series of Faculty Assembly meetings followed and were very well attended, with widespread participation, as I remember them, in which these proposals were intensely but civilly debated, culminating in summer faculty workshops, funded by the college. From these came guidelines for determining the specific requirements for any course in any given G-category as well as procedures for evaluating proposed new courses and for periodically reviewing existing ones. Although the tangible results here took bureaucratic form (G-subgroups), many of the participating faculty remember these workshops as involving some of the most sustained and collegial intellectual work of their Stockton career.

A proper assessment of the enduring significance of this early elan lies beyond the scope of this essay. No assessment of any kind would be complete, however, without calling attention to the unanticipated fecundity of the General Studies structure in facilitating the emergence of programs not anticipated in the original design. Within a decade, topical concentrations of courses of interest to students and generally created in response to a broadened view of "the requirements of citizenship" emerged, becoming in later years more specifically denoted as interdisciplinary minors.

Among the originally unanticipated programs, however, one in particular needs to be singled out, the BASK or Basic Skills program. Faced with a significant number of matriculating students judged to be unprepared for serious academic work, many members of this early faculty, generally trained as research scholars, willingly and voluntarily took on, in addition to their program and other required General Studies teaching, the task of teaching fundamental writing skills and analytic reasoning where needed, initially under the direction of Ken Tompkins and subsequently under the leadership of Bill Daly. No other development in my opinion so perfectly epitomizes the

determination of the early Stockton faculty to bring the abstract experience of the ivory tower to the needs and lives of students and society alike than does this departure.

What then of a legacy? Subsequent formal assessment among later faculty members indicated a high level of enthusiasm for the opportunities and value offered to them by General Studies. Survey studies among graduating and graduated students reflected similar widespread enthusiasm (2001 General Studies Self Study, Executive Summary, V). Whether continuing popularity of this sort constitutes a warrant for continuing into the new century with its opportunities and problems the structures of the original founding and the first fruits of their realization is for others to decide.

The Real Bonus

I attended Stockton State College from 1979 - 1982 to complete my bachelor's degree in nursing. As far as my major was concerned, it was everything I hoped it would be. It laid the foundation for my success in both master's and doctoral programs.

However, the real bonus was in the form of general education. I was raised in a working class family, had limited exposure to arts, humanities, music, politics, etc. I was the first in my family to obtain a college education. The general education courses I took at Stockton opened up an entirely new world for me. I became intensely interested in these topics and after having a course that introduced me to art, actually took a trip to Taos, New Mexico to visit Georgia O'Keefe's territory. This is just one example of what general education did for me. I continue to this day, 30 years later, to cultivate the interests that were sparked during my time at Stockton State College. I am eternally grateful; general education has made my life much more enriched than it might have been.

General education is the Stockton component that must be preserved. It has the potential to open up people's lives in important and meaningful ways.

Linda Aaronson

Designing the Self—Creating General Studies at Stockton

Ken Tompkins

An important place to start describing General Studies at Stockton would be the original description written in July 1970. Each of the founding deans was asked to describe his division; this description is mine:

A Note on General Studies at Stockton

July 1970

The Division of General Studies is founded on the idea that among the student's first college experiences there need to be specific courses designed to separate out of his past that knowledge which will be of value in independently designing and pursuing his education. The whole Stockton faculty, and especially the Division of General Studies, will have to lead, prod, urge, and coax the student to initiate his own learning. To do this, and do it early, this Division will have to provide a series of wide, radical, pedagogically untraditional, exploratory and introductory courses. These courses will question what students have critically accepted, illuminate what they have not understood, challenge them to confront what they are used to evading.

To do this, if it can be done, we shall avoid committee-run, syllabus-style courses, offering rather a wide range of courses, seminars, tutorials, and independent projects to prepare our students, not for specialized study, but for intelligent exploration and productive independence. These courses will "represent the belief of the academic community that it is valuable for amateurs to reflect on, talk about, and inquire into the artistic, scientific, and intellectual questions of contemporary civilization." We expect each student to take six to ten general courses; at some point, we expect each student to initiate a series of what we call Liberal Studies: independent, self-designed, and at least partly self-evaluated studies and projects following the implications or developing the interests of earlier investigations.

The Division of General Studies must also initiate, develop, and maintain new interdisciplinary studies, both for General Studies and for degree programs. The Division itself can originate and investigate possible programs; the Division can draw together faculty and students to propose and produce new programs. We will, then, play the catalytic role of connecting a variety of endeavors and interests.

Four categories for interdisciplinary programs can already be recognized:

1. Foreign Area Studies—we propose a far more thoroughgoing involvement of the sciences and the fine arts than is usually seen.

2. Period Studies—these would focus the student's educational experience on a particular era, again involving as many disciplines as possible. Our first program in this category will probably be in

the History and Philosophy of Science.

3. Topical Studies—will be concerned with broad approaches to a particular theme like war, racism, beauty, ecology.

4. Methodological Studies—perhaps the most exciting of all these programs would consider the methods men use to communicate, to learn, to express, to worship.

Finally, the opportunities for pedagogical experimentation are legion. Indeed, it is our hope that this Division might be the leading exporter of innovative teaching at the College. The single vice we are stalwartly against is that of being merely traditional. We will meet the student where we find him; we will also declare that we will not leave him there.

What seems to me significant in this description are the *ways* that I propose these goals might be achieved. I argue that General Studies should teach the student how to "initiate his own learning," that General Studies would create nontraditional courses to do this, that along with General Studies courses, each student would take a set of Liberal Studies courses based on interests identified earlier. Finally, the Division of General Studies would be the place for pedagogical experimentation in collections of courses found nowhere else in the College curriculum.

To understand the eventual shape and position of General Studies, it might be helpful to understand some events and personalities in the years just before 1970.

My first full-time teaching job was at Millikin University in Decatur, Illinois. I had not yet finished my dissertation, and I wanted to be close enough to Indiana University to be able to drive there for consultations and research. Decatur was about three and a half hours from Bloomington. I didn't know it at the time, but even more important for my career was the Chairman of English at Millikin—Wes Tilley.

I had been interviewed by Wes Tilley at an MLA meeting in Chicago; we immediately became fast friends. Tilley, an experienced academic politician, was very bright, hilarious, and terribly widely read. Though I had been offered other positions, I took the one with him when it was offered.

During the two years that I taught at Millikin, Wes and I were constant friends. His knowledge and experience was limitless—it seemed—and I learned most of what I know from him. He was, in hindsight, particularly insightful regarding higher education, especially in humanities and literature. One of the constant

B-wing gallery (1976)

discussions we had was about general education.

The other important fact about Wes Tilley was that he could "think the unthinkable." There was no subject, no idea, no proposal that he would reject or mock.

In 1967, we both left Millikin. He went to St. Johns on Staten Island, and I went to Central College in Iowa. I became Chairman of the English Department at Central, so I had both administrative and teaching responsibilities.

It was in March 1970 when Wes Tilley called me to ask if I'd "like to build a college in New Jersey?" He had been appointed at this yet-to-be-built college as Vice President of Academic Affairs. He was hiring deans (we were called chairmen) and wondered if I would come east for an interview. He offered me two possible positions: Dean of Arts and Humanities or Dean of General Studies. I interviewed for the latter, was hired, and arrived in late June.

To understand General Studies at Stockton you have to understand the role of questioning and the informed choices that can result from the right question asked at the right time. Wes Tilley makes this point in his Academic Working Paper #1, Principals 7 and 8:

7. *We are paying special attention to the significance of questions in education. We should be able to identify the kinds of questions we expect students to raise at any given stage of education; we*

should be able to show how such questions are formulated, and how they lead to choices of materials: principles and methods of expression, communication and proof. And we think there is probably no better indication of how much students are learning than the kinds of questions they raise, both in their classes and in the general dialogue of the community.

8. *We are distinguishing with some care between merely offering choices to students and educating students to design choices for themselves. However slow the latter process, it seems to hold the greater promise for education.*

Hence, if we could teach students to ask questions, this would lead to making informed choices.

The practical structure of General Studies was to create a curriculum out of courses offered by every faculty member. By contract, each faculty was to teach two General Studies courses per academic year.

This meant that from the First Cohort of fifty-five faculty, General Studies would be able to count on 110 individual courses. These were to be arranged in seven categories: GA (Fine Arts), GH (Humanities), GS (Social Sciences), GN (Natural Sciences), GM (Mathematics), GT (Topics), and GX (Experimental).

Traditional general education requirements serve as a "foundation" for courses in the major. I early rejected this idea because I didn't find it true in my own education. Wes Tilley did not find it true in his either. As an undergraduate, my first two years were solely devoted to general education. Like many Americans then and now, I was required to take two introductions to science, two introductions to social science, two introductions to the arts, and two to the humanities. I also had to take writing courses. The rest I don't remember. Note that I was not required to take math or business courses, though I was required to take two courses in a language. I suspect that these courses had pretty much been taught the same way with the same content for decades.

The assumptions underlying this curriculum was that such courses would (1) provide a liberal arts education exactly the same as everyone else had had for a century, (2) that these courses would provide a foundation for, in my case, literature courses I would take in my last two years, and (3) like the Medieval *trivium* and *quadrivium*, what I would learn in those courses was what every well-educated male in America knew. These courses would mark me as "civilized."

It didn't take me long to realize that the courses did not prepare me to read literature, that there were all sorts of information about the world I lived in that these courses omitted, and, that after an introductory chemistry course, I knew almost nothing about the subject even though, as I remember I got an A in the course.

So, I decided that we had to create another set of desiderata for General Studies courses—ones that did not assume that everyone had to take a specific set of courses and that did not assume a foundational role for the rest of the curriculum. The desiderata for General Studies courses at Stockton was that they were not introductions, they could have a current perspective, they did not have to be in the teacher's discipline, and they could, for the faculty, have an element of risk either from approach or content. Originally, it was the Dean of General Studies who solicited courses and had approval over what was handed him by the faculty. Later, the generation and approval of General Studies courses was transferred to the divisional deans, effectively cutting the Dean of General Studies out of the construction of the curriculum.

I want to comment, briefly, on the desiderata for a General Studies course. In a document (written after a few terms from the opening of the College in fall 1971) entitled "General Studies at Stockton" I wrote the "philosophy" that informed the early concepts of general education at Stockton.

First of all, the basic idea of GS does not encourage institution-wide course requirements. We do not see ourselves in the role of determining what GS experiences all students should have regardless of their age, background, or skills. We insist that each student comes to Stockton as a responsible individual; curricular-wide requirements prohibit that insistence from being effective.

Secondly, we do not see ourselves as "redeeming" the student. We have

avoided, and continue to avoid, telling the student he needs certain educational experiences because of their quality. Coming up against the great historical battles does not necessarily prepare one to deal with life; reading a few pages of poetry or a play does not make one more tolerant of others and their beliefs.

Thirdly, we do not see ourselves at the beginning of education as if that process started upon arrival at the main entrance. We are not specifically concerned about introductory learning experiences to a discipline or an idea. All new experiences are introductory in the widest, and, for GS, the best sense. Whether a student continues in an area of search is up to him and his Preceptor. GS makes no rules about it. GS, then, seems to be a fairly simple idea: students have interests (though they are not always aware of them or very precise about them) and faculty have interests. The GS curriculum seems to be an effective means of bringing these interests together in the form of courses. We have no desire to unnecessarily determine the outcome.

General Studies courses, then, were not to be specifically introductory. I felt that some faculty would simply transfer, say, Psychology 101 into the General Studies offerings. Had this been permitted, the General Studies curriculum would, without question, have become a second-class citizen. Also, such transfers would have replicated traditional general education at Stockton. I was determined not to let this happen.

I also felt that, within reason, General Studies courses could offer content outside of the teacher's discipline. I found during my interviews that all of the First Cohort faculty had fascinating outside interests. For example, I happened to uncover the fact that one of our Chemistry faculty had extensive experience with recorders. Indeed, he was somewhat of an expert on eighteenth-century recorder music and had long experience playing and teaching recorders. He proposed a course replete with the study of composers, culture, the history of the recorder, and the challenge for his students to write recorder music. He and his students frequently sat in the Gallery entertaining us with wonderful recorder playing. While he did not have a degree in recorder musicology, he had more than sufficient content for a General Studies course.

I hasten to add that I did not encourage or permit courses in silly skills or irrelevant content to be offered. I was well aware of the wider community's perception that we were a "hippie" college where students studied basket-weaving or chicken-raising. I assiduously avoided any courses that could be considered by anyone as frivolous.

I also strongly felt that faculty—as well as students—needed a place to grow and that if we didn't provide such a place in the College, faculty would more and more turn to safe courses like those in their disciplines. Most faculty leapt at the opportunity, confirming my sense that most faculty have all sorts of fascinating courses hidden away in their minds waiting to be birthed.

Given the 110 courses during the first year, it was obvious that there had to be an emphasis on choice. If the earliest documents are examined, one will find that they are laced with serious discussion and postulations about the centrality of choice and how to encourage students to make informed choices. I very much wanted to confront our students with a smorgasbord of course offerings. Our earliest General Studies courses were only organized in a very general way—primarily around the content and discipline of each instructor. While the seven categories linked General Studies courses to traditional disciplines, I urged faculty—and they eagerly responded—to teach courses in others of the categories. This resulted in chemists teaching recorder music, physicists teaching urban planning, literature instructors teaching maritime history, etc. So, if choice was the central means of meeting the General Studies requirement, the relationship between the preceptor and the student was the arena for those choices.

What, then, would happen if we structured the Stockton version of general education vertically instead of horizontally as traditional schools had? What if we said to Stockton students: we want you to take courses in your major when you are a freshman as well as a senior and we want you to do the same with your general education courses? So, Wes Tilley turned the traditional structure on its side. This, effectively, made General Studies courses the equal of courses in the major. It also meant, we argued, that as students matured they would be able to make more informed, mature choices as well.

To recognize this maturing choice process, we created Liberal Studies. In a way, Liberal Studies was like a minor in General Studies. My thinking was that once a student began to accrue a few courses, under the guidance of her preceptor, she would want to take more courses in one discipline. Imagine, for example, a Literature major taking General Studies courses until she developed an interest in psychology. Needing more concentrated training than the General Studies courses offered, she would develop a Liberal Studies plan to take courses from the Psychology program faculty. In a sense, for a knowing student, the course offerings from the whole College would be available in a Liberal Studies plan. Note that a student could not plan a Liberal Studies sequence until she had taken other General Studies courses and only when the student's preceptor felt she was ready to do so.

It can be seen, then, that the preceptor was at the center of the success of General Studies and of the way that students chose their General Studies courses. Others have written in this text about the preceptor; here I want to stress the importance of the role. Preceptorial activity was part of the teaching load at Stockton, and all faculty were preceptors.

Within five years General Studies had been changed. The second Dean of General Studies created a set of categories still in use today and the requirement that students had to take at least two courses in each. Certain faculty complained that they didn't want to teach in the General Studies curriculum, and many were released from that obligation; these were primarily faculty in the Professional Studies division. Programs broke a rule that I had established that NO General Studies courses could count in program requirements. I had tried to maintain a nonporous barrier between the General Studies curriculum and the curricula of the programs. Programs saw that there was a benefit in counting General Studies courses as Program courses so they broke that rule. Conversely and finally, programs began to offer their introductory courses as General Studies offerings, breaking another barrier that I had set up. This allowed faculty to teach, say, Introduction to Psychology in the PSYC program and to teach the same course as a General Studies course.

Some maintain that the General Studies curriculum is still vibrant, imaginative, and innovative. Perhaps. It is still one of the most distinctive aspects of the Stockton experience, though if you were to ask newer faculty exactly what a General Studies course was, most would be hard pressed to answer clearly. From my standpoint it has been weakened over the years, losing its definition, and becoming routinized. I have hopes that, given the structure, it can be revived and take its place as the jewel in our crown. But I have my doubts.

Dance professor, Henry van Kuiken

Joyous Serendipidity

G. Jan Colijn

The origins of the General Studies curriculum are firmly rooted in the *zeitgeist* of the Sixties. The College's founders, in particular the Dean of General Studies, Ken Tompkins, wanted no part of a traditional core curriculum (to which many had been subject in their college days) and had little interest in unimaginative distribution requirements to provide liberal arts breadth. Instead, it was argued that the cognitive map was seamless, not departmentalized in fiefs; that students should grapple with perennial questions facing humanity; and that, were they to do so, it was abundantly clear that no singular discipline held all the answers. Thus, the faculty set out to implement a commons heavily slanted toward cross-disciplinarity, and experimentation and, mindful that students had different interests and brought different experiences and knowledge to the table, the faculty wanted students to chart their own paths through the arts and sciences under the pastoral eyes of their preceptors, who could steer them to discovery and self-actualization without stultifying and overarching College-wide requirements and also without the fear that experimentation would have an effect on grades. Grading, therefore, consisted of a simple system (i.e., H, S, and N). You had done well with an H (high), well enough with an S (satisfactory), and not well enough with an N (not satisfactory or no credit).

Faculty were encouraged to teach subjects in which they had a strong interest or passion—subjects that might stray well beyond their disciplinary background because teaching on and about a passion would create excitement in the classroom, and students could see how the faculty was actually learning with them, another presumed pedagogical nugget. Finally, all faculty would contribute to this commons: the liberal arts were everyone's business.

Thus, the early General Studies "requirements" barely warranted that term. Categories were very broadly construed, e.g., Methods of Inquiry. And for those courses that could not find a home in even the most liberally defined categories, there was a category called General Topics.

By the mid-seventies, it became clear that the original intentions underlying the design of General Studies continued to be sound in an epistemological sense but that students, in a "let a hundred flowers bloom" curriculum, did not necessarily get the requisite skills to underpin an optimal liberal arts education and that others were simply underprepared for the rich menu that had been created for them.

Henceforth, the history of General Studies can be summarized as a movement from freedom to constraint. The first change was the creation of a Basic Studies program for underprepared freshmen, with required courses in writing, mathematics, and critical thinking—a program that would become a model in the state and proved highly successful, with students completing College at the same pace as those who had been exempt from the program. Shortly thereafter, a college-wide, four-year writing requirement was created, among the first writing-across-the-curriculum programs in the nation, followed by a quantitative reasoning program, supported with National Science Foundation and American Council of Learned Societies seed grants. Both programs would mature into cornerstones of the liberal arts in the same fashion as the Basic Studies program had. In the meantime, the grading system was slowly replaced by a more traditional A through F system, presumably to accommodate market forces and graduate schools.

Next up was a re-examination of the General Studies categories, and, after considerable debate, they were replaced with categories that aligned to a significant degree with the College's internal organization in divisions (now schools). Students subsequently were to undertake coursework in the Arts and Humanities (GAH), Natural Sciences and Mathematics (GNM), and Social Sciences (GSS), with retention of the General Topic category in (General Interdisciplinary Skills) GEN courses, an area wherein many skills-based courses would soon find a home. On top of this, (General Integration and Synthesis) GIS courses were to be the *de facto* capstone of the curriculum, wherein the faculty hoped students would experience Max Weber's *Aha-Erlebnis*—that magic moment when the whole undergraduate experience would come together in a celebratory leap of understanding.

When it turned out that students, even with these more precise categories, would still opt out of certain experiences, e.g., by taking arts but no humanities, a thin line of four subscripts was added in the 1990s to address that issue as well. Throughout the 1980s and 1990s, interdisciplinary minors were added, from Africana to Holocaust and Genocide Studies—a trend that continues.

The College's General Studies approach has played a great role in constantly revitalizing faculty (and allowing some to build national reputations well beyond their disciplines). The College has avoided canon fights or the kind of departmental sovereignty that has led to repeated failure to reform the liberal arts at places such as Harvard. The curriculum, by constantly adding new courses, has been responsive to changing times. The ambitious and hugely popular Understanding 9/11 course is a prime example of all these points. Its designers, David Emmons and Paul Lyons, received national recognition; the course was in place in the spring after September 11th; and the course responded to a strong need as many students had lost family in the attack on Manhattan.

The curriculum remains a work in progress and a current task force is looking at what else needs to be done. General Studies has served the College well and has added to the College's reputation in a central way, but it would be hard to claim true excellence as long as the College continues to lack robust language requirements and as long as the curriculum lacks a modicum of sequential scaffolding that would allow more depth rather than just breadth. Those students who have benefitted from four years of General Studies perform exceedingly well on some national tests that indicate they are conversant with the cognitive landscape, indicating that General Studies continues to meet its prime objective.

Regrettably, the joyous serendipity of early experimentation is gone. Higher education lives in philistine times, yet the College remains young enough to have the *élan vital* and the readiness to continue improving its liberal arts commons.

The Tsardeana of the Stockdons—Ingie Lafleur

Penelope Dugan

"Like the fella says, in Italy for 30 years under the Borgias they had warfare, terror, murder, and bloodshed, but they produced Michelangelo, Leonardo da Vinci and the Renaisssance. In Switzerland they had brotherly love—they had 500 years of democracy and peace, and what did they produce? The cuckoo clock."—Harry Lime in The Third Man

Stockton had no cuckoo clocks on the walls—no clocks at all in fact—when Ingie Lafleur arrived in June 1980. But the scars of warfare, internecine rivalries, and wounded veterans were still visible. Not all land mines had been unearthed and disarmed in the College's common and contested ground of General Studies. Ingie, an historian of European history and a refugee from Yugoslavia, knew peace is always provisional, negotiations never really end, and despair the only sin of the revolutionary. She loved and understood Stockton—its faculty, curriculum, and founding ethos from the first. The renaissance in General Studies began with her.

Had Stockton's "founding fathers" been able—Zeus-like—to pull a General Studies dean from one of their hammer-struck heads it would have been Ingrun Gerlinde Lafleur. Born in Novi Sad in its final three weeks as part of Hungary in June 1941, she spent 1945 to 1950 in displaced person camps in Austria, before coming to Chicago in 1951. (She kept on her desk her framed enemy alien card with her childish thumb print on it.) Ingie learned English in the Chicago public schools, commuted on a scholarship to Northwestern's Medill School of Journalism, was awarded fellowships by Columbia University where she earned her MA in the interdisciplinary Averell Harriman School of Soviet Area Studies and her PhD in Russian history. She played the violin, spoke German, Hungarian, Serbian, English, Spanish, and Russian fluently, and studied Hindustani singing. It was a pleasure to go with her to restaurants around New York's Upper West Side where she spoke to waiters in their own languages. But English was the language Ingie loved best because, she said, one could change one's mind mid-sentence. She relished the suppleness and flexibility of thought and conversation English made possible.

Her first job out of graduate school was at Staten Island Community College, whose history department was home to many Columbia graduates, where she taught Western Civilization. Then in 1972, she joined the faculty of William James College in Michigan. Like Stockton, its founding is recounted in Reisman's *The Perpetual Dream*, about the public alternative colleges established in the late 1960s. So when Ingie came to Stockton, she was accustomed to permeable interdisciplinary boundaries and programs, to faculty stretching and renewing themselves teaching courses of their own design. The only tradition Stockton has, she would say, is innovation.

A question Ingie failed to ask in her initial interview was how many Deans of General Studies had preceded her. I believe in eight years, there had been seven—some of whom were "acting" and some of whom had clearly not been given the script. Although every Stockton faculty member, the Stockdons as Ingie called them, was contractually obliged to teach at least one course yearly in General Studies, the Dean of General Studies had no contractual authority over them. Her sole authority was that which the faculty gave her through respect and devotion to the same curricular vision. Ingie cut an unlikely charismatic figure. She was under five feet tall, plump (my flesh, she would say, is made of the finest food and wine), yet moved, as Bill Daly commented, with the speed of a mongoose. Energy incarnate, passion personified, she inspired us. Every candidate for a faculty position at Stockton was and is still interviewed by the Dean of General Studies. Thirty years later, the Stockton faculty I spoke with said the most memorable part of their interview day was their time with Ingie. Dave Burdick remembers the excitement she communicated to him about Stockton, how she drew out from him thoughts about the General Studies courses he might teach, how hopeful she made him feel. He turned down other offers to come to Stockton because he felt he had been recruited by Ingie for a very special mission. Says Dave, "She gave me a sense of possibility and freedom."

Looking through Ingie's date books and their lengthy lists of daily things to do, I see "Write thank you to Ken Harrison," "talk to Paul Lyons about 1984 theme," "ask Ralph about best place to get tee-shirts made for union bug," "get travel money for Pat Reid." The entire faculty was Ingie's faculty. She nurtured them, encouraged them, and rejoiced in them. In March of her first year as dean when the College underwent a reorganization, replacing appointed deans with elected divisional chairpersons, Ingie, who had faculty rank but not a line, resolved to run for Chairperson of General Studies, a brave decision. She was elected by the college-wide faculty and was the only chairperson without tenure.

The sole faculty members Ingie had contractual authority for were the seven of us in General Studies. In 1976, when the Basic Studies program began, Academic Affairs decided to move those of us who taught full-time in the program from our disciplinary divisions to General Studies. It was to be a one-year experiment; it continues to this day. As she did with the college-wide faculty, Ingie nurtured and encouraged us, but she also fought for us like a mother wolverine. We had never been treated like full-fledged faculty members. Instead of regarding us as part of the remedy for the problem of underprepared entering freshmen, some faculty seemed to think we were part of the problem. So we kept our heads low and our eyes peeled for openings elsewhere. We had not been included in any of the groups to interview the Dean of General Studies candidates.

Ingie Lafleur was a dean who stressed the *pares* not the *primus* of *primus inter pares*. She signed up to teach BASK 1101, College Writing, and attended all the workshops we ran to learn how to teach it. We wrote and received grants; we presented at conferences; we published. As a faculty and as individuals we came alive; it was impossible not to in the presence of so much heat and light. Ralph Bean talked about his first vision of Ingie: "She threw out her arm to point to the world beyond the room, then pulled her arm back with all of us in it. I felt like she hugged me."

Ingie did bring the world to Stockton. She realized that faculty development could take many forms, that we as a faculty could feel stuck in the Pine Barrens, that budgets should be spent fully and quickly. She brought in Leo Horowitz, the filmmaker, for a one-week residency; Kenneth Boulding, as an exemplar of interdisciplinarity; Hubert Dreyfus for a lecture and workshop on artificial intelligence; Eva Brann to conduct St John's-style seminars for the faculty on teaching great books; Peter Elbow for writing-across-the-curriculum workshops; Ira Shor for pedagogy sessions. She supported Ken Tompkins in the acquisition of parts for a robot he and a class would build. He called it "Little Ingie."

The General Studies curriculum strengthened through her leadership. Groups in the General Studies categories of GAH (General Arts and Humanities), GSS (General Social and Behavioral Sciences), GNM (General Natural Sciences and Mathematics), GEN (General Interdisciplinary Skills and Topics), and GIS (General Integration and Synthesis) met regularly not only for course approval presentations but discussions of what the categories could do to advance student learning. Every semester before preceptorial advising, she issued "The State of the Art," a collection of the course syllabi for every General Studies course being offered that semester as well as articles pertinent to teaching and learning. She never stopped celebrating what faculty did in their courses, stressing the advantages of a separate General Studies curriculum of courses unique to the faculty members offering them. Many of us still have the 1984 buttons issued for the commemoration of the first college-wide theme, and some of us may fit into the black tee-shirts we were issued for preceptorial advising days with college-wide requirements emblazoned on the front.

The African American Studies and Jewish Studies certificate programs, which have now evolved into interdisciplinary minors, developed during Ingie's time and with her support and encouragement. Pat Reid-Merritt reminisced about Ingie's assistance with her first published article on teaching African American dance in General Studies. Now the author of numerous articles and three books, Pat did not then think of herself as a writer.

The Comprehensive Writing program and graduation requirement in writing came into being with Ingie's assistance and leadership. It would not have been possible had she been a dean trying to replicate what every other college does. She gave us the time and support to develop a writing program congruent with Stockton's founding ethos, growing out of the 1976 Basic Studies program with its structure of core faculty and rotating faculty from across the disciplines trained by the core and the writing-across-the-curriculum effort begun in 1978. She wrote the grant for the first Summer Faculty Writing Institute in 1982 and secured administration support for the subsequent institutes in 1983 and 1984 conducted by Mimi Schwartz and me. The average life span for a writing-across-the-curriculum program is three years. Stockton's program, despite changes in administration and academic trends, has persisted for thirty-three years under the aegis of General Studies.

Ingie Lafleur was denied tenure at Stockton in 1984. Speeches and protests disrupted the Board of Trustees meeting. Faculty raised money for a defense fund. Ralph Bean hosted a farewell party at his house on Nacote Creek attended by over two hundred members of the faculty and staff. Max and Stan of the custodial staff provided fresh-caught crabs for the multitudes.

Ingie was hired as Associate Vice President for Academic Affairs at SUNY Plattsburgh where she continued the work she loved, opening up the world and expanding opportunities for state college students. She died on June 7, 1993, at her home on Lake Champlain cared for by colleagues from every college where she had taught. She was fifty-two years old. Scholarships in her memory are offered at William James College, SUNY Plattsburgh, and Stockton.

One of two experimental classrooms where hexagonal platforms could be arranged in any order or height (1977)

Not Left Behind

Gordon William Sensiba

When I interviewed at Stockton in the spring of 1973 and heard about General Studies, the liberal BA, and independent studies, I thought I had died and gone to academic heaven. I was sure of it when I met my new colleagues that fall at the union picnic at Gerry Enscoe's. I don't believe there was another college in the country at that time where a committed political lefty and human potential activist could have felt more at home.

My first attempt to take advantage of the invitation to try new pedagogies was challenged by the new Dean of SOBL, Bob Brown, a retired US Army officer, who was never happy at Stockton. The course, Group Experience, sounded to him like psychotherapy and was therefore inappropriate. He was wrong. The course used the T-Group model developed at the National Training Laboratories to encourage individuals to examine their interpersonal behavior in light of feedback from other group members. As participants become more aware of the motivations and strategies they employ in social situations, they are encouraged to experiment with new ways of interacting that might be more effective.

Carl Rogers argued that the intensive group experience was "the most rapidly spreading social invention of the century and probably the most potent." He was referring not only to the popularity of encounter groups, in which middle-class Americans were seeking self-actualization, but to its use worldwide, like the "Guatemala guerilla" technique the Student Nonviolent Coordinating Committee was using to organize in the South, for example, or the "speak bitterness" campaigns in Mao's China. Fortunately, the Dean of General Studies, Bob Helsabeck, agreed with me, and I was allowed to teach the course.

Group Experience provided both theoretical and experiential learning, with the emphasis on the latter. In addition to the readings, students were required to keep a journal in which they applied the ideas in their reading to an understanding of the events they were experiencing in the group. I made the course "permission of instructor only" so I could interview students and explain what they could expect from the course and to get their commitment to providing honest feedback about the behaviors they would be observing. I also made the distinction from psychotherapy clear. I explained that while we would discuss the emotional reactions of group members, our focus would be on the within-group behavior of individuals and its consequences there, a process that generally leads to self-insight and the acquisition of new social concepts and skills.

The course met for four hours once a week but after students kept clamoring for a Group Experience 2, I added a marathon weekend to the course. The current class members along with the course veterans still in the area would gather at my house in Leeds Point with their sleeping bags starting on Saturday morning with things winding up on Sunday afternoon. I usually cooked a turkey. Group Experience, judged by enrollment pressures and student ratings, was the most popular course I ever taught at Stockton.

In 1975 I introduced a course called Politics in the 70s, designed to provide an overview of world politics for nonmajors. It was a large lecture class capped at 125 students. Although my teaching received an enthusiastic response from students, I became frustrated because the lecture format tended to reinforce the passive role that the political analysis was trying to undercut. One of the course goals, after all, was to create an active citizenry. After thinking about the problem and discussing it with students, I decided to try an alternative.

The core of the new model was the division of the class into a dozen permanent discussion groups of ten students plus a facilitator. The latter were chosen by me from among former Politics in the 70s students, political science majors, and campus activists. They met with me in an independent study seminar twice a week in which we went over the course material for the following week, shared the experiences they were having in their discussion groups, and monitored the effectiveness of the experiment.

The discussion groups provided the students with an opportunity to talk about the political ideas and analysis they were encountering in the lectures, reading, and films. In addition, each group was required to design an action project of its own choosing, the specifics of which were to be worked out over the course of the term. After an initial confusion over what that might involve, the small groups proved to be very inventive. The projects varied from pure library research (e.g., on daily life in Cuba) to activities in the local community (e.g., spending a weekend at the Life Center in Philadelphia, a political community whose members lived communally).

Several of the projects had an impact on the institutional life at Stockton, one of them even generating some controversy. The latter was the research done by one group that revealed how little student input there was on how the money collected via the student activity fee was allocated. Another project investigated how the moribund student government might be resurrected. And when the president of the college resigned, one group ended up running the election for student reps on the search committee for a new president.

I realized that if I wanted students to buy into the activist thrust of our new model, I would have to share my power to grade them. I decided that the final grade would be a composite of three grades averaged equally together. The first was the one each student received for participation in the small group as agreed upon by the other members. The second was the one the group project received as determined by the group facilitators. And the third was the grade I gave them for a paper describing their emerging political philosophy. The hope was that giving each member of the class a piece of the power would contribute to our goal of creating an active and involved community.

Did it work? Yes and no. Daily attendance was down from previous years, and the student course evaluations were lower than in the past. I believe the uniqueness of what we were demanding was difficult for some students because they came into the class expecting a traditional pedagogy. Many of those who enroll in a large lecture class like POLS 1100 are nontraditional students who find the extra time or effort that an alternative pedagogy involves burdensome due to job and family responsibilities. In contrast all of the facilitators, who were more typical undergraduates and participated in the design of the course, spoke very highly of their experience. I personally found it a lot of work and was exhausted by the end. I realized I would need more resources if I were to try it again (e.g., course teaching credit for the seminar).

I felt comfortable offering both of these courses at Stockton because of the general atmosphere that prevailed during those years. My interest in the ideas and practices of the human potential movement, for example, were shared by a number of other faculty members, and many offered courses similar to Group Experience. That helped to legitimate what I was doing in the eyes of others, especially the students. That also applied to my teaching as an avowed Marxist who wore a red star around his neck. I was not alone. There was a sizeable group of colleagues who were strongly identified with the Left. We used to meet once a week for lunch to keep in touch and share experiences. I remember the laughter one semester when I sent out a memo announcing that the Monday Club was meeting on Wednesday this semester.

We took the innocuous name because even at Stockton, people without tenure felt they had to be worried about seeming too radical. Several colleagues told me they were amazed when I got tenure, for example, because I had always been up front about my politics. In fact that trait got me in trouble with my left-wing colleagues one time. I was featured in an article in the *Atlantic City Press* entitled "The Marxist Wears Tennis Shoes" (November 13, 1983). In it I was quoted as saying that "12-15 faculty members sympathize with the cause and another 30 are on the 'periphery.'" An emergency meeting of the Monday Club was called, and I heard in no uncertain terms that I was out of line making such a public statement. But that was me—and they forgave me.

I was frequently in the local paper for organizing teach-ins, bus trips to Washington, D.C. for various protests, a coffee-picking brigade to help the Sandinistas in Nicaragua, and a group to help shut down the nuclear power plant in Seabrook, New Hampshire. But despite this local notoriety, I always felt supported by the college community. And not just by the faculty. People in the administration, many of them veterans, came to appreciate my anti-war efforts as we talked and they got to know me. Even the men and women who cleaned the building, worked in the mail room, or delivered audio-visual materials, most of whom tended to be very conservative politically, became real friends as they began to see the method to what they at first saw as my madness. Would this have happened at Duke (I had an in there if I had wanted)? I doubt it.

In Broughton's Tank

There was nobody in the tank but me, and the little sounds were all me. Thump thump thump, and little gurgles in the stomach and intestines, and something in the ear, amazing how many little sounds there are that normally you don't hear because the outside world is making so much noise…so what….

I let everything go. I had been holding my head up, unconsciously. It didn't drop as far into the salt water as I thought. Nothing to do…. Certainly is black in here. Wherever you go normally, you're never in complete blackness, there's always some light….

I had a momentary vision of some bicycle riders at twilight, a country road. Ah, Altered State of Consciousness. Let go, let go, let go, let's go… …and so on.

The building with the tank room was new. The main hallway connecting the several college buildings was several stories high, quite striking architecturally, with kiosks for various college notices. Big posters with bold colors broke up the spaces. Outside, a sunny day, the leaves of the shade trees making nice patterns on the grass. A bit of a breeze. Some people on the college tennis courts, in the distance. I couldn't remember whether my car was in parking lot 3 or parking lot 4, they looked almost exactly alike. The speedometer said 15279. I had a fleeting worry— what if I have a flat tire? Then I thought: that's a bit silly, why should I worry about a flat tire, I don't normally. Now, where are the keys, I had them—in my right pocket, of my pants, my pants, my pants are on the

chair, the chair in the tank room, the tank room? THE TANK ROOM? EEEEEEEEEEEEEEEeeeeeeekkkkkkkkk I'm still back in the tank! Zoooooooooooop!…..

I heard footsteps. The lid opened, a silhouetted figure in dim light up there.

"Hi, how you doin?"

"Not ready yet."

"That's an hour and a half. Blink your eyes. In a minute, I'm going to turn the light on in this room."

I said the last hour had certainly gone by quickly. I climbed out. My professor was grinning?

"Why are you grinning?" I said.

*"Why are **you** grinning? You're giggling. You look very rested."*

I said I felt somewhat rested. My fingers and toes were quite wrinkled. I got dressed.

"This course has turned out well," my friend said. He described the reading list for the course. Some of the papers written by the students had been quite interesting.

"Some of the kids logged a lot of time, three, four hours at a stretch."

"No bad experiences?"

"Not one. The administration was worried, but the course turned out extremely well."…

I took a couple of psychological tests. We chatted.

"You look much more serene than when you got here," said my friend. Well, they always say that, the people that run the resort, when you're leaving.

Bold posters in the corridor. The sun was still out, the shade trees making nice patterns on the sunny grass. Some people on the college tennis courts, in the distance. The car was in lot 4. I got in. My keys were in my right-hand pocket, and my pants were on. The speedometer said 15279.

Excerpted from Adam Smith (George J.W. Goodman), *Powers of Mind*, Random House, 1975

Dancing in Chains

Leonard Solo

I was hired in 1971 to create a teacher education program at Stockton State College, this new public college that wanted to bring what existed in small, private, liberal arts colleges to South Jersey.

This "I" was a long-haired, bearded, freshly minted EdD, a thirty-two-year-old with his head filled with K-12 progressive education and little experience in higher education. In the two plus years I had been at the School of Education at the University of Massachusetts, I had helped reform the MAT program, and I had developed a very small teacher education program, which placed students from area colleges—UMass, Amherst, Smith and Hampshire—in select innovative elementary schools throughout New England. I also ran a national organization that was an active clearinghouse of information on alternative and innovative schools.

As I began to consider what kind of teacher education program would be best for Stockton students, I learned the following about the college's prospective students:

• Most would probably be the first generation in their families to attend college, many of whom worked, and a number of these could be older, working students who would probably need evening classes.
• Most, if not all, of the prospective students would have attended conventional elementary and secondary schools.

This information was important because, as far as I could tell, there were literally no schools in the area that had a hint of innovation. There were no local schools that would fit my vision of "good" schools, places where I would be able to send prospective teachers for practicum experiences. There were such schools nearer to Philadelphia and in northern New Jersey, but they were too far away for me to place students there for short- or long-term practicums.

A good school, for me, was a place where education was personalized, where building community was emphasized, where learning was based on students' experiences (see John Dewey), where deep engagement with intellectual, moral, and social issues was the norm and grew out of the other factors just mentioned, and where students were excited to be on a daily basis, and where they were actively involved in their education.

There were other issues that helped shape my initial thinking about teacher education at Stockton:

• The program was to prepare secondary teachers.
• The program was housed in the Experimental Studies Division, with, initially, one faculty position.

• The program was to draw on faculty from other divisions for much of the teaching, supervision, and student support that would be needed to make the program work.
• Education students would, like all other students, also take courses in General Studies.

So, one of the things I had to do was to identify faculty in each of the divisions who could develop courses appropriate for students seeking certification as English, science, mathematics and social studies high school teachers. Hopefully, this same faculty would supervise practicum experiences and have this count as part of their workload.

It was not an easy task because faculty were not being hired with this in mind, and the various divisions were not thinking of offering specialty courses just for Teacher Education students.

Finally, I had to create a program that would be approved by the New Jersey Department of Teacher Education. When I met with the relevant people in Trenton, I was excited to discover that the department had a category called "experimental," which was undefined. But, as I explored this option with the officials, it became clear to me that the department was mostly concerned with teachers-in-training taking appropriate courses that would prepare them to teach this material to high school students. This translated into, for example, a social studies teacher taking approved American history courses, European history courses, and the like. So, the bottom line was that I could submit a program for approval in the "experimental" category (which I did), but it could not appear to be too experimental and too far out of the norm and had to contain the required education courses and the required courses in a student's academic major. The teacher education courses had to include a supervised student teaching experience, a methods of teaching course, and several other conventional courses. We had not only to submit titles of courses but their descriptions, too. The Teacher Education officials also made it clear to me that, in a real sense, I would be acting as their agent and representing their standards when I certified each student's application for a teaching license.

At this point, I thought of Nietzsche's saying that "the artist is he who dances in chains." I had figured out what the chains were; now, I had to figure out how to break some of the chains and/or how to dance within them.

Here's what I thought and what I developed:

The real power in a program is in what students experience in the content of what is taught and how it is taught in courses and in other experiences they have in the program—regardless of its title and description in a catalogue.

For example, students were required to take a methods course in our TDEV program. Students were shown how to develop "meaty" courses with significant intellectual, moral, and social content, with lessons that would truly engage students. They were taught how to use a range of methods instead of just lecturing and going from page one to page three hundred in a textbook. These included ideas like cooperative learning groups, role-playing, use of primary documents, use of projects, use of manipulative materials in math, use of experiments and "hands-on" activities in math and science classes as well as in other disciplines, use of journals in all subjects, use of assessment alternatives to testing, use of community resources, planning backwards, and the like. More often than not, students would be assigned to develop a lesson using these methods and ideas and to teach that lesson to their classmates in the course.

Students were also shown how to engage in developing what is now called a community of learners in their classrooms: how to involve students in decision-making, how to have them work closely together, how they could become responsible for their own learning and for the learning of their peers.

Obviously, the idea was to design courses to explore alternatives to traditional education. For example, I taught an introductory education course in a large room that I filled with many magazines, articles, books, videos (of schools, of innovative ways to teach), audio tapes, lists of schools to visit, and the like. Students were asked to explore the items in the room, to go into depth with a number of the items and to dig deeper by going to the library and beyond, to write regularly about their explorations, and to discuss them with me and their fellow students.

Each education course in the TDEV program was listed for four credits, because every course involved students in a relevant practicum. Students were encouraged to spend time in an extraordinarily good alternative high school in Cinnaminson, New Jersey. I took students to observe there on a regular, almost weekly basis. Starting in the second year of the program, I had every Teacher Education student do a practicum in a small K-8 alternative school that I had founded in Atlantic City since Stockton's president would not approve of the development of a lab school at the college. The school was based on John Dewey's philosophy and featured multigrade, open classrooms. Many Stockton faculty either taught part-time in the school or opened their labs and classrooms to the school's elementary students.

Ralph Bean, head of the Mathematics program, developed a math lab for college students that contained a wide range of manipulatives. Ralph taught students how to use these math manipulatives (multi-based blocks, tanagrams, algebra tiles, etc.)

and how to develop lessons that were project-oriented. He also taught them how to teach concepts as well as skills.

In the first year of the program, I was the lone Teacher Education faculty. In the second year, we hired Dave Tilley who came with a background in humanistic education. Dave offered courses that emphasized the social and emotional aspects of teaching and learning. As the program grew, we were able to add a third member to our group.

The TDEV program sponsored a series of evening lectures from prominent educators of that era, such as John Holt, Jonathan Kozol, and Nat Hentoff, which were also open to the area's public and private school teachers. Each of these speakers spent time in our education classes talking with students. (We, of course, read their books and articles in the TDEV classes.)

I had made connections with each of the superintendents in the area and attended their monthly "round table" meetings. I visited the high schools in the area, spoke with principals, and tried to identify solid teachers with whom I could place our practicum students.

Research tells us that the most important experience teachers-in-training have is their senior practicum. Most of the TDEV students did their student teaching in these local high schools. I encouraged our students to identify their own placements, with an emphasis on trying to find quality teachers who would model good practices. The students were mostly supervised by TDEV faculty, but a few professors from other divisions also did some supervision.

Obviously, these arrangements were not what I would have preferred for the TDEV student teachers, but there were really no other options available to the program since, as I noted earlier, the "good" schools that I knew about were too far away for our consideration. It was a programmatic weakness that I could not overcome.

Before leaving Stockton in 1974, I made connections with a school for the deaf. It was a school where students learned in ways that paralleled my ideas of a good school. With its director, we began to explore the possibility of adding courses to our program so that TDEV students might be able to get certification in teaching the deaf.

Of course, Teacher Education students had to take courses and fulfill the requirements in their divisions and they, like all other students, took General Studies courses. The TDEV program had no control over these courses. What we did do, though, is advise our students about the state's requirements for certification. A student wanting certification in science would need to have courses in biology, physics, and chemistry, for example.

For me, teaching Stockton students was much more than

interesting. I had come out of a very exciting time in K-12 public education, a time when teachers were trying a wide range of new ways to teach and to reach students. We used many of these methods in our TDEV courses, some for the first time. We used methods like those in the two courses noted above: trust activities to build a sense of community and shared goals in a class, small group discussions, students teaching part of each class, and the like. Another example is the Experiental Writing course that Ken Tompkins, a student, and I taught, where we developed interesting experiences at the beginning of a class as springboards for students' writing. I enjoyed the challenge of developing these methods and modeling them for the TDEV students, and the students' feedback to me was that they both truly enjoyed and learned a great deal in their education courses. The deeper issue for me involves whether the Stockton students internalized the ideas and concepts of the program. Did students really come to believe that schooling had to be personalized, that they, as future teachers, needed to learn how to actively involve students in their learning and that they needed to work in collegial ways in their schools in order to develop a community of learners among adults and students?

My sense is that a fair number of students did embrace our philosophy, but this number was less than half of the TDEV students. Those were the ones who really ate up the courses, spent considerable time in the Atlantic County New School and in the Cinnaminson alternative school and did their student teaching with innovative teachers. The other half of students did not buy into the program's beliefs. They took the courses and did the work, but they believed they would go out into schools where they would be expected to be traditional teachers.

I was moderately successful in getting faculty in other divisions to offer courses that supported the TDEV program and to supervise students' practicums. Ralph Bean's efforts, noted above, were an exception, though we also got significant help from "Mic" Mikulak for our social science students.

Few of the faculty in other divisions shared our program's philosophy. For me, this was a very large issue because the bulk of our students' learning was in their major areas of study, and we had no control of these.

Even the courses that students took sometimes became a problem. For example, several students sought certification in social studies. When I checked their transcripts, the only American history course they had taken was The Italian-American Experience. When I contacted state officials about this, they explained that unless it truly was a course that covered the history of the country, it would not be acceptable. Luckily, I was able to justify the course by showing that the course used the history of one ethnic, immigrant group as a lens to open up an examination of America's history—i.e., by examining what makes America America.

That is the Teacher Development program I created at Stockton State College in the early 1970s. From my perspective, it was a program built on compromises. I would have preferred having a truly experimental program, one where most of a prospective teacher's experiences were in classrooms with children, working with master teachers. College classroom work would then have been an examination of and a deepening of their experiences. But the program had to be developed within the state's and the college's frameworks, and that was what I did, trying as much as possible to impart the program's philosophy, ideals, and practices within that framework—i.e., to dance in chains.

An Early Exchange

From 1972-1977 I was part of Stockton's second faculty cohort in ARHU. With President Dick Bjork's support and approval I was able to set up an academic exchange program between Stockton and the University of Cluj in Romania. At that time Romania was still under the rough socialist dictatorship of Ceausescu. The exchange program focused on the art and science of teaching English to foreign speakers, both in Romania and on the Pomona campus.

A major result of the exchange was the 1973 publication in Bucharest of An English Teaching Methodology Handbook. Stockton State College's contribution is prominently acknowledged on the title page. The book became the standard pedagogic text used in Romanian teacher training colleges for about ten years. Copies of the book are probably still in the Stockton College library collection.

A second significant event allowed me to take three Stockton EDU/ARHU students to Romania to do practice teaching in Romanian secondary schools and to field test a set of ESOL visual aids. The experience in Romania fulfilled a State of New Jersey TESL certification requirement for the three Stockton students—Charlotte Simsen, Bill Higgins, and Neil Naughton. In 1978 the result of their work was published as Teaching English as a Foreign Language: A Set of Visual Aids with Teacher's Guide. The text was the first of its kind available to Romanian ESL teachers at low cost.

Dave Filimon

The Origins of Teacher Education

Ronald J. Moss

When Stockton State College was new, the administration decided to create a teacher preparation program that fit in with the new type of institution that Stockton sought to be. A new approach to the preparation of teachers attempted to create agents of change for the public schools. These new teachers underwent a training program that encouraged them to modernize traditional approaches to teaching.

As is true in all states, the state government had responsibility for and control over the means of preparing teachers and what these teachers had to know. Most states ran their programs through a Department of Education. Because teacher education programs, in the period before 1980, were run through colleges, a state's Department of Higher Education also had responsibilities for the programs run through colleges. In New Jersey, both departments had responsibilities for creating and evaluating teacher education programs at the colleges that offered them. Most used American Association of Colleges of Teacher Education (AACTE) standards, and those in the vanguard of traditional reform programs used the standards of the National Association of Colleges for Teacher Education (NACTE). New Jersey initially used its own program standards that included specific certification standards for each certification program offered in the state. The New Jersey Teacher Education Regulations and Standards book (hereafter referred to as the Standards) spelled out these requirements. In the 1970s and 1980s, one was required to follow these regulations, as they had the force of law behind them.

I did not know the creators of the initial Stockton Teacher Development (TDEV) program. It's my understanding that early Stockton teacher educators did not often attend state or New Jersey Association of Colleges of Teacher Education (NJACTE) meetings, as most New Jersey college program leaders did. I knew that after much state coaxing and encouragement concerning program requirements as stated in the Standards, Stockton's TDEV program underwent state accreditation review, and, I believe, failed to meet requirements. Indeed, the college was required to close down its program within two years or completely redo it. It was unheard of that the Department of Education would close out a New Jersey state college's teacher preparation program. As I understand it, this shocked the administration at Stockton, who sought a solution for this public embarrassment.

During my graduate studies at Rutgers University, I was invited by my department to assist and supervise student teachers as part of my assistantship, as I had completed a teacher education program at a college in Connecticut. I developed a program of "band-aid" seminars for student teachers I supervised. At the time, it was a new concept, and it worked well for my students. Soon other departments asked that I supervise student teachers for them. The Rutgers University Department of Teacher Education encouraged my activities and supplied more students for supervision. Upon completion of my degree, they invited me to apply for a new position that they had created, Coordinator of Laboratory and Field Experiences, which involved helping student teachers who were having difficulties, among other activities. I also attended state Department of Education meetings, NJACTE meetings, and other teacher education conferences.

In the fall of 1976, I was invited to apply for the position of Director of Teacher Education at Stockton State College. On visiting the college, it became clear that its Teacher Preparation program was in great difficulty. Perhaps a wiser mind would have run from the interviews. It was, on reflection, a life-changing opportunity. When offered the position, I accepted. Meetings with New Jersey Department of Education personnel made very clear what had been wrong with Stockton's program. Promises of consultation and help were made and lived up to.

At Stockton, it was clear that teacher preparation programs had to be recreated from scratch. Even a new acronym, EDUC for "Education," was created, though some faculty missed the old TDEV name. A series of more traditional and regulation-compliant programs with new EDUC courses were created utilizing EDUC associated faculty and field-based practitioners. State regulations were followed closely as were AACTE standards. "Approved Program" documents were created that detailed Stockton EDUC certification programs, and the documents were signed by state officials without requests for amendment. Two new programs in psychology and in comprehensive science were also created and approved as well. These were possibly the very first Approved Program documents for Stockton filed with the state Department of Education's Bureau of Certification.

Stockton's EDUC program also worked hard to rebuild relations with Atlantic County's school district administrators, who welcomed promises of higher quality and consultation. These promises were lived up to, and fieldwork placements for EDUC courses were made. Students were supervised and evaluated by school teachers and administrators, and college faculty also visited schools regularly. Some Stockton faculty had activities of their own in the schools, especially NAMS faculty.

Standards and measurements of success were increased, particularly in the introductory and new reading course sequences and in the new Practices and Techniques of Teaching course. Students were more regularly visited by EDUC associated faculty in student teaching placements, and the Director of Teacher Education visited all student teachers as well. Written evaluations were created and shared with students. Students in EDUC seemed pleased with the new standards, and there were few student complaints about workload. Most EDUC associated faculty went along with the new program, though a few faculty opted to reduce their involvement. Success was a great reward for students. The administration supported the new EDUC program. The support included supplemental funds for many years for the development of a Curriculum Center with computers and for purchasing prepared computer programs in all certification fields, as computer-assisted production developed. At that time, Stockton favored a small Teacher Education program, just in secondary education. I left in January 1991 for a position elsewhere.

The Wright Stuff

During the 1982 fall semester, a new era in my life was begun by reading a book. The book was Richard Wright's autobiography, Black Boy. *During the first semester of my freshman year, I discovered a new experience—reading. I had just graduated high school and could honestly say that I had not read a book cover to cover during my four years. I was assigned works from Shakespeare, Dickens, Steinbeck, Fitzgerald, Vonnegut, and Wilder; however, I was always able to make it through my English classes without completely reading any of these texts.*

At Stockton, I was assigned two BASK classes, College Writing and Critical Thinking—courses that are focused on reading, writing, and analyzing texts. I remember going to the bookstore to purchase the books for these classes, only to learn that there were seventeen required books. One can only imagine my trepidation about remaining in college at that point; how was I to read seventeen books for two courses, when in four years I had not fully read one? In the back of my mind, I heard the voice of my preceptor, Dr. Lowenstein, who had apprised me of the consequences of failing and/or receiving a "D" in either of the two courses, the greatest of which was dismissal from the college. "How can I go home at the end of the semester," I asked myself, "and tell my parents that I was academically dismissed from college for not doing the assigned readings—especially since I used their money to purchase the books?" I envisioned their reaction, the least of which would probably mean homelessness for me. With these thoughts in mind, I resolved to read each book to its end.

Of the seventeen books, one stands in the forefront: it was my discovery of an African-American writer who was unknown to me. The book was Their Eyes Were Watching God *by Zora Neale Hurston. I was at intrigued by Hurston's use of language. Her characters spoke a language that would have been regarded as substandard by my former English teachers. However, Dr. Nelson, my professor, explained that the language of Janie, Phoebie, Joe, and Teacake was part of the novel's aesthetic as it captured the many aspects of African-American culture. I never realized that a novel could bring a culture or one's experience—especially my own—to life. This new awareness ignited in me a thirst for learning about other African-American writers and their literature.*

At the conclusion of the semester, after having read the seventeen aforementioned books, I realized that reading was indeed an activity of which I had robbed myself, and I was on a mission to compensate for my dearth of reading experiences. This mission commenced one Thursday evening with my going to the Stockton library and checking out a copy of Richard Wright's autobiography, Black Boy.

As I began to read, I became enthralled by Wright's storytelling prowess. I traveled with him back to his Mississippi home and the harsh upbringing that he experienced in the Jim Crow South and was intrigued by this "coming of age" story. The more I read, the more I wanted to further read to understand Wright's story. Despite having parents who were both reared in the South, my knowledge of Jim Crow was limited to what I had read in my high school history texts and the footage of the civil rights movement that was usually aired on television around January 15th each year. I had never read a firsthand account about life for African-Americans in this setting and was captivated by Wright's realistic and unapologetic portrayal of race in America. His forthrightness about race and racism in this country awakened in me a consciousness of what it really meant to be an African-American man in this society and how much more I needed to learn about who I was and the struggles of those who came before me.

Reading Black Boy *became a coming of age experience for me. Today, twenty-eight years later, I have the pleasure of teaching a course in African-American literature at Atlantic City High School. I hope that my students, like their teacher, will experience a new era dated in their lives as a result of reading a book.*

Ricky Epps-Kearney, 1988, 2001

A Brief History of NAMS

Roger Wood

In its early years, Stockton was an exciting and rather chaotic environment for the first cohorts of NAMS faculty. To a considerable extent we could not teach traditional college-level science courses because we did not have adequate lab facilities. Knowing this, the original NAMS dean (Dan Moury) tried to recruit individual faculty members with broad ranges of interests who could create a credible science curriculum without the traditional academic infrastructure (i.e., labs and library resources such as scientific journals) found at any college or university that aspired to offer a well-rounded undergraduate science curriculum.

Compounding this problem was the fact that Stockton students in the early years spanned a much broader range of academic preparedness for a college education than is characteristic of Stockton students today. Some were extraordinarily bright and would have been exceptional students at any college or university in the country. Others were woefully unprepared for college, lacking the necessary reading, writing, and critical thinking skills. The faculty spent large amounts of time in program meetings trying to figure out how to teach classes to students like these with such a broad range of abilities. Should we teach up to the level of our best students and risk leaving behind those who were ill-prepared for college? Or should we leave no students behind by teaching down to the level of the most unprepared students, necessarily watering down our courses to the point that our best students were deprived of the kind of intensive learning experience they deserved? These ongoing debates, as well as the constraints imposed by the lack of adequate lab space and teaching resources, were responsible for shaping much of our early curriculum.

Some interesting decisions about the NAMS curriculum were necessarily made by Dean Moury well before any faculty had been hired. These included the establishment of the ENVL (Environmental Studies) and MARS (Marine Science) programs. At the beginning of the 1970s, environmental studies was a fledgling academic discipline in the United States and undergraduate programs in marine science were rare indeed. Today, most colleges and universities offer environmental studies curriculum of one type or another. But it is still true that Stockton is one of a handful of academic institutions offering an undergraduate major in marine science.

Originally, ENVL attracted the greatest proportion of NAMS majors, but over the years ENVL enrollments have decreased while the number of Biology (BIOL) majors has mushroomed. By the 1990s BIOL produced more graduates annually than any other programs in the college except for Business (BSNS) and Psychology (PSYC).

Recently, a new component has been added to the NAMS curriculum—graduate education. At present there are two master's degree programs in which some NAMS faculty participate, the Master of Science in Computational Science and the Professional Science Master's in Environmental Science.

Over time the NAMS faculty has changed, too. The early cohorts of faculty were hired for their breadth of knowledge and willingness to teach a very wide range of subject matter. Now, forty years later, we have developed a fairly typical undergraduate science curriculum and new faculty hires are recruited to teach specific courses needed for a particular academic program.

Like good cheese (or wine), the NAMS faculty has also inevitably aged. In the fall of 1971, when Stockton offered its first classes, there were fourteen NAMS faculty positions. (One of these, interestingly, was jointly held by a husband-and-wife team, Mark and Martha Pokras.) The composition of the original NAMS faculty was almost all folks who were fresh out of graduate school and hired at the assistant professor level. Included in this cohort were only one full professor (Ralph Bean) and one associate professor (Don Plank), both in the MATH program. Other deans (e.g., ARHU), hired a more traditional mix of faculty at all ranks that one would expect to find at any long-established college or university. Over the years, the demographics of the NAMS faculty have normalized, being characterized today by a fairly typical range of assistant, associate, and full professors.

The original fifteen NAMS faculty gathered at Dean Moury's home in Absecon for a week of meetings and discussions in August 1971, prior to the start of the first classes at the Mayflower Hotel on Atlantic City's boardwalk. These meetings generated a strong sense of cohesion among this very disparate group of people, perhaps more so than was the case in the college's other academic divisions. This shared sense of community is a tradition that has largely persisted to the present.

Good laboratory facilities are necessary not only for science education but also research activities. Stockton has never had, and still does not have, first-class teaching labs or research space. Despite this fact, until recently Stockton has managed to graduate more science majors year after year than all the other state colleges combined. This is no longer true, however, and Stockton is losing its preeminence as a center for undergraduate science education among publicly supported colleges in New Jersey.

At the Mayflower Hotel, in the fall of 1971, lab facilities were virtually nonexistent (nothing more than a hotel room with an adjacent bathroom equipped with a toilet and bathtub but no wash basin). There was a large closet down the hall where a few microscopes and some field equipment were stored. By January 1972, A- through D-wings were ready for occupancy at our new campus. A temporary all-purpose NAMS lab occupied part of the ground floor of B-wing. In order to make sure that this new lab space would be ready for the start of classes in January, the dean and several members of the NAMS faculty spent part of a day over Christmas break coating the lab's floor with a very smelly and probably toxic sealant. (This was before OSHA had come into existence. Nowadays, such an initiative would undoubtedly be prohibited.) The NAMS faculty made do with this rather minimal facility for several years until F-wing was completed. The entire ground floor of F-wing was the site of our first permanent lab space.

Like the curriculum, the F-wing lab was designed solely by Dean Moury. It had a radical floor plan based on a recently constructed lab facility at a small liberal arts college in North Carolina. It was basically a huge open space with no partitions where several different labs could be conducted simultaneously. While conceptually intriguing, this innovative, open lab design did not work at Stockton. Specialized, dedicated spaces were needed for Chemistry and Physics labs, so within a short time the lab was partitioned into three still very large areas. The windowless end of the lab was curtained off for Physics labs, and the central part was reserved for Chemistry labs. No one could enter this area without wearing the appropriate safety gear. The remaining third of the lab was left for BIOL, ENVL, and MARS labs.

Then the fire happened.

A year or two after F-wing lab was occupied, there was a fire in the chemical storage area of the lab in the early summer. Because the lab shared a common ventilating system with the Library (either through design or construction error), smoke and fumes from the fire spread not only throughout the lab but also throughout all three floors of the Library. Both the lab and the Library had to be completely shut down for several months after the fire while these two areas were decontaminated and cleaned by a crew wearing Tyvek coveralls and respirators. Fortunately, both the lab and the Library were ready for use by the beginning of the fall term.

As the college continued to grow, F-wing could no longer provide enough space for all the labs that needed to be offered. Physics labs were created on the ground floor of C-wing, while the acquisition of nearby property on Nacote Creek enabled the construction of a field station (including some lab space) for the MARS program.

Then, finally, the F-wing lab underwent a major redesign. The enormous open lab was partitioned into a series of walled BIOL and CHEM labs. And, for the first time, a small amount of dedicated research space was created for faculty to use.

These lab renovations were followed by the construction of the Arts and Sciences Building adjacent to A-wing. This provided classrooms, labs, and offices for ENVL, GEOL, and two BIOL faculty members.

So now Stockton's science labs are scattered through the college. Currently, a new science building is in an advanced stage of planning. When built, it will only be one third of the size originally planned as minimally meeting the needs of the NAMS faculty.

Giving Teaching a Shot

I am a relative newcomer to RSC. After a long career as a practicing veterinarian I came to RSC in 1995 as an anatomy lab adjunct. Since college I had wanted to try teaching but circumstances led me in a different direction.

When I finally sold my veterinary practice my intent was to give teaching a shot. My first semester as an anatomy laboratory instructor was exciting and the students and faculty were very impressive. As time went by I became a 13 D Visiting Professor and had physiology as my teaching responsibility. After three years as a 13 D a tenure track position opened up in the Biology Program. With some reservation, I applied, knowing that my teaching credentials weren't the greatest. But my dreams came true and I landed a position as an Assistant Professor of Biology.

Eventually I was tenured (at age 64) and promoted to Associate Professor. There are very, very few milestones in my life that compare to this accomplishment. The quality and dedication of my colleagues continues to astound me. At age 70 I still look forward each day to going to RSC, interacting with the faculty, and, most of all, working with some really great students.

The only negative thing I can say about RSC is the lack of up-to-date science laboratory facilities. I think that we lose many talented science applicants because of our outdated labs. I'm sure that in the future this will be corrected but it is frustrating for those of us who lose good prospects to other schools.

In summary I would like to say that my colleagues, my students, and the staff are the best and they all keep me enjoying every day at RSC.

Ralph Werner

A History of the Psychology Program

David Lester

THE EARLY YEARS

The Psychology program was shaped to a large extent by the first Dean (or, as they were called initially, Chairpersons) of SOBL (Woodworth Thrombley). Although the Vice President for Academic Affairs (Wesley Tilley) had in mind an innovative liberal arts college, perhaps modeled on private liberal arts colleges, Thrombley, who came to the college from the Political Science department at Indiana University, was more traditional. Thrombley hired as coordinators for the programs in his division, young, seasoned, orthodox faculty members, myself in Psychology, John Reiss in Economics, William Daly in Political Science, and John Richert in Criminal Justice. Only Mark Sanford in Sociology (an experiential sociologist) was nontraditional. Under Thrombley, the coordinators had power and functioned much like department chairs.

As Coordinator of PSYC, I had two concerns. With Esalen making news on the West Coast, the administration was horrified by "touchy-feely" psychology, as they referred to it. I had to keep the PSYC program, therefore, free from such accusations. One faculty member in the Management Sciences Division did run encounter groups (sometimes in the nude), but PSYC did not.

Second, President Bjork was adamant about not providing counseling services for the students. His philosophy was that, as adults, they should use community resources like any other adult. The descriptions of preceptorial duties often were written so that preceptors were described as counselors, and the PSYC faculty fought this whenever the words were used.

I liked the philosophy of the new college, but I also valued traditional academic styles. For example, I wanted faculty who were researchers and who published scholarly articles. Before arriving at the college, I had met a young African American psychologist who had interviewed at the suicide prevention center in Buffalo where I had been Director of Research, Jacqueline Stanton. I persuaded the College to interview her, and she joined the program. The third member (Karen Bogart) was not hired by me.

In the early days of the college, there were Collegia, whose goal was to provide both social activities and a political base for faculty and students. Each Collegium consisted of five faculty and their seventy-five preceptees. Unfortunately, Karen was in the same Collegium as the president, and he took an immediate dislike to her. At the time of the first faculty evaluation, the president decided to terminate three faculty out of the initial fifty or so,

and Karen was one of the three. The faculty protested this harsh decision (to let faculty go after only one year and with only a few months notice), and a faculty committee of three members was formed to adjudicate. The committee recommended that two be rehired for a second year, but not Karen. As a result, she was not retained. Since I did the recruiting for the new faculty to begin in the second year of the college, by fall 1972, all of the PSYC program had been hired by me.

There were several interesting events in this initial year. The college permitted each program to hire whomever the program wanted. General Studies, under Kenneth Tompkins, hired a psychologist, Bernard Silverman. Silverman was unhappy from the beginning and wanted to transfer to the PSYC program. Much as I liked him as a person, I did not want him in the program. Silverman immediately began applying for jobs elsewhere and left after the first year. A few years later, a psychologist was hired by PROS, and he too did not last long at the college. The lesson was that, while it was permissible to hire psychologists in other divisions, it was not a good idea.

The second interesting event was that the president removed Wes Tilley as vice president at the end of the first year (and reassigned him as a "Professor of the College"), and the SOBL Dean, Woody Thrombley, became Vice President for Academic Affairs. This changed the tone of the college, making it a little more realistic given the nature of the student body. For example, Wes Tilley refused to let me hire a psychologist with a PhD from the University of Florida because he did not have a good undergraduate education! (The individual had a BA from Glassboro State College, now Rowan University.)

Third, several of us urged the formation of professional programs. With the support of Robert Helsabeck in Sociology, I argued for a Social Work program and recruited the first coordinator of SOWK, Sherman Labovitz. Later in 1977, when the Criminal Justice (CRIM) program was in danger of being abolished, Thrombley (still vice president) went to a CRIM program meeting and told the CRIM faculty that he wanted me to be coordinator. The CRIM program elected me coordinator, and I spent the year of 1977-1978 recruiting a new coordinator (Malcolm Goddard) and imposing more rigorous standards. (For example, the previous coordinator had hired primarily faculty without terminal degrees who had no chance of tenure.) Of the CRIM program then, only Larry Nutt, who was a well-credentialed sociologist, remains.

I wanted the PSYC program to be free of any disciplinary bias. I did not want it to be Skinnerian or Freudian but rather to encompass all perspectives so as to expose students to the breadth of the field. For the first year, the PSYC faculty consisted of myself, Jacquelyn Stanton, and Karen Bogart. For the second year, I hired Marshall Levine, Lewis Leitner, William Miley, and Mark Thomas. Miley was hired as our animal psychologist, while Levine and Thomas rounded out the program.

For the third year, I hired Israel Posner (another laboratory and animal psychologist) and Michael Costaris. Costaris was in counseling and had an EdD degree.

This account may sound, so far, as though I had great power in the program. In fact, this was the case. As I indicated, Thrombley allowed his coordinators a great deal of influence while he was dean and later vice president. The collegiality of the PSYC program was, however, strong. We met most paydays for dinner together at the Pitney Tavern, a practice, which, over the years, became less and less common.

From the beginning, I wanted accountability. I implemented the rule that all PSYC majors had to take either the GRE in psychology or the UGRE (a two-hour version that was available then). I wanted each graduating student to know how they stood with regard to PSYC majors in the U.S. I also insisted that all PSYC faculty evaluate their courses. I used a form brought by Tony Marino from Cornell University. Later this form was used by all faculty in SOBL and, still later, by the college as a whole, only recently being replaced by the IDEA system.

In the early years, the faculty members were members of a school teachers union, and so tenure was granted after three years. The SOBL personnel committee awarded tenure to everyone on the committee, including myself! The college had always said that it would be willing to hire both members of a couple, but it had not actually done so. The president agreed to hire my wife, who had taught as an adjunct for the college, on condition that I step down as coordinator. The result was that the program became more typically "Stocktonian," with the coordinator becoming much less powerful.

CHANGES IN THE PSYCHOLOGY PROGRAM
THE STUDENTS
In the early days of the college, the 1970s, the "hippie" culture was still strong, and the students were a mix of traditional, academically oriented students, primarily from the local area, and those who had come to the Pine Barrens to relax (often helped by recreational drugs). Almost all of the instructors were called by their first names by the students, and faculty and students often became close friends. The range of abilities of the students was, therefore, broad, but many were outstanding. Over the years, the students became much more traditional. Calling instructors by their first names became rare, and the students became more career-oriented. Although the college has documented a rising trend in the SAT scores of entering students, the Psychology

majors continue to span a broad range in abilities, from very poor to outstanding, although the proportion of outstanding students has risen.

THE PSYCHOLOGY FACULTY TODAY
The program has grown in size so that now it is the second largest in majors (10.3 percent, second after BSNS), with sixteen faculty members. As the early faculty retired, beginning in 2005, the program hired PhDs in their twenties, so that now almost half of the Psychology faculty is young. The criteria for hiring, tenuring, and promoting these instructors have also become more traditional, and faculty are expected to have ongoing research programs that result in scholarly publications.

In the 1990s, the Psychology program had become less vibrant, but the addition of the younger members has revitalized the program. The Psychology Club and the honor society (Psi Chi) have become active again, and there is much more involvement of the Psychology faculty in college-wide activities (such as the Stockton Center on Successful Aging and the Living Learning Community project).

THE CURRICULUM
The Psychology program curriculum has always been traditional. The courses offered have been in the standard areas in psychology (such as learning, abnormal psychology, and cognitive psychology). The program has avoided "topics" courses except in the seminars.

There is discontent in the program concerning graduate programs. The program has proposed master's degree and doctorate of psychology programs, both of which have been rejected by the administration, primarily because of cost considerations. These programs have been established at many of the state colleges in New Jersey, and Stockton is lagging behind. Indeed it may be too late, and there is disappointment among the faculty about the lack of support from the administration.

THE PROGRAM AND THE COLLEGE IN NEW JERSEY
When the college opened in 1971, it was innovative. The structure of the college (advising, curriculum, and style) was different from the other state colleges. Inevitably, the college became more traditional and more like the other colleges in the state system. Today, the college is no longer cutting edge. The plans at the beginning to have ancillary facilities on the large campus were scaled down. Although graduate programs have been established, they are far fewer than we expected back in 1971 when we were thinking that we would soon have a medical school! Other colleges in the state system have developed these programs: Engineering at Rowan, a new PsyD program at Kean University, and a proposed medical school, again at Rowan. Indeed, whereas in 1971, Stockton was poised to become the leading state college in southern New Jersey (and perhaps all of New Jersey), easily surpassing Glassboro State, Rowan now threatens to surpass Stockton. This impacts the growth of the Psychology program and the enthusiasm of its faculty.

Recent Trends in Teaching

Untitled Landscape #34 by Wendel White

In a sense, teaching in the very earliest years of the College was "pure" in that there were no assessment tools, no faculty training, no Writing Center, no minors, no graduate studies, and no infrastructure. As Mark Hopkins said, "The best school is a log with a teacher on one end and a student on the other." That is essentially what Stockton was early on.

The support system that the College now proudly offers its teachers took years to produce and the elements of that support system have been responses to wider, cultural changes in higher education.

The writers in this section generally embrace this support though Alan Arcuri regrets what he sees as a shift from student-centered teaching to research interests and teaching that doesn't always place the student firmly "on the other end of the log."

Assessment is, of course, a fact of teaching life these days, and Sonia Gonsalves reviews Stockton's efforts to create acceptable tools for assessing learning while providing support for new teachers with workshops and semester-long training.

Penny Dugan and Frank Cerreto focus on writing and quantitative reasoning training. Stockton was one of the earliest colleges to offer Writing Across the Curriculum and, later, Quantitative Reasoning Across the Disciplines. We can rightfully be proud of these efforts, especially because early models for both skills were minimal though faculty-wide.

Dugan and Tom Kinsella delineate the role of the disciplinary program at the College. (There are other reviews of programmatic history elsewhere in the volume.) Both see their programs as constantly changing, challenged by technology, struggling to acquire resources, and proud of their program's efforts and achievements up to the present time. The same can easily be said about the various interdisciplinary minors at the College; Linda Nelson surveys their growth and impact. The Women's Studies minor, for instance, is one of the largest and most active in the lives of women at Stockton.

There was, of course, almost no technological infrastructure at the start of the College. Stockton was a "node" in a larger, state network as Jim McCarthy notes in his review of the phenomenal growth of technology on campus.

Perhaps the most obvious impact Stockton has had on national higher education is with the concept of "advising as teaching."

Making each faculty a preceptor and defining that role as teaching has, in the years since 1971 when Stockton began the practice, become a national mantra for advising. Peter Hagen, who has been at the center of defining advising this way, thoroughly discusses this history and the effect we have had on the whole nation.

Finally, in the earliest days, transfer students were half of the student population, and we had arranged with all of the state's community colleges to admit anyone they sent us. The result of this agreement has, over the forty-year history, continued to provide Stockton with a generous supply of capable transfer students. As Tom Grites points out, we have been and continue to be the "most transfer-friendly institution in the state."

Cheerleader or Dreamer?—Stockton's Teaching Excellence

Alan F. Arcuri

Stockton's defining characteristic is teaching excellence. Paraphrasing Distinguished Professor William Daly, the College was founded on the rock of providing state college students with an Ivy League education at a bargain basement price. The fifty-five founding faculty members embraced strong elements of populism and idealism. Many in this highly credentialed group were nontraditional academics. They taught freshmen in basic skills courses, experimented with new pedagogies in General Studies and made precepting—academic advising—a central part of their teaching mission.

Stockton was, and is, a special place. This is how I viewed it in 1972. Stockton's *gestalt* appeared to be different and certainly more exciting than that of other state colleges. I sensed a broad and deep commitment to students. The so-called Mayflower faculty, in my mind, began a tradition of putting teaching first, scholarship second. Luck was with the nascent college. Faculty recruitment for much of Stockton's history was a buyer's market. Every year a group of new faculty came from prestigious universities. Recruitment in the Political Science program may be representative of others in the School (formerly Division) of Social and Behavioral Sciences. First, as previously mentioned, there was an usually large pool of able candidates. Second, the interview process had a heavy element of socialization. Did the applicant enjoy teaching? Was he/she committed to assisting students? Was graduate school's gravitational pull toward research and publications unbreakable? Candidates heard storied tales of POLS Program teaching. Some found both our passion and our expectations "unrealistic." In a couple of instances, I think, we lost excellent prospective colleagues because of our messianic zeal. Over the years, painful decisions had to be made in retention decisions. One colleague, for example, was not retained because only six students completed his class out of the thirty-five originally enrolled. Another, if I recall correctly, missed far too many classes. The "no" votes still leave a bad taste in my mouth. However, I would not change my negative vote if similar situations arose again. All faculty members at Stockton cannot be master classroom teachers, but they must put students first, show up to teach, and be accessible and supportive.

By my lights, virtually every program in the College has a core of superior teaching professors. Like successful first-round draft choices in professional football, they make others around them better. Here we are talking about a subtle teaching socialization. Good teaching professors keep office hours and are often seen assisting students. They are role models, having earned their reputations for excellence among students, faculty, and administrators. This spirit of excellent teaching has a salutary ripple effect. In my mind, most of the two hundred-person faculty are excellent teaching professors; some are stars—though I don't want to name names for fear of leaving someone out.

What else accounts for my laudatory comments about colleagues? A smidgen of "hard" data comes from an unpublished study of fifty tenured faculty at Stockton that dealt with providing additional assistance to struggling students. Colleagues were overwhelmingly enthusiastic about teaching. Many expressed a passion for their profession. This enthusiasm mirrored my own feelings.

More convincing evidence of teaching excellence was garnered by my serving on over a dozen division personnel committees and one two-year stint on a college-wide committee. I spent countless hours reading hundreds of files, which included thousands of student evaluations of teaching forms (SETs – Now replaced by IDEA Forms). Colleagues' academic futures were at stake, after all. The aggregate data were telling. The pattern of "soft" responses was particularly helpful. My overall conclusion was that the teaching mission at Stockton was (and is) alive and well. Those faculty who had strong teaching credentials, and high teaching scores, were tenured and promoted. Others were turned down for promotion, and a few were not retained. The evaluation process and the SET/IDEAs are far from perfect, but teaching success in the classroom was—and is—the "gold standard." What always impressed me on these committees was the careful discussion of the importance of teaching.

The most persuasive thread in the commentary on teaching excellence comes from students. Compliments over the years abound. Students seem to thrive on the friendliness and informality of faculty and staff. Interesting, but statistically insignificant, are the views of transfer students from four-year colleges or universities. Over the years I have asked hundreds of students, "What, if anything, is different at Stockton from your home institution?" Virtually every student mentioned "friendliness." Faculty who have an open-door policy are my heroes. It speaks to their special commitment and dedication to students. This situation encourages a healthy learning atmosphere.

Yet, as Stockton grows in size and budgets shrink, some serious slippage has occurred in our commitment to teaching excellence, one-on-one advising, and availability. Very sad. Great teaching never just happens. It takes an enormous commitment, energy, and encouragement. If taken for granted, excellent teaching can flounder. We all can improve, increase our knowledge, "discover" a colleague's teaching strengths, and refine our classroom presentations. Stated differently, successful teaching is a daunting task. It takes tremendous commitment and dedication. We should always keep our eyes on the prize. To that end, I'd like to conclude with a few modest suggestions.

Senior administrators and faculty should champion teaching excellence whenever they speak in a public forum. No audience is too large or too small. The Fall Faculty Conference, for example, provides an ideal opportunity to remind faculty of their quasi-sacred mission. Cheerleading is very important. It acknowledges and re-acknowledges our core mission. There should, in my mind, be a constant drumbeat of why Stockton is different—and better—than other institutions. Different and better because of the dedication to students and teaching excellence.

There should be teaching seminars every semester. The new faculty orientation would be a great place to begin. This would be a part of the socialization process. New faculty fresh out of graduate school should have an opportunity to see and hear a few of Stockton's teaching stars. Senior faculty would also benefit. Faculty talking to colleagues can also have a pep rally effect. Bringing together new and seasoned faculty can make everyone feel good about a marvelous profession and confirm our commitment to our high standard of excellence.

The provost and deans should acknowledge their faculty's teaching excellence. After the IDEA Forms arrive each semester a brief note of thanks would go a long way.

At present there is a deafening silence from senior administrators and senior faculty concerning individuals who do a great job in the classroom. Why not encourage our colleagues? If college leaders showed that they know and care about quality teaching, the teaching spirit would get a much needed boost.

Senior administrators and faculty should also try to resurrect the pivotal, but moribund, precepting function. The Office of Academic Advising is outstanding by any measure. Its staff embraces the central idea that "advising is teaching." However, because of online registration students do not have to visit their preceptors. Many whom I deal with do not even know who that person is. It now takes a titanic struggle to coax students to visit. We can do better. Students will benefit because excellent advising goes far beyond just suggesting courses.

Cheerleader or dreamer? Perhaps a little bit of both. Thirty-eight years in the classroom gives me some license to assert that Stockton has a unique and precious ethos of teaching excellence. It encompasses an accessible and supportive faculty. Indeed, this broad and deep commitment to students defines the College. It is our brand, and it must be nurtured, encouraged, and rewarded.

Teaching Impact

I remember some interesting and gratifying experiences from teaching courses in the history of Ancient Hellenism, from the Homeric Age to the Roman Conquest. A lady of 72 years became so fascinated to the extent that one summer she went to Greece and visited every major area that we had covered in our courses, from Minoan Crete, through the Peloponnesus to Delphi. Upon her return to the States she invited me to hear her lecture to the Ladies Society of her church in Brigantine. Another woman, in her fifties, became so enthusiastic with ancient Hellenism that she decided to attend Greek language courses at the summer Aegean Institute in Poros in order to learn classical Greek and pursue post-graduate studies for a doctorate in the Classics. A young man of 27 took several courses with me as independent studies, in addition to Latin courses with my Latinist colleague, Fred Mench, and he is now a professor of Classics in a Maryland State University.

Demetrios Constantelos

Assessment—Good Teaching Practice

Sonia V. Gonsalves

The assessment of student learning has been and continues to be an important institutional focus. It is now so integrated in the lexicon of higher education discourse that it would be easy for early career faculty in 2010 to assume that this was always the case. In 1980 when I joined the Stockton faculty, the assessment of student learning was informal, voluntary, and sporadic. Since then, we have been moving incrementally towards a more cohesive college-wide approach to assessment.

Stockton was an early responder to the call from the accrediting agencies for more accountability on the part of faculty, programs, and institutions in demonstrating the value that college adds to student learning. Years later we are still refining a systematic campus-wide approach and working to ensure more even progress across programs in implementing assessment plans and in using assessment results to make changes that help students to do better.

Although faculty and programs have always been engaged in testing and measuring student learning, progress, performance, and attitudes, the organized approach of asking questions about what and how course and program learning goals for students are being met and answering these questions empirically by following a logical sampling and measurement plan did not become the norm, in terms of expectations, until the 1990s. Under the direction and leadership of then-President Vera King Farris, the College established the Institute for the Study of College Teaching (ISCT), a faculty initiative, to support research in pedagogy. At about the same time, the scholarship of teaching became more accepted in teaching institutions such as Stockton. Faculty were happy with the broader definition of scholarship as Boyer (1990) described it and with the option to be teacher-scholars as well as disciplinary scholars.

Newly hired faculty were oriented into the emerging culture of assessment through the work of the ISCT with its Faculty Fellows, who served as their mentors. and its technological and research support. Some senior faculty viewed the ISCT with reservations, while most newly hired faculty accepted, used, and welcomed its services. In the same generational split, most junior faculty integrated the assessment of student learning into their instructional plans while a few more senior faculty saw it as an add-on to their existing duties and argued against its value.

The ISCT (started in 1999) was renamed the Institute for Faculty Development (IFD) with a more applied mission to support all faculty development efforts. The establishment of the IFD (started in 2005) provided faculty with an organizational structure and personnel to coordinate the resources related to teaching and scholarship. The IFD continues to offer workshops on teaching that are mandatory for newly hired tenure-track faculty during their first semester of employment and optional for other faculty, including adjuncts. Newly hired tenure-track faculty members teach a reduced load during their first semester, and the release time is devoted to improving instructional strategies and to reading, discussing, and planning for their courses. The workshops are led by senior Stockton faculty, and the participants rate all the workshops on several dimensions of effectiveness. The Director of the IFD chairs the College's assessment committee and coordinates program assessment work for all undergraduate programs. More recently, with the expansion of institutional research, the faculty-led work has been supported by the Office of Institutional Research.

Between 1998 and 2010 the College invested in outside consultants, seminars, and workshops to upgrade the assessment knowledge and skills of faculty, administrators, and students and to disseminate the importance of, and the College's commitment to, assessment of student learning. In 2003 we started a print and electronic assessment newsletter, *Evidence*. We used *Evidence* to share assessment work and the diversity of perspectives and experiences within the institution. During this period and using this medium, we had several public discussions about the results of the National Survey of Student Engagement (NSSE), the Collegiate Learning Assessment (CLA), and the i-Skills tests. These are standardized measures of students' reports of their experiences (NSSE) and actual intellectual performances (CLA and i-Skills) that are reported at the institutional level and for which there are published norms. Here again faculty responded in a variety of ways. Some faculty challenged the sampling, the questions, and the usefulness of these standardized tests. Others took a more responsive approach, discussing the results with students and trying to address deficit findings in whatever ways they could.

In the earliest stages of the College's assessment journey, Provost David Carr gave programs the option to begin their assessment work in whatever way they wanted. Some programs started with faculty-developed affective measures, others with required standardized measures, and still others with measures that were shaped by disciplinary guidelines. Additionally, the provost did not at first require programs to share their findings with the administration. This latitude gave faculty the confidence to explore assessment questions that could uncover deficits without leaving them vulnerable in an administrative evaluation of program effectiveness. Later program coordinators were required to plan, carry out, and report program assessment work to their deans.

For the past ten years the impetus for the assessment of student learning has come from the faculty, through the IFD and the assessment committee members, from the administration under the guiding hand of the deans, and both directly and indirectly from the provost. Our home-grown assessment plans were allowed to emerge under program faculty leadership, and the approach was encouraged and supported by the provost.

The role of the assessment coordinator and IFD director has evolved as the assessment climate has changed. One of the biggest changes was precipitated by the current personnel process that now requires early career faculty to include peer evaluations of their teaching in their personnel files. These observations are a significant part of the work that is done by the IFD director. Additionally, because the student rating system has a more in-depth reporting structure than did the earlier Student Evaluation of Teaching (SET), faculty use the resources of the IFD to decipher, manage, and respond to their Individual Development and Educational Assessment (IDEA) reports. The College now expects more from faculty than it did twenty years ago in the areas of planning for teaching, scholarship, and service as well as in providing evidence to support claims of effectiveness and excellence.

Over the years, I have had several opportunities to describe to the wider academic community many of Stockton's initiatives and programs that support faculty work and assess student learning. Faculty and administrators from colleges across the country have routinely characterized Stockton as innovative and trendsetting. Although many of our own faculty also see the College policies and practices as dynamic and cutting edge, there are many different views as faculty within an institution are often more critical of in-house status than are outsiders.

Assessment of student learning is an important and necessary part of the work that faculty do. As the mix of faculty generations changes to reflect a more recently minted group of instructors, the attitudes toward assessment will likely change to be more in line with the theory and the philosophy. It is impossible to overdo assessment; it is an important part of good teaching. We cannot overdo good teaching practice.

History with Passion

During the summer of 2010, I had a life-changing opportunity thanks to the incredible people who support the ICHS [Interdisciplinary Center for Hellenic Studies] at Stockton.

As I flew to Istanbul, Turkey, I had a few things on my mind: will I deliver my presentation right? What if I don't like this country, and this trip makes me want to drop my interest in my major?

No worries on both accounts—Turkey is without doubt the most fascinating country I have been to and the experiences I had have been some of the most fulfilling to date.

For a history major passionate about Middle Eastern studies, I cannot tell you how exciting it is to present a paper in front of some of the most brilliant Anatolian history scholars on the planet! I am indebted and incredibly thankful to ARHU and the ICHS for allowing me this opportunity.

Our trip would also not have been complete without the theatre students who performed in [Pam Hendrick's and Tom Papademetriou's] Stones from God. I was proud of my new friends and was glad to have had the chance to take on a new country with them—together we made Turkey a truly unforgettable experience.

Lillian Hussong, 2012

Michael Frank teaching a stats class using one of the original, full-length, metal blackboards (1977)

The Quantitative Reasoning Across the Disciplines (QUAD) Program

Frank A. Cerreto

Students appear to have a math switch. Consider Maria, who, in her precalculus class, is ready to engage with mathematical ideas and communicate mathematically. Later that day, in her business class, she does not associate the future value problem she is now solving with the lecture on exponential functions she had a few hours earlier in her math class. Why? Her math switch is turned off. How do we help students keep their math switches on so that they can apply the mathematics they learn to other subjects? During the late 1980s, a series of reports confirmed that Maria's story is a common one by documenting the poor performance of American students in applying mathematical principles to realistic situations. In the early 1990s, Stockton decided to address this problem.

In 1993, President Vera Farris established four divisional (now called school) task forces and a central task force whose mission was to develop a proposal for a college-wide mathematics program and whose tasks included the following:
• Reviewing mathematics requirements for all majors
• Surveying faculty members, alumni, and local employers to determine what mathematical skills and understandings were needed in various fields
• Studying approaches taken at other institutions
• Determining a course-labeling system and a graduation requirement that would advertise the new program and communicate its importance to students and faculty
• Piloting new courses designed to integrate mathematical principles and applications

- Creating a faculty development program that would provide a forum for discussing the teaching and learning of mathematics
- Developing an assessment plan

After a two-year planning period, the Faculty Assembly, by a nearly unanimous vote and with enthusiastic support from the Student Senate, approved a proposal to implement the Quantitative Reasoning Across the Disciplines (QUAD) program in fall 1995.

The general goals of the QUAD program include:
- Increased numeracy of graduates
- Improved learning and teaching of quantitative reasoning, informed by relevant research
- Increased student and faculty awareness of the importance of quantitative reasoning throughout the disciplines

Associated with these goals was a clear set of objectives for students, faculty, the curriculum, and research.

The architects of the QUAD program recognized and exploited the mutually reinforcing nature of the relationship between mathematics and other disciplines. Not only can a mathematical perspective increase one's understanding of topics in other disciplines, but problem situations in other disciplines can provide concrete grounding for and appreciation of the utility of mathematical concepts.

Based on this theoretical foundation, we distinguish between two types of quantitative courses. In a Q1 (quantitative-reasoning-intensive) course, mathematical thinking is the primary focus, the majority of class time is spent on mathematical thinking, and instructors are encouraged to emphasize applications of mathematical principles and tools to a variety of other subjects. In a Q2 (quantitative-reasoning-across-the-disciplines) course, while the primary focus is on disciplinary or interdisciplinary content outside of mathematics, the instructor agrees to portray mathematics as a vital tool for understanding this content. Q1 courses include not only traditional program course offerings in mathematics and statistics but also a variety of general education courses designed for the nonspecialist. Q2 courses can be found throughout Stockton's curriculum in program and general education courses.

Although other colleges and universities implemented mathematics-across-the-curriculum initiatives around the most recent turn of the century, Stockton's approach remains distinctive in many ways, some of which relate to special characteristics of our College.

In comparing Stockton's QUAD program to similar initiatives at other institutions, the feature that stands out most is the breadth of infusion of quantitative reasoning throughout our curriculum. At most colleges, efforts at integrating mathematics often consist of a small set of special courses on the applications of mathematics to one or several other disciplines, usually taught by mathematicians. Alternatively, at some colleges and universities, small teams of faculty members develop interdisciplinary courses combining mathematics content with, for example, other content in the natural sciences. By contrast, at Stockton, Q-designated courses can be found in every school and in almost every program of the College. During the first academic year of the QUAD program, 134 Q1 course sections (including forty-two distinct courses) and 157 Q2 course sections (including seventy-eight distinct courses) were offered. By June 2010, a total of seventy-three different Q1 courses and 217 different Q2 courses had been developed.

This shared commitment to and responsibility for quantitative-reasoning instruction is a function of four main factors: broad participation of faculty members throughout the College in the development of the program, Stockton's flexible curricular structure in general education, its tradition of involvement with college-wide programs, and its firm commitment to faculty development. Almost fifty faculty members, representing all academic divisions, were actively involved in an open and flexible planning process. The collective ownership of the resulting proposal almost assured its Faculty Assembly approval and broad-based faculty support.

Unlike many other institutions, Stockton provides students (and faculty) with a significant degree of flexibility with regard to the general education curriculum. As a result, faculty members who wish to infuse quantitative reasoning into existing or new courses can rely on a supportive review process.

Stockton, since its founding, has fostered a series of college-wide academic initiatives, including the General Studies, Basic Studies, and Writing programs, within a culture of interdisciplinary collaboration. Faculty members from all disciplines are expected to contribute to college-wide programs. Willingness and ability to teach in such programs are considerations upon hiring and in reappointment, tenure, and promotion decisions.

With internal support and external grants from the National Science Foundation and the American Council of Learned Societies, QUAD leaders developed summer institutes and seminars offered during the academic year for those who were interested in exploring mathematical connections to other disciplines. The QUAD Summer Institute continues to provide a supportive forum for learning about the program, designing courses, developing curricular materials, and discussing the teaching and learning of quantitative skills and understandings in context. In addition, Stockton has hosted three well-attended regional conferences on quantitative reasoning across the disciplines.

The QUAD movement has not been without obstacles, however. For example, during the planning stages, there was serious debate over the number of Q-designated courses that would be required for graduation, with some faculty members arguing for a two-course requirement and others a four-course requirement. Through patient discussions with a wide array of interested faculty members, the task forces fashioned a compromise three-course requirement.

Over its brief history, the QUAD program has evolved. As stated earlier, new Q-designated courses continue to be added to the curriculum. Currently, the program is undergoing a large-scale assessment project in order to determine the extent to which we are achieving our stated objectives. Based on these findings, we will recommend changes.

The QUAD program at Stockton serves as a model of institutional reform and a reminder that enduring change requires a kernel of "true believers," broad-based faculty support, a willingness to compromise, and an appreciation of the need for ongoing reflection and adjustment. These principles should guide future efforts. One that is on the horizon targets the special academic needs of first-year students. A small working group composed of faculty and administrators is developing a proposal for a First-year Studies program that will enhance the academic experience of entering Stockton students. Given our record of college-wide initiatives, I am pleased to be working with this group and optimistic that our efforts will result in another successful, innovative response to an educational challenge.

Turning on the Math Switch

I came to Stockton from Buena High School in 1997, and I wanted to major in Biochemistry/Molecular Biology. I was really lucky, though, because I had a chance to take a class in Math with Charlie Wu. I had been pretty decent in Math at Buena, but I hadn't passed AP Calculus, and I hadn't intended to carry on with it at Stockton. But Professor Wu was a very different kind of professor. He was funny and engaging in the classroom like many teachers. But what made him really different was that his door was never closed, and there would always be five to ten students who would come to his office to work at his table or even to sit on the floor in the corridor. And he would be there until about 10 at night, always ready to help his students. Now that I am a forensic scientist working for the New Jersey State Police, I feel really fortunate to have had Professor Wu. I went on to get a minor in Math, and I would never have done this without him inspiring me. The funny thing is that people are always talking about girls and women having Math phobias; but because of Charlie Wu many female students overcame their Math fears and learned a love for Math just like I did.

MaryAnn Catto (Kahoe), 2001

Planting a Program with Deep Roots and Good Growth—Writing at Stockton

Penelope Dugan

In assembling this overview of writing instruction at Stockton, I looked at the College *Handbook*s and *Bulletins* going back to 1971, read interoffice memoranda between faculty and college administrators, reviewed my own reports to the faculty and administration from 1982 through 1987 when I was the founding Director of the Comprehensive Writing program and from 2002 to 2006 when I coordinated the Writing program, and talked with former and current faculty colleagues.

Contradictions and inconsistencies abound in what was expected of student writing and what assistance the students were given. In the 1971-1972 *Bulletin*, the word "writing" appears in a course title once; students are told the Literature program offers creative writing seminars. The 1971-1972 *Handbook* tells students that a number of degree programs will require students "to stand for comprehensive examinations in the final week of the fall term of the academic years in which the students expect degrees. . . . Comprehensive exams will not ordinarily exceed sixteen hours." It further states that a number of programs will require a senior thesis instead of comprehensive exams.

In January 1972, President Richard Bjork writes to Academic Vice President Wes Tilley, "Your memo indicates that we are now prepared to admit that regular coursework, conducted by regular faculty cannot be relied on to assist in the development of such skills as reading, writing, math, etc. especially if student deficiencies are pronounced. . . . [T]he early hope that 'remedial work' could effectively be done within the framework of the regular coursework, without special courses, has not been realized." He directs Tilley to organize the "skills" programs "at once" under the Dean of Academic Development or the Dean of Experimental Studies. The 1972-1973 *Bulletin* lists no formal writing courses other than Creative Writing. The Skills Acquisition and Development Center makes its first appearance. It does have a reading/writing specialist, Stephen Phelps, but it seems from the Bulletin description that students went there to learn Fortran, which is defined as a basic skill. Dean of Academic Development Gordon Davies writes in Academic Working Paper 26 (3/27/72) about students being able "to acquire a needed skill as soon as the need is perceived." He estimates a student can learn Fortran in two weeks and then proceed with the study of psychology, which was interrupted by the perceived need to know Fortran. Davies and Woody Thrombley, the next academic vice president, have a memo exchange in August and September 1972 about the idea of credit for skills courses. Davies suggests the acronym SADC but doesn't want to use it or give credits for "language skill" courses. He writes, "I have been committed to

offering courses and individual study which attack language skill problems through valid academic subject matter in such areas as psychology, history and the other disciplines."

In November 1974, Paul Elliott of the Office of Academic Development writes to Woody Thrombley and Dean Bob Helsabeck about the reorganization of skills development within General Studies. He speaks of the growing concern on the part of the faculty, as expressed through the institutional self-study committees, about the adequacy of students' basic skills both for entering and graduating from Stockton. He suggests the College could continue to make remediation an option for the individual student, with a few credit courses a semester and noncredit work in the Skills Center, or it could establish a skills competency for either admittance to a program or for graduation. He cautions that requiring competency would be very costly and notes that because "it appears that Stockton has large numbers of students with deficiencies, we might want to consider setting more astringent admissions standards."

In March 1975, Woody Thrombley puts out a call for a Skills Development Planning Committee to be chaired by Assistant Professor Dave Filimon of the LITT/LANG program. Thrombley writes, "It has become increasingly clear that Stockton, like most American colleges and universities, has not been paying sufficient attention to the teaching of basic reading, writing, and mathematical skills." He proposes a "modest but carefully planned skills program next fall," which, through mandatory testing, would identify those seriously deficient whom he would remediate through the Skills Center, excepting those who can be "most economically served through classroom instruction."

In an undated proposal, the Task Force on Verbal Skill Courses, Group 4-A of the Skills Development Task Force, recommends the creation of Types A, B, and C writing courses. All entering students scoring below 400 on the verbal SAT would be strongly advised to take Type A, basic writing courses; students scoring between 400 and 500 would be urged to take a Type B, "intermediate formal writing courses designed to further develop already existing basic skills," or Type C, "more advanced writing courses which emphasize writing in the context of subject matter courses." The criteria for Type B courses were that the instructor be able to meet with colleagues teaching similar courses, that enrollment not exceed twenty students a class, that the focus of instruction would be only expository writing, and that proficiency was to be evaluated at the end of the term. Type C courses had a subject orientation, were to have a minimum of six writing assignments, including a major paper, and would be evaluated on form as well as content.

The 1975-1976 *Bulletin* lists all three types of courses. The sole Type A course is one section of GM 2110, College Writing Skills; Type B courses, nine in all, are taught by full-time tenured or tenure-track faculty and are offered in GD, GM, and GT categories. Type C courses, four, are offered by full-time faculty in the GT category. Clearly, there were not enough Type A or Type B courses for students having a verbal SAT below 500 to be "strongly advised" or "urged" into. The Type A, B, and C designations disappeared by the 1976-1978 *Bulletin*.

Fall 1976 marked the beginning of the BASK program and the beginning of a competency requirement in writing. Three hundred students, one third of the entering class, were placed in fifteen sections of BASK 2101, College Writing and Reading, on the basis of their placement essays (read holistically by the core and rotating faculty in the BASK program as trained by first BASK Coordinator and Professor of Literature Ken Tompkins) and their scores on the standardized Nelson Denny Reading Comprehension Test. These 300 students were not given the option of achieving competency when they perceived the need; they were not strongly advised or urged to take BASK 2101. They were required to take it and pass it or face dismissal from the College. BASK courses each offered four credits toward graduation, like any other course at the College.

Much was expected of BASK students and their teachers. Nine of the fifteen sections of College Writing and Reading were taught by "core" writing faculty whose primary teaching obligation was in the BASK program. The remaining six sections were taught by "rotating" faculty from across the College, recruited for their reputations as good teachers and their willingness to participate in six days of faculty development divided between the month of June and the month of August. Teaching a BASK course partially fulfilled their obligation to teach one or two General Studies courses a year.

January 1978 saw the beginning of Writing Across the Curriculum (WAC) at Stockton. Core BASK faculty member Christopher Burnham had been selected to participate in the National Endowment for the Humanities seminar on that topic conducted by Professor Robert Parker of Rutgers University in the summer of 1977. Burnham invited Parker to give three days of workshops for the Stockton faculty during the winter intersession. The ground was prepared for Parker's visit by our institutional history. The idea of WAC did not seem strange to a faculty used to teaching outside their disciplinary boundaries in their General Studies courses, accustomed to the practice of nonwriting teachers teaching BASK writing, and familiar with the position papers of Wes Tilley and others on teaching academic skills within the context of content area courses. The Type C courses of 1975 were proto writing-across-the-curriculum courses. The ground was ready and the seedlings

carefully tended. The growth of WAC was deliberately slow and incremental. A system of model WAC courses was put in place, so participating faculty could act as exemplars and mentors for other faculty. By 1980-1981, nineteen faculty members from five disciplinary divisions, eleven percent of the total faculty, taught twenty-five WAC courses (twelve program courses, thirteen General Studies courses) with a capacity of 750 students.

Chris Burnham, the first Director of Writing, left Stockton in July 1981. He was succeeded by Professor of Literature Phil Klukoff, who was directed by Academic Vice President Phil Nanzetta to generate a graduation requirement in writing. Klukoff chaired a Writing Task Force composed of two representatives from each division: Aida Lalalian and Royce Burton from ARHU; Lee Hoxter and Jan Colijn from SOBL; Jon Griffiths and Don Plank from NAMS; Alex Don and Len Wollack from PROS; Mimi Schwartz and me from GENS. (Burton, Colijn, Plank, and Wollack were elected divisional chairpersons following the dean to chair reorganization of 1981.) The proposal from the task force drafted by Mimi Schwartz, revised and represented by Jon Griffiths and me, built on the twin foundations of BASK and WAC and their traditions of cross-college faculty participation, melding them into a Comprehensive Writing program.

The proposal passed the Faculty Assembly in December 1981 and was to go into effect for students matriculating in fall 1983. 1982-1983 was the pilot year. I became Director of Writing in May 1982 to implement the proposal.

The graduation requirement in writing would consist of three writing-designated courses (W1 stood for a writing course, W2 for a writing-across-the-curriculum course), two to be taken before the Junior Writing Test and one after it. I conceived the Junior Writing Test as a rite of passage. Tribal elders would meet to assess writing proficiency; all candidates would do the same thing after the test, i.e., take another writing course, either W1 or W2 depending on their level of proficiency. The purpose of the test was community building around writing—faculty from across the College meeting each semester to read student writing and discuss it, students striving to excel in their efforts to join the tribe.

The first task was to increase faculty recruitment and training to generate the number of writing courses needed. In the summers of 1982, 1983, and 1984 Mimi Schwartz and I led intensive two-week Faculty Writing Institutes based on the theme, Teacher as Writer/Writer as Teacher. Forty-four faculty members participated over that three-year period; they became the exemplars and mentors for other faculty. 1982-1983 was a year of rapid expansion. Whereas in 1981-1982, thirty-six faculty members, twenty-one percent of the total, offered fifty-eight WAC courses, in 1982-1983, seventy-four faculty, forty-four percent, offered 136 WAC courses. By 1983-1984, when the requirement went into effect, eighty-five faculty members, fifty percent, offered 203 WAC courses. Over the three years, capacity went from 1,885 to 3,597 to 5,130 seats in WAC courses. Through college-wide faculty commitment, we generated the classes to fulfill the requirement. In 1984, our Comprehensive Writing program was given the G. Theodore Mitau Award for Innovation and Change in Higher Education.

I stress the early history of writing at Stockton to demonstrate how integral and congruent writing at Stockton is to our founding ethos and development. The average life of a college-wide WAC-based writing program is three years. Our program, with few changes, has persisted for twenty-seven years. It was not built with external money but with the sweat of a faculty sharing a curricular vision and refusing to pass responsibility or blame onto others. Our current Writing Program Coordinator, Emari DiGiorgio, is a product of the Stockton Writing program. The trees from the original seedlings send off new seeds.

Penelope Dugan at registration (c. 1975)

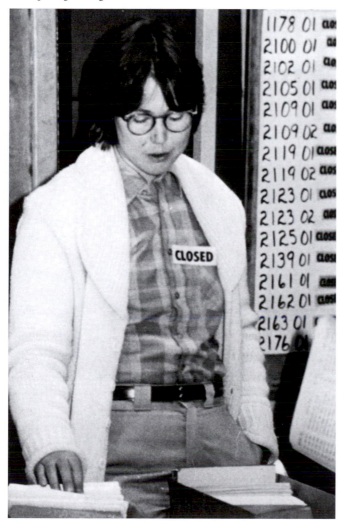

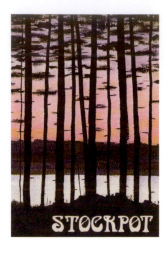   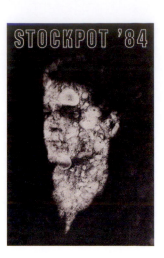

Born (and Reborn) Within the Currents of Academia—The Shifting Literature Curriculum

Thomas Kinsella

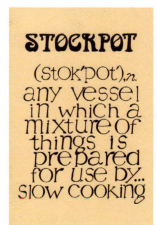

Sometime in early 1987 Ken Tompkins was called a whore by a colleague in the Literature program (LITT). Ken ignored the insult and pushed forward an innovative curriculum, the reason for the taunt in the first place. This marked the opening of a period of cooperation during which the faculty pursued particularly well-focused and well-articulated academic goals. For a few years in the late 1980s and early 1990s, the LITT program asserted that it could prepare students for specific job markets. To prove it, tracks were offered in a range of literary areas, each with a more or less marketable end in view. It was a remarkable achievement for a program in the humanities, and one that has not been equaled since. It serves to remind us that excellence can be achieved despite the competing demands of the academic environment. Those demands, and the ways they impact curricular decisions, are the focus of this brief essay.

The original Literature curriculum wasn't much of a curriculum at all. The fathers of the program (the first cohort of LITT professors was male) had a one-time problem: where to start. Instead of following traditional, well-delineated models for English departments, they voiced their support for student choice: "The Literature curriculum by its nature makes it possible for a variety of students to make a variety of choices, each of which is unique, all of which are coherent" (1972-1973 *Bulletin*). It is easy to believe that unique choices were made; it is

less clear that "coherence" was a sure bet.

Within three years, the Language program (LANG) had merged with LITT. The stated reason was to create a program that would deal "with the literary and linguistic manifestations of the human experience of our own and other cultures" (1973-1974 *Bulletin*). The two-track curriculum that was adopted, although an obvious choice, was unsatisfactory. In theory, both sides of the program benefitted from the merger. Certainly, a more robust range of literature courses was offered. The Language faculty, however, were caught in a long-standing bind. For the first twenty years of their existence, they staffed each non-English language with one to 1.5 faculty members, not enough to attract numbers of majors to language study. The situation became a point of contention in the relationship between program and administration. In order to fully develop languages and reach larger numbers of students, more faculty were needed, but additional resources would not be allocated given the current small number of majors.

A recurring demand upon the curriculum is first seen here: student numbers drove faculty positions. Numbers were the bottom line, and during the first twenty years, the program did not have numbers. Coordinator reports during the early 1980s read like exercises in quantitative reasoning as they presented figures for "aggregate load enrollment and accounting," "enrollments per FTE faculty," "enrollments/quota," and "percent SCH quota met." Their clear goal is proof of numerical adequacy. With enrollments low and flat, the program sought to justify its existence by demonstrating that it really *did* teach an adequate share of students. Curricular design took a back seat to the need to fill seats.

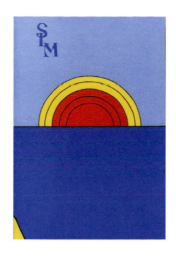 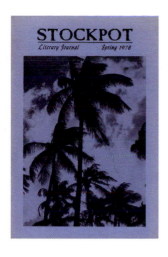 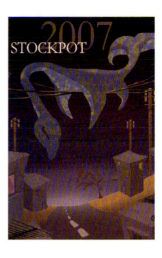 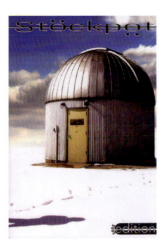

Another point of curricular pressure derived from a surprising source. For many years LITT/LANG had difficulty finding a comfortable fit between General Studies and program courses. Early on, some faculty offered individual courses within General Studies, but program-approved courses such as Introduction to Literature (GD 2101) and later Experience of Literature (GAH 1150) were the primary contributions. In the late 1970s, Expository Writing, a LANG course offered in multiple sections, was allowed to stand for credit in General Studies. In 1982, the program recast a significant portion of its lower-level courses as GAH courses, including its two-semester Literary Traditions course, its two-semester surveys in British and American literature, and first-year language and linguistic courses. This was done "to make literature and language courses, which at most other institutions are considered fundamental to students' general education, more accessible to the Stockton community" (1981-1982 CR). In the following year, the program reversed itself, noting that program offerings were weakened by the move. The line between program, service, and general education courses was blurry. The fact that service courses might be created within the program or in General Studies seemed to muddle the situation even further. For the first decade of its existence at least, LITT/LANG demonstrated an uncertain attitude toward General Studies, viewing it as another demand that had to be met but failing to understand the juncture between curricular demands of the program and of the college.

Not surprisingly, faculty turnover often had an impact on curricular decisions. In 1985-1986, the unexpected absence of the program's Americanist, coupled with the imminent departure of Gerry Enscoe and Phil Klukoff, two founding members of the program, postponed the implementation of one new curriculum and paved the way for a second. The inability of the program to retain qualified professors in the Communications program in the early 1990s and a qualified professor of new media studies in the first decade of the twenty-first century also led to dramatic changes in the curriculum.

Over the last twenty years, however, the largest impact upon the curriculum derived from enrollment spikes. The first occurred in the late 1980s and was fueled by enrollment in the Communications track. A direct result was the creation of Communications Studies as a free-standing program. When LITT/LANG split into two programs in the late 1990s, enrollment spiked again within Literature. The response was an efficient curriculum that stressed skills rather than coverage. The final enrollment spike (so far) was precipitated by the implementation of No Child Left Behind. Between 2003 and 2007, the number of majors in Literature nearly doubled, reaching an all-time high. During this influx, the program changed in ways that it would not have done in more stable times. Selected faculty stopped teaching courses in General Studies in order to offer adequate numbers of program courses. Three tracks were collapsed into one, maximizing efficiency by cutting the range of offerings. A four-semester foreign language component was added, at least in part to quell rising numbers. Unable to staff multiple sections, the program reluctantly abandoned Literary Methodologies, a core course that emphasized close reading. Perhaps the most significant change was the re-tasking of a line from New Media Studies to Creative Writing. Low enrollment in one track balanced against high enrollment in another induced the program faculty, not the administration, to make hard decisions based on numbers.

As the program enters its fifth decade, with new faculty and new demands, it will surely once again review its curriculum, and it will do so within the varied pressures of the academic environment. There will not be enough money or enough space to assure low faculty-to-student ratios. If numbers of majors drop, there will be pressure to make them grow; if numbers grow, faculty resources will increase slowly and only in response to dramatic increases. There will be pressures deriving from faculty politics, faculty turnover, administrative initiatives, and just plain chance. Nevertheless, program faculty need to keep in mind the most important question—the question that Ken Tompkins and his colleagues attempted to answer in 1987. How will courses taken at Stockton help graduates to live productive lives? When the program has once again thoughtfully addressed this question, it will build for the future.

Changing Lives—The Interdisciplinary Minors

Linda Williamson Nelson

Stockton's mission has always emphasized a commitment to a liberal arts education, one that assures students will graduate with concentrated study within a field of their choice, as well as significant exposure to courses outside of their majors. One consequence of this exposure is that students understand that knowledge is often constructed at points where disciplines intersect and not solely within the discrete theoretical boundaries of individual fields of knowledge. The five subdivisions of the General Studies curriculum, for example, are especially designed to insure that this breadth is part of every student's experience. Specific skills as well as social and historical issues are addressed within the range of the General Studies categories: GEN (General Interdisciplinary Skills and Topics); GAH (General Arts and Humanities); GSS (General Social Sciences); GNM (General Natural Sciences and Mathematics); and GIS (General Integration and Synthesis). Integral to this interdisciplinary focus is the expectation that faculty can and should teach outside areas of their specialization when they have the expertise and the passion to do so.

While not always interdisciplinary, courses that fulfill the requirements of the minors also reflect the institution's commitment to graduate its students with skills and competencies beyond those directly related to employment or further study. Minors may be the primary area where students are exposed to cultural practices and beliefs that depart significantly from what students have learned in their own enculturation. While this is not exclusive to the minors, those who pursue a minor often have had the opportunity to interrogate class, gender, and racial hegemonies that can obscure a complex understanding of challenges inherent in a multicultural society. In order to fulfill the requirements of a minor, students must complete twenty credits, or five courses, formally approved as core or cognates.

Since the inception of the first minor in the early 1980s, the list, as noted below, has grown continuously in response to both student and faculty interest and currently includes courses within one specific discipline as well as others more interdisciplinary in scope:
• Africana Studies
• Gerontology
• Holocaust and Genocide
• Holistic Health
• Jewish Studies
• Latin American/Caribbean Studies
• Women's and Gender and Sexuality Studies
• Writing Minor

Depending on the extent to which their content is specific to the minor, courses are designated as core or cognate. Each minor concludes with a capstone course in which students generally complete a significant research project. Completion of a minor is then noted on the student's degree. While faculty members develop particular courses to augment the minor, many core and cognate courses come from various disciplines, associated with a particular division within the college. For example, the courses African American Women Writers and The Contemporary African American Novel are both Literature program courses, in the Schools of Arts and Humanities, but they also qualify as core courses for the Africana Studies minor. A cognate would be the GSS course Dealing with Diversity, which, in part, treats issues related to people of African descent but is also concerned with a range of other social locations. Because courses in the minor are drawn from the wider curriculum, a course taken to meet the requirements of a minor may also fulfill a student's major study or General Studies requirements.

A distinct characteristic of the minors is the special commitment of the faculty who teach these courses. In nearly all cases, a minor course of study is devised by instructors who believe that a critical examination of the history, the culture, and the social challenges faced by a specific group of people should be a part of Stockton's curriculum. Faculty teaching in the Holocaust and Genocide minor, for example, help students to comprehend the way an atrocity such as the Holocaust could be fueled by a theory of racial inferiority and the presumed legitimacy of eradicating an entire group of people. Students report a profound personal change provoked by such study and a heightened sensitivity to the ongoing threat of genocides the world over.

Similarly, as a consequence of their work in Women's, Gender and Sexuality Studies, students are able to critically examine the way heterosexual and male hegemonies have marginalized other identities. Their studies have inspired original research, presented at regional and national conferences as well as activism here and abroad. One Middle Eastern student's independent study of feminist initiatives in her native country inspired her own work with women's groups on her return home. Almost from their inception, courses within the minors have directed students toward further study and praxis, occasionally garnering international as well as well as domestic acclaim. Most notably, a young woman named Naomi Natale who was preparing to work with orphaned children in Africa took the Africana Studies course, The Literature and Culture of South Africa. While her classmates prepared for a South African Study Tour, she prepared to spend time in an orphanage in Kenya. In her own words, "That South African literature course changed my life." After graduation, she went on to establish a nonprofit organization to benefit children in need worldwide. She earned a senior research fellowship, spoke to ambassadors at the United Nations, and launched two acclaimed art installation projects. Her most recent, "One Million Bones," is designed to call attention to genocides across the globe. Also noteworthy are the numbers of students who pursue the Writing minor and then distinguish themselves as poets or essayists; graduates of this minor have moved on to earn the MFA and professorships as they continue to write and publish.

These minors have been sustained and augmented by the personal commitment of a dedicated faculty. In addition to their academic credentials, many bring lived experience and embodied knowledge to these particular courses. While this can benefit students, these personal affiliations can be a unique challenge to the instructor. The words of a gay or lesbian, an African American or a Jewish instructor, for example, are at times dismissed as self-serving. It might take weeks before students take on the difficult intellectual work of questioning their deeply embedded assumptions. Notwithstanding these challenges, over the last three decades faculty efforts have resulted in increasing numbers of students choosing minors that are not directly related to their own ethnic or gender identity and cultural experience. In this way, the minors have become focal points for the timely work of understanding difference, encouraging inclusion while fostering dynamic curricular innovations and intellectual exchange.

Art & Architecture: New Jersey Style

Around 2002 I got an idea that creating a website devoted to the artists and architecture of New Jersey, both historical and contemporary, would be an interesting project for a class. I'd already started researching New Jersey art and architecture with the idea of teaching a general studies course based on the material – basically an introduction to American art using New Jersey examples. This is the kind of personalized yet interdisciplinary approach to a topic Stockton encourages in its general studies courses. I thought that the students could research and write essays for the website, and that eventually I'd be able to teach the class using the images on the site.

Colleagues were immensely helpful. Wendel White, who teaches photography in the Visual Arts Program, recommended that I ask Phil Polsinelli to design the site. Phil is a former student of Wendel's who works at the ETTC. He's also a musician and former music producer whose new career as computer guru gives him exactly the right skills to create the kind of website I wanted. As we sat together working on the design – both the aesthetics of the website and the format the information would take – Phil would ask me, "Are you feelin' it?" Apparently that's music-speak for "Is it working? Does it look right to you?" The result of our collaboration, "Art & Architecture of New Jersey" (www.artofnewjersey.net), went live in 2003.

Most contemporary artists have been willing to let me use their artwork free of charge. Museums, the more famous artists, and artists' estates often require a fee, however, and sometimes the fee is as high as several hundred dollars. Beth Olsen and the Grants Office were extremely helpful at this point, making suggestions on grant proposals and shepherding outside applications through the application process. Two grants – one from Stockton, one from the New Jersey Historical Commission – allowed me to purchase most of the expensive illustrations I wanted.

Art & Architecture of New Jersey now has more than one thousand pages, each dedicated to an artist, a building, or a film with a connection to the Garden State. The artists include painters, sculptors, photographers, printmakers, draftsmen, and artists making "new forms" of art like computer generated imagery, installations, and performance art.

The course and website have been a collaborative enterprise, with students choosing their own subjects and often suggesting new ones. Colleagues among the faculty and staff of the college have also suggested artists to include; Alex Marino, director of the Carnegie Library facility, jokes that if he gives me any more ideas he'll have to start charging a finder's fee.

The students taking the class have often been excited to have their research "published" on the Internet. Their essays have varied widely, both in the quality of the research and writing, and in the types of subjects. One semester I assigned gravestone carvings, a particular interest of mine, and the students really seemed to enjoy their research; it wasn't a topic most had considered before. We had to flip a coin to decide who would write about the most unusual examples: the life-size Mercedes Benz in Linden, for example, or the Three Stooges gravestone in Metuchen. One student voluntarily photographed the pet cemetery in Linwood. Over the years, a number of students have gone above and beyond their assignments by taking photographs of buildings, gravestones, and public sculpture they thought I should include on the website.

In recent years I've taught my "Art of New Jersey" class using the website instead of 35 mm or PowerPoint slides, which has allowed me to teach it in different locations – the Carnegie Center in Atlantic City and St. Joseph's High School in Hammonton, for example. With only an Internet connection and a projector, the students and I take a virtual tour of art and architecture in the Garden State.

Kate Ogden

The Information Age at Stockton

James McCarthy

The use of technology, especially computing technology, has dramatically changed over Stockton's first forty years. The information age began, as did Stockton, near the last quarter of the twentieth century. During this period, many colleges and universities transformed technology and were transformed by technology. In liberal arts institutions, where teaching is paramount, innovative technology-based teaching methods emerged and materially transformed the art of teaching. Some institutions quickly and eagerly adopted emerging technology-based teaching methods, while others were cautious or reluctant.

In consideration of the full forty years of our history and comparing Stockton with peer institutions, it is fair to characterize Stockton overall as an early adopter of technology. Stockton was an early participant in the building and evolution of the various computer networks that eventually combined to form the Internet. Additionally, from inception to the current day Stockton's faculty have taught about and with technology. In the beginning, however, it didn't appear the College would necessarily have the mettle for early adoption. On May 8, 1972 the College's job description for a Director of Computer Services and Information included the following admonishment, "the Director should be able to recommend those directions which best support the college's educational and administrative programs and not his professional empire." At the time, the director reported to the Dean of Education Services. Sensibly, the position of director was soon realigned to report directly to Vice President of Educational Services, James Judy, where the department could garner executive support and access to budget and thereby better assist in delivering a liberal arts education in a contemporary fashion and also automate administrative operations.

It is somewhat tempting to write about the technology that was part of our history and wax nostalgically about bits and bytes, chips and CPU cycles. However, such things won't likely capture the interest of many readers, and much of yesterday's technical jargon (e.g., core, MIPS, Hollerith code, Winchesters) has become irrelevant and redacted from today's lexicon.

More pertinent than bits, bytes, and the like was (and remains) the actual use of technology. Early and innovative academic use of technology is evident below in the titles of select courses from 1970-1975. These course titles unveil early faculty perspectives and student experiences with technology. These examples also show wide-ranging attention to technology and related issues from across the curriculum:

- Computer Application in Health Care
- Computer Assisted Instruction
- Computer Managed Instruction
- Computer Methods For Behavioral Science
- Data Communications
- Electronic Music
- Information Science
- Technology and the Human Reply
- Technology and Human Values
- Man-Machine Communications
- Operations Research, Programming
- Technology as a Religion
- Readings in Technology and Society
- Urban/Rural Information Systems

The early and innovative use of technology at Stockton emanated from all quarters of the college. Faculty in the Arts and Humanities seem to have recognized early on the ways in which technology would revolutionize the creation, distribution, and presentation of images and the written word. Faculty in the Natural Sciences, Social and Behavioral Sciences, Mathematics, and Professional Studies infused number-crunching and data-analysis technology into their lectures and research. There has never been a shortage of faculty at Stockton who were eager to develop technology-based teaching and learning methods.

Below are examples showing early and innovative teaching about technology and use of technology in teaching:

- In the 1970s, well before the term "geographic information system" was coined, Stockton's students were digitizing spatial data and generating maps using computers. The maps were printed using character printers that created gray-scale images by overstriking alphabetic characters. Today, Stockton has a computer lab devoted to geographic information processing and spatial analysis.
- In the 1980s, over a decade before teaching and learning systems became commonplace on college campuses, a substantial portion of Stockton's faculty had begun to use electronic conferencing systems to engage students outside of the classroom. The use of technology to support face-to-face lectures continues to be a common practice at Stockton. Today, a third of Stockton's face-to-face lecture courses utilize computer-based teaching and learning tools to augment lectures and engage students outside of the classroom.
- In 1994 Stockton designed and built its first electronic classroom, which featured a podium, projector, document camera, and computer with access to cable TV, satellite feeds, the In-

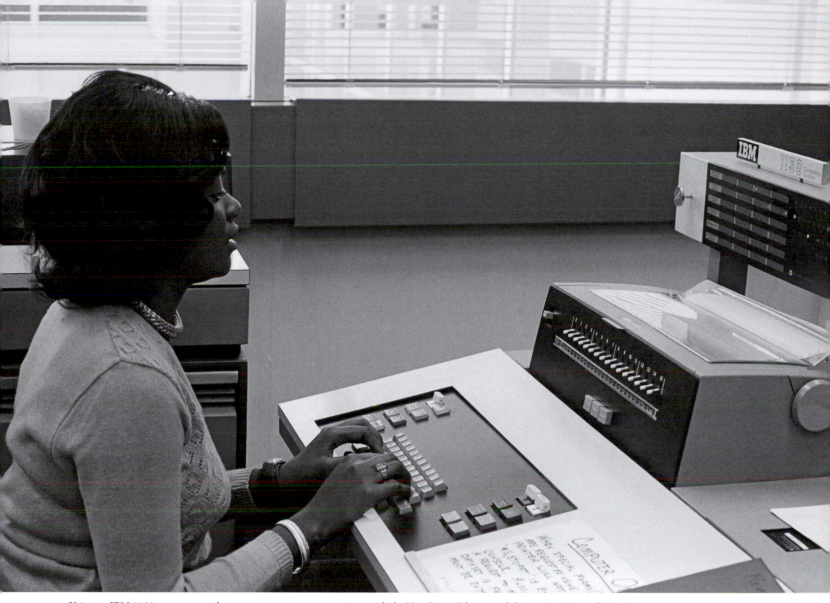

Using an IBM 1130 as a remote job entry computer to communicate with the New Jersey Educational Computing Network (1977)

ternet, and the college's data, voice, and video network. Today, nearly all of the college's classrooms are similarly equipped.

Further examples of Stockton's use of technology over the past four decades can be seen in the table on the following page. The table contains a timeline of select examples of Stockton's early technology adoptions juxtaposed with benchmark advances in computing and communication technology.

Forty years of technological innovation has made a mark on teaching and learning at Stockton. Information technology is now substantially infused into the fabric of college curriculum and pedagogy. It is difficult to find a course where technology isn't in use by faculty and students.

The word, technology, refers to the study of tools and technical arts and also refers to the actual tools and technical arts. Technology is both topic and tool. It has changed the way we teach, learn, and work and has changed what we teach and learn and work upon.

At Stockton information technology serves as an essential tool used in the study of arts and science. It has been the topic of

study in courses dating back to the 1970s and emerged as a master's degree program in 1997. The college has also created a technology training center, the Educational Technology Training Center (ETTC), in response to the important role technology has garnered and the need to train New Jersey's teachers in the use of technology.

A contemporary liberal arts college arguably should append technological literacy to the liberal arts *trivium* of grammar, rhetoric, and logic. Our graduates, the future workers in this age of information, are expected to be as fluent in the use of technology as they are in the use of grammar, rhetoric, and logic. However, what we learn about technology today, unlike what we learn about the core subjects of the *trivium*, cannot endure. Technology and change are inseparably linked. Faculty and students can at best only become apprentices of technology, never masters. Technology is unfortunately akin to the stone in the Greek myth of Sisyphus. For the past forty years Stockton's faculty, students, and staff have willingly leaned a strong shoulder to the stone.

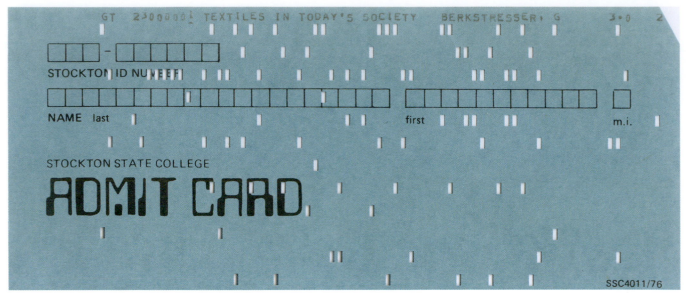

Original punch card used to register for a course (1972)

1971: Intel 4004 microprocessor developed and marketed for calculator manufacturers. First test of email using ARPANET, a military computing network.

1972: Stockton connects to one of the first college and university computing networks (later named NJECN).

1973: Ethernet networking protocol invented at Xerox Palo Alto Research Center.

1974: Stockton offers first courses in electronic music, computer-assisted instruction, and computer-managed instruction.

1976: Stockton first uses geographic information systems and computer mapping in the Environmental Studies Program.

1977: Apple II microcomputer released.

1978: Stockton offers its first computer graphics course.

1979: USENET established for the purpose of posting categorized messages and files.

1981: IBM PC released.

1985: Stockton builds its first academic computer lab and creates the AcademiaNet bulletin board.

1985: ARPANET and National Science Foundation form NSFNET. The Whole Earth 'Lectronic Link (WELL) online bulletin board founded.

1986: Stockton renovates D-wing and creates a computing center, computer labs, and a local area network. Stockton sets up an electronic text-based conferencing system for online discussions.

1988: Stockton establishes a network connection to Bitnet and ARPANET, obtains a National Science Foundation grant to connect to NSFNET, registers a class-B IP license and creates the stockton.edu domain, and installs a fiber optic network that extends from A-wing to the Performing Arts Center.

1989: Virtual reality, 3-D, computer-generated, simulated environments emerge.

1989: Stockton begins using electronic conferencing and creates a computer lab for its residential students.

1990: Stockton students use Internet (external) email for the first time.

1991: First commercial use of NSFNET.

1993: Stockton builds a fiber optic network and expands the College's local area network campus-wide, including high speed, port-per-pillow network access in all residential facilities.

1993: Mosaic web browser released.

1993: Stockton becomes one of the first colleges to build an institutional web site. The first www.stockton.edu web site was spearheaded by Arts and Humanities faculty members (Ken Tompkins and Wendel White) who immediately recognized and seized the sea change that would soon transform methods of inquiry, research, collaboration, and information dissemination in general.

1994: Stockton equips its first electronic classroom.

1995: ARPANET civilian network renamed the "Internet."

1995: Stockton awards internal grants to faculty to develop innovative and "virtual reality" computer applications.

1995: Stockton builds a geographic information systems lab.

1996: Stockton begins distance education.

1997: Stockton establishes the Education Technology Training Center (ETTC), a training and demonstration site for instructional technology, and develops a Master of Arts in Instructional Technology program of study.

1998: Google established.

1999: Stockton installs wireless network services in campus buildings.

2001: Wikipedia established.

2002: Stockton acquires and begins implementation of the Banner Enterprise Resource Planning System.

2005: Stockton begins project to convert all conventional classrooms into electronic classrooms.

2010: Thirty-three percent of Stockton's lecture courses that are taught face-to-face (nondistance-education) utilize computer-based teaching and learning tools to augment lectures and engage students outside of the classroom.

[*National trends in black; Stockton's use of technology in green.*]

advising @ stockton.edu

Peter L. Hagen

When you invent a college from the ground up in 1969 you have a lot of opportunities to get it right. You can take the best of what's around already and avoid the mistakes that other colleges have made by virtue of having been created in an earlier century.

At many colleges in 1969, advising was regarded as little more than a bookkeeping function; anyone capable of reading the college bulletin could help steer students toward the completion of degree requirements. In fact, the students themselves could do it as long as they knew what majors they wished to go into. Being undecided about the choice of major was generally frowned upon; some colleges regarded being undecided as a pathological condition requiring "cures" by the counseling center. Having full-time professional advisors on staff was not widely practiced and, if it was, such practitioners were found in the Divisions of Student Affairs and not in the Divisions of Academic Affairs. Such professionals tended to regard successful academic advising as the development of the student to his/her fullest potential. On the faculty side, successful academic advising—for those that regarded it as more than just checking off boxes on a worksheet—was providing the student with a degree, an education, and a push toward a career or graduate school.

Stockton's original vision for academic advising was a noble plan that skirted the prevailing attitudes toward advising at other colleges. It was the only fair thing to do, after all, because the curricular vision enacted at the beginning (and one largely present to this day) was for an education that did not merely pay lip service to the notion of breadth. Breadth was found all across the curriculum. Every degree program offered in the first years was as wide as it was deep—perhaps even more so, because even in most of the majors (called "programs") there was a wide array of choices in how requirements could be fulfilled. The requirement of cognates—usually a long list of disciplines related in some way to a student's program—further broadened the ways that a student's major requirements could be fulfilled.

The truly iconoclastic vision of General Studies was nothing like the "distribution requirements" one typically found at other colleges. Instead of a short list of arts, humanities, social sciences, science, and math courses (all of which were typically the first courses in majors), at Stockton there was a separate array of courses that were not intended to provide a student with the complete scope of, say, Western civilization in just two easy installments. Rather, faculty were able to "teach their bliss," in the parlance of Joseph Campbell, and students were introduced to the social sciences not by taking PSY 101 and SOC 101, as

is still the case at so many colleges, but rather by taking courses with titles like Violence in America, African Americans and the Law, and Writing About Popular Culture.

The original curricular dream at Stockton also included a requirement that caused students to step outside of their comfort zones and take a quarter of their coursework in areas that were not at all related to their home disciplines. Originally called Liberal Studies, this requirement became known by the deceptively vague At Some Distance in the 1974-1975 *Bulletin*. The name for this category was and is actually quite precise. The requirement calls for each Stockton graduate to have substantive exposure to courses that cover a different area of the cognitive map than the student's major field of study. For example, the student majoring in business has to have at least thirty-two credits in any of the nonbusiness areas of study, lest s/he not graduate due to insufficient study in the traditional liberal arts areas.

Such a curriculum, with bewildering arrays of choices for nearly every requirement, required a strong academic advising program. For how could a student be expected to construct the best possible education without guidance at every step? But it wasn't just guidance: it was to be teaching. Hence, advisors were called "preceptors"—Latin for "teachers"—and this practice remains, at least in name, to this day. From a 1971 document found in Stockton's archives ("A Note on Preceptorial Teaching" by Wes Tilley, who was Stockton's first Vice President for Academic Affairs) we learn that "the preceptor's basic function is teaching; that is, his constant goal is "to show or make known." To achieve this he may use a variety of devices, both traditional and radical, but his objective is clear; each student must be encouraged to define what he wants and needs to know and how to go about learning it."

It would be many decades before the National Academic Advising Association would catch up with Stockton. In 2006 that organization ratified a very influential manifesto that proclaimed that advising was teaching, indeed a necessary component for fulfilling the teaching/learning mission of any institution of higher education. That manifesto, called "The Concept of Advising," was written by a task force that included two members of the Stockton staff: Thomas J. Grites, Special Assistant to the Provost and myself, Peter Hagen, Director, Center for Academic Advising. We were both very familiar with, and advocates of, the notion of preceptorial teaching as it existed at Stockton. It is not going too far to say that the "visionary gleam" of preceptorial teaching instituted at Stockton in the early days and remaining in at least vestigial form today has had a strong national influence on how advising is viewed. This document, which has spawned myriad conference presentations and scholarly papers, can be found at: http://www.nacada.ksu.edu/Clearinghouse/AdvisingIssues/Concept-advising-introduction.htm.

It was the preceptor's role in 1971 to acculturate the student to the life of the mind, the life of the college community, and to serve as a sort of Socratic dialectician. As Wes Tilley put it, "When a student's choice seems hasty or capricious, the Preceptor should challenge the student's assumptions and goals. In the give-and-take of their meetings both the Preceptor and the student may come to understand themselves and the choices that arise out of such an understanding" (1971). Only through such rigorous dialectic could the student be made to understand the real demands of the curriculum, especially General Studies. The preceptor, then, was modeled on the very highest ideals of higher learning.

Students back then were also assigned to a major advisor, whose more quotidian task was to make sure that the student did not neglect to schedule courses that would complete degree requirements. But clearly the greater task was shouldered by the preceptor.

In 1979 Stockton instituted a program whereby two days that would have been devoted to class instruction were instead turned over to the preceptorial process each semester. Still practiced, this plan, which started out as a noble response to the unique needs and demands placed on Stockton students, has deteriorated somewhat, as has the noble goal of preceptorial teaching itself, which probably ended up crushed under its own weight. What used to be the time devoted to the lofty goals of a liberal education has now become days for schedule planning. All too often in this decade we hear of students and preceptors alike who equate precepting with course registration and think that it can only happen on those two days each semester.

Certainly it is the case that throughout much of the 1980s and 1990s advising was more of a chore than a teaching experience for most faculty members. The responsibility for certifying students for graduation rested then, as it still does, with the preceptor, whose certification is checked and ratified by the program coordinator, the dean of the school, and the Dean of General Studies. This meant an enormous amount of bookkeeping on the part of faculty. Each faculty member was required to do a junior-year audit of their preceptees' progress toward the degree and then essentially repeat the process when the student came up for graduation. The tedium of this accounting process was alleviated for the most part when the College converted to the Banner database. This created the opportunity to have an automated degree audit for the first time. It was made available to faculty and staff in fall 2006 and to students in fall 2007. This degree audit, called CAPP (Curriculum, Advising, and Program Planning), has been the most radical change to advising at Stockton in recent years. It has not only enabled students to keep track of their own degree requirements, but it allows them to recast their existing credits into any major, thus providing a great service to undecided students.

Within the past several years, advising at Stockton has started back toward the original vision and thus toward the vision of advising promoted by the National Academic Advising Association: "advising as teaching." A group of faculty interested in advising, called the Stockton Advising Council, was created in 2009. This group, aided by members of the Center for Academic Advising, has done much to promote the idea of "advising as teaching." Thus we have recently seen more and more faculty at Stockton, especially the newer ones, for whom training is provided during their first year, making use of an advising syllabus and structuring learning outcomes for their advisees. After all, if advising is teaching, then it is possible to think in terms of a pedagogy of advising, a curriculum of advising, and of learning outcomes.

The story of advising at Stockton is not really complete without discussing the accomplishments of some of the staff and faculty at the college. Stockton's name is well known nationally in the field of advising. The above-mentioned "Concept of Advising" manifesto is one of many efforts on the part of Stockton staff and faculty, who have published books, articles, and monographs that have had a tremendous impact on the field of advising. Stockton, along with a very few other schools like Penn State, Kansas State, and Arizona State, sets the tone for advising across the nation. Salient examples of published works include Associate Provost Marc Lowenstein's *NACADA Journal* article, "If Advising Is Teaching Then What Do We Teach?" (*NACADA Journal* 25.2 [2005]), which is now one of the most often-quoted articles in research on academic advising. Thomas Grites co-edited the now-standard work in the field, *Academic Advising: A Comprehensive Handbook*, 2nd edition (Jossey-Bass, 2008), that included chapters by myself on advising theory and Marc Lowenstein on the ethics of advising. In 2010 I was the lead editor of a monograph stemming from my role as Chair of the Research Committee of the National Academic Advising Association. This monograph, *Scholarly Inquiry in Academic Advising*, contains contributions by Marc Lowenstein and several Stockton faculty members.

So in 2010, the future of advising at Stockton looks rosy. The CAPP degree audit system has removed the onerous clerical tasks of advising and has cleared the way for the educative function of advising to occur. Our collective mindset still tends to regard advising as only occurring on those two Preceptorial Advising Days each semester. But as new faculty come on board each year, we are seeing advising stretching out beyond those two days. The Banner database has also allowed a great deal of email communication to take place between student and advisor, and so it is not for nothing that I have titled these remarks "advising @stockton.edu." Advising via email, Facebook, Twitter, and Second Life seem to be not just on the horizon but with us now.

The Most Transfer-friendly Institution in the State

Thomas J. Grites

Stockton has always recognized the importance of its transfer student population, as evidenced by various internal reports as well as by external constituencies. Consequently, the College has earned and maintains the well-deserved reputation as (perhaps) the most "transfer-friendly" institution in the state. How did this happen? It was certainly not by accident but rather by conscious and sustained efforts, along with a flexible curriculum and academic policies that enabled the simple transfer of credits to be a much less complex endeavor than it is elsewhere.

The number of transfer students enrolled at Stockton has grown; transfers now constitute nearly sixty percent of the students walking through the galleries each day. Yet, their identity remains a mystery to most of us. Recent efforts to address this condition, and ones that have advanced Stockton's "transfer-friendly" reputation, will be described later.

ENROLLMENT PATTERNS

The first significant shift in the balance of newly enrolled first-year (freshman) and transfer students occurred in the 1984-1985 academic year. That year the college enrolled fifty-five percent new freshman, down from approximately sixty-seven percent in the fall terms of the previous five years (Jassel 1985). The reasons for this shift are not clear, but the fact that eighteen percent of these students did not return after only one semester was of some concern. Lucinda Jassel's Freshman Year Planning Report, though initiated to enhance Stockton's implementation of a Freshman-Year Experience through a Department of Higher Education grant, identified the need to accommodate transfer students as well. Her summary suggested that "alternative ways of easing transfer transition to Stockton and trauma of first registration should be examined" (41). Suggestions included: advance mailings of graduation requirements to each student; immediate evaluation and allocation of transfer credits; early (summer) precepting, even though actual registration was not possible at the time; relocation of all transfer processing to one wing of the College; and provision of a special "transfer" brunch for faculty, staff, and new transfer students. (These suggestions encompass essentially what we do today.)

The next observable shift in the population of newly enrolled transfer students occurred in the fall term 1999, when the actual number of new transfer students was larger than that of new freshmen. This proportion was gradually increasing by design, since the reduction in the freshman class was accompanied by a substantially higher freshman class academic profile (SAT scores and class rank). The larger number of new transfers each

fall has remained a feature of Stockton's enrollment since then (Institutional Research Council). When coupled with the 300 to 500 new transfers enrolling each spring term, it is easy to see why you are more likely to meet a transfer student in the galleries than a "native" freshman.

CURRICULUM AND POLICIES

There is no question that the flexible Stockton curricula, both in programs and in General Studies, permit a wider range of transfer-credit acceptability and applicability. Similarly, Stockton's academic policies are flexible enough to accommodate transfer students and credits without sacrificing curricular integrity. Both the curricula and the policies have been designed and administered with a single principle in mind: treat transfer students the same way we treat our native students, that is, require no more and no less of transfers and provide them with opportunity up to the point where it would become more advantageous to be a transfer student than a native (freshman) student.

The General Studies "twenty-five percent rule" (whereby every transfer student needed a quarter of his or her coursese to have the G acronym) is the best example of the consistent application of requirements between the two types of students. Every student must meet this requirement. However, realizing that most transfer students, especially those from community colleges, enter Stockton with a fair number of traditional general education courses and credits, the distribution requirement in General Studies was modified so that certain traditional general education (liberal arts) courses could be substituted for a portion of the Stockton General Studies curriculum. The "twenty-five percent rule" is always preserved, however.

Two examples of the flexibility in Stockton's transfer policies are especially evident with graduates from the New Jersey community colleges. The first example is that of accepting the best sixty-four credits that these students have earned and that will apply to their chosen curriculum. These students usually enter with more credits than the sixty-four-credit maximum allows, but they are able to manipulate their total credits in order to make the best use of them for Stockton's graduation requirements. Obviously these manipulations are done in consultation with and approval of the preceptor and the Center for Academic Advising.

The other example of flexibility comes from permitting students to return to their community colleges to complete a specific degree requirement so that they are able to take advantage of having an associate's degree. Sometimes a student must "trade" a new course for one already taken (no additional credit), but the financial and academic advantages are worth it.

Stockton's curricula and policies regarding transfer students have met the tests of all of the New Jersey state policies and legislation that have been enacted to remedy the inequities that have existed across the state for many years. In the mid-1980s Stockton was identified in an external consultant's report as the only institution in the state that even came close to meeting the Full Faith and Credit Transfer Policy at the time. As the state legislature, the Presidents' Council, and the Commission on Higher Education have enacted various laws, policies, and the current Comprehensive Statewide Transfer Agreement, Stockton has received no criticism or recommendations for changes in its policies. In fact, no appeals have been made beyond the campus throughout this time.

SUPPORT EFFORTS

Specific efforts were initiated when the General Studies distribution requirement was approved and substitutions were permitted. The Director of Academic Advising (this author) reviewed all transcripts and indicated which courses would be used as substitutions in the General Studies curriculum. This effort facilitated both the students' early knowledge of the substitutions and the preceptors' time to administer the task.

When the Office of Academic Advising was expanded with two full-time academic advisors (1987), three significant efforts were undertaken. First, curriculum worksheets were designed for every major and used to plot both transfer and Stockton courses for degree progress. Second, in order to expedite this process, the advising staff began determining all course equivalencies (always subject to approval by programs) so that the transfer students' initial registration was more efficient. The third enhancement was the introduction of summer advising programs for transfer students in 1988. Since online registration was not available at the time, students still had to return to campus during the pre-term to register, but they were much better informed and prepared to do so.

Since that time a number of ongoing initiatives for transfer students have occurred. Visits to the community colleges by the advising staff have been made on a regular basis; prospective transfer students are able to make appointments on campus to review transcripts and curricula even prior to their application for admission; Instant Decision Days for transfer students have been initiated by the Office of Admissions; transfer students are encouraged to attend and welcomed at Open Houses; the Summer Transfer Orientation and Registration programs have been enhanced; processing of transcripts and preparation of CAPP audits are completed in timely fashion; and more of the campus staff and programmatic efforts consciously include transfer students.

The most significant effort has been the introduction of the transfer seminars in the fall term of 2002. Modeled on the freshman seminar concept, four to six courses are made available exclusively to new transfer students each fall and spring term. Anecdotal evidence is quite positive regarding the success of these courses in making the transition to Stockton thorough, smooth, and productive. Two related transitional efforts are also being explored: creating a peer-mentoring program led by students who have taken a transfer seminar and who will mentor students from their previous community college and extending the transfer seminar concept into the community colleges via one of their courses or a Stockton course taught on their site. To date, five students have volunteered to be mentors, and three of the community colleges have expressed interest in beginning the seminar concept on their campuses.

In summary, Stockton continually strives to create a transfer-friendly environment so that transfer students may achieve the best academic and career success the College can provide.

References

Institutional Research Council. *Enrollment Reports, Fall 1992-Spring 2010. Richard Stockton College of New Jersey.* Retrieved August 21, 2010 at *http://intraweb. stockton.edu/eyos/page.cfm?siteID=54&pageID=2* Jassel, L.S. (1985). *The Freshman Year Planning Report. August Orientation.* Pomona, NJ: Stockton State College.

The Spaces We Occupy

Stockton's Cedar Swamp by David Carr, 2002

It is wonderfully ironic that the word "sustainability" first appeared in a printed text in 1972—a year after the College's founding. The *Oxford English Dictionary* has this quote from the original work:

> 1972 T. Sowell *Say's Law* iii. 100. An increase beyond limits of sustainability existing at any given time would lead only to reduced earnings and subsequent contraction of the quantity supplied.
> 1980 *Jrnl. Royal Soc. Arts* July 495/2. Sustainability in the management of both individual wild species and ecosystems is critical to human welfare.

In this sense, Stockton's emphasis on the concept of sustainability and the word that describes it grew up together.

In a very real way, the Environmental Studies Program (ENVL) was the progenitor of sustainability here. It is doubtful that, without the ENVL faculty, the College would have been so prominently recognized for its efforts to preserve and continue its projects. From the very beginning—even before the land was purchased—it was supposed to be an institution centered on the environment and preserving it.

As Claude Epstein so clearly states, Environmental Studies hardly existed in 1971 as a separate discipline and while student interest in the courses was well-intentioned, student participation was more romantic than realistic. In addition, there was the credibility of the discipline as a concern in the surrounding communities. Even if students worked their way through the ENVL curriculum, there weren't any jobs for them to seek. Also, in the 1980s, the College itself set up personnel policies that worked against continuing an effective environmental program.

The ENVL program has, in spite of these setbacks, survived and has strongly advocated for rational and sustainable growth matched with preservation.

Tait Chirenje and Patrick Hossay write a long and comprehensive history of what "sustainability" means at the College, what has limited it, and what the future holds as the College tries to balance the forces pressuring it from all sides. They discuss four issues: (1) sustainability across the curriculum, (2) institutional structures, (3) energy use and conservation, and (4) energy generation and purchase. They also discuss solutions that have been or need to be adopted. They are honest in identifying the time when there has been little or no collaboration between the administration and the faculty.

Through a thorough discussion of what has worked, what hasn't, and why, the two authors still seem optimistic for the future of our efforts. Curricula are being designed to stress sustainability, students are graduating and finding employment, and our national reputation for these efforts is solid and held in much esteem. Their essay ends:

All of us understand that Stockton College must now commit itself to growing in a way that ensures a clear commitment toward environmental stewardship, energy efficiency, and addressing the great threat of climate change. We can set a new standard in green design, efficiency, and stewardship that could serve as a model for other public and private institutions; we can earn the title of New Jersey's Green College.

Jamie Cromartie's essay is less positive. His argument is based on his experiences when trying to protect the site's biodiversity and its water quality. These are, as he points out, serious issues for any complex located within the Pine Barrens. He suggests that the problems come not from lack of environmental expertise or from innovative plans for protection but, rather, from a lack of clear collaboration between the ENVL faculty and administrations from the beginning of the College to the present. Specifically, Cromartie objects to the lack of implementation of the 1971 Master Plan in three areas of concern: professional management of forested areas, innovative use of native plants, and, finally, planned runoff from College buildings (to avoid damage to Lake Fred).

These are warnings to all of us that this precious environment cannot be maintained without careful planning and an understanding that our need to develop and grow must be matched with our need to preserve what we have inherited. The lesson—an old one—is that we are but stewards and that, in some absolute sense, we do not own the spaces we occupy.

Environmental Studies at Stockton

Claude Epstein

NAISSANCE

The Environmental Studies program (ENVL) was born on the first Earth Day. The original report of the Educational Policy Committee stressed that Stockton was to be New Jersey's environmental college, especially as it was to be the *only* college in the Pine Barrens. Moreover, the report stressed that there should be an Environmental Studies program at Stockton. Dan Moury, the first dean of Natural Science and Mathematics, included Environmental Studies as one of the five original programs in the Natural Science and Mathematics division. Since then, this program has become one of the oldest, largest, and most stable undergraduate environmental studies programs in the nation.

EARLY DAYS OBSTACLES

Environmental studies was a new field. There were few precedents on which to build such a curriculum. Its definition was vague in the early 1960s. At the same time, many academics considered environmental studies a fad, soon to disappear. Early ENVL students' idea of environmental studies was also fuzzy. Typically, they wanted to be Ralph Nader and save the planet. Programs in environmental studies were attractive to colleges as a way to increase enrollments, tapping into the enthusiasm of graduating high school students and returning Vietnam veterans. Some colleges tried to patch together programs by borrowing faculty from traditional departments. But there was always a stress for the faculty involved in becoming the servant of two masters. This obstacle was avoided when Stockton established an Environmental Studies program with its own multidisciplinary faculty.

Credibility with the local community had to be developed. There was a local environmental citizens group in the early 1970s made up of a small minority of Atlantic County residents coming from different interest groups. There were hunters, fishermen, nature enthusiasts, bird watchers, antivivisectionists, and people looking to "jump on a band wagon." They could never overcome their partisan disagreements to form a common front against unplanned development, which was viewed as the biggest local environmental issue in the early 1970s. At first, ENVL faculty and students joined in local community stream "cleanups" and Girl-Scout Jamboree nature walks. In addition, many of our first students were members of local hunting clubs and employees of state forests, wildlife refuges, and local government agencies.

These students helped us develop contacts to our mutual benefit. ENVL gained further credibility when our faculty and students conducted environmental resource inventories for Galloway, Hammonton, and many other South Jersey townships. We also conducted site-specific research for local stakeholders (e.g., Makepeace Lake, the Oswego River, Adams Branch, Franklin Parker Preserve, Atlantic White Cedar Regeneration). The ENVL faculty also participated in local government. Libby Marsh served on the Galloway Township Planning Board. John Sinton became a member of the Pinelands Commission, while George Zimmermann and Jamie Cromartie served respectively on the Weymouth and Galloway Environmental Commissions. We also put our "green" innovations (i.e., the sewerage spray irrigation facility, the geothermal well field) on display for the benefit of outside communities through campus field trips and conferences.

The Pinelands Act, establishing the Pinelands Commission, was a major turning point for the South Jersey environment and for ENVL. It preserved large tracts of the Pine Barrens. ENVL faculty wrote parts of or provided information for the original comprehensive master plan. Water supply was another major issue facing South Jersey. Both water quantity and quality were at stake because of increasing water demands with development, chemical contamination, and the threat of saltwater intrusion. I served on committees that developed the various New Jersey water supply plans.

Another obstacle involved employment of our graduates. There was little employment for environmentalists in the early 1970s, but we anticipated that employment opportunities would develop, and they did. A civil service job description called environmental specialist was created at about that time to meet the need created by environmental regulations. Each regulation required two kinds of jobs—private sector consultants to undertake environmental impact statements and research as well as government regulators to review them. The job market has never been a problem for most of our students since then. Our reputation is such that our graduates are sought out by consulting firms and "head-hunting" employment services.

The College itself provided several obstacles to ENVL program development. During the administration of Stockton's first three presidents, the Board of Trustees set a tenure quota and job requirements that worked against ENVL. ENVL reached its quota rapidly, costing the Program some excellent faculty. We lost Alice Gitchell, who did major work establishing the curricula in Environmental Chemistry and Environmental Regulation. We lost Dennis Slate and Peter Plage, two good wildlife biologists, and Carl Dury, a good forester. Another obstacle was and is presented by Stockton's Plant Management, which replaced more and more natural forest cover with lawns and ornamental trees. These changes required additional resources for irrigation, mowing, fertilizing and other kinds of care. At the same time it required the consumption of gasoline and the creation of noise pollution (that was heard within the classrooms). These activities have been noticed and criticized by faculty, students, and visitors alike and have been an embarrassment to the ENVL program.

The ENVL faculty has a professional stake in the college environment and has on occasion been embarrassed by some administrator's environmental decisions. Some administrators, realizing that environmental issues benefitted their own goals, set up environmental initiatives without much consultation with the ENVL faculty. By not keeping the program "in the loop," administrators denied ENVL the opportunity to help the college "do the right thing" environmentally. Citations by the Atlantic County Mosquito Control Commission and the New Jersey Pinelands Commission could have been avoided with the program's help.

PROGRAM DEVELOPMENT

The program focus and curriculum were developed by the first ENVL faculty, Libby Marsh and myself, who were joined in 1972 by John Sinton. Subsequent additions to the faculty—Jamie Cromartie, Mike Geller, Ray Mueller, George Zimmermann, Wei-hong Fan and Tait Chirenje—shaped the program further. There were also many contributions by faculty no longer at Stockton.

The faculty developed the ENVL Program based on shared pedagogic values. Our approach is *multidisciplinary*. (For example, we have stressed regional planning, which involved not only environmental sciences but also included economics, politics, and history.) We are *field-oriented*, using the Pine Barrens and the Jersey Shore as our classrooms and research areas. Our faculty and students are *focused on local issues.* Specifically we have worked for the Pinelands Commission, town planning boards and environmental commissions, the New Jersey legislature, the NJDEP, as well as for South Jersey businesses. We have developed a *profession-oriented curriculum*, preparing students for careers in government and at consulting and non-governmental agencies. (Consequently, we have stressed the skills needed to characterize the "natural" and "human-impacted" environments as well as those needed to formulate and enact environmental policy.)

The current ENVL core courses and track structure was developed in 1975. The core included courses in physical geography, ecology, and environmental issues. The original tracks included Biological Resources, Water and Soil Resources, and Planning and Regulation. Environmental Chemistry and Environmental Policy (in cooperation with the Political Science program) were added as new curricular needs arose. Laboratories were added to the core courses in the 1980s. Courses in environmental statistics, global positioning, and geographical information systems were added through the efforts of Weihong Fan, George Zimmermann, and Ray Mueller.

Student Action Volunteers for the Environment (S.A.V.E.) banner (1976)

STOCKTON—THE "ENVIRONMENTAL" COLLEGE

ENVL faculty has demonstrated for over forty years principles we now call "greening," recognizing our role as New Jersey's environmental college. In the early days, the program studied the college's innovative sewerage disposal facility—the sprayfield—to assess its impact on the natural environment and its applicability to other institutions. It also assisted many communities with environmental resource inventories. Beyond these efforts we conducted research to expand our understanding of the South Jersey environment. This included such things as compiling a Pine Barrens insect collection, establishing wetland delineations, determining best management practices (BMPs) for South Jersey's Atlantic white cedar, assessing the impact of the college's innovative geothermal well field, one of the largest in the world, on the aquifers and associated wetlands on the campus, working with the US Geological Survey in their study of radium isotopes in South Jersey public water supplies, assisting the New Jersey Conservation Foundation in assessing the environmental resources of their newly acquired Franklin Parker Preserve in the heart of the Pine Barrens, and providing public information transfers on "green" and "sustainable" conservation, building, and operation practices. In recent years some of our faculty and students have turned their attention beyond South Jersey, assisting with environmental issues in Oaxaca, Mexico, South Africa, and China. These activities have enhanced Stockton's reputation as the environmental college.

ENVL AND COLLEGE DEVELOPMENT

ENVL has been a pioneer in environmental education, creating environmental education opportunities where few previously existed. ENVL developed environmental curricula beyond the program itself with bridging tracks in Public Health, Chemistry, Geology, Computational Science, and Criminal Justice. (These tracks have varied from the Environmental Chemistry track shared with the Chemistry Program to clusters of ENVL courses required by the Environmental Policy and Sustainability track offered by the Political Science Program, the Environmental Health track offered by the Public Health Program, and the Environmental Crime track offered by the Criminal Justice Program. We developed a Certificate in Geographical Information Systems (GIS), including the newest developments in global positioning systems, remote sensing and LIDAR, to serve any discipline requiring this technology.

We have developed programs beyond the college's undergraduate programs. We were selected by the state to develop the Governor's School on the Environment for gifted high school students. We have established the Professional Science Master's (PSM) in Environmental Science for working professionals, the first such degree in New Jersey. We have formulated articulation agreements with the ENVL programs at various community colleges (Ocean County College, Burlington County College, Union County College, and Sussex County College). We have also helped coordinate our curriculum with those of the magnet schools in Ocean County (Marine Technology and Environmental School) and Atlantic County (Cedar Creek High School).

The program has been active in the college's extracurricular life. Our students founded SAVE, an environmental action group, which has organized the campus Earth Day festivals and helped the college in various "green" initiatives, such as developing and maintaining campus nature trails and setting up various recycling efforts. In addition, the ENVL faculty and students helped establish a folkdance club, which did many Macedonian and Bulgarian line dances. The lines regularly included myself, Jamie Cromartie, Mike Geller, Dick Colby, Alice Gitchell, and many ENVL students.

WHAT HAS ENVL ACCOMPLISHED IN THE LAST FORTY YEARS?

When ENVL started in 1971, there were no curricula, no laboratories, no field study sites, no internships, no outside contacts, and hardly a job market. The ENVL faculty and students had to make the program a reality. The faculty grew to include many disciplines and designed the present curriculum. The quality of this curriculum is cited by employers that specifically seek ENVL graduates for the private and public sectors. It has also been cited in various nationwide environmental education studies. We have had approximately 2,000 graduates since 1971, and many of these are employed in all levels of business and government, and at nongovernment agencies. Our faculty has developed good research programs, resulting in many publications that have made us known to the academic world.

Faculty efforts to help local governments deal with environmental issues have spread the word that Stockton is the environmental college. Some of us have served on the Pinelands Commission, on the State Water Supply Study Board, consulted with the Bureau of Land Use Regulations (NJDEP), the US Forest Service (USDA), the Natural Resource Conservation Service (USDA), the US Geological Survey, the Fish and Wildlife Service (USDA), the Environmental Protection Agency, and many New Jersey townships. The faculty developed the laboratories, computer facilities, and collections in the Arts and Sciences Building and field study areas throughout South Jersey. We have held seminars and field trips to inform the outside community about local environmental issues and the college's innovative "green" technologies. The students developed SAVE and other environmental groups to assist the college and hold the annual Earth Day celebration. We have spread our educational expertise beyond the ENVL program, partnering with other Stockton programs, nearby magnet high schools, the Governor's School, community colleges and now our Professional Science Master's program in Environmental Science.

We have built all this from scratch to make Stockton the Environmental College of New Jersey. Our program mission was to provide environmental education and opportunities for the citizens of New Jersey to help meet the state's need to overcome environmental problems and to preserve our natural environment. ENVL was in the right place at the right time to meet our mission, which is still valid, and is in an excellent position to continue the work it has accomplished in the last forty years.

Sustainability at Stockton

Tait Chirenje and Patrick Hossay

As the Richard Stockton College of New Jersey celebrates its forty-year anniversary, it is important to reflect on what we have done and where we are headed in the area of sustainability. Dr. Claude Epstein, an Environmental Science professor who has been at the College since its founding, has written a review of Stockton's Environmental Science Program. His review includes the origins of the Program, its evolution through the decades, and the opportunities and challenges that face it.

This discussion will specifically focus on some of the things Stockton, New Jersey's Green College, is doing in the area of sustainability. Generally speaking, sustainability can be defined as the use of resources in a way that does not compromise the ability of future generations to be able to use them. This includes the stewardship of (i) atmospheric resources, (ii) water, (iii) soil resources, (iv) biodiversity, and (v) natural resources. This discussion is by no means a comprehensive analysis of how the college meets specific goals in these five areas. Rather, the major activities that play a significant role in the college's ecological footprint will be discussed (e.g., energy use and generation for electricity, heating and cooling as well as transportation). These discussions will also be based on Stockton's progress in meeting the provisions of the American College and University Presidents' Climate Commitment (ACUPCC), an agreement made by college and university presidents to work towards achieving climate neutrality.

Specifically, it focuses on the following issues:
• Sustainability across the curriculum, including courses, programs, and tracks
• Institutional structures
• Energy use and conservation
• Energy generation and purchase

Wherever possible the challenges that the college faces and viable solutions will be discussed as needed. For example, a lot of the deficiencies apparent in Stockton's pursuit of environmental sustainability could be traced to the lack of collaboration between the physical plant, administration, and faculty. A number of construction projects have gone on with little or no college-wide collaboration, resulting in considerable missed opportunity for students, faculty, and other members of the campus community. Some of these projects are highlighted in the proceeding discussion.

SUSTAINABILITY ACROSS THE CURRICULUM (COURSES, PROGRAMS, AND TRACKS)

A big reason behind the Richard Stockton College of New Jersey's claim to be New Jersey's Green College is its innovative liberal arts curriculum, which is anchored by a nationally recognized Environmental Science Program. However, Stockton College is not only strong in environmental and marine science, but it also boasts a number of sustainability-related courses across its college-wide curriculum.

COURSES

Faculty in the School of Natural Sciences and Mathematics' (NAMS) Biology, Chemistry, Marine Science, Computational Science, Geology, and Environmental Science Programs offer a wide range of courses in the field of environmental sustainability. Chemistry, Biology, Computational Science, and Marine Science faculty often crosslist their courses as ENVL courses. Additionally, other faculty in the Schools of Arts and Humanities (ARHU), Social and Behavioral Sciences (SOBL), Business (BSNS), General Studies, and Health Sciences also offer a considerable number of supporting courses. At least two dozen sustainability-related courses are offered outside NAMS, i.e., in the other six schools at Stockton.

PROGRAMS

Stockton's Environmental Science program ranks among the best in the nation. It offers students a wide range of experiences in tracks spanning Water Resources and Environmental Quality, Environmental Chemistry, Environmental Education, Environmental Policy and Sustainability, Natural Resource Management, and Geographical Information Systems. The program is interdisciplinary in nature and offers field experience opportunities at every level. The Environmental Science program is discussed in detail in another chapter of this volume.

A new graduate program, the Professional Science Master's in Environmental Science (PSM) was started in 2009. Program faculty worked very closely with industry partners to identify practical industry needs and created the required curriculum to fulfill those needs. Some PSM coursework incorporates topics also covered in professional examinations and certifications. Additionally, leading-edge technologies and processes being developed or considered as potentially interesting by industry are regularly assessed for inclusion in the curriculum. This has often included discussions with local industry to assess new technologies and bench test new methods.

The Marine Science program also ranks among the best in the nation, offering tracks in Marine Biology, Marine Resource Management, Marine Education, and Oceanography. Like the Environmental Science program, it is interdisciplinary in nature

Hal Taylor – on the left – instructing students on the workings of a solar oven

and provides field experience opportunities through the Coastal Research Center, located about ten minutes from campus. The Environmental Science and Marine Science programs share many double majors and many Marine Science students often carry an Environmental Science minor and vice versa. Additionally, professors in these two programs also collaborate on a number of research projects.

Plans for a bachelor's degree Sustainability program, partnered with the Environmental Science and Geology programs, are at an advanced stage. It is anticipated that this program would allow students to prepare for careers in a vital and growing field, with a rigorous and interdisciplinary undergraduate education. The program will cement Stockton College's commitment to be New Jersey's Green College by becoming an academic leader in this field. Furthermore, the sustainability degree could define Stockton College as New Jersey's leading source of innovative and engaged education in sustainability. Additionally, this program could help define an academic core for the multiple sustainability-related projects that take place across the college. Multiple faculty members, representing every school, teach courses related to sustainability or conduct research and service in related areas. The program would not only allow students the opportunity to incorporate these courses into a coherent and focused curriculum of study, but it would also encourage cross-disciplinary cooperation and collaboration in the development of

these sustainability-related academic endeavors.

TRACKS

Stockton boasts two tracks that directly support the sustainability field. The first, the Sustainability and Environmental Policy track between the Environmental Science (NAMS) and Political Science (SOBL) programs is one of the most popular tracks at Stockton. This track allows students who are interested in the area of advocacy and related fields to take a select number of natural science and political science courses in the Environmental Science and Political Science programs. Students who have taken this track have gone on to work as community activists, sustainability managers, and in other related fields. Others have gone on to graduate schools in the areas of environmental education, environmental planning, and related fields. The second track, the Environmental Chemistry track between the Environmental Science and Chemistry programs, is also a very popular track for students interested in careers in the environmental pollution and remediation fields.

INSTITUTIONAL STRUCTURES (INCLUDING COLLEGE COMMITTEES AND STUDENT GROUPS)

If there is an area in which Stockton College lags behind all the other colleges in the region, it is in the strength and coordination of institutional structures. Stockton has a large number of outstanding faculty and staff who are involved in projects that fall under the umbrella of sustainability, yet none of them knows what the others are doing. There is very little campus-wide coordination between Academic Affairs, Administration and Finance, and Student Affairs. The Offices of Academic Affairs, Administration and Finance, and Student Affairs do not collaborate as effectively as they could on many projects. The lack of a designated Sustainability officer for the college makes it difficult for the different offices to coordinate activities. Such an officer (or office) could also effectively act as a clearinghouse for projects and activities.

Noting the lack of coordination at the college level, Stockton faculty created two committees on their own, the Biodiversity Working Group (2004) and the Sustainability Committee (2006). These two committees work to promote the implementation of sustainable policies in campus development and management as well as through the curriculum. The President's Office has recently moved to formalize these committees and make them more inclusive, i.e., involve staff and student members. However, the composition of these new formal committees is not yet clear.

Student Action Volunteers for the Environment, SAVE, the oldest student environmental group in the state, continues to attract a large and dedicated membership. This club engages in various environmental activities and, most recently, has been administering the student bike loan program for residential students in conjunction with the Sustainability Living Learning Community (SLLC). Stockton's SLLC is an innovative student housing project that infuses specific academic activities into select residential areas and allows faculty and housing staff to jointly offer experiences to residents of these dorms/apartments. The SLLC partners with different student groups and offers a core living community for students committed to environmental engagement. The bike loan program entails resident students checking out a bike for a semester and using it for on-campus transportation, reducing automobile use on campus. Other projects include stewardship and education efforts from campus vegetarian barbeques to the design and planting of rain gardens in the local community.

Water Watch has been a very active campus group, focusing on surface water testing, community education, local landscape cleanups, and outreach to local primary and secondary schools. Until recently, this group enjoyed the benefit of a paid Americorps organizer on campus. This support was shifted in 2009 by the New Jersey Public Interest Research Group to a newly established PIRG effort, Energy Corps. Taking the Water Watch model as its starting point, this group focuses on energy efficiency and alternative energy, promoting energy education in schools and the community, conducting basic energy assessments in local homes, and even conducting weatherization for local homeowners.

Smaller clubs and organizations like the Geology Club, the Marine Science Club, and others offer discipline-related experiences to like-minded students and often collaborate with the bigger organizations and SLLC on public lectures and field trips, among other things.

ENERGY USE AND CONSERVATION

After signing the ACUPCC, Stockton College conducted an environmental audit of its campus in 2007. The first of three steps in the ACUPCC commits college and university presidents to set up institutional structures to ensure the implementation of this agreement within two months of signing, conduct an inventory of greenhouse gas emissions within one year, and develop an action plan within two years for becoming climate neutral.

This audit was done to fulfill the second commitment and was done in several stages. First a baseline emissions index was established to gauge progress on Stockton's move to carbon neutrality, and then campus energy use patterns were studied in order to determine the areas most in need of energy-use reduction strategies. The audit included an evaluation of:
1. Energy use in college classrooms, labs, and offices
2. Energy use and behavior in campus residence halls and apartments
3. Energy use in college-related transportation (commuting, campus fleet, school trips, and employee travel)
4. College purchasing of equipment, materials, and other supplies
5. Campus food purchasing
6. Landscaping practices
7. Waste management, disposal, and recycling practices

The results showed that Stockton's greenhouse gas emissions are significant and that transportation contributed the most, accounting for about forty-seven percent of the 35,000 metric tons of eCO_2 (equivalent carbon dioxide).

Source	Metric tons eCO_2
Transportation	17,000
Electricity	12,000
Natural Gas	3,000
Purchasing	2,000
Food	2,000
Waste	300
Landscaping	100

This includes faculty, staff, and student commutes, resident student travel, faculty and staff work-related trips, and the campus vehicle fleet. This figure is large because Stockton is still generally a commuter college, and very few of those commuters opt for public transportation or rideshare options. The car-centered infrastructure of southern New Jersey does not help the situation. A considerable percentage of resident students also used to drive from their dorms to the academic parking lots and go home on weekends instead of staying on campus.

The second largest source of climate-changing emissions at Stockton, at thirty-three percent of total emissions, is electric use. This includes electricity used in all campus buildings and residential dorms and apartments. Over the past two decades, energy demand at Stockton College has been generally increasing, led by a large increase in electricity demand from the addition of campus buildings and housing, increased student enrollments, and the increase in the number of computers and related instructional technologies on campus. Around nine percent of electric use is a result of interior lighting used in campus buildings. The college has already taken advantage of these results by implementing energy and cost savings through reductions in illumination levels, improvements in the efficiency of the lighting equipment, reductions in operating hours, and the increased use of daylighting. On the basis of this report's findings and cost benefit analysis, the college has upgraded most interior lighting on campus and is installing motion sensors and light sensors where they are not already in place. Other changes include dorm policies for appliances (a significant drain on electricity) and computer lab equipment and operations. Other options for energy are discussed in a separate section.

One of the more significant changes implemented by the college was to restrict parking in the academic lots and open it to nonresidential students, faculty, and staff until 6 pm on weekdays. A campus shuttle was then introduced for the benefit of residential students so that they would not be tempted to drive to the main academic lots. This shuttle runs until 10 pm to the North Lot, located near the Port Republic-Pomona Road. This lot also serves as an overflow parking lot for staff, faculty, and commuter students during the day.

An experimental shuttle was introduced to and from one of the train stations (Egg Harbor City) to accommodate faculty, staff, and students who commute from the southwestern part of the state, principally the Philadelphia-Camden region. The shuttle schedule was made to coincide with the train schedule to encourage commuters to take the train. This service had mixed results and efforts to revive it with an extended schedule are underway.

Other changes and improvements have been implemented in several areas (discussed under energy). A separate write-up on biodiversity by other authors addresses landscaping, water use, and other areas. However, these authors are frustrated with the way Stockton has chosen to implement the ACUPCC. The ACUPCC clearly lays out the specific steps that need to be taken by signatories to this pact. Stockton seems to be skating through them without putting any real structures in place to implement the plan. Not only have we not set a target date for maintaining climate neutrality, but we do not have explicit interim targets for goals and actions that will lead to climate neutrality. If the college has taken any steps to expand research and develop mechanisms for tracking progress they have not been clearly articulated.

Stockton has also not established any policies that require new construction to meet a minimum of silver LEED (the US Green Building Council's Leadership in Energy and Environmental Design) certification or energy-efficient appliance purchase.

Nothing has been done to offset carbon releases from official air travel, and the vehicle fleet's smallest vehicle for personal travel for employees in Academic Affairs is still a seven-passenger van. This means that if one professor wants to attend a conference more than 300 miles away s/he will have the use that van, while two Toyota Priuses remain out of bounds for faculty. Although these vans are rated E85, the highest percentage of ethanol ever used in these vehicles is ten percent, the norm found at most local gas stations. A formal Stockton Sustainability Committee has been discussed for a number of years now and yet is still to get off the ground. A number of separate committees and individuals are doing amazing things, but coordination is dismal.

In all fairness, the college has met the barest minimum requirements set by the ACUPCC. Stockton has entered into power purchase agreements (PPAs) to increase our energy purchase from renewable to a minimum of fifteen percent, and the administration is supporting efforts to create the new BS and BA in Sustainability. The college has also designated sustainability as one of the four themes in which it seeks excellence. (The other three are engagement, learning, and global perspective.)

The college has also participated in the national Recyclemania Tournament and won. However, we seem to be regressing on this front as we have not changed our campus recycling program to align with the new single-stream recycling policies of the local utility authority. The President's Office has also sponsored a study to assess the availability of wind on campus in anticipation of putting up wind generators on its grounds. In our minds these efforts do not cut it for a college that claims to be New Jersey's Green College. We need to be leaders and pioneers in this field, and the opportunities are there.

A few low-hanging fruits currently exist at Stockton. The presence of very strong Environmental Science, Geology, and Marine Science programs, with vibrant dedicated faculty, makes it easy for the administration to tap experts on a number of issues. More consultations and collaborations are required in this regard. For example, the F-wing expansion carried out in the last five years could have gone better had faculty been brought on as participants as the project was being planned. Similarly, the Campus Center is now complete and there was little to no faculty input in some of the designs and energy saving mechanisms in the building. More importantly, the College is the midst of developing a forest management plan, but the consultative process is, at best, troubling. The contractor who was paid more than $1 million to address tree loss on campus planted hundreds of trees randomly in places for which they are not suitable and left town. It was only through tough criticism from a local forester, a Stockton professor, that the College has considered bringing in a well-known forester to address some of the problems at hand. Even then, it is not clear where this process is at the moment. Currently the administration has consulted with a few faculty members in the Political Science and Environmental Science programs on the new College Walk project. However, there is still a lack of proper coordination and communication between the different departments on campus, and the mechanism of providing feedback on a number of issues is not very clear. Faculty are not in the know about the specifications of the proposed Unified Science Center beyond their assigned interior spaces.

ENERGY GENERATION AND USE
The most feasible means for the College to meet its ACUPCC obligations will be through a combination of alternative energy generation and efficiency measures in existing and new facilities. Hence, it is useful to review College efforts toward the use of wind and solar energy and infrastructure efficiency.

WIND
Stockton College is a promising site for the generation of wind energy. The main campus offers buildable space, interconnectivity, high energy use on site, and viable wind resources. However, as of yet, no such installation has taken place.

In 2004, a Wind Turbine Feasibility Study was completed by South Jersey Energy Company of Folsom, New Jersey. Using what have turned out to be conservative estimates for wind speed, this report recommended the installation of a 1,650 kilowatt turbine. The report estimated a total project cost of $2.59 million with very positive financial returns. The calculated simple payback for this installation was estimated at slightly over nine years with a positive cash flow in one year of $440,500, as well as a project new present value (NPV) of $41,817,575. This report also considered the installation of a 950 kilowatt turbine and found the financial prospects to be very positive but not quite as promising as for the larger unit.

One of the necessary first steps in the continued consideration of a campus wind energy installation was an on-site wind assessment. As a result, in spring 2009, a fifty-meter meteorological tower was erected on the Stockton College campus, in an open field near the campus arboretum. The results indicate a consistent northerly wind with a mean speed of slightly over ten miles per hour. These results indicate strong wind energy potential for the College, significantly exceeding the estimated wind speeds used in the 2004 Wind Turbine Feasibility Study. These results indicate the likely economic feasibility of a wind turbine installation. These data may be used to project production estimates for specific turbine types and heights in the future as the examination of a campus wind turbine moves forward.

Tower instrumentation included six anemometers located at 102, 128, and 164 feet. Two wind vanes were also located at 128 and 164 feet. Winds appear strongly focused in the north-northwest quadrant, with relatively little variation in general direction. The overall average wind speed for the year at 164 feet was found to be 4.52 meters per second or 10.11 miles per hour, with a standard deviation of .93. At 128 feet, the speed was 3.24 meters per second with a standard deviation of .77.

Wind speeds varied over the course of the year, with predictably higher speeds in winter and lower speeds in summer. Similarly, the standard deviation was slightly higher in winter and lower in summer months. These wind speeds are slightly above, but consistent with, expectations and available data for the region.

Because an estimated mean wind speed of 3.87 meters per second was used in the 2004 Wind Turbine Feasibility Study, these data indicate possible energy production that would be roughly thirty percent higher than that provided by the 2004 report. Hence, the financial estimates provided by that initial report are likely to understate the economic desirability of a wind turbine installation on campus. It was therefore recommended that the college move forward with the investigation of a wind turbine installation on campus, using these data, and projections to actual hub heights based on these data, to create more precise estimates of likely energy production and economic feasibility.

With the recent acquisition of the Seaview Golf Resort and Spa, the college now has the option of placing a turbine on this site, or perhaps on both the main campus and the Seaview site. Given the Seaview's closer proximity to the shore, and the measured winds at similar sites including the ACUA wastewater treatment site and Atlantic City High School, it is likely that the Seaview has generally higher wind speeds than does the main campus. Hence, it is likely that a turbine at the Seaview would produce significant and relatively consistent output.

SOLAR
Stockton College owns very little solar electric capacity. An aging array atop the Arts and Science Building now maintains roughly twelve kilowatts of generating capacity, or less than half its original capacity. Installed in 1996, this array was once one of the larger installations in the region. After a period of in-operation, the array is now operating at diminished capacity, with the still-functional panels rewired to a new inverter. A twenty-six-kilowatt array atop the F-wing overbuild is now producing electricity as well. This installation was used to help this new construction achieve basic LEED certification. The inverter is not now running at full capacity and could allow for the addition of a few more panels; however, it is clearly the most significant solar resource owned and operated by the college. An additional small array at the campus daycare center has not produced energy in several years.

Stockton is also the site of much larger solar installation that is not owned by the college. These arrays are the result of PPAs entered into by the college. Such PPAs define a contract between an energy provider, who typically maintains ownership of the solar equipment for a set number of years, and the college, which commits to purchase of the generated electricity at a set price. PPAs on campus include a 320-kilowatt array mounted on the roofs of the Multipurpose Recreation Center, a 383.6-kilowatt array on Parking Lot 7a, and a 468.2-kilowatt array on Parking Lot 7b. Stockton does not own the facilities, nor does it maintain the Solar Renewable Energy Credits. Hence, these installations have little impact on the college's environmental footprint or carbon emissions profile. However, Stockton may claim credit for "hosting" such a significant solar array and has pointed out that by allowing on-site generation, the approximately one-percent loss in energy through transmission is reduced.

A cooperative project with Professor Hossay and Stockton Facilities is now evaluating the installation of additional photovoltaic and solar thermal panels on residence halls and apartments. Funds from a $3.46 million award through the state's Innovation in Energy Efficiency and Renewable Energy—Public Entities will be used for this effort and improved energy-management systems in college residence halls. The solar thermal arrays will be owned by the college and are likely to reduce hot water energy demand in the installed units by one third.

BUILDING DESIGN

In recent years, Stockton College has expressed a desire to seek energy and environmental performance from all new campus construction and to pursue efficiency upgrades in existing buildings. However, this goal has been pursued with an uneven level of commitment, and the endeavor has often seemed to reflect a desire to appear green rather than a commitment to actually be green.

The F-wing expansion of 2006 was the first attempt by the college to obtain LEED certification for a campus building. Over the past five years, the LEED criteria have become an industry standard for green construction, recognized nationally as the principle scheme for the evaluation and verification of the environmental performance of new construction and existing buildings. The F-wing expansion included classrooms, offices and an atrium, and was constructed atop the already existing science laboratories.

While the building did indeed incorporate some important environmental features, it also reflected a desire to meet the letter of the certification requirements rather than their spirit of intent. Notable green features include waterless urinals, the use of environmentally preferable materials, the proper management of construction waste, and the use of environmentally desirable paints and adhesives. However, other features too often demonstrated only the desire to achieve the LEED certification rather than actually produce a greener building. For example, occupancy sensors in the individual faculty offices were placed in the switchbox. Such an installation is contrary to industry standards and violates basic best practices in lighting design. Indeed, these units would be expected not to function properly by anyone trained in basic installation. It seems likely that this mode of installation was chosen because it was inexpensive and would allow the building to achieve a point on the LEED rating system for lighting design. Predictably, within a short period of operation, all of these sensors were replaced with standard manual switches as they began to malfunction. Another example

might be drawn from the installation of Car pool Parking signs in the campus main parking lot, allowing the building to achieve another point in the LEED rating system for the encouragement of efficient transportation. However, since no effort was made to develop a verification, enforcement, or incentive process, these signs had no discernable effect on commuter behavior. The signs were largely ignored, and campus police had no way of knowing if the vehicles parked in any given "carpool" spot were actually carpoolers. These signs were removed a short period after the building achieved its certification. It goes without saying that a real carpool program would have been preferable to the ploy used to gain an easy certification point, and the installation of well-designed occupancy sensors would have been preferable to the cheap and ineffective installation used to wangle another one.

Stockton College is now promoting its new Campus Center as a major green project. As the largest single building project in Stockton's history, it would be important for this building to integrate green design features and set a tone for future campus construction. The college has registered this project with the U.S. Green Building Council (USGBC) and has targeted the gold level of certification. This is, of course, an admirable aim that could help underscore the college's commitment to sustainability in the design and operation of its facilities. Based on basic design criteria available to the authors, the building does seem to have adopted some important green features, including energy efficiency, green materials, environmentally desirable paints and adhesives, and water-saving features; however, this building is not without controversy. The building's location required that a large portion of the campus' main building be isolated from the existing geothermal field. So, while the new construction utilizes this field, and claims this as a green feature for LEED certification, this represents no net expansion of geothermal capacity on campus but rather the shift of geothermal from an existing building to a new one. The portion of the main campus now isolated from the geothermal field is heated and cooled by newly installed conventional rooftop units, reducing its efficiency by likely a third. The choice to build this new construction on the largest remaining grove of natural vegetation on the main campus was also controversial and difficult to justify.

Lastly, the College also highlights the building's use of green energy, claiming that it uses "a new 30,000 sq. ft. photo voltaic array on the adjacent athletic center." However, as previously discussed, this array represents a power purchase agreement, and Stockton College does not maintain the Solar Renewable Energy Credits, or green tags, representing the production of green energy from this array. Hence, the college has neither the right nor justification for claiming the use of green energy by this building; that right belongs to the holder of the green tags.

Energy-efficiency upgrades on existing buildings have been moving ahead slowly but with good effect. Lighting across the college has been upgraded. This includes more efficient lighting and motion sensors where appropriate. Outdoor lighting has also been significantly upgraded, with relatively few inefficient units left on campus. It is hoped that the upgrade of the lighting in the main campus corridor will be completed soon. This might include photovoltaic sensors and motion sensors as well as more efficient lighting units. Similarly, there is potential for the improvement across the college—in the operation of the electric doors (ADA doors) on the main campus, the lighting in residence halls, and other features. Many of these changes were outlined in the campus carbon inventory, completed in 2008. There is also promising discussion of green roofs and other visible green features on campus. It is worth noting that the leadership in Facilities and Plant has demonstrated a keen interest in many green features and a genuine concern for improving Stockton's environmental performance. So, there are reasons to be optimistic.

As the college expands its facilities, it has the potential to truly define itself as New Jersey's Green College. Stockton's current advantage is in the relatively high intensity of use of its existing facilities. As Stockton increases its campus facilities, this relative efficiency is likely to decrease, making the aim of carbon neutrality that much more challenging. A commitment to the adoption of cutting-edge green design and a real dedication to

the development of truly high-performing, environmentally sound construction would do a great deal to help Stockton maintain the veracity of its self-proclaimed "Green College" status. Unsubstantiated claims to achieve the appearance of green will fool no one.

CONCLUSION

Achieving a more sustainable campus is a tremendous but vital challenge, and a closer cooperative relationship between faculty specialists and the college administration can help foster this achievement. We have made important steps in this regard that point the way forward. However, an institutionalized Sustainability Committee and campus Office of Sustainability that can be dovetailed with the forthcoming academic program in sustainability could serve as a vital nexus in this effort. All of us understand that Stockton College must now commit itself to growing in a way that ensures a clear commitment toward environmental stewardship, energy efficiency, and addressing the great threat of climate change. We can set a new standard in green design, efficiency, and stewardship that could serve as a model for other public and private institutions; we can earn the title of New Jersey's Green College.

Aerial view of the College (c. 1980)

The Natural Environment

Jamie Cromartie

From the very beginning, Stockton faculty and students have been engaged in many activities that fall under the currently popular term "sustainability." Early efforts included valuable studies of the flora and fauna of the campus directed by Sandra Bierbrauer and Roger Wood, of the morphology and hydrology of Lake Fred by Claude Epstein, and of deer management. Later there were studies on the cedar swamps and upland oak pine forests by George Zimmermann, soil surveys by Ray Mueller, and surveys of fishes, amphibians and reptiles by Rudy Arndt, of mammals by Mike Geller, of birds by Jack Connor, and of insects by myself. Many of these surveys were carried out by students working independently under the guidance of the faculty. Students who got their start on research on campus have gone on to earn doctorates and pursue research across the globe. There has also been a wide range of activist projects carried on by students and faculty, ranging from recycling to animal rights to organic farming. A few of these lasted for more than one academic year, and the recycling efforts, in particular, were gradually taken over by Plant Management. More of these undertakings are described in the history of the Environmental Studies (ENVL) program, which, along with the Marine Science (MARS) program, has been responsible for Stockton's greatest effort in the area of sustainability over its forty-year existence.

Yet, despite its many positive achievements, Stockton has failed to protect biodiversity and water quality, key values in the Pine Barrens.

The 1971 Comprehensive Architectural Master Plan emphasized the natural environment. It recommended setting aside areas for research and for aesthetic and recreational value. It stated, "the identification of the most desirable natural areas on the campus and administrative action now, to assure the recognition of their unique values and to insure their perpetual protection, will demonstrate the vision of the College's founders." In 1977, John Rokita and Lester Block, two students who now work in the Natural Sciences Lab at Stockton, and I spent a summer assessing the campus to delineate areas for future ecological research. The administration, however, did not act on subsequent faculty requests to permanently designate ecological research areas and to insure perpetual protection, except as required by outside agencies. The one bright spot has been the former Kennedy farm, developed by George Zimmermann, Pete Straub and others into an arboretum, but even this was threatened by proposed plans until faculty protested.

In 2010, Stockton requested changes to agreements made in 1990 to protect specific areas, so that virtually the entire upland habitat remaining on the campus could be developed and preservation limited largely to legally restricted wetlands and parcels of land located away from the campus, inaccessible for research or recreation. While the total quantity of lands said to be "deed restricted" from further development remains about the same as in the 1990 plan, the willingness of the Pinelands Commission to overlook past promises when new proposals are brought forward has led several outside environmental groups to protest the proposed changes. Nevertheless, the new Master Plan was approved by both Galloway Township and the Pinelands Commission.

The 1971 Master Plan gathered more ecological information than any previous plan for a similar institution. The goal was to continue to develop a management plan that would serve as a model for others. Today, the only interest on the part of the administration in these data seems to be finding ways to develop the land as far as state regulations allow. Until 2010 Stockton had not contracted for a professional management plan for its forested areas. Despite recommendations from the ENVL Program, no management has been done beyond limited prescribed burns.

The 1971 plan recommended innovative use of native plants, even for lawns, but Stockton has replaced natural forest and field cover with turf and ornamental trees, which require irrigation, fertilizing and mowing. Besides noise, soil compaction, and air and water pollution, this has led to declines in plant and animal diversity on the campus. Moreover, ENVL students and faculty have documented the spread of a number of harmful invasive plant species in several areas on the campus. Stockton does not follow the best management practices developed by environmental groups and the Pinelands Commission for maintaining roadside biodiversity, so it is a follower, not a leader, in this area.

In 1971 runoff from buildings, parking lots, roads, and sidewalks was channeled directly into Lake Fred and surrounding wetlands. One stream was converted into a drainage ditch. These were legal methods at the time, but despite changes in the laws and the science, they remain in use. The 1990 revision of the Master Plan emphasized that they were "grandfathered" and suggested that they be utilized for the indefinite future. Although new rules require ending direct discharges when new development takes place, Stockton and the Pinelands Commission seem content to let things be. During the building of the Campus Center, the Natural Resources Conservation District issued a citation for allowing sediment to enter Lake Fred via the old storm water system. Thus, one of the ecological jewels of New Jersey's Green College continues to be abused.

Stockton's environmental faculty and students are not only part of the College's educational mission but also professionally committed to the environment. This has led to collaborations among faculty, students, and administration on such projects as the original sprayfield, the geothermal and related energy systems, and the nonstructural elements of storm water management. At times, however, faculty have been left out, given limited information after major decisions have been made, or have only been asked to fix problems when regulators rejected Stockton's proposals. Too often, faculty and students have been denied the opportunity to help Stockton lead with innovative solutions. Stockton has preferred to work with professional consultants, who focus on getting development permissions, while doing the minimum that the law or public relations requires for biodiversity and water quality.

The Lost is Found

In the Fall of 2006, I wrote that "In some ways Stockton can be seen as a gem of lost opportunities. Let me suggest that you take a walk to the west of parking lot 7, following the wooded path to the cedar bog. In its natural state, the area is enchanting. It could be a showpiece of beauty and environmental teaching on this campus; instead, it is littered with trash and left in dangerous physical disrepair."

At that time the foot bridge across the creek was thoroughly rotten, a very large television had been carried into the woods and smashed near the bridge, and even more shocking, one of the tallest cedars in the area – "Big Spiral" – had been cut down by vandals and left to rot. One of Stockton's most accessible, most beautiful areas, was a mess. Today, however, the area is once again a showcase.

The trash is gone, the path to the bog is well marked, and in the Fall of 2010, the downed cedar tree was repurposed, thanks to the efforts of Steve Brown and Russell Conrady in the carpenters shop, as part of the new cedar bog bridge and walkway. The area may still be a hidden gem, but it is no longer lost.

Thomas Kinsella

Promoting the Professions

Labyrinth by Hannah Ueno

Unlike the other divisions, the birth of the School of Professional Studies (previously called the Division of Professional Studies and originally called the Division of Management Sciences) was not easy. For the other divisions, the person hired as dean created a collection of programs), and hired faculty who fleshed the programs out with curricula.

Not so Management Sciences.

First, the original Vice President for Academic Affairs, Wes Tilley, didn't really like curricula that offered vocational courses. He knew that, eventually, the College would have to offer professional courses, but he insisted that they be taught by a faculty who gave allegiance to the liberal arts. The other deans pretty much concurred.

So, while the four deans of traditional liberal arts subjects were hired in the spring of 1970, the Dean of Management Sciences was not hired until the fall of 1970. That person was not part of the conceptual planning, not part of recruiting of the First Cohort of faculty, and not part of the community-building that was so central to the work of the original deans.

In addition, the first candidate for Dean of Management Sciences—shortly after the position was offered to him—developed an inoperable brain tumor. We were forced to do a second national search, thereby delaying the vital planning it takes to create a college division.

The candidate we did hire, John Rickert, seemed the right fit for what we had already created, but personal problems prevented him from full participation in the planning process. While he hired the first faculty and created the necessary structure, he was never effective.

The wider community—in contradistinction to the founding vice president and deans, who insisted on a liberal arts focus—wanted the College to offer wide vocational curricula. The Atlantic City hoteliers asked for students trained in hotel management, the FAA Technology Center requested engineers and safety technicians, and local school districts strongly urged us to produce quality teachers.

Some professional curricula were needed; it was a matter of what kind of faculty and what kind of courses would be offered by the Management Sciences division.

These tectonic faults are at the center of Marc Lowenstein's excellent survey of the creation of Management Sciences. For Lowenstein, the two points of view are Vice President Tilley's and President Bjork's. Bjork insisted that Stockton was not a "liberal arts college" and that it would certainly have professional programs. John Rickert, for his part, argued that whatever curricula the division finally produced, they would be based solidly on the liberal arts. It should be clear that Rickert was securely in the vice president's camp—to no avail.

As the national academic culture changed, Bjork's perspective prevailed. Management Sciences became more specifically vocational, less influenced by the liberal arts, and, unfortunately, less connected to the other divisions at the College.

Nancy Davis' essay also outlines the struggle to produce a variety of Health Sciences programs at the College. Resistance came from students who didn't see the value of Biomedical Communications, or the president—Peter Mitchell—who saw the health sciences costing too much, or faculty asked to initiate programs with no experience in that discipline. Davis' long and solitary struggle is both a warning and a confirmation to faculty. It warns faculty that new programs can be designed on paper but take on a life of their own when fully created. It is a confirmation that one faculty member committed to a cause can succeed when nimble and clever and, most of all, persistent.

It took years before support for graduate programs developed, as Bess Kathrins suggests, though from the very earliest days they were anticipated. Deb Figart thoroughly reviews the history and process of creating graduate programs; there are thirteen at the College as of 2011. The earliest was the Business Program—now an MBA—started in 1997. In 1997, 165 students had enrolled in two graduate programs; in 2009 enrollment had grown to 746 students.

The growth of Professional Studies at Stockton reflects that same growth nationally. Students have become very practical expecting that their courses lead to employment. This is understandable given a present unemployment rate of nine percent. But one wonders what will support these same students when, in the middle of their lives, they consider retirement or second careers. Will they not be limited given the narrowness of their early training? Somehow we need to seek a middle ground in the competing ideas of the liberal arts on one hand and professional studies on the other. Given its innovative history, the College needs to bridge this gap more effectively.

Professional Studies—Competing Perspectives

Marc Lowenstein

What is the role of professional studies at a liberal arts college? There have always been multiple perspectives on this question at Stockton, and these perspectives have often been at odds.

When I interviewed and began teaching here, my colleagues in ARHU certainly told me about the liberal arts mission of the institution, sometimes summarized in a metaphor like "the public Swarthmore." Certainly most of the faculty with whom I worked in the 1970s saw it that way. But the college's first president, Richard Bjork, always denied that Stockton had ever been, or was intended to be, strictly a liberal arts institution.

Expressions such as "arts, sciences, and selected professional programs" occur frequently in official documents developed under his administration. Some of the early innovations of which the Mayflower faculty are rightly proud are actually quite compatible with the academic mission as Bjork saw it: he thought General Studies, the encouragement of interdisciplinarity, the permeability of degree programs, significant freedom of choice for students, and the preceptorial system were every bit as appropriate for professionally oriented programs as for the liberal arts.

Professional programs were part of the curriculum from the very start, mostly within a Division of Management Sciences. But even then there were two very different visions of what these programs were about. The initial dean, John Rickert, wrote that the division would focus on the "common principles and methods of virtually all administration, private and public; and the pervasive role of the social and behavioral sciences in effective administration." In other words, professional programs were appropriate at this liberal arts-focused institution because such programs are themselves intellectually rooted in liberal arts disciplines.

President Bjork saw it differently, which may have been one reason why Dean Rickert's tenure was brief. Bjork thought the professional programs were legitimate on their own terms, that they "bring the students here." Where Rickert's view would appear to imply that faculty in professional programs ought to have liberal arts backgrounds, Bjork wanted to make room for more people with industry experience, even if their academic credentials were nontraditional. Rickert's vision was reflected in at least some of the initial faculty hiring, including a Business professor with a philosophy background, but Bjork's predominated in the long run.

Against the background of these ideological differences, from the start the curriculum on the ground included some courses reflecting Rickert's vision (Bigotry as an Organizational Problem) but a larger number that would be recognizable as characteristic of business curricula at most institutions—in accounting, management, and marketing. The Information Science curriculum was heavy on programming courses although the above-mentioned philosopher was teaching logic and offering independent study in the philosophy of language.

By the mid-1970s the college had added programs in health sciences as well, and in 1976 they were combined with the Business/Management programs in a new Division of Professional Studies. That step clearly presupposed that these groups of programs had more in common with each other intellectually than either did with the college's liberal arts and sciences programs. I suggest that this idea represented the clear victory of the Bjork vision over the Rickert vision. It was precisely the professional nature of the programs that set them apart, whether or not they had any intellectual foundations in the liberal arts, or any common intellectual foundations at all.

Professional Studies faculty, as such, are not exempted from the requirement that Stockton faculty contribute to the General Studies curriculum. The different ways in which they have done so are illustrative of some of the themes we have been looking at. Some have offered courses that bring their specific professional knowledge to the general student, for example, in a course by an Accounting professor on personal finance, or a Nursing professor's course on women and their bodies. Others might have pleased Dean Rickert more, such as an interdisciplinary course on psychopharmacology taught by a professor of pathology. Still others drew on undergraduate backgrounds in liberal arts subjects, as in the case of a Statistics professor who has taught Virtue and Moral Philosophy for thirty years. That these faculty participate in General Studies as peers of the liberal arts faculty and indeed have occasionally played leadership roles sends an important message that Stockton sees the two areas as integrated, not isolated from each other.

On the other hand, the way the expectation of participation applies in Professional Studies sends a slightly different message. For many years it has been understood that while liberal arts faculty are expected to teach one third of their load, two courses a year, in General Studies, the expectation of Professional Studies faculty is one course a year. This is not because they are thought to have less to contribute. Rather, it reflects a tacit decision, reached early on, that by allowing Professional Studies faculty to teach more courses in their programs, it is possible to deliver those programs with fewer faculty than would otherwise be necessary, and more of the total Stockton faculty can be in the liberal arts.

By the 1980s there could be no disputing that professional programs were here to stay. Specifically the Business Studies program was far and away the largest at the college in both faculty lines and student enrollments. Business alone produced 36% of the college's graduates in academic year 1986, thirty-nine percent in 1988. The dominance of PROS was really that of BSNS. Some faculty found this phenomenon disturbing—at odds with their concept of the type of institution Stockton was. There were proposals to "cap" the program, limiting the number of majors it could have. The program took some steps internally, adding more quantitative requirements, to counter any perception by students that business was the default major for mediocre students.

A separate step taken in the mid-1980s had long-term implications for the role of professional programs at Stockton and for other institutional issues as well. Mainly on the initiative of President Farris, the college established a program in physical therapy. Initially a five-year bachelor's degree program, PT became a master's degree in the 1990s and a clinical doctorate in the 2000s, in both cases breaking new ground for the college but also having immediate impact on the character of Professional Studies.

PT was very attractive to prospective students and thus led to a first for Professional Studies: a professional program with highly selective admissions. Considerably more students than the program could accommodate matriculated at Stockton as would-be PT majors. Many had higher academic profiles (and specifically SAT scores) than were typical for Stockton at the time, and they played a role in the college's substantial gains in this respect over the next decade. Another side effect was the creation of a new type of link between professional and arts and sciences programs, since students hoping to enter PT spend their first three undergraduate years studying natural sciences. When PT became Stockton's first graduate program a part of the impact was that a substantial number of undergraduate PROS/PT majors became NAMS/BIOL majors. By fall 2000, BIOL had become the second largest program at the college in terms of self-described majors, and PT had shrunk from 7% of the college to near zero.

In the mid-1990s Governor Whitman did away with the Department of Higher Education and introduced new mechanisms for the creation of new programs and other curricular changes, which made such steps much easier to effect. Institutions could object to each other's new programs only if they were either "unduly duplicative or expensive." In reality institutions have rarely invoked these criteria. New programs, location of programs at new sites near other institutions, and strategic alliances are largely deregulated. This environment encourages aggressive entrepreneurial players, often from out of state.

The impact of the new environment on liberal arts programs is minimal; the competition it engenders is felt almost entirely in professional programs. Although the college's leadership had supported the governor's actions, Stockton was not well prepared to take advantage of the new system or even to defend its territory against competition that was not long in coming. One of the first places competition was felt was in Stockton's upper-division Nursing Program, whose pipeline of students was partly cut off when a major employer formed a strategic alliance with another "provider." Still another type of alliance that poses a potential threat to Stockton is formed between a community college and another senior institution.

In the late 1990s and thereafter Stockton created a number of graduate programs, almost all in professional areas, in order to expand its markets, serve regional needs, and provide opportunities for its own undergraduates to "stay at home" for their graduate education. This trend continues, with new programs in educational leadership and communication disorders coming online in 2010 and 2011. State approval was obtained for a programmatic mission change to accommodate this, and subsequently an "exception" to offer the Doctorate of Physical Therapy. New baccalaureate programs were added as well, in hospitality and tourism management and pre-licensure nursing, both of which attracted new students to Stockton. At the same time moving into these new territories rendered the college more vulnerable to competition from other institutions. It was largely in order to strengthen its hand in meeting that competition that Stockton decided a few years ago to disassemble Professional Studies as an administrative unit, creating in its place Schools of Business, Health Sciences, and Education. (There were other reasons as well: one was that PROS had simply become too large and diverse to be effective, with over seventy faculty at one point.)

Initially the rationale focused specifically on the Business Program. The Business faculty had determined to seek national accreditation, partly to meet regional competition and partly as a way to measure and demonstrate excellence. That the institution was willing to support this project was emblematic of an understanding that it was no longer tolerable for quantity to be more important than quality in this area, as it perhaps had been in the 1980s. Pursuing accreditation would require strong, focused leadership that was expert in this specific project and that would not be distracted by responsibility for other areas of the curriculum—in other words a separate dean. Once that decision was made, it only followed that the remaining programs should similarly have leadership with specific disciplinary expertise, and the Schools of Education and Health Sciences were created just a year later. The Computer Science faculty reached with some difficulty a decision that they had more affinity for business than for natural sciences, and PROS was no more.

If the creation of PROS in the 1970s represented a victory of the Bjork vision over the Rickert vision regarding the role of

Weavers in the Gallery (c. 1976)

professional programs at Stockton, its disassembly did not signal a change of philosophy. Rather it represented a recognition that in the current environment, in order for professional programs to flourish they would need singularity of purpose and a vigorous, tightly organized effort to interface with the regional employers, governmental units, and other organizations that are their stakeholders. Success in such efforts is far from guaranteed, but the new structure is Stockton's best effort to position itself to be effective.

Health Science Education at Stockton

Nancy Taggart Davis

THE DIVISION OF HEALTH SCIENCES: THE EARLY YEARS

Late in the summer of 1973, I called Stockton's Biology department to see if they might have a job for me, a new PhD in comparative pathology from the University of Pennsylvania, doing research at the Penrose Research Laboratory at the Philadelphia Zoological Garden. I was told that Biology had no openings, but they transferred me to the dean of the brand new Division of Health Sciences (HS). I spoke to the dean, Dr. Ted Martin, who invited me to an interview and a tour of the college.

Ted Martin was exciting and full of life; he was a brilliant and fun person to work under. His persuasiveness and energy enabled the Division of Health Sciences to get established during those first five years. He had come to Stockton as part of the Business faculty and had both a science and a business background. He was thought to be a mover and shaker and someone who could get the new Division of Health Sciences off the ground.

The original plan was to offer degrees in public health, speech pathology and audiology, biomedical communications, nursing, physical therapy, and nutrition. Ted hired me on the spot, and I began working right after Labor Day. At about the same time, he hired Bruce DeLussa to head up the Public Health program. Bruce held a master's degree in public health from the University of Michigan and had extensive experience in the public health arena in New Jersey. He was a good organizer and expert at networking.

This was a very exciting but confusing time because there were no programs or students in these areas. I had never taught a course in my life and didn't have a clue about nursing or any of the health-related professions except medicine. Ted seemed to think that I would be valuable to the Nursing program because I could teach anatomy, physiology and pathology. Ted Martin, like me, did not have a degree in a professional area. He had a PhD in an area of science and had been involved in a number of research projects in the health field. I distinctly remember his stories about research projects relating to health problems in outer space.

Bruce and I had the task of helping to hire faculty for the Division of Health Sciences. Neither of us taught that semester, but we were on just about every college committee as each had to have a representative from HS. In addition, we were given little projects like organizing and implementing continuing education programs.

I remember putting together a program for licensed practical nurses (LPN); I didn't even know what an LPN was at that point in my career. On the day that all the LPNs appeared, I met Dick Berry who was visiting Stockton for an interview. Everything was falling apart in regard to this LPN continuing education program; the speaker and the donuts didn't show up, but all the LPNs were there, and they were very unhappy. (I wasn't sure if they were most unhappy about the lack of a speaker or having no donuts.) This was the first thing of any consequence that I was assigned at Stockton, and it was a total failure; I was sure this was the end of my career. During this day, I was also squiring Dick Berry around the campus. I remember this so very distinctly as Dick brought a great sense of humor to an otherwise dismal situation. I was delighted when Dick arrived the next year to implement the Speech Pathology and Audiology program. Dick, who is still working at Stockton, holds a PhD in audiology and speech pathology and previously taught at Northeastern and Boston Universities.

During that first year, we also hired Robert Dixon to develop Biomedical Communications and Alma Wooly to implement Nursing. I had taught a pathology course for nurses the first year, but the program really didn't get started until Alma arrived. Alma Wooly was an extremely motivated and capable leader; she later became the dean of Georgetown's Nursing School and was nationally known and respected in her field. Regardless of this, Alma didn't fit very well into the Stockton culture. Everyone was afraid of her—students, faculty, and administrators.

During this time we had Florence Wimburg as the administrative secretary, and later we engaged Betty Wessler as her assistant. Back in those days there was a great deal of camaraderie, both at the work place and at home. We were all one big happy family— dean, faculty, and staff. Florence and Betty did everything for all of us. They took dictation, deciphered the worst of handwriting, handled the finances, and dealt with student problems. Everything we did was handwritten, and it all had to be typed, edited, and retyped. Dick Berry's handwriting looked like a straight line; the only person who could read it was Betty Wessler. How did we survive without computers?

PROFESSIONAL STUDIES: THE MIDDLE YEARS

After Ted Martin left, in order to save money, a number of programs were moved into the catch-all Division of Professional Studies (PROS). During the reign of President Peter Mitchell there was talk of eliminating some of the Health Science programs, as they were more costly to run. There were very few

Health faculty at that time, and in order to create a stronger bargaining group and to show the administration that we could save money, Dick Berry and I came up with the idea of combining all the Health Science programs under the umbrella of "Allied Health," with one coordinator and subcoordinators. We would coordinate the in-teaching responsibilities throughout the programs; we came up with a core curriculum for all the programs except Nursing. Nursing was an accredited program and could not join the group, but the rest of us formed the subdivision of Allied Health Sciences. This included Public Health, Biomedical Communications, and Speech Pathology and Audiology. Dick and I actually wrote a proposal, which was accepted by the administration and faculty. I believe that this saved us, as there was very little administrative and faculty support for Health Sciences at this time.

Health Sciences again became a priority under President Vera King Farris' leadership. At the beginning of her tenure, she called me into her office and asked me, commanded me, to help develop and promote a program in physical therapy. I was enthusiastic about this project, as I believed there was a community need. The most difficult part of this task was finding the right person to develop and run the program. I was getting desperate and discouraged when I had a call from Vice President of Finance Rob Trow who gave me the name of Bess Kathrins, whom he had heard about when attending a conference in the Boston area. The rest is history. Bess developed one of the best Physical Therapy programs in the area. We started offering a baccalaureate degree and now we offer a Doctorate of Physical Therapy.

We lost Biomedical Communications during the period we were developing Physical Therapy. It wasn't from a lack of enrollment, but from the administration's perception that the program wasn't offering sufficient job opportunities, among other things. Retrospectively, I think this was a poor decision, since, with the use of computers and online education, there is a great need for biomedical communications. This type of major lends itself to interdisciplinary study. This was a popular major and attracted large numbers of students.

Also during this time we tried to develop a program in biomedical record keeping, utilizing faculty from the Allied Health Sciences and Information Sciences. Dr. Joy Moll, along with the rest of us, drafted detailed curricular plans in an attempt to implement this concept. Unfortunately we did not have enough support at that time.

Nursing at Stockton was originally a BSN completion program. Students came in with an RN with the intention of earning a baccalaureate degree. At that time Stockton didn't want to incur the expense of a four-year generic program in nursing. Today the RN to BSN is a very common degree, and most nursing schools offer it. Back in the 1970s the New Jersey Board of Nursing as well as the National League of Nursing frowned upon this type of program. Stockton was one of the first institutions of higher education to offer this degree in the state of New Jersey. Today we also offer a four-year generic program in nursing as well as an Advanced Practice graduate program. The number of students applying to the RN to BSN program is dwindling as nursing education changes, but the four-year program and graduate program are very competitive, and we have to turn away many students.

Back in the 1980s, when I was Chairperson of the Division of Professional Studies (PROS), we investigated the possibility of a four-year generic Nursing program. Unfortunately the commitment on the part of the faculty and the administration was not sufficiently strong. We were able to find the commitment under the leadership of President Herman Saatkamp, and last year we graduated our first class. Ninety-four percent of the students passed the nursing boards on their first try.

Toward the end of the PROS period, President Farris wanted an Occupational Therapy program at Stockton. This is strictly a graduate program with a strong emphasis on the social sciences. It is a popular program, which is growing at a rapid rate. A Health Sciences building was also erected to house these programs as well as health-related student services; this is the West Quad Building.

THE SCHOOL OF HEALTH SCIENCES (SHS)

Three years ago the Health Sciences programs were given their own division, the Division of Health Sciences. Today we are known as the School of Health Sciences. We have our own dean, Brenda Stevenson-Marshall, who has a doctorate in public health. Physical Therapy now offers a doctorate, which is the terminal degree in the field. Speech Pathology, under Amy Hadley, is developing a graduate program in speech communication disorders, but they will still continue to offer the baccalaureate degree. Nursing, as I mentioned earlier, offers three separate tracks as well as off-campus programs in hospitals throughout the area. We are outgrowing the West Quad Building.

SUMMARY

The early years of the division were exciting but unsure. We never really knew how committed the administration was to the health sciences. In addition, we were looked down on by much of the faculty. We didn't really fit into the vision of a liberal arts college modeled after a place like Swarthmore. My perception was that the trustees wanted a DHS as they felt that we were answering the needs of the community at large. Faculty meetings were often stressful as there was a lot of resistance toward these new expensive programs as well as toward graduate degrees. I, in particular, felt torn, as I wasn't a professional certified in a health field. I was a PhD trained in research. I was moved around from program to program; nobody really wanted me, and the administration didn't know where to put me. Because of a tenure quota during the early years, having me in a program made it difficult for others to receive tenure.

Somewhere along my career path I decided to invest my energy and talents in promoting and supporting the health sciences. I have seen these programs get stronger and more credible over the years. We are a leader in developing graduate programs. We are a well-respected school in southern New Jersey. We have supported the needs of our community. Over the years we have gained more respect from the faculty at large. We embrace the newest technology, and our curriculum utilizes the newest research in our different fields. Our students go on to become productive and respected members of their communities and are in demand.

I expect our school to grow and thrive in the future, as the need for good health care providers has never been greater. We are in the process of developing a graduate degree in communication disorders, which is greatly needed. We are working on an undergraduate degree in the health sciences that will enable students to apply to graduate programs in health-related fields as well as offer students with associate degrees a way of achieving a baccalaureate utilizing their credits from two-year colleges. There are opportunities for new programs and tracks that will enable majors in other fields to become more marketable. Perhaps we might want to rethink a track in medical record keeping and biomedical technology. The possibilities are limitless.

In summary, you might equate us to the phoenix. We started out as the Division of Heath Sciences, morphed into the Division of Professional Studies, almost died, and have been reborn as the School of Health Sciences. We are stronger than ever, with excellent undergraduate and graduate programs. We certainly are a presence at Stockton and in the southern New Jersey medical arena.

What the Community Advised

Early in 1970 meetings were held between college officials and representatives from local business and organizations with a view to considering what professional programs the College should develop in the future. A list of the programs and the local organizations that suggested them follows:

Health Professions:
Atlantic Community College (ACC)
Atlantic County Health Department
Children's Seashore House

Engineering Programs:
Institute for Electrical and Electronics Engineers (IEEE)
American Chemical Society (ACS)
National Aviation Facilities Experimental Center (NAFEC)
Atlantic City Electric Company (ACE)

Teacher Preparation Programs:
Atlantic County Schools
Cumberland County Schools
Cape May County Schools
Center for Research and Experimentation in Higher Education

Management Programs:
Atlantic City Chamber of Commerce
Cape May County Chamber of Commerce
Law Enforcement Program, A.C.C.
Cumberland County College
Ocean County College

Science Professions:
Environmental Center
Conservation District
American Chemical Society
Atlantic City Electric Company
Marine Sciences Consortium
Institute for Electrical and Electronics Engineers (IEEE)

Hotel/Motel/Restaurant Programs:
NJSMHA
Atlantic County College

Embracing Graduate Education

Bess Kathrins

It could be equated to Bob Dylan going electric at the Newport Folk Festival in 1965. Some booed him and saw it as the downfall of civilized music; others watched and waited in silence, while others embraced a new era of music. Faculty had similar reactions to the idea of offering graduate education at Stockton. That is how the journey of graduate education began.

It was the early 1990s and the college, having just initiated a Physical Therapy program (the first major academic program to be added to Stockton's offerings since the college's inception), now needed to convert this program to the master's level. Though Physical Therapy was the impetus for the change, faculty in the Nursing and Business programs, who had similar intentions of introducing new programs, were also waiting in the wings.

How would an institution developed with a vision for change face change itself? Stockton considered graduate education in the same way it considered all important matters, carefully, methodically, and with lively discussion. Ultimately, the concept of graduate education was approved by the Faculty Assembly. On June 30, 1994, President Vera Farris walked into the last meeting on the last day the Department of Higher Education of the State of New Jersey was in existence and saw to it that graduate education and the Master of Physical Therapy Program at Stockton were approved. In short order, January 1999, the Master of Nursing and Master of Business degrees were the first graduate degrees awarded.

Dr. Marc Lowenstein took the initial leadership role in developing graduate education at Stockton. Others contributed to the early development, and, eventually, Dr. Deb Figart left a faculty position at Stockton to significantly grow our graduate programs. In time, the School of Graduate and Continuing Studies was established.

The next test of graduate education occurred when the Physical Therapy faculty once again announced that the program needed to develop a Doctor of Physical Therapy Program in order to meet expectations within the discipline. Stockton had come a long way as evidenced by the Faculty Assembly's unanimous approval of the doctoral program. President Herman Saatkamp and Provost David Carr shepherded the doctoral proposal through all processes to ultimately achieve approval of doctoral education at Stockton in 2006.

To this day, Stockton has worked hard at maintaining the important balance of offering graduate education at a primarily undergraduate institution. Graduate education has flourished and is now infused into all aspects of Stockton life, including additional graduate programs, a Graduate Student Council, and graduate housing. However, unlike the electric guitar displacing the acoustic in popular music, graduate education should never become primary at Stockton. Stockton should remain a nationally renowned undergraduate institution with outstanding graduate education, and we should continue to challenge and cherish this balance.

Growth and Change—Graduate Study

Deborah M. Figart

On Saturday, April 5, 2008, Stockton's School of Graduate and Continuing Studies threw itself a birthday party with the theme, "You Only Turn Ten Once." All 828 graduate degree alumni were invited back to campus to share in the anniversary celebration. Alumni, faculty, staff, and friends of the college had an opportunity to reconnect, to network with colleagues, and to meet and greet new friends. The graduate school, now with over 1,000 alumni on the occasion of our fortieth birthday, has matured along with the institution.

Stockton started planning to meet the region's need for graduate programs in the mid-1990s. The administration, faculty governance bodies, and other stakeholders on campus and in the surrounding community thought the College needed to supplement its primary focus on undergraduate education in order to more ably respond to emerging professional career opportunities, especially in health and business services, in the southern part of the state. The graduate programs that Stockton wished to offer would help aid the placement of qualified employees in high-growth occupations.

On August 5, 1997, the agency that governs Stockton's mission and degree programs, the New Jersey Commission on Higher Education, visited the College to determine the institution's readiness for programmatic change from a bachelor's granting institution to a master's-level institution. Stockton received the approved change in mission authorizing the offering of additional graduate programs on an incremental basis (dated November 21, 1997). This fit well with Stockton's placement in the then-Carnegie Classification system: an Undergraduate Liberal Arts College with selective graduate programs. The Stockton Board of Trustees subsequently amended the College's mission statement by adding a graduate mission statement:

Graduate Education Mission Statement
(Adopted by the Board of Trustees on February 18, 1998)
The Richard Stockton College of New Jersey provides quality graduate programs, which promote advanced inquiry and application of new knowledge, foster advanced-level career opportunities, and transmit our cultural and intellectual heritage in all its diversity. Its graduate programs are consistent with the College's commitment to the liberal arts and support the undergraduate program through enriched resources, the discovery of new approaches to teaching and learning, and the creative use of new technologies. Through accessible graduate education the College responds to State and regional needs.

Students began taking graduate courses in business in the spring 1997 term and in instructional technology in the summer 1997 term. At that time, the Physical Therapy program also planned a transition from a baccalaureate to a master's degree program, with a new graduate student cohort beginning full-time study in the fall 1997 term. A graduate degree program in occupational therapy was in development as well.

Off to a running start, in September 1998, Stockton initiated its fourth graduate degree program, the first Master of Arts in Holocaust and Genocide Studies in the United States. The Master of Science in Nursing program and the Master of Science in Occupational Therapy program also accepted their first students in the fall 1998 term. During the fall 1998 commencement ceremony held in January 1999, Stockton awarded its first graduate degrees to two students who received the Master of Business Studies, now termed the Master of Business Administration.

After the initial spurt of planned master's degree programs, new programs were added gradually to respond to regional needs. According to the College's official enrollment reports, new graduate students were welcomed into degree programs in the following terms (see below):

Graduate Degree Program	Degree acronym	Starting Term
Business	MBS ➡ MBA	Spring 1997
Instructional Technology	MAIT	Summer 1997
Physical Therapy	MPT	Fall 1997
Holocaust & Genocide Studies	MAHG	Fall 1998
Nursing	MSN	Fall 1998
Occupational Therapy	MSOT	Fall 1998
Education	MAED	Fall 2004
Criminal Justice	MACJ	Fall 2005
Physical Therapy	DPT	Fall 2006 (replaced the MPT)
Computational Science	MSCP	Fall 2007
Social Work	MSW	Fall 2009
Professional Science	PSM	Fall 2009
Education Leadership	MAEL	Spring 2011

These new programs have been designed to utilize Stockton's strengths, to meet student interest and needs, and to reflect changes in professional credentialing in local, regional, and national labor markets. In fact, Stockton's Professional Science Master's program was the first in the state of New Jersey and also in the mid-Atlantic region. The master's degree program in physical therapy was also replaced with a professional doctorate (DPT) to meet the vision of the American Physical Therapy Association.

When the Carnegie Classification system revisions were released in November 2005, Stockton's classification changed to: Master's Colleges and Universities (smaller programs).

With its steady growth over the years, Stockton ensured that graduate students would have access to first-rate student services. Stockton became an institutional member of the Northeast Association of Graduate Schools in 2002. To further learn about and follow best practices in graduate education, the College joined the Council of Graduate Schools (CGS) in 2005. CGS member institutions enroll approximately two thirds of graduate students nationwide. CGS members also award seventy-five percent of master's degrees annually in the US and nearly all of the nation's doctoral degrees.

And the administration of graduate programs evolved. With substantial growth from 165 graduate students (in fall 1997) to 746 students (in fall 2009) has come major changes in the School of Graduate and Continuing Studies. The Office of Graduate Studies was renamed the School of Graduate and Continuing Studies at the opening of the fall 2008 term. In its first phase, the graduate school

- Took on responsibility for and offered continuing education programs and credit-based certificate programs
- Opened the Graduate Admissions Office responsible for recruitment and retention
- Started an online newsletter, *Headway*, for students and the community
- Helped to foster and sustain graduate student clubs and organizations for each of the graduate degree programs
- Rekindled interest in and aided in the development in a new Graduate Student Council
- Developed the Board of Trustees-funded Distinguished Research Fellowships for graduate students
- Developed policies and procedures to facilitate the College's first defenses of student master's theses
- Began a program to recognize outstanding graduate alumni during Homecoming weekends

The tenth anniversary of Stockton's graduate school in the spring of 2008 coincided with maturity in some graduate degree programs and produced the College's first master's theses, successfully defended by students in the Holocaust and Genocide Studies and Criminal Justice programs. These are "published" and available in the Stockton College Library. More examples of the outstanding work completed by graduate students, called final projects or capstone projects, can also be found in the Library. Some of these projects include a companion CD or DVD, especially in programs such as Instructional Technology.

There will definitely be a phase two and growth and change in graduate study at Stockton. With Stockton's reputation to respond quickly and effectively to ever-changing labor markets and educational needs, future graduate students—from those enrolled in post-baccalaureate and certificate programs to those pursuing post-master's programs and professional doctorates—can look forward to Stockton's continued innovative leadership in higher education.

To fulfill Stockton's **Graduate Education Mission Statement**, the graduate school's goals are:

- To recruit and retain excellent, diverse students from the mid-Atlantic region, and especially the State of New Jersey
- To work with Stockton's other academic Schools to support the academic enrichment of existing graduate degree and certificate programs
- To support the development of new graduate degree and certificate programs
- To adopt "best practices" in graduate education
- To serve graduate student needs in their programs through opportunities for research and applications
- To support graduate student clubs, organizations, and activities
- To help provide graduate students with excellent services across the units of the College
- To complement the College's commitment to and strength in the liberal arts and sciences by encouraging regular communication and consultation across graduate programs and between undergraduate and graduate programs
- To assess the impact of graduate students' programs on their knowledge, skills, and personal growth and to continuously improve our services to the campus community

Lew Leitner
Dean, School of Graduate and Continuing Studies

Looking Forward

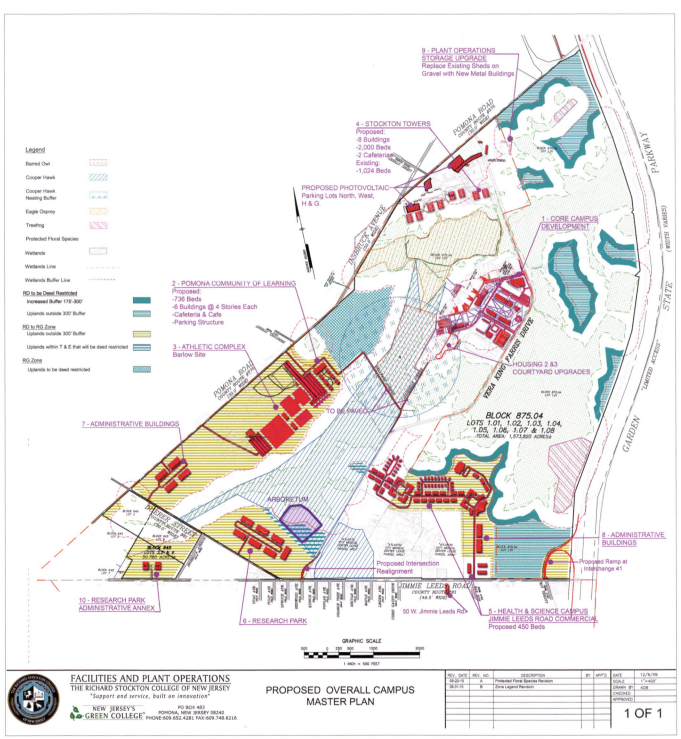

Map of proposed campus (2009)

The final substantive section of this volume focuses on the recent past at Stockton with an eye to how we are moving forward. Stockton is now positioned in a way that it can become a major force for educational advancement in the region. In part this is due to sound fiscal management over the last ten years, which has allowed the college to invest in new buildings, as well as do so without falling dangerously into debt as other colleges have done. The college has come through the last few lean years of the economic downturn and declining state support, better off than many other public and private institutions in the mid-Atlantic region. In part, though, it is also because of the college's heritage, drawing on the innovations of the past and being willing to adapt to the changing educational landscape. Here the Stockton Idea has been of importance in helping the College retain its critical and creative edge, while remaining committed to benefitting the surrounding communities by its presence in southern New Jersey.

In the first essay, Rob Gregg describes the significant contributions Stockton's fourth president, Herman J. Saatkamp, Jr., has made to the College. This is then complemented by two pieces that focus on the Stockton strategic plan, the 20/20 Vision, and the changes that have occurred since the mid-1990s. Stockton began to undergo a major transformation from being a college that was divided between an administration that tended to be very hierarchical in its approach and a faculty that was quite belligerent in its opposition to administrative initiatives, to being one that is very much more harmonious in the relations among all the various constituencies. The unions remain powerful and respected, the faculty assembly has been replaced by a more effective governmental body (the Faculty Senate), and, while conflict has not evaporated entirely, there has been a greater sense of cooperation with the administration.

In 2001, Stockton witnessed one of its faculty members receiving a Pulitzer Prize for poetry. Stephen Dunn had been well respected for many years and had published a great many books of poetry – some of the best known works being *Between Angels*, *Landscape at the End of the Century*, *Loosestrife*, *Everything Else in the World*, and his most recent, *Here and Now*. But the Pulitzer Prize was certainly an honor of a greater magnitude than he or any other Stockton faculty member had ever received. Dunn was awarded the honor for his work—"Different Hours"—from which "The Metaphysicians of South Jersey", printed below, comes. This is accompanied by two other Southern New Jersey poems, "At the Smithville Methodist Church," and "Landscape at the Turn of the Century." Stephen also has a great reputation as an inspirational teacher and a taskmaster who is able to provoke the

will to search for great writing in his students. Poet BJ Ward, who graduated from Stockton in 1989, highlights this element of Stephen's accomplished career at Stockton.

Much of the published work produced by Stockton's faculty has been supported by college funding. Beth Olsen's discussion of grant seeking highlights an important element of Stockton's future, namely the ability of the faculty to secure funding for their innovative research and creative endeavors. Such funding will help the college build on its reputation both regionally and nationally.

In the next part we return to the contributions Stockton has made to the community. The first of these essays draws on the expertise of Economics professor, Oliver Cooke, who outlines the College's economic contribution to the region – which has been very significant in the past and looks like it will only grow in the future with the acquisition of the Seaview Hotel, a new educational center in Hammonton, and other projects throughout Atlantic County and southern New Jersey. Harvey Kesselman and Patricia Weeks then provide a brief history of the Southern Regional Institute & Educational Technology Training Center, which has had a great impact on all area public schools, through the services and training it has provided to area teachers. Diane Falk then discusses the development of the Baccalaureate Child Welfare Education Program, an innovative venture that has dramatically enhanced the state's Public Child Welfare System. Once again, Stockton has made contributions to the area through the arts. In addition to the on-going efforts of the Performing Arts Center, (led by Michael Cool), Beverly Vaughn and Henry van Kuiken, with more than 30 years of service to the college each, have been electrifying audiences with their dance and choral concerts that have been generated in the classroom and have been performed to area audiences. Beverly Vaughn, in particular, has been one of the premier ambassadors for the college, increasing awareness of Stockton among residents of all the surrounding communities.

The last word goes to a recent editor of the *Argo*, Emily Heerema, describing her work as a recent editor of the student newspaper, which has been appearing continuously since the earliest days of the college (the first issue being published on October 29, 1971). Through her service as editor, Heerema helped revive interest in the student newspaper, making it once again an important voice for students.

Toward the Environmentally Responsible Learning Community—Herman J. Saatkamp, Jr.

Rob Gregg

Herman J. Saatkamp, Jr. arrived at Stockton to become the college's fourth president in June 2003. A scholar of George Santayana, President Saatkamp brought with him more than thirty years of experience in higher education as a philosophy professor and administrator at universities in Florida, Texas, and Indiana. He came to Stockton having had considerable success as Dean of the Indiana University School of Liberal Arts.

During Dr. Saatkamp's tenure as president, the college has witnessed significant growth and improvement, in terms of the size of the student body, the funded assets and endowment, and the physical environment. All of these developments fit within the president's overarching vision—one that is in accord with the college's history and mission—that Stockton is and should remain an environment for excellence. In his view, the college should be "an environmentally responsible learning community of engaged citizens embracing a global perspective." As such, he believes that even though Stockton is a state-funded institution, this does not preclude it from having the highest aspirations for its students and the highest expectations of all its employees.

In particular, there have been many new construction projects completed and many more envisioned for the future. A master plan for the college was developed with the architectural firm RMJM Hillier. When completed, this plan will see the campus that has been in place largely since the college's founding utterly transformed; where the college had been organized along a single spine, the intention is to have a new quad develop in front—the first two elements, the Campus Center and the Unified Science Center, already completed or under construction. The first major construction under President Saatkamp, however, was the F-wing overbuild, which provided additional space for teaching and for offices, and which also created an atrium outside the Library—a feature that was very much the president's own hallmark. As he predicted it would, this has become an excellent space for interaction among students, faculty, and administrators, as well as increasing use of the Library itself.

The major project has been the new Campus Center, which will almost double the floor space of the college. Running parallel to the main spine that had comprised the college, this dramatically conceived building will house all of the offices of Student Affairs and many of the services needed by students (the Registrar, the Bursar, advising, etc.), as well incorporating a bookstore, dining services, a theater, and conference space. Its opening in the spring of 2011 is likely to be transformative in the life of the

college, changing the campus from one that empties out on the weekends to one that is vibrant seven days a week.

Additional projects have been completed, are in the process of construction, or are planned for the near future: the A-wing auditorium has been remodeled and renamed in honor of Elizabeth Alton; residential space has almost been doubled with new dormitories built around a renovated Lakeside Center; the former swimming pool in L-wing is being rebuilt as an art gallery with additional teaching spaces; and, groundbreaking for a Unified Science Center occurred soon after the completion of the Campus Center. This Science Center will be the first building to encroach on the parking spaces that have up to now provided visitors with their first impression of the college.

While President Saatkamp has transformed the campus physically, the influence of Santayana is nonetheless also very evident. Santayana would remind those who erect new edifices to symbolize the strength of the institution that an institution cannot flourish if it should become an "intellectual slum." In tandem with this building program, therefore, President Saatkamp has worked hard to improve the condition of faculty and students at the college. When he arrived Stockton's student-faculty ratio was one of the highest in the state, so he immediately freed up funding to increase the number of faculty lines. Each school of the college has thus been able to hire faculty who have substantially increased college offerings.

Moreover, as has been a characteristic of the college since its founding, the quality of these hires has been exceptional. Along with the numerous departures occurring as a result of the Mayflower faculty reaching retirement age, the faculty body has been markedly transformed. More than fifty percent of the current faculty began their employment at the college since the beginning of Herman Saatkamp's presidency.

Such new faculty, treated poorly, might only have swelled the ranks of the disenchanted. This has not occurred because the level of support provided to junior faculty has been greatly increased, and the new arrivals have been made to feel welcomed and nurtured. With the active support of Provost David Carr, new faculty have been mentored through the Institute for Faculty Development and provided with funds for their research. In addition, the personnel procedures have been rewritten to ensure that all faculty members coming up for reappointment, tenure, and promotion are aware of the College's expectations. Gone are the days of the

President Herman Saatkamp, Jr. at Lake Fred

tenure quota and the sense that a tenure-track appointment at Stockton was a misnamed temporary position. The result of these changes has been a boost in the morale of the faculty generally and an increase in the productivity of faculty members—in areas of teaching, research, and service to the community.

In addition, like Santayana, Saatkamp does not fear debate; he is willing to engage with faculty about all issues. In a letter of 1939, Santayana wrote: "Of course, I like agreement, it warms the heart, but I don't expect it; and I like disagreement, too, when it is intelligent and carries a thought further, rather than contradicts it *a priori*, from a different point of departure." In this vein, President Saatkamp has engaged with the faculty, both in the Faculty Assembly and the union, in ways that have helped to move the college beyond the fractiousness of its founding years. The president has been met with good leadership from the faculty—from Joe Rubenstein, Mary Ann Trail, Marilyn Vito, and Bob Helsabeck in the Faculty Assembly (now Senate), and David Emmons, Mike Frank, and Tim Haresign in the union.

Of course, sound fiscal management and the sense that the college is still growing has helped reduce some of the tensions from the College's earlier years. Whereas many colleges have felt the impact of funding cuts, leading to increased disenchantment among state employees, Stockton has seen continued construction and few cuts in funding. With the deep cuts in state funding and the resultant freeze in new lines, however, this overall sense of well-being may be more difficult to sustain.

President Saatkamp has also made his mark in helping to transform relations with the surrounding community. He has continued strong support for the Performing Arts Center, but he has expanded Stockton's reach, taking over and renovating the Carnegie Library in Atlantic City, working with Hammonton Township to convert an old factory into classroom space near to the railroad station, creating an affiliation agreement with the Noyes Museum of Art, and, in perhaps the most audacious move, acquiring the Seaview Hotel. In short, owing to these and other initiatives, the college receives considerably more attention from the local community and has a much stronger reputation regionally than was the case prior to President Saatkamp's arrival.

The new Campus Center—photograph by Margot Alten

20/20 Vision

Claudine Keenan

The Richard Stockton College will receive national recognition for excellence in education through its focus on learning, engagement, global perspectives, and environmental sustainability.

LEARNING

Stockton College is committed to fostering a climate of lifelong learning that challenges and continually transforms all members of the Stockton community. As an institution of higher education, we strive towards a 2020 in which graduates are solidly grounded in the foundations of interdisciplinary understanding, deeply engaged in learning that reflects the ability to move across disciplines as well as between theoretical understanding and the subtleties of implementing knowledge, and capable of understanding the limits inherent in a single frame of reference, whether it be a disciplinary perspective or a cultural perspective. As a community, we aspire to learning that is intentional and cumulative.

ENGAGEMENT

Our concept of engagement is broad and includes the intellectual involvement of students with deep learning and the cocurricular, as well as the community activities of students, faculty, staff, and administrators on the campus and in the wider community through active civic work. We aim to create meaningful opportunities for Stockton stakeholders to develop personally by supporting engagement and reflection.

GLOBAL PERSPECTIVES

We envision laying the foundation of our global theme by building a community capable of developing opportunities to collaborate across a diverse world of cultures, race, gender, orientation, and age, one that prepares us for global participation. We understand that building a global perspective is not limited to travel abroad. We do believe that in this effort we should strive to capture the wealth of diversity and opportunity that exists locally, regionally, and nationally. Accomplishing this theme is an ongoing project.

SUSTAINABILITY

Stockton's theme of sustainability recognizes the need to use, maintain, and enhance resources in a way that safeguards the ability of future generations to use those same resources. Sustainability encourages stewardship of air, water, soil, biological diversity, and carbon/associated energy production (and this list is not exhaustive). Institutionally, this theme means actively managing our own operations with an explicit goal of sustainability. This theme also involves building the capability of our students, faculty, staff, and other stakeholders to be stewards of natural resources through education, research/scholarship, and service/outreach. Stockton seeks to have a positive impact on the environment locally, regionally, nationally, and globally.

Changes at the Turn of the Century

Rob Gregg and Claudine Keenan (with assistance from David Carr and Marc Lowenstein)

Stockton has seen many changes from the 1990s through the first decade of the twenty-first century. These changes reflect the college's constant desire and capacity to improve itself. While the college has matured since the heady days of the 1970s, it has not settled into a state of complacency; it recognizes that it will always be a work in progress.

Here is a brief listing and elaboration of a few of these developments:

DEVELOPMENT OF UNDERGRADUATE PROGRAMS AS WELL AS INTERDISCIPLINARY MINORS:

Programs:
- Bachelor of Fine Arts in Visual Arts
- Hospitality and Tourism Studies
- Four-year Bachelor of Science in Nursing
- Computational Science

Interdisciplinary Minors:
- Latin American and Caribbean Studies
- International Studies

EXPANSION OF GRADUATE AND CONTINUING STUDIES, INCLUDING FIRST DOCTORAL PROGRAM

New Graduate Programs:
- Doctor of Physical Therapy
- Master of Business Administration
- Master of Arts in Criminal Justice
- Master of Arts in Education
- Master of Arts in Educational Leadership
- Master of Science in Computational Science
- Master of Arts in Holocaust and Genocide Studies
- Master of Social Work
- Professional Science Master's in Environmental Science

REORGANIZATION OF DIVISIONS INTO SCHOOLS

In 2008, the six divisions were renamed schools. In addition, the Division of Professional Studies was broken out into different entities. Originally housing Education, Health Sciences, Business, and other Professional Studies, and having been in place since the founding of the college (though originally called Management Sciences), PROS no longer exists. In its place are three new schools, Education, Health Sciences, and Business, each headed by its own dean. This change reveals growth and change at the college. Once primarily a liberal arts undergraduate institution, Stockton now incorporates a much stronger graduate and professional studies component.

INSTITUTE FOR FACULTY DEVELOPMENT (IFD)

President Vera King Farris established the Institute for the Study of College Teaching (ISCT) in 1999. Headed by Sonia Gonsalves, the ISCT provided support for junior faculty and mentoring for all aspects of the teaching enterprise. Necessary funding cuts led to the disbanding of the ISCT in 2003, but it was replaced two years later with the Institute for Faculty Development, with a broader mandate to assist in all aspects of faculty development. The IFD has spearheaded the college's efforts to increase assessment of teaching outcomes in compliance with the requirements of Middle States accreditation.

JUNIOR FACULTY SUPPORT

Stockton has flourished owing to its strong faculty. However, for many years little support was given to new faculty, and the threat of the tenure quota was such that there was considerable insecurity among the new arrivals. The arrival of President Saatkamp led to a sea change in this area, with junior faculty receiving additional funding to support their research and attend conferences, as well as mentoring through the Institute for Faculty Development. A transformation in the morale of the faculty has resulted from this initiative.

RESTRUCTURING OF FACULTY EVALUATION

New procedures and policies for reappointment, tenure, and promotion were adopted in 2007. These procedures made much clearer to faculty the expectations of the college in terms of the three main pillars of evaluation—teaching, service, and scholarship or creative endeavor. Gone are the days when faculty members feared that they would be denied tenure owing to a quota, or felt uncertain what their program or school expected of them.

EXPANSION OF STUDY ABROAD

Study Abroad declined briefly following the events of September 11, 2001, but it has been growing steadily over the last five years under the leadership of Janice Joseph. With the inclusion of globalization as one of the themes in the strategic plan, it will grow alongside other initiatives to foster a more internationalized environment at Stockton.

HONORS PROGRAM

In order to attract high-achieving students, the college established an Honors program in 2005. Under the leadership of Michael Hozik, and now Lisa Rosner, the program provides Honors students with a unique, fully integrated educational experience, involving both curricular and cocurricular elements. Students actively engage in college life, take Honors General Studies courses together, and finish with an enriched capstone experience, usually in the major.

FRESHMAN-YEAR EXPERIENCE

In contrast with many other colleges in the New Jersey system, Stockton has always had very high retention rates. In part this has been owing to the fact that the college has made constant efforts to improve the freshman-year experience. It has instituted freshman seminars, more intimate classes of no more than fifteen students, organized around topics of the faculty's choosing but including segments that introduce students to the college's learning environments—from the library to online resources. It has established a common freshman reading tied to the re-established Freshman Convocation. Including works like Warren St. John's *Outcasts United* and Ishmael Beah's *A Long Way Gone*, the reading allows students across the campus to consider issues of pressing concern in contemporary society.

EXPANSION OF GRANTS AND CONTRACTS

As discussed in the essay by Beth Olsen that follows, the Grants Office has grown significantly in the last ten years. This reflects and has helped cement Stockton's reputation regionally and nationally for undertaking strong research and creative endeavors.

EXPANSION OF ENGAGEMENT WITH THE COMMUNITY AND REGION

In 2010, the college earned the Carnegie Foundation's prestigious Community Engagement Classification. The application that garnered this award included (among other things) the following:

The Performing Arts Center (PAC): For more than thirty years, the PAC has provided the community with a wide range of cultural offerings: the Children's Imagination Series and Summer Playhouse, Stockton Goes to the Beach concerts, as well as the very best in jazz, dance, theatre and opera.

Service Learning: Stockton now partners with about one hundred businesses and organizations throughout southern New Jersey.

New Centers: Several new centers have been established, including the William J. Hughes Center for Public Policy, the Stockton Center on Successful Aging, the Lloyd D. Levinson Institute of Gaming, Hospitality and Tourism, the Center for Economic and Financial Literacy, the Interdisciplinary Center for Hellenic Studies, and the Stockton Text Center.

Seaview Resort: The college has acquired this historic building and plans to continue running it as a luxury hotel and golfing resort, in conjunction with the rapidly growing Hospitality and Tourism program. The college will also benefit from the hotel's potential as a site for conferences and other public programming.

The Noyes Museum of Art of Richard Stockton College: In 2010 the college created an affiliation with the Noyes Museum in order to safeguard and expand the reach of an important community resource into the future.

The Carnegie Library: In July 2010, the Middle States Commission on Higher Education approved Stockton's satellite facility in Atlantic City, the Carnegie Library Center, as an "additional location." This designation permits the institution to offer more than fifty percent of any degree program at this venue, thus greatly expanding all academic offerings. Graduate programs in social work and special education are scheduled to be solely offered and held at Carnegie. As of August 2010, the facility, operated by Alex Marino, has hosted 226 graduate and undergraduate courses with 3,917 student registrations since opening in 2004. Additionally, Carnegie hosts a considerable amount of continuing education and professional development programming offered by the institution, as well as hosting a number of meetings, retreats, and conferences sponsored by regional businesses, nonprofit organizations, and governmental agencies. Carnegie is home to the newly established Lloyd D. Levenson Institute for Gaming, Hospitality, and Tourism, a comprehensive institute offering research and educational programming in support of the region's largest economic industry, and to the offices of the Small Business Development Center (SBDC) of Atlantic, Cape May, and Cumberland counties. Under Stockton's umbrella since 2003, the SBDC is part of a networked national partnership between state and federal government, the private sector, and higher education. Since locating its offices at Carnegie in January 2005, the SBDC has counseled more than 3,300 clients and trained over 8,400 people at more than 380 events, seminars, and workshops.

Stephen Dunn

A Tribute to Stephen Dunn

BJ Ward

When I entered the Master's in Creative Writing program at Syracuse University, people asked me what it was like studying under Stephen Dunn for four years. I said the first two years were fine, but then he started to bring his shotgun to class.

He named it "Little Harold Bloom." He never aimed it at anyone, of course, but if someone had a cliché in his poem, he'd discharge it in the air, as if warning a trespasser on his property to back off.

This is when they moved the Creative Writing classroom from lower C-wing to upper C-wing.

One workshop, several of us had moments of pathetic fallacy in our poems. He grasped the brim of his cap, pulled it even to his brow, and said, "Follow me, Poetasters."

He marched us to the shore of Lake Fred, had us crumple up

the offensive poems. He yelled "Pull!" and we all tossed them into the air. Then he shot them onetwothreefourfive justlikethat. And Lake Fred was snowed upon by shattered words, a blizzard of Dunn, a strange alphabet soup, which, Stockton legend has it, served as inspiration for the acronym system used in Academic Affairs to this day: ARHU, NAMS, SOBL . . . they were all once parts of lousy poems in my workshop.

In any case, the lesson that day, as he tucked Little Harold Bloom back into his AWP tote bag, was "Write better." So many of his former students who've enjoyed a certain level of accomplishment since graduation still ponder his shotgun.

In all seriousness, it's a diminishment to merely state that he taught me for four years at Stockton State College. I took every class Stephen offered and took either the Poetry Workshop or Advanced Poetry Workshop seven times. After the first time in each course, he arranged for me to get credit by renaming the experience I would have and listing it as an independent study. The titles we came up with together in my sophomore year seemed appropriately edentulous: "The Creative Process" and "Sound and Meaning." But by my senior year the names had progressed to the point where it was clear to me that Stephen, ever the rebel, was seeing what he could get away with: "Studies in Verbal Flight" and "Refutations of Deconstruction." Taking his cue from Donald Justice, he was creating the maximum amount of wildness a dean could bear.

I can honestly say I never learned more from a single teacher in class than I have from Stephen—and I have learned even *more* from him since I stopped being a formal student of his.

When he won the Pulitzer, he asked me to teach his courses for him at Stockton. That invitation remains the single highest professional honor of my life—that my greatest teacher would ask me not to work for him, but to work with him. We team-taught the Advanced Poetry Writing Workshop in the spring of 2005, once a week talking for an hour on the phone about the thirteen students' poems. It was my favorite hour of the week every week. Over the fifteen-week semester, what I learned from those one-hour conversations about poetry and teaching rivaled what I learned over two years in graduate school. What made the experience even more extraordinary is that Stephen was just talking to me—not even trying to be a teacher then.

And he gave me my own shotgun, which he named, "Little Aggravated Helen Vendler."

I want to emphasize this: he never pointed his shotgun at anyone—only our poems. And when he discharged it in the air, we young writers—like quails that had grown slightly complacent—rediscovered flight in a crucible of sound. A great teacher he is, who knows how to say both, "That ain't flyin'" and "Well flown."

Poems by Stephen Dunn

Landscape at the End of the Century

The sky in the trees, the trees mixed up
with what's left of heaven, nearby a patch
of daffodils rooted down
where dirt and stones comprise a kind
of night, unmetaphysical, cool as a skeptic's
final sentence. What this scene needs
is a nude absentmindedly sunning herself
on a large rock, thinks the man fed up
with nature, or perhaps a lost tiger,
the maximum amount of wildness a landscape
can bear, but the man knows and fears
his history of tampering with everything,
and besides to anyone who might see him
he's just a figure in a clearing
in a forest in a universe
that is as random as desire itself,
his desire in particular, so much going on
with and without him, moles humping up
the ground near the daffodils, a mockingbird
publishing its cacophonous anthology,
and those little Calvinists, the ants,
making it all the more difficult
for a person in America
to close his office, skip to the beach.
But what this scene needs are wisteria
and persimmons, thinks the woman
sunning herself absentmindedly on the rock,
a few magnificent words that one
might want to eat if one were a lover
of words, the hell with first principles,
the noon sun on my body, tempered
by a breeze that cannot be doubted.
And as she thinks, she who exists
only in the man's mind, a deer grazes
beyond their knowing, a deer tick riding
its back, and in the gifted air
mosquitoes, dragonflies, and tattered
mute angels no one has called upon in years.

At The Smithville Methodist Church

It was supposed to be Arts & Crafts for a week,
but when she came home
with the "Jesus Saves" button, we knew what art
was up, what ancient craft.

She liked her little friends. She liked the songs
they sang when they weren't
twisting and folding paper into dolls.
What could be so bad?

Jesus had been a good man, and putting faith
in good men was what
we had to do to stay this side of cynicism,
that other sadness.

OK, we said, One week. But when she came home
singing "Jesus loves me,
the Bible tells me so," it was time to talk.
Could we say Jesus

doesn't love you? Could I tell her the Bible
is a great book certain people use
to make you feel bad? We sent her back
without a word.

It had been so long since we believed, so long
since we needed Jesus
as our nemesis and friend, that we thought he was
sufficiently dead,

that our children would think of him like Lincoln
or Thomas Jefferson.
Soon it became clear to us: you can't teach disbelief
to a child,

only wonderful stories, and we hadn't a story
nearly as good.
On parents' night there were the Arts & Crafts
all spread out

like appetizers. Then we took our seats
in the church
and the children sang a song about the Ark,
and Hallelujah

and one in which they had to jump up and down
for Jesus.
I can't remember ever feeling so uncertain
about what's comic, what's serious.

Evolution is magical but devoid of heroes.
You can't say to your child
"Evolution loves you." The story stinks
of extinction and nothing

exciting happens for centuries. I didn't have
a wonderful story for my child
and she was beaming. All the way home in the car
she sang the songs,

occasionally standing up for Jesus.
There was nothing to do
but drive, ride it out, sing along
in silence.

The Metaphysicians of South Jersey

Because in large cities the famous truths
already had been plumbed and debated,
the metaphysicians of South Jersey lowered
their gaze, just tried to be themselves.
They'd gather at coffee shops in Vineland
and deserted shacks deep in the Pine Barrens.
Nothing they came up with mattered
so they were free to be eclectic, and as odd
as getting to the heart of things demanded.
They walked undisguised on the boardwalk.
At the Hamilton Mall they blended
with the bargain-hunters and the feckless.
Almost everything amazed them,
the last hour of a county fair,
blueberry fields covered with mist.
They sought the approximate weight of sadness,
its measure and coloration. But they liked
a good ball game too, well pitched, lots of zeros
on the scoreboard. At night when they lay down,
exhausted and enthralled, their spouses knew
it was too soon to ask any hard questions.
Come breakfast, as always, the metaphysicians
would begin to list the many small things
they'd observed and thought, unable to stop talking
about this place and what a world it was.

The Metaphysicians of South Jersey **woodcut by Michael McGarvey**

Not Taken for Granted—Grants and Grant-Seeking

Beth Olsen

EARLIEST EFFORTS

Throughout our short history, Stockton has searched for balance between our devotion to the pedagogy of teaching and learning in the liberal arts and our integrity in promoting scholarship and knowledge. However the tensions for competing values see-sawed over time, the foundations for grant-supported scholarship were established early on.

The founding policy for providing support to faculty at Stockton State College was signed on April 28, 1977 by the Board of Trustees and then by the president on June 6, 1977 to establish the Research and Professional Development (R&PD) Committee. Funds for these awards were provided by the (then) New Jersey Department of Higher Education for programs of "separately budgeted research" for the faculty and professional staff at the New Jersey state schools. This fund for Stockton began at approximately $70,000 and remained constant for nearly thirty years. Alongside R&PD awards for projects, a sabbatical leave program began in April 1977 when policy was first authorized. Review of applications fell on the R&PD committee, and guidelines governing the timing of a sabbatical request have been defined by the faculty union agreement. This original structure of internal support—the review procedures and the committees themselves—has remained fundamentally constant since the beginning. Then, and now, awards were determined by a committee of peers: two from each division/school, one each from the Library, and a union representative.

The original Research and Professional Development Committee was chaired in 1978 by Roger Wood, followed by a two-year term by John Richert. The R&PD committee received $70,000 to allocate. Seven sabbatical semesters were supported in 1978.

Mining the reports of R&PD chairs over the years, several trends began during these early days that strike familiar chords even now:
• New applicants have always been "strongly encouraged" and the R&PD committee has shown a bias toward them, encouraging committee members to make an effort to contact new faculty members. Untenured faculty received up to thirty-five percent of funding during the 1980s and early 1990s.
• The Business division has historically submitted by far the fewest proposals (some years submitting no applications and other years maybe two or three at most). Consequently Business faculty have regularly received less than ten percent of the overall funds.
• NAMS and ARHU have historically submitted about equal numbers of proposals and together have won the majority (sixty

to seventy-five percent) of the awards. SOBL faculty have been a strong third place in both number of submissions and receipt of awards. Even though GENS has been consistently outnumbered by faculty size, GENS faculty have also consistently been at the table, involved in scholarly work and receiving support.
• The number of applications has historically exceeded the number of awards, but support has generally been given to approximately sixty to seventy-five percent of applicants.
• The committee has historically declined to support any one person for both R&PD and sabbatical simultaneously as a matter of principle, preferring to share scarce resources more widely.
• Committee members have always been encouraged to take active roles in promoting scholarship and intentionally serve their colleagues and the college in building a scholarly culture. Thus a scaffolding of assistance and encouragement for developing projects has slowly risen to promote scholarship.

New Guidelines were approved in fall 1987 under the leadership of the committee chair, Margaret Marsh, ARHU, so they might conform to the policies and procedures of our sister institutions. Former chair Alan Arcuri provided "valuable leadership" over the preceding few years wrote Neil Kleinman, Vice President for Academic Affairs, in a September 1986 memo to faculty. The guidelines were revised again in 2003 to reduce the application size and tighten the requirements.

Early examples of research supported by R&PD include Roger Wood's project on diamondback terrapins, Anne Birdwhistell's research on Shao Yung's Non-orthodox synthesis of Chinese philosophical traditions, Dennis Wildfogel's work on *Intuitive Calculus: A Textbook*, and John Sinton's book on the Pine Barrens, *Water, Earth and Fire*. Faculty artists—David Ahlsted, Josh Cabot, Pat Hill Cresson, Mike McGarvey, Stephen Dunn, Liane Schneeman, and Al Corpus—received summer stipends during the early years for their time in studios and their creative thought. Looking back, awardees accomplished an enormous body of work. Summer stipends in 1989 ranged from $1,700 to $1,900 (at a time when adjuncts were paid $1,400 a course) with the expectation that significant progress could be made—and it was!

Sabbatical leaves spawn a life's work for some faculty members who have used their time away from teaching to immerse themselves in more personal interests. Given time to follow their passions, scholars can spend long days writing (sometimes award-winning) books. For example Mimi Schwartz took the 1989-1990 year to work on two book projects, including one based on her work in autobiographies; Paul Lyons was given a sabbatical during this same year to begin work on a book on the Baby Boomers of the 1960s. Jean Mercer received a sabbatical in 1993 to write a textbook on adolescent development.

Of course, not everyone writes books, but what seems universally true is that a sabbatical from teaching can be the catalyst for very significant changes—at times causing a turning point in one's professional pathway that may fundamentally affect the institution. For example, John Searight spent a semester in 1993 to study "recent research and literature on social work practices and child welfare." Later John and Diane Falk would receive federal and then state funding to address this critical topic, which led to deep and broad changes in child welfare education and practices throughout New Jersey. Stew Farrell spent fall 1992 compiling New Jersey shoreline trends for the state legislature that eventually altered state regulations governing the coastline. Stew's policy-related work contributed to his reputation as an expert, which has reeled in millions of dollars in external funding over the years for the Coastal Research Center. In 1994 Lynn Stiles spent time on computer simulation models used in geothermal-based energy systems and during a later sabbatical worked on super efficient UTES—projects that have informed Stockton's growth in energy-saving systems.

Thus the college support for R&PD and sabbatical programs has always been the foundation for launching scholarship among faculty and, in turn, has improved the institution. Throughout this forty-year period the College community looked to the R&PD committee as the primary mechanism for financial support for the faculty as well as the body symbolic for promoting a culture of scholarship. This role within the College historically caused some tension as the numbers of faculty increased and the expectation for scholarly engagement expanded beyond the means of the R&PD budget. In response, internal funding programs slowly grew, offering support for a variety of purposes. The Career Development Awards were mandated earliest, targeting members of the bargaining unit who request support following their five-year assessment process. The rules for applications have remained consistent; decisions are made by a committee of three, which includes a tenured faculty member, someone appointed by the bargaining unit, and an administrator. The Career Development Committee, chaired in 1978 by Ralph J. Bean, received an appropriation of $24,000 (of which $1,650 was given to the chair for administrative duties). Twelve faculty members received support then. Awards are given mostly for professional development rather than scholarship.

The Distinguished Faculty Fellowship (DFF) program began in 1996 as a way to expand the support for scholarship and research; the program encouraged and rewarded large, summer-long projects. Decisions were made by a committee that included faculty, deans, administrators, and presidential appointees. Twelve fellowships were awarded during the first year. The program expanded the second year to include a new category of awards that encouraged innovation in teaching. When the program began, each award carried a stipend of $5,000 to be given during the summer months, which was substantially more than one could gain from an R&PD award since R&PD stipends were tied to faculty overload payments. As the overload payments increased over the years, the financial value of a fellowship paled. The last year the DFF program ran was in 2007, when five fellowships were awarded.

Over the years, some projects funded through DFF continued far beyond the fellowship period. Readers may recognize a scattered few, including Development of Self-Directed Readings Courses for Literature Majors by Tom Kinsella and A New Calculus I Course Based on Cooperative Learning and the Use of Modern Technology by Juan Tolosa from 1998. In fiscal year 2000, Stephen Dunn received a fellowship for *Different Hours: A Collection of Poems*, which later earned a Pulitzer Prize. Bill Gilmore-Lehne was supported for his *A Republic of Knowledge: Communications and the Rise of an Age of Reading in America to 1861*. In 2003 David Emmons and Paul Lyons were awarded fellowships to develop their ground-breaking course, Teaching September 11; Alex Alexakis for his study, *The Life of Leo of Catania*; Peter Straub for *Pollution Effects on Gene Expression in Winter Flounder;* and Wendel White for *Small Towns, Black Lives.*

From 1994 to1998 the college invested $90,000 for eighteen projects in Virtual Reality—New Teaching and Learning Strategies as a category of funding from the DFF. These were course-based projects to promote new pedagogies in electronic classrooms, integrate technologies, and rework courses. SOBL, ARHU, NAMS, and PROS all were equally supported, transforming or introducing eighteen courses before the program ended.

In March 1998 President Farris issued a "Faculty Gram" to announce two new programs: Excel 2000 and Transition to Retirement. The Excel program, which gave full salary to two faculty members to engage in projects that would benefit the community or the state, lasted only one year. (Rudy Arndt and Yingyi Situ were only recipients.) The "pioneers" for the Transition from Classroom to Retirement program, first offered in spring 1998, included Allen Lacy, Mimi Schwartz, John Searight, Bill Sensiba, John Sinton, Alan Steinberg, and Joe Walsh. This program set a standard for ways to support senior faculty members for our sister institutions.

Other funding programs emerged over the years, smaller in scope, but adding to the broad cloth of faculty development. In 1998 President Farris responded to faculty requests for support during their sabbatical terms, which, until fiscal year 2010, provided only three-quarter salaries for one semester and one-half salary for a full year of sabbatical leave. The new program provided a subvention of $2,000 per semester to offset project-related costs to sabbatical awardees, when requested. In 2008 the Stockton Federation of Teachers and Provost Carr instituted a Summer Research Fund (whose purpose and process coincided with R&PD) and its $45,000 was folded into R&PD pot in 2010. The Junior Faculty Awards came from money distributed to the deans by the provost's office based on the number of nontenured faculty members within each school. The money was intended to fund opportunities for new and junior faculty to make progress in their scholarly goals by traveling to conferences, buying software, student research assistance, or small pieces of equipment. The Divisional Grant Development funds were fairly short-lived (running from fiscal year 2007 to 2009, and modestly in 2010). The money was intended to encourage grant-seeking for school-wide or college initiatives. Time and talent spent on developing a competitive proposal was money well spent, or at least that was the idea. The Summer Technology Academy provided instruction to faculty who infused the academic curriculum with technology-rich courses. Some of these programs morphed into other funding opportunities, and some survive as long as they seem relevant and affordable. The dynamic quality of internal funding programs during the last few decades seems characteristic of greater institutional agility.

Throughout the history of internal award programs, the cry for more support became a constant subtext to a need to participate in scholarship and the costs of doing so. The original $70,000 in R&PD seemed insufficient for the growth of the faculty and the increased expectation for faculty to engage in scholarship. In a February 20, 2001 Faculty Assembly meeting, for example, the agenda included "discussion and vote on resolution to request doubling of the R&PD money over the next five years." The R&PD budget finally did grow in 2007 through efforts of Provost Carr and President Saatkamp.

REGARDING GRANT-SEEKING OUTSIDE THE COLLEGE

The official policy for applying for outside grants dates from June 1, 1982, likely in recognition that the college should broaden grant-seeking activity. In 1983 the state established a competitive grant process for programmatic and technical educational programs. Stockton was particularly successful in the next couple of years in winning several substantial grants from the state to purchase energy technology equipment to support our new Energy Studies Certificate program, to computerize the Physics labs, and to develop freshman and senior seminars among other projects. Harold Taylor, Yitzhak Sharon, Lynn Stiles, and Robert Helsabeck were major players. But during this time, the college lacked a formal grants office to support and encourage grant-seeking.

Then-Vice President of Academic Affairs, Neil Kleinman, asked Lynn Stiles to organize seminars for faculty to help them write successful grants. Kleinman's September 1986 memo marked a new commitment to grant-seeking for support from outside the college: Margaret Marsh, ARHU dean, was charged to identify grant sources from outside the College for ARHU faculty, Lynn Stiles in NAMS to identify grant opportunities for the sciences, and "one more faculty member" to do so for business and the social sciences. The vice president also announced the allocation of funds to hire someone for twenty hours a week during the academic year to serve as staff support for grant-seeking. Under the direction of Margaret Marsh, I was subsequently hired part-time to promote grant-seeking, serve faculty efforts, and lay foundations for a new office. Early years were critical for building structure and practices: policies were instituted, and procedures for gaining institutional support and approval were practiced. The position was made full-time in 1998. Gradually, a culture was taking shape that asked scholars to look beyond the institution for assistance.

During the period from 1986 to 1994, grant-seeking focused primarily on grant programs offered by the New Jersey Department of Higher Education. This state agency was rich with funds and dedicated some of these to grant competitions for equipment and curriculum development.

At the risk of neglecting significant awards, only a few are described below to illustrate the impact of awards and their effects on institutional growth.

Among the total awards ($92,231) received from external sources in 1994 was an award that helped tip Stockton's path toward becoming an "engaged" institution. Afterschool at Pleasantville: Science and Service, directed by Rogers Barlatt and myself, received an award from the New Jersey Department of Higher Education for $34,668. This program mapped the beginning steps for service-learning at Stockton—also through DFF support to Marcia Steinbach for surveying institutional interest in service-learning—and put Stockton faculty and students into the surrounding community to assist disadvantaged neighborhoods. Rogers' program (later joined by Tim Haresign) received further funding to continue this work the following year from the US Department of Energy for Pre-Freshman Enrichment. Stockton's service efforts were again rewarded by the US Corporation for National and Community Service with one of the first AmeriCorps programs: Project SafetyNet, directed by Sonia Gonsalves and myself, received $500,000 over five years to integrate peer-mediation programs into a number of Atlantic City elementary schools. More service-oriented programs were funded over the years, which deepened and widely embedded service practices and activities throughout the culture of the College.

In 1996 the curriculum experienced a profound shift when the National Science Foundation and the American Council of Learned Societies funded Quantitative Reasoning Across the Curriculum programs. These grants followed two years of work by a Central Task Force, convened by then President Farris, to study and plan for a mathematical literacy requirement. The task force presented their findings in spring 1995, at which time the proposal for a new graduation requirement was approved by the Faculty Assembly and the Student Senate. Grant awards followed this intensive work and supported a college-wide implementation plan, with faculty workshops and course development to include numerical literacy, materials, and programs. The QUAD program dove deeply and spread widely across institutional programs, and Q-courses are now offered throughout the curriculum. The faculty included Frank Cerreto, as project director, and team members Alan Mattlage, Renga Iyer, Melaku Lakew, John Quinn, and Joy Moll. A second National Science Foundation award was received for the purpose of writing several guides, or text books, which would disseminate the QUAD efforts to a wide, national audience. This team (during a grant period that ran from August 1, 1999 to July 31, 2002) included Frank Cerreto as principal investigator (PI) and co-PIs Renga Iyer, Melaku Lakew, John Quinn, and Marilyn Vito. The project also involved Juan Tolosa, Hannah Ueno, and Lance Olsen. The quantitative reasoning requirement is now totally embedded throughout the curriculum and continues to serve other institutions as a model. Such is the power of grants.

In the years since the grants office was initiated, grants and contracts award amounts have increased, sometimes leaping ahead with the successes of large awards. Not until 2001 could the College begin claiming millions of dollars in outside funding—with $2.37 million received in support for new projects, the majority of these (approximately $1.5 million) from federal agencies. Over the years, significant amounts of money (more than $1 million) have distinguished the projects and their directors—Diane Falk and John Searight for child welfare, Cynthia Sosnowski for continuing studies, Patty Weeks

and Harvey Kesselman for education, Stew Farrell for coastal research. In fiscal year 2010, awards amounted to $8.76 million in new project funding.

In 2004 the Grants Office expanded for the first time from a one-person operation to include a clerical staff position and a financial analyst to assist in post-award monitoring and activities. And again in 2006, the office expanded with an assistant director position. Activities emanating from the Grants Office now include an annual Report of Scholarly Activity (since 2000), an annual Day of Scholarship (since 2000), workshops about grant-seeking, programs about compliance and developing successful proposals, support for the Institutional Review Board, and most internal award programs.

It's critical to note that the real impact of all the awards over the years is not the money. The money simply made it possible for labs to expand, faculty and students to dig deeper into research, stronger connections and collaborations with community and colleagues to be made, and courses to be developed. These long-term programs and short-term projects depend on faculty and staff for their interest and their passion, their hard work and care. The grant-seekers truly have made a tremendous difference and significant impact on the College.

The Stockton Faculty Band - David Lechner, Paul Lyons, David Pinto, Anne Pomeroy, Frank Cerreto, Peter Hagen, Warren Ogden, and Rodger Jackson (2008) - photographs by Margot Alten

Stockton's Regional Economic Contribution

Oliver Cooke

It has long been recognized that institutions of higher education have important economic impacts on the communities in which they operate. Those located in smaller communities tend to have larger impacts. It is thus perhaps not surprising that economic considerations played an important role in Stockton's earliest history. Minutes of the October 1, 1969 hearing in which Stockton's Board of Trustees solicited public comments regarding its announced intention to site the college in Galloway Township suggest that economic motives played a key role in delineating site detractors from supporters. Indeed, at one point during this charged meeting—which included debate over county population statistics—the Mayor of Absecon, Joseph McGahn, argued that opposition to the site seemed largely based on selfish motives (RSC Archives, "Summary of Public Hearing–Site Selection" October 1, 1969).

Needless to say, Stockton has had a significant economic impact on the greater southern New Jersey region. This impact has grown considerably over the course of the College's history. An institution whose initial state allocation (for planning and preparation purposes) totaled $150,000, and whose first academic semester was held in a rented Atlantic City hotel now boasts a $125 million operating budget, capital assets of approximately $92.5 million, and a 1,600-acre main campus.

Relying on archival material and other internal data, this essay pieces together some basic economic and financial statistics in an effort to provide a modest assessment of the College's "narrow" economic impact. The essay does not constitute a comprehensive economic impact statement, and its use of the word narrow is intentional. All economic assessments are incomplete in numerous ways. For example, highly-trained critical thinkers and engaged world citizens ostensibly represent the College's ultimate final products. The social and economic value of these thinkers and citizens (Stockton has granted a total of 41,425 undergraduate and graduate degrees since its inception) escapes easy quantification. Similarly, how does one value the economic activity of the thousands of interns and volunteers the College has provided the greater southern New Jersey community since its inception? What is the real economic value to a community of a performing arts center, an art gallery, a library, and all of the myriad events and activities that constitute the fabric of any institution of higher education? In short, all of these things produced by institutions of higher education are socially and economically valuable but escape the type of quantification that comprises the heart of traditional economic assessment exercises. The primary determinants of the College's narrow economic impact include: salaries, vendor outlays (input purchases), student spending, and capital expenditures. The theoretical underpinnings of economic impact research hold that each of these forms of expenditure results in positive spillover or multiplier effects for the local and regional economy. For example, College faculty members use their salaries to consume goods and services produced by local businesses. Similarly, a college's purchases of the various inputs required to produce higher educational services support the myriad local and regional businesses that produce those inputs. College students' consumption of higher educational services, unlike the consumption of many other services, necessarily requires additional expenditures (e.g., food, entertainment, and transportation spending) that nourish the local economy in which a college is located. Finally, the college's capital expenditures, like its outlays on inputs, support various types of businesses in the local and regional economy.

COLLEGE EMPLOYMENT AND SALARIES

Planning documents for the college's first official semester (fall 1971) indicate that an anticipated first-semester enrollment of 500 students would require approximately twenty-six administrators and a minimum of thirty-one faculty members. (The latter figure reflected a state-mandated 16:1 student-faculty ratio.) The 500 student figure turned out to be a significant underestimate, however, as the college's initial enrollment turned out to be approximately 1,000 students. As classes began, the college's employment comprised ninety-seven staff and sixty full-time faculty members (who had been chosen from a pool of over 4,000 applicants). The college's state appropriation for 1970-1971 totaled $842,000, with $461,200 of this amount representing salaries. Today, the college serves 7,300 undergraduate and graduate students and employs approximately 850 individuals, making it among the region's largest public-sector employers (outside of the local school districts and the Hughes FAA Technical Center), and one that rivals several of the largest private-sector employers (outside of the region's casinos and health care facilities). Stockton's fiscal year 2011 total salary outlay will equal approximately $71.5 million (excluding fringe benefits).

The larger economic implications of these salary figures can be better grasped by putting them in some context. Specifically, the 1970-1971 salary cited represented 0.05 percent of Atlantic County's total personal income. The College's current salary outlay represents approximately 0.7 percent of the county's total personal income. In other words, college salaries' contribution to the local economy's total personal income has increased by a factor of twelve. The casino industry payroll's share of total county personal income (about 18 percent in 2009) has roughly doubled since the industry's inception. It is also worth noting that while the College's employment is considerably smaller than any Atlantic City casino's, five of the eleven casinos have payrolls that are smaller than Stockton's. This, of course, reflects the difference in the occupational structures (and, thus, average employee salary) of casinos and institutions of higher education.

NON-SALARY EXPENDITURES

Beyond salary and fringe benefits expenditures, as well as student aid commitments, the bulk of the remainder of the College's operating budget is used to purchase all of the "inputs" an institution of higher education requires in order to operate (e.g., utilities, office supplies, information technology, food/dining services, etc.). A significant portion of the monies used to secure these inputs supports local and regional businesses. (Some suppliers are not local, and, thus, the monies they receive effectively leave the local economy.) Stockton's 1970-1971 state allocation, for example, included $128,400 for materials and supplies, $44,500 for outside professional services, and $75,000 for library acquisitions. For fiscal year 2011, Stockton's non-salary expenditures (excluding student aid commitments) comprise approximately $22 million or 0.2 percent of total personal income in Atlantic County. Additional contracts managed by Stockton's nonprofit auxiliary organization, Stockton Affiliated Services, Inc., represent additional input purchases (related to housing, dining, safety, and transportation services) that further enhance the College's impact on the local and regional economy.

STUDENT SPENDING

As noted, college students' consumption of higher educational services is somewhat unique as it generally necessitates additional local-based spending (e.g., food and entertainment outlays). These types of expenditures enhance a college's local economic impact. Research on college student spending habits suggests that today's college student has significant discretionary income (often ranging between $600 and $1,100 per month). This income reflects, among other things, increased access to financial aid and grants, students' willingness to work while in school, and evolving student demographics. (More than half of college students are older than twenty-one.)

While a fully-documented estimate of the total local economic impact of Stockton student spending lies beyond the scope of this essay, a back-of-the-envelope calculation suggests that this impact is far from insignificant. Assume that one-half of Stockton's student body (roughly 3,500 students) is present on campus on any given weekday. Assume each of these students spends $2 per day in the local economy (gas, food, entertainment, etc.) = $7,000. Over the course of any given school week this yields $35,000 in student spending in the local economy. Over the course of the academic year this spending totals roughly $910,000—a sum equal to 2.7% of total proprietors' (small business) income in Atlantic County. Given the steady growth in the College's enrollment since inception (in 1971, the College's student body accounted for 0.6% of Atlantic County's total population, whereas today it accounts for 2.7%) this impact has undoubtedly increased significantly.

CAPITAL EXPENDITURES

From its humble beginnings in the Mayflower, Stockton's capital plant has grown significantly during its forty-year history. The capital expenditures associated with this institutional growth largely flowed to private sector entities. Despite these expenditures' transitory nature, they can have significant economic impact on the local economy—especially when the entities involved are local or regional ones. The price tag associated with the College's initial (Phase I) academic building construction totaled approximately $5.7 million. College archival materials indicate that these expenditures flowed to regionally based construction firms. The largest contract ($2.7 million) went to the Costanza Construction Company of Pennsauken, New Jersey. By way of comparison, the cost of the new Campus Center is estimated at $60 million.

I hope this brief sketch underscores what I think is obvious—at least to those who are (or have been) associated with the College as well as those who are only indirectly touched by it—Stockton's economic contributions to the local and regional economy have been and continue to be significant. I should add what I hope is equally obvious: while the numbers and statistics presented here offer some modest means by which these contributions might be contextualized, the college's real impact (like so much in life) escapes easy quantification.

The following individuals graciously gave their time and/or provided invaluable research assistance: Louise Tillstrom (whose research efforts were invaluable to me in writing this essay), Richard Colby, Claudine Keenan, and Robert D'Augustine.

Beverly Vaughn in Israel - photograph by Wendel White

Impacting the Region—The SRI & ETTC

Harvey Kesselman and Patricia Weeks

Beginning in the late 1980s, Stockton College recognized its responsibility to help address the needs of the K-12 educational sector and drew on the professional expertise of its faculty and staff to contribute to the initiatives of regional school districts. Through grant-funded programs, including Goals 2000, Comprehensive School Reform, and the New Jersey Statewide Systemic Initiative (NJSSI), which was funded through the National Science Foundation, local school districts regularly sought support from the College in the development and delivery of continuing professional education for K-12 personnel.

The College's Holocaust Resource Center was providing prejudice reduction programs to thousands of students from K-12 schools each year and offered in-service training programs to teachers under New Jersey's Holocaust and Genocide Education program. The College also created and hosted a unique series of conferences designed to reduce prejudice and promote racial harmony. These conferences, entitled CHEER (Civility, Harmony, Education, Environment, and Respect), were supported by then-Governor Christie Whitman and boasted over 2,000 participants, including students and teachers from higher education and the K-12 sector.

By 1996, when the New Jersey Department of Education (NJDOE) released a Request for Proposal (RFP) to establish an Educational Technology Training Center (ETTC) in every county in the state, Stockton had gained the trust and respect of the K-12 community and under the leadership of the Vice President for Student Affairs, the college helped to organize a county-wide response to the RFP that would include representation and participation from all twenty-four public school districts and municipalities in the county. The college suggested to school districts that rather than compete against each other for this competitive funding, they should form a consortium of schools that would all be able to benefit from the establishment of a county resource to assist teachers as they learned to introduce the emerging educational uses for technology into their classrooms. And to validate its commitment to the program's success, Stockton College offered to house the program—the Atlantic County ETTC—on its campus in Pomona.

The purpose of that initial county-wide proposal was to seek funds to develop and implement comprehensive educational technology training programs for the 4,000 teachers and educators in Atlantic County's K-12 public and nonpublic schools. The Atlantic County ETTC acknowledged unequivocally that technology would fundamentally alter the teaching and learning

process. The need to offer teachers comprehensive professional staff development opportunities was greater than ever as pedagogical methods adjusted in order to effectively infuse rapidly emerging technologies within our schools and curricula. The ETTC would provide coordination and collaboration for schools across the county in their efforts to prepare students for the challenges they would face in a highly technical society.

Through creative and multiple scheduling options, teachers throughout the county would be provided flexible opportunities for professional development well beyond what any individual school district could provide. The consortium approach would promote a wide range of alternative instructional delivery methods by utilizing such technology as distance learning, telecommunications, on-site workshops, and weekend and summer institutes.

The proposal to NJDOE was successfully funded in the amount of $450,000. Stockton provided the physical space and technical support to the Atlantic County ETTC, which opened in July 1997 in a small classroom in F-wing. Although a center was funded in each of the twenty-one counties in the state through this initial RFP, the Atlantic County ETTC was the only program that was designed and operated as a voluntary consortium of dues-paying school districts and other members. This unique governing and financial structure is the primary reason the center in Atlantic County remains the state's most successful after fourteen years.

The state-mandated goal for ETTCs was to prepare teachers to utilize technology to address the multiple levels of cognition embedded in each of the New Jersey Core Curriculum Content Standards. Additional training areas included basic technology literacy, technology planning, telecommunications, distance learning, and strategies that fuse curriculum with existing and emerging technologies, such as the World Wide Web and multimedia design.

Stockton College realized that the programming provided through the ETTC would generate an increased interest from K-12 educators to become more fully engaged with these new instructional tools, and the college proposed the establishment of a Master of Arts in Instructional Technology degree to be offered beginning June 1997. The program would provide educators, prospective technology consultants/coordinators, and technology trainers with the means to integrate the latest interactive technological tools into the instructional environment. Communication, research, and productivity through technology provided the foundation for course offerings as students formulated technology's role in teaching and learning. This program contributed significantly to the partnerships between Stockton and the K-12 community.

State funding for all centers ended in 2001, but because the Atlantic County ETTC, through its consortium underpinnings, began with a strong business plan for sustainability, there was a sufficient funding stream to continue to provide services as project staff sought additional financial support through new grants and contracts. The end of funding for the statewide network of ETTCs also provided an opportunity to extend membership in the Atlantic County ETTC to districts in neighboring counties that had recognized the quality of programming and services available to consortium members. Membership quickly doubled and then tripled in just a few short years.

In July 2002, the New Jersey Department of Education recognized the success of the Atlantic County ETTC and renamed it the Southern Regional ETTC. Shortly thereafter, NJDOE administrators strongly encouraged the Stockton Board of Trustees to continue to expand and enhance the programming provided by the center to include research and other activities that would fully explore issues relevant to K-12 education. In response, the college established the Southern Regional Institute (SRI), which today serves as the umbrella for the ETTC, now a consortium of ninety-six school districts and not-for-profit organizations from six counties throughout the southern region of the state. While professional development for K-12 educators remains its primary function, the SRI&ETTC has expanded its menu of services to include such diverse topics as strategic planning and feasibility studies for school districts, district technology audits, educational program evaluations, curriculum planning and alignment, instructional mentoring, grant-writing, and educational leadership development.

Nearly 80,000 participants have attended the workshops and programs of the SRI&ETTC, which is now under the administrative leadership of the School of Education. The SRI&ETTC is well known for the depth and breadth of its programming and for a strong technological infrastructure that supports the delivery of nearly 600 workshops each year. College faculty and staff members regularly present workshops and programming to school districts across the region on behalf of the SRI&ETTC and provide suggestions and support for the continued exploration of topics germane to K-12 education as well as those that address and strengthen connections to higher education.

Most importantly, the SRI&ETTC has been able to participate in and secure numerous grant-funded and long-term systemic initiatives in area school districts for the past decade. Direct funding to the college has included a Safe Schools Safe Communities grant ($150,000), two Improving Teacher Quality grants (ITQG) from the New Jersey Department of Education ($1.8 million), a Mathematics and Science Partnership grant ($1.5 million), a National Endowment for Humanities grant ($150,000), and most recently an Improving Active Partnerships and Collaboration in Teaching (IMPACT) grant ($75,000).

The SRI&ETTC has also participated in numerous grants received by school districts including a federal Teaching American History grant, NJDOE grants such as ACE, ACE Plus, Star-W, Comprehensive School Reform, Include, and Talent 21, as well as projects funded by the National Science Foundation, to name a few. Most recently, the SRI&ETTC received a $1.2 million contract to develop the Intervention and Referral Services (I&RS) Technical Assistance Project, which provides workshops and services to school districts across the state in the implementation and review of intervention services for struggling learners as required by New Jersey administrative code.

SRI&ETTC staff regularly participates in local, county, regional, and statewide committees and organizations and develops and hosts programming that brings educators from across the state to Stockton's campus. The SRI&ETTC has played a pivotal role in the development of Stockton's position as the educational hub for the region by creating a venue for all educators to share and learn from one another about the issues facing today's classrooms. Through training and conversations about the value of preschool education through the analysis of instructional design at the graduate level, Stockton College provides leadership to a community of educators whose goal is continuous academic improvement for all students in New Jersey.

A Part of Something

My name is Christina Birchler and I work in the Accounts Payable department. My first day was April 28, 2010. I remember it well. Anyway, during my second week at Stockton, I was asked if I wanted to attend the "Annual Employee Recognition Day". Well, of course! Working in the Parkway Building hadn't yet allowed me to mingle with many other staff members, so I gratefully accepted. I was overwhelmed by the number of employees who had attended. But, that turned out to be nothing compared to my shock at the number of people actually being recognized. What an honor it was to be among peers that had their "first day" at Stockton 5, 10, 15, 20, 25 years ago. And though my journey here at Stockton had just begun, that day it was a privilege to be a part of something that began back in 1971!

Cristina Birchler

Enhancing Public Child Welfare

Diane S. Falk

In January 2003, police discovered the beaten and decomposing body of seven-year- old Faheem Williams in a Newark basement. This event precipitated a series of newspaper articles by investigative journalists, all raising serious doubts in the minds of the public about the effectiveness of New Jersey's public child welfare agency, the Division of Youth and Family Services (DYFS). The *New York Times* picked up the story, bringing New Jersey's crisis to the attention of the nation and the world. Compounding the crisis was a lingering lawsuit, filed in 1999 by the advocacy organization Children's Rights Inc., which focused on the rights of children in foster care. Unable to continue fighting the lawsuit in light of the embarrassing details revealed in the media reports about DYFS's shortcomings, Governor James McGreevey moved to settle the lawsuit, acknowledging that the state's child welfare system was in need of repair.

In 2004 the state launched a comprehensive and ambitious plan to transform New Jersey's child welfare system. The plan, A New Beginning, called for a dramatic increase in the number of caseworker positions, with the intent of reducing caseloads to manageable levels. It also placed considerable emphasis on workforce development, calling for enhanced internal training programs, as well as the involvement of experts from colleges and universities across the state. Furthermore, the transformation plan proposed to expand internship programs for Social Work students.

As Social Work program coordinator at the time, I recognized a potential synergy between the needs of New Jersey's public child welfare system and the needs of students enrolled in Stockton's Social Work Program. First, I noted that the state, local communities, and network of agencies making up New Jersey's child welfare system needed professionals who were prepared to work effectively to help New Jersey families cope with the complex problems they face in today's society. Second, I knew that many Social Work students expressed a strong interest in careers in working with families and children but that many of these students confronted barriers to fully pursuing their interests.

A very high percentage of students who receive degrees in social work have transferred to four-year institutions from community colleges. A significant proportion of these students are from lower income families; many are first-generation college students; and many are members of minority groups, predominantly African American with a growing percentage of Latinas. Many have chosen social work as their profession because they have had to struggle with difficult personal and family circumstances. They come into social work strongly committed to the profession's values and to working with populations at risk. They have a compassion bred out of their own experiences. Empathy for oppressed people does not have to be taught.

I began working with Social Work Program Field Coordinator Barry Keefe and recently retired Social Work program faculty member John Searight. Added to the mix were Dave Oldis and David Mallory, both District Office Managers for DYFS. We professors, seeking to reconnect with the realities of community-based social work, went out with DYFS workers on their visits; we met with workers and supervisors in the local offices; and we networked with faculty members who had established partnerships with child welfare agencies nationwide. In these exchanges, we learned that a large proportion of the workers entrusted to protect the lives of children had educational backgrounds that could not have prepared them for this work.

In April 2004 we learned that the Children's Bureau of the US Department of Health and Human Services had posted a request for proposals. Professor Searight and I contacted DYFS and easily persuaded the agency to partner with Stockton should the college be successful in obtaining funding. We then wrote and submitted a proposal, summarizing the dramatic events that led to New Jersey's child welfare crisis and citing a large body of evidence documenting the positive outcomes of partnerships between public child welfare systems and institutions of higher education. We also cited research that demonstrated that the most effective preparation for public child welfare casework is a baccalaureate degree in social work. We described the students who had expressed interest in careers in public child welfare, stating that the proposed project would not only bring compassionate, knowledgeable, and skilled workers into the child welfare system but would also ease the financial and time burden for students who were often working long hours in low-paying jobs to support themselves and pay for their education.

The proposal called for offering a $5,000 stipend to fifteen senior Social Work students who were committed to pursuing careers in public child welfare. In exchange, students would agree to work as caseworkers in the Atlantic, Cape May, or Cumberland County offices of DYFS for at least one year following graduation. On September 29, 2004, a letter arrived from the Children's Bureau, congratulating Stockton College on being one of five Social Work programs in the nation to be awarded a Title IV-B, Section 426, discretionary grant—$100,000 a year for five years. In October 2004, Stockton held a press conference to announce receipt of the federal grant. New Jersey Commissioner of Human Services Jim Davey attended, and three student applicants for the stipends spoke movingly about the ways in which their life experiences had led them to pursue careers in child welfare.

Touched by their stories, Commissioner Davey met with the students following the press conference, asking them to share their ideas about bringing change to the child welfare system. Later that month, Professor Searight and I were asked to bring all of the students who had received stipends to Trenton. There, in a surprise move, Director of Human Resources Linda Dobron offered paid internships and guaranteed caseworker positions upon graduation to all of the students. At the same time, she expressed interest in finding a way to involve all of the New Jersey undergraduate Social Work programs in a program modeled after the one created by Stockton for the southern part of New Jersey.

As president of the New Jersey Baccalaureate Social Work Education Association, I called a meeting of representatives of New Jersey's accredited undergraduate Social Work programs. This group enthusiastically endorsed a plan to submit a proposal to the state to fund a statewide program identical to Stockton's existing one. The then-President of the New Jersey Chapter of the National Association of Social Workers (NASW-NJ), Allison Blake, was an employee of the state's Office of Children's Services (OCS) and a longtime advocate of enhanced services for New Jersey's children and families. At her initiative, NASW-NJ brought in a consultant from Pennsylvania, Professor Ed Sites. Professor Sites shared his experience in forming a statewide consortium in Pennsylvania.

By July 2005 Professor Searight and I had prepared a proposal to OCS. Within a few weeks, we met with OCS executive staff, presented our proposal, and received immediate endorsement to proceed with the project. The new program, the Baccalaureate Child Welfare Education Program, affectionately known as BCWEP, began with nineteen students from the newly formed consortium (which included the Social Work programs at Stockton College, Georgian Court University, Kean University, Monmouth University, Ramapo College, Rutgers University—Camden/Newark/New Brunswick, and Seton Hall University) for the spring semester and accepted sixty-five students statewide for the following academic year. The Stockton College Social Work program, in offering its expertise, emerged as the acknowledged consortium leader.

Stockton continues as the lead institution in a statewide consortium of baccalaureate social work education programs that, in partnership with the New Jersey Department of Children and Families and NASW-NJ, is preparing Social Work students each year for careers in public child welfare. Since its inception, 441 students have applied for child welfare traineeships, 289 (sixty-six percent) have been accepted. As of September 2010, 240 have completed the program and accepted positions as Family Service Specialist Trainees at DYFS. This means that approximately eleven percent of the DYFS caseworker workforce is made up of graduates of BCWEP, bringing social work values, knowledge, and skills, as well as competency in child welfare, into New Jersey's public child welfare system. A follow-up study of BCWEP graduates suggests that the program has already made a real difference in the lives of the state's most vulnerable children and families.

Canoes on Lake Fred (2011). See page 13.

Tales from an Argonaut

Emily Heerema

In 2004, I joined the *Argo* as a copy editor. It was my first semester, and I was looking into ways I could get involved in campus life and make friends. That first semester was a transition period for the staff and overall reputation of the paper. At the time, it was slightly under the radar and had more of a cult following than a general readership. The staff I worked with at this time was trying to give the paper a makeover, to transform it so that it fit in with the other clubs and organizations at Stockton. We felt that the student population was isolated, that only classmates or club members really knew each other. Students knew that clubs existed and had meetings by reading flyers on tables or bulletin boards, but it wasn't widely known what was happening around campus. The idea was to work together to build a stronger community within so that every Monday other students, faculty, and staff could see what the student community was doing.

I worked in different sections of the newsroom until fall 2006 when I became Editor in Chief. *Argo* veterans Lori Lepelletier, Donna Huneke, Joe McMahon, Keith Jacobsen, and Nikki Carpenter were the exceptional editorial staff at that time, and all held their positions until graduation. By this point, each one of us was involved in other campus activities and clubs and was able to bring ideas, experiences, and, most importantly, stories in from all areas of life at the college. Together, we knew it was imperative to reach out to students—all students—for story ideas. Our tagline was "Your Newspaper. Your Voice," and we felt soliciting story ideas from peers was the best way to gain readership and loyalty on campus. The paper's popularity grew consistently throughout this period because of stability, teamwork, and leadership from within.

The 2006-2008 era included many thematic spreads, highlighting special college events like Alternative Spring Break, Welcome Week, Writers for Change, Homecoming, Unity Week, Greek Week, Student Senate Informer, and various Study Abroad trips. We came together following the death of our friend Gina Durham in January 2008 and dedicated many pages to her life and work. Anything that we could do to keep the sense of community, engagement, and positive spirit in print was our main priority.

Our relationship with the faculty, staff, and administration was, overall, positive and friendly. We were proud to continue printing the Chief's Corner, the Police Blotter, student activity calendars, and an entire page filled with over fifty school club/organization meeting times and locations. Since the *Argo* is independent, we were completely on our own when it came to content. We were never an "if it bleeds, it leads" organization, but we never pulled a piece due to potential controversy or backlash if we felt it was important. We heard criticism from many sides about our general spelling, punctuation, and grammar. Most of the time, though, this criticism was limited to anonymous notes left in our mailbox. Other times, we felt heat from groups that felt underrepresented, or that thought information we were printing would create a safety risk. Whether the criticism was trivial or serious, we took it seriously and tried to improve for the next issue.

Our yearly April Fool's issue, the *Rago*, was the best issue of the year to put together. Both years, we stayed late at the office, eating pizza and consuming way too many stimulants (mainly Diet Coke, Red Bull and coffee), hoping that extreme caffeination, mixed with sleep deprivation, would trump our seriousness and bring out a hilarity that would transfer itself to the pages of the *Rago*. Wonderfully enough, many people didn't quite grasp the idea of the *Rago*. Those who thought this issue was real and true paid us the highest of compliments.

The writing staff was mostly recruited from club fairs and by word of mouth. Many of the editorial staff started off as writers, and we reached out to our classmates, encouraging them to submit pieces as freelance writers, or to join the staff if they felt a passion for it. We had a diverse staff, populating a variety of majors and serving up a variety of general interest topics, including health and wellbeing, fashion, sports, current events, and music/entertainment. It also became apparent early on that people loved to submit opinion pieces and original art. When I started in 2004, the paper struggled to reach sixteen pages, and by 2006-2008 we were pushing twenty-four to twenty-eight pages every week. This wouldn't have been possible without the outstanding financial management of our business manager Katie Monacelli.

Katie's business skills were crucial to the survival of the paper. The *Argo* had an annual operating budget from the student activities fund, but with payroll, color pictures and extra pages, it was necessary to print ads to cover our costs. Without Katie, I'd surely have run us into bankruptcy! Katie, a management major, single-handedly transformed the business end of the paper into a fully functioning department that was able to host an intern in our final semester together. Her responsibilities included managing the payroll, communicating with budget heads, soliciting advertisements, and managing all of the relationships with those customers. Her job was tricky and stressful, but she pulled it together with ease and confidence. Because of her, we managed to finish every year under budget and employ a full staff of editors, writers, and contributors.

In 2007, it was sad to see Lori, Donna, Joe, and Nikki graduate. It was also exciting to fill four staff positions for the fall 2007-spring 2008 year. I was happy to promote staff writers Marisa Sanfilippo to Arts and Entertainment Editor, Mark Cantiveros to Sports Editor, and copy editor Amanda Ismail to News Editor. Keith became the Assistant Editor. Working with Keith and Lori as Associate/Assistant Editors made my experience exceptionally fulfilling. You can't have a good paper without an amazing assistant editor.

Spring 2008 was Keith's and my last semester. Together, we began to start recruiting for future operating staff. We were graduating seniors that year, and many of the editorial staff were also leaving. That semester was a fun and interesting time as we were still putting out the highest quality paper we could, but we were also training a brand new staff on all of our office operations and computer programs. I'm happy to say that Lina Wayman, who began as a staff writer her freshman year, was promoted to Editor in Chief her sophomore year and continues to hold this spot going into her senior year at Stockton.

Because of my time at the *Argo*, I learned about teamwork, management, personal reflection and improvement, and the value of being an engaged citizen and community member. I was lucky enough to be presented with dozens of opportunities to attend events and go on trips, even traveling to different countries to study journalism with other school newspaper editors. I'm thankful that I was able to do it at a smaller school with a community like ours.

Inspired

My experiences of Stockton are unique from those of most people, but they can be simply described by two words: community and family.

Community

Down by the riverside a hanky panky where the bullfrogs jump from bank to bank saying e-a-e-a . . . east, and west and a bull. . . frog!! Oh! You're out! And the circle gets smaller, and smaller as we continue to play one of our favorite Stockton day camp games, in the center of K-wing circle, on a beautiful late June day.

Much like the role K-wing circle played as a meet and greet for the Stockton day campers, like myself, the many encounters I have experienced here at Stockton College, as a child and as an adult, have done wonders opening my mind and leaving me yearning for knowledge. For this I am grateful.

A-K groups of day campers were led by the enthusiastic Paul Chambers with his megaphone in hand, and by the unforgettable Larry James. With the inspiration of Margaret Simons, each day was filled with seven hours of engaging activities such as swimming lessons, in which I proudly boasted of winning races, learned how to execute the back stroke properly, and overcame my fear of the diving board. In upper N-wing we would meet to analyze colors and play with ideas for arts and crafts class.

I walked away every afternoon feeling I had accomplished something great. Owing to the Stockton day camp I have wonderful memories as well as experiences, and these flashbacks bring nothing but a smile to my face.

Stockton day camp, you're the best; Stockton day camp rules; you're number 1 for summer fun, you even have a pool for swimming, counselors and kids alike come back every year, for Stockton day we all give a great big cheer hooray!

Family

Many children have an array of stories about growing up that shaped them. Mine focus on the various role models and inspiration that constantly surrounded me. I was a blissful mixture of ARHU and the Bursar's. With my father [Dominick] as the Bursar of the College for a great many years, and my mother [Nancy], then Assistant to the Dean, and now Assistant Dean of ARHU, I saw firsthand what the true meaning of hard work really was. I got to build long-lasting relationships with individuals such as the wonderfully charismatic Beverly Vaughn, the knowledgeable Ken Tompkins, and the classically talented Wendel White; with Rodger Jackson, an amazing thinker, professor and friend; and with Kate Ogden, an excellent motivator for anyone. I have been privileged to grow up and experience all of their accomplishments along the way, and they have praised all of mine as well. With the presence of Stockton in my life I have had the opportunity to have such a vast multitude of admirable influences surrounding me, and this leaves me inspired.

Sarah Messina, 2008

More Than the Sum of Its Parts

The Climb by Arnaldo Cordero-Román

It is easier to start a book than end one. Starting means that there are almost endless possibilities before you; ending one means that all of those hopeful possibilities have been chosen or rejected and there aren't many more in the sack.

We both feel this very keenly.

We started by asking ourselves what sort of history book we wanted. Did we, for example, want to focus on events in time? We rejected this approach because we knew it would turn into a list of events (e.g., the President was appointed, the faculty were hired, the Board said NO, there was a strike, etc.) We also considered focusing on personalities – and there have been MANY of note at Stockton – but while we knew a considerable amount about events, we knew little about our colleagues especially ones who broke the rules. Perhaps we should write about roles? We could have a chapter on teachers, a chapter on administrators, on staff, on students, etc. That one didn't appeal to us at all. Who would want to be limited to a single chapter on teachers or teaching?

Finally, we agreed early in the process that we wanted many voices. If Stockton is nothing else it is a place of many voices. Sometimes all those voices create a cacophony, many times empty confusion, and sometimes great verbal power about great issues of the head and heart. We wanted all of this in the book.

We thought then about folks who had something to say, who had spoken to us before and, by that speaking, changed the college and our lives. That's where we started: listing those voices.

We worried a good deal about missing someone who should have added their voice to our lives but, for whatever reason, didn't. We wanted them in the book also. Almost everyone we asked quickly agreed, though a few thought about it for a time, and a very few rejected our request. A few promised and then never sent us their words. We fretted over these but, finally, realized that not writing was also saying something. So we moved on.

Each of these discussions—and we had hundreds over the two years we have worked on this project—informed decisions about what the book would be and also what it wouldn't be.

Nonetheless, there are many, from the highest to the lowest rung of the institution, whose contributions are most worthy of recognition, but who escaped direct attention in the foregoing pages of this volume. Among the faculty, there are, of course, all those people who have been exalted with the title of Distinguished Professor owing to their contributions to the college, to the community, or to their academic fields.

The first of these to be so honored was Demetrios Constantelos, one of the very first faculty members hired by the college, who become the Charles Townsend Distinguished Professor of History and Religious Studies. In addition, to his luminous work as a scholar of Byzantium, he has also helped establish and fund the Interdisciplinary Center for Hellenic Studies.

The faculty who have been distinguished in this way comprise a very impressive group:

Demetrios Constantelos (1971)
Charles Townsend Distinguished Professor of History, 1986.
Bill Daly (1971)
Distinguished Professor of Political Science at Stockton, 1997.
Stephen Dunn (1974)
Distinguished Professor of Creative Writing, 2001.
Janice Joseph (1989)
Distinguished Professor of Criminal Studies, 2011.
David Lester (1971)
Distinguished Professor of Psychology, 2008.
Paul Lyons (1980)
Distinguished Professor of Social Work, 2009.
Patricia Reid-Merritt (1976)
Distinguished Professor of Social Work and Africana Studies, 2011.
Carol Rittner (1994)
Distinguished Professor of Holocaust and Genocide Studies, 1999.
Ken Tompkins (1970)
Professor of Literature, Distinguished Service Award, 2010.
Wendel White (1986)
Distinguished Professor of Visual Art, 2009.

Other faculty contributions have also been most noteworthy, and while not celebrated with a title should be acknowledged for their significant contribution to the college. We refer here in particular to the Stockton Faculty Band, an ensemble formed through a blending of various musical groups that had been playing around campus as far back as the late 1970s. Throughout its various incarnations the band has played a wide range of music from jazz to classical to country to rock and performed at an incredible number of events over the years, from informal gatherings, like union roasts and college holiday events, to the most formal, such as Stockton's annual Spring Gala. They even recorded a CD, Pop Quiz, and headlined a concert of faculty bands at the Atlantic City House of Blues, dedicated to longtime band member Paul Lyons (sax, clarinet and vocals) who passed away in 2009. The common thread woven through all these activities is the donation of all proceeds from their gigs and CD sales to support student scholarships.

The members of the band should be noted here: Frank Cerreto (vocals, guitar), Michael McGarvey (vocals, saxophones), Rodger Jackson (guitar), Anne Pomeroy (vocals, flute) Lance Olsen (alto saxophone), David Pinto (drums, mandolin), Warren Ogden (keyboards), Richard Hager (guitar), David Lechner, (saxophones, trumpet), Peter Hagen (vocals, bass).

Beyond the faculty there are other important people who need to be acknowledged. Most significant of these, perhaps, is Chuck Tantillo. He was an assistant to President Bjork in the 1970s, and was very much a force at the college throughout the Peter Mitchell and Vera King Farris presidencies, as Vice President for

Student Affairs, Senior Vice President for Administration and Finance, and a Professor of Political Science, before leaving the college in 2002. Many faculty and administrators have reminded us that his contributions need to be acknowledged, and many of those who now hold high rank in the college feel a great debt of gratitude to him for his inspiration and mentoring.

But there are others who are more difficult to name and yet who play an incredibly important role at the college. Unlike faculty, who need to be seen and heard in order to move up the ladder at the college, those who are behind the scenes, administrators and staff, are frequently only functioning at their best, if they are not being noticed. This is true from those working in the police force under Chief Glenn Miller, to the people in grounds and plant, and to the janitors and other employees who have worked at the college quietly, efficiently, and frequently anonymously, acknowledged only in the yearly employee recognition breakfasts for the number of years they have been at the college. While they cannot be named here, or fully represented, their lives and work need to be acknowledged.

* * * * * * *

For better or worse, there is much of both of us in this book. We have written a few of the sixty-two essays, we have written all of the introductions, have chosen the photos, the design down to the paper, and the buckram of the cover.

But we hasten to add that we never could have done this volume without the tireless support and assistance of many others. There are those, mentioned in the prologue, who helped conceive of the volume, which had been about to move forward under Paul Lyons' stewardship. Herman Saatkamp needs to be recognized for believing in the importance of the book, and Jan Colijn needs to be also, for proposing that a volume such as this one would be an appropriate way to celebrate the fortieth anniversary.

But there are others as well. Here we list their names so that you will understand that while our names are on the title page, these names were much on our minds as we pulled this work together.
- Richard Colby and Louise Tillstom of the Library Archives who found documents with alacrity and eagerness.
- Julie Bowen and her Graphics Staff, but especially Margot Alten who designed and formatted the book.
- Ingie LaFleur, William Gilmore-Lehne, Paul Lyons and Jan Colijn – each of whom wanted to write this text.
- Sharon Schulman, Kim McCabe, and Dan Gambert who supported the project and created our public websites.
- The staff of the Phoenix Diner who fed us and allowed us to work on the book over uncounted cups of coffee
- Debbie and Mark at Barista's Coffee House who provided unlimited wifi, Almond Mocha and walnut muffins.
- Wendel White who made the past visible, and was a pillar of strength.
- Joan Bjork who graciously got us started by sharing her collection of photos and clippings.

- The ARHU secretaries – Marieann Bannan, Susan Zennario, Meghan Smith, and Madeline Perez—who steadfastly typed, copied, mailed and organized whatever we sent them, and especially Deanna Tumas, who oversaw our finances.
- Lisa Honaker – our copyeditor – who brought consistency to wildly different essays.
- A group of other advisors who provided assistance whenever called upon: Madeline Deininger, Nancy Messina, Claude Epstein, Michael Hozik, Melissa Hager, Brian Jackson, Jean Mercer, and Kristin Jacobson.
- Martha Zechman for her invaluable assistance in locating early Stockton photographs in *The Press of Atlantic City* Archives.

* * * * * * *

Finally, we want to end by asking ourselves what this all means. Because it is only forty years old, Stockton has been living in the shadow of its founding. As a result, all its members, from faculty to administrators and staff, refer back to the early days of the college almost as a habit. For some of the newer members of the college, this can be overbearing, as an action will either be seen as continuing a tradition or departing from it. For someone, who arrived in the 1980s or 1990s, or whose career doesn't extend back beyond the beginning of this century, this might even be seen as annoying. "Enough already!" one faculty member exclaimed in a meeting, when someone was talking about how distinctive the college has been. He was tired, he continued, of the reflexive way in which people referred back to the Mayflower days, though as discussion continued he happily acknowledged that the college was a pretty unique institution.

What makes it so, we believe, is reflected in this volume. The ability to be self-critical and self-aware is at the heart of the Stockton idea, so that looking at the history of the institution is not undertaken as an endeavor to praise ourselves in a wave of self-congratulation. Such a work could only elicit and deserve the response, "Enough already!" Rather, to fulfill the spirit of this college and to love it fully is to be constantly challenging it and oneself to be better, and to be constantly attuned to the fact that not all the decisions made are the right ones, that what we may believe is for the best at one moment may be shown to be false at another. Discourse and disputation, reflection and analysis, must be at the heart of any project that is worthy of the title education, and that project can never be allowed to become a prescriptive one. Many different visions came together to make Stockton, and because it allowed for choice for its students, flexibility for its faculty, and respect for all its employees, it has become more than merely the sum of its parts.

If the next forty years are to be worthy of the love that so many have poured into this place—all the blood, sweat, and tears described in the foregoing pages that went into creating this educational gem—then we need to keep that respect for difference, and desire for engagement with ideas, that sense that we are all participating in an intellectual adventure from which we all may benefit, alive!

The Contributors

David Ahlsted began teaching at Stockton in 1976, and retired as Professor Emeritus in 2008. While at Stockton, Professor Ahlsted received two Distinguished Faculty Fellowships, and the New Jersey Governors Award for Excellence in Teaching. He has shown his work in 26 solo exhibitions, 230 group exhibitions, and has completed commissioned art works for the New Jersey State Capitol, Rutgers University, and Stockton's new Campus Center. His art is in numerous public & corporate collections throughout the United States.

Margot Alten is a Philadelphia native who honed her graphic design and photography skills there and abroad before coming to Stockton in 2007. She and her husband share a home in Monroeville, NJ with 2 dogs, 4 goats and any strays that need shelter, but Jamaica is where she considers herself truly at home.

Alan F. Arcuri earned his BA and MA from Michigan State University and his Ph.D. in Political Science from Brown University. He has been a college professor for 40 years, 38 at Stockton, and has been recognized for both his teaching and advising excellence. His major field of study is American government and politics.

David Carr came to Stockton College in 1992 as Dean of Social and Behavioral Sciences. He served as Vice President for Academic Affairs and later Provost from 1998 to 2010. Returning to the faculty Dr. Carr is Professor of Political Science and Senior Fellow at the Hughes Center for Public Policy. An avid nature photographer, Dr. Carr's photographs have been featured in many College publications, as well as two public exhibitions.

Frank A. Cerreto has been a member of the faculty of General Studies at Stockton since 1976. For most of his career, he has coordinated and taught in the College's Basic Studies program, while designing and teaching undergraduate and graduate mathematics courses for liberal arts students and for pre- and in-service teachers. He was instrumental in developing and implementing the college's Quantitative-Reasoning-Across-the-Disciplines (QUAD) program, which has been supported by three external grants, including two from the National Science Foundation. He leads and plays in the Stockton Faculty Band, a musical group that raises money for scholarships for Stockton students.

Tait Chirenje holds a PhD in Trace Metal Biogeochemistry from the University of Florida, an MS in Earth Science from the University of Guelph (Canada) and a BS from the University of Zimbabwe. He works in the area of aquatic chemistry, brownfields assessment and redevelopment, and the urban geochemistry of trace elements. He has worked on baseline studies of trace elements in both urban and rural areas of Florida and performed geochemical characterization of water bodies including Hammonton Lake, the Delaware River, Crosswicks Creek and the Great Egg Harbor River. He advises local communities on storm water quality and watershed management projects.

G. Jan Colijn joined the College as visiting political science instructor in 1974. Decades later, having served as divisional chair and dean of a school, he continues to be fascinated by the College's growth and energy. He is especially proud of the College's international reputation in Holocaust and genocide education, of the institution's continuing adherence to the interdisciplinary approach to the liberal arts, and of its commitment to provide public access to quality higher education.

Oliver Cooke is an Associate Professor Economics. He produces *The South Jersey Economic Review*, a bi-annual electronic publication that focuses on the economy of southern New Jersey. His primary research interests lie in urban economics and political economy. He began his teaching career at Stockton in 2005, having earned his doctoral degree from the University of Massachusetts, Amherst.

Arnaldo Cordero Román earned his PhD in Comparative Literature at the University of Maryland, College Park after having attained a BA/MA in Hispanic Studies at the University of Puerto Rico, Río Piedras. Since 1999, he has been teaching at Stockton and is now Associate Professor of Spanish. His research fuses photography and literature. *The Climb*, a composed image, is from his series *Imágenes del Quijote*, a photographic essay that portrays literary reflections from *Don Quijote, el caballero de la triste figura*.

Jamie Cromartie has been in the Environmental Studies Program since 1974. He teaches Ecology, Environmental Issues, Entomology, Population Biology, Green Politics, and a freshman seminar on primates and humans. His research has ranged from colonization behavior of agricultural pest insects to biology of rare and endangered species of moths and butterflies in New Jersey and North Carolina. Recently, he and his students have been working to inventory, protect and restore biodiversity on the Stockton Campus, and assisting with an inventory of the insects of the Parker Preserve in Chatsworth, NJ. He has also worked to improve the biomonitoring of streams in the Pine Barrens.

Bill Daly is Distinguished Professor of Political Science at Stockton. He was a member of the first cohort of faculty hired when the College opened its doors to students and he has taught in both General Studies and Political Science for the entire 40 years of the College's existence. He has received awards for excellence in teaching at all three of the colleges at which he has taught, including Stockton. He has also served at Stockton, for short periods, both as Dean of General Studies and as Vice President for Academic Affairs, and he was selected by the New Jersey Department of Higher Education to serve as Chairman of four separate statewide task forces assembled in the 1980s to shape state higher education policy.

Gordon Davies served as the Director of the State Council of Higher Education for Virginia from 1977 until 1997, and as President of the Kentucky Council on Postsecondary Education from 1998 until 2002. He has taught at Yale University, the Teachers College of Columbia University, and Birzeit University in Palestine. He was a founding staff member of Richard Stockton State College in New Jersey. Born in New York City, he is a Navy veteran and worked for several years in computer sales for the IBM Corporation. He currently serves as a senior adviser to a Lumina Foundation project, the Productivity Grant Initiative, and to the Miller Center of Public Affairs at the University of Virginia. From 2002 through 2006, he directed a project to improve state higher education policy making, with funding provided by The Pew Charitable Trusts. In 2007, he served on a panel appointed by Virginia Governor Tim Kaine to investigate shootings at Virginia Tech that left 33 people dead and 17 wounded on April 16, 2007.

Nancy Taggart Davis, Professor of Pathology. Geographically, she spent her life between Bryn Mawr, Pennsylvania and Beach Haven, New Jersey. She graduated from Rollins College in Winter Park, Florida with a degree in Biology and Theatre Arts. She earned her Doctorate in comparative Pathology from the University of Pennsylvania and spent a number of years doing research and pathology at the Penrose Research Laboratory at the Philadelphia Zoological Gardens. She came to Stockton in 1973 where she went through the ranks to Professor and served as Dean/Chairperson of Professional Studies for three years in the 1980s. She has a husband who is retired and two sons who both live in Europe and are involved in the Political arena. She enjoys sailing, traveling, reading and the arts.

Penelope Dugan came to Stockton in 1976. Ken Tompkins picked her up at the bus stop, bought her a cup of coffee and piece of pie, and told her about the founding of the college. Dugan trusted the teller, trusted his tale, and fell in love with Stockton before she laid eyes on it.

Stephen Dunn is the author of sixteen poetry collections, including *What Goes On: New and Selected Poems 1995-2009*. He was awarded the Pulitzer Prize for his collection *Different Hours*. He has also been a finalist for the National Book Critics Circle Award and has received an Academy Award in Literature from the American Academy of Arts and Letters. He came to Stockton in 1974 and became a distinguished professor in 2001.

Claude Epstein, Professor of Environmental Science, founded Stockton's undergraduate and graduate programs in Environmental Science and brought the Governor's School on the Environment to Stockton. He has conducted research on Pine Barrens Hydrology and served as a consultant to many New Jersey Towns as well as to the State Legislature and the New Jersey Water Supply Master Plan.

Diane S. Falk has been Professor of Social Work, Director of Stockton's Master of Social Work Program, Principal Investigator of New Jersey's Baccalaureate Child Welfare Education Program, Member of the AtlantiCare Behavioral Health Board, Clinical Director of the Raritan Bay Mental Health Center, and President of the 7000-member New Jersey Chapter of the National Association of Social Workers.

Deborah M. Figart came to Stockton in 1995. She is currently a Professor of Education and Economics and Director of the Stockton Center for Economic & Financial Literacy. From 2003–2010, she served as the graduate dean, steering and shaping new graduate programs and helping then-termed "graduate studies" grow and evolve to the School of Graduate and Continuing Studies. From 2001–2002, Dr. Figart was a faculty co-chair of Stockton's Middle States Reaccreditation Executive/Steering Committee.

Richard Gajewksi: Military Service – 1952-1954 US Army – Fifteen months in Korea Education – BBA St. John Fisher College 1958 1958-1964 – served on the staff of a National CPA firm. From 1964 to 1989 he served in financial administration positions in a variety of institutions. During that time he was able to computerize financial systems, improve telecommunications, purchasing, printing and other logistic services. At Stockton he was responsible for developing administrative and financial systems from the ground up and learning to work with the many state agencies responsible for the state's finances. His most recent service was with St. Francis University in Loretto, PA until he retired in 1989.

Sonia V. Gonsalves joined the Stockton faculty 20 years ago and is now a professor of psychology. For six years she directed the Institute for Faculty Development and served as the assessment coordinator for the college.

Rob Gregg came to Stockton in 1996, and is grateful that the college would hire him. He has endeavored to repay this debt. He is Professor of History and Dean of Arts and Humanities.

Tom Grites has served as Director of Academic Advising, Interim Director of Teacher Education, Interim Dean of Social and Behavioral Sciences, Assistant to the Vice President for Academic Affairs, and currently as Assistant to the Provost in his 34 years at Stockton. He was one of the founding members of the National Academic Advising Association (NACADA) and served as its President for two terms. He has written over 50 journal articles, book chapters, and professional reports; he has delivered more than 70 conference presentations; and he has conducted faculty development workshops and academic advising program reviews on over 100 campuses. He has also served on the Absecon Board of Education for over 20 years.

Peter Hagen serves as Director of the Center for Academic Advising. He was the founding Chair of the NACADA Theory and Philosophy of Academic Advising Commission, served as Guest Editor of the NACADA *Journal* for its Fall 2005 issue on the theory and philosophy of academic advising, and was a member of the task force that wrote "The Concept of Academic Advising." For NACADA he also served as Chair of the Research Committee. He is currently a member of the NACADA *Journal's* Editorial Board and the Publications Review Board. He won the 2007 Virginia Gordon Award for Service to the Field of Advising.

Emily Heerema graduated from Stockton in 2008 with a BA in Literature and minors in Political Science and Holocaust Studies. As an undergraduate, she was the Editor in Chief of *The Argo*, president of the English honor society Sigma Tau Delta, and president of the student anti-genocide movement S.T.A.N.D. Emily was also an Orientation Leader and SOAR Mentor. Since graduating, she was a corps member with City Year New York and has worked as a substitute teacher in New Jersey. She will be returning to Stockton in 2011 for a Masters in Occupational Therapy.

Bob Helsabeck was a charter member of the Stockton Faculty. While at Stockton he has been active in matters of governance. He was the first informal moderator of the Faculty, served two terms as President of the Faculty Assembly, did his dissertation and a book on collegiate governance, served two three-year terms as a dean of General Studies, chaired two separate faculty committees on the faculty constitution and is just completing a term as president of the newly formed Faculty Senate.

Nancy W. Hicks, Special Assistant to the President for Affirmative Action and Ethical Standards, joined the Stockton staff in 1988.

Patrick Hossay has directed and advised sustainable development projects and community conservation initiatives in various communities in the Caribbean Basin, and he currently advises community and municipal sustainability projects throughout New Jersey. He maintains a strong interest in wildlife conservation, municipal planning and sustainability, alternative energy, and green design. His own home is a model for green design, producing nearly as much energy as it uses.

Elaine Ingulli was a Legal Services attorney before she began teaching in the early 1980s. She has taught business and computer law and a variety of General Studies and Women's Studies courses at Stockton since 1986. During that time, she has been active in faculty governance, serving as President of the Faculty Assembly and as local negotiator for the SFT, and co-authored a text, *Law and Ethics in the Business Environment*, now in its 7th edition.

Bess Kathrins is Professor of Physical Therapy. She came to Stockton in 1984 and developed the original Bachelor of Science in Physical Therapy. She led the conversion of the Program to a masters then doctoral program. She served as Program Director for 25 years.

Claudine Keenan is the Chief Planning Officer at Stockton, where she integrates academic, enrollment, financial, facilities, strategic and assessment plans in collaboration with the President's senior leadership Cabinet. Prior to working at Stockton, she was a Program Development Specialist for SunGard Higher Education, a Director of Graduate Programs at the Marlboro College Graduate Center in Vermont and she was a faculty member at Penn State University and Program Administrator for a K-12 National Writing Project site. Claudine earned her Doctorate in Higher Education Leadership from the University of Massachusetts, Amherst.

Harvey Kesselman serves as Provost and Executive Vice President at Stockton. He is a former "Mayflower Student," has also served Stockton as Dean of Education, Interim Vice President for Administration and Finance, Vice President for Student Affairs, Director of Institutional Research and Planning, and Director of the EOF Program during his more than 30 years in administration. He also represents the senior public college and university sector of higher education on the Higher Education Student Assistance Authority, the agency responsible for overseeing the $1 billion financial aid system in New Jersey.

Tom Kinsella has been a student of literature for most of his life. He arrived at Stockton in 1989 in time to meet and befriend several of the Mayflower faculty and to experience the bulk of VKF's tenure at Stockton. He has published studies on James Boswell, Arthur Murphy, and the history of bookbinding in Britain and America. While at Stockton he has developed a curious and satisfying interest in grammar and punctuation.

Melaku Lakew joined Stockton College in 1982, as a professor of economics. He has been involved in several curriculum transforming grant-writing projects at the

College. Melaku is the co-author of two successful major grants to the National Science Foundation to infuse quantitative skills across the curriculum. In the mid-eighties he was also one of the major players in internationalizing the curriculum in the college. His South African Study Tour program is quite popular among a large number of students.

Joyce Lawrence, a native of the Jersey Shore, studied art at Stockton, Pennsylvania Academy of Fine Arts, and Studio Incamminati, Philadelphia, PA. From 2003 – 2007, Lawrence operated her own gallery in Tuckerton, NJ. She has taught at various art centers in New Jersey and has won many awards and honors for her work. Her oil paintings have graced the covers of books and magazines and can be found in numerous public and private collections throughout the US. Currently Lawrence paints full time at her Bay Moon Art Studio in Little Egg Harbor. She is a member of the American Artist Professional League and The Catherine Lorillard Wolfe Arts Club in New York City. To see more of her work visit www. joycelawrenceart.net

Jeanne Sparacino Lewis has worked for Stockton, as Director of Financial Aid, for nearly 40 years. Professionally she has served as Chairperson of the State Directors of Financial Aid, as a member of the National, State and Eastern Association of Financial Aid Administrators and as a member of a national advisory group on financial aid related matters. Personally, she has been an active member of her community having served on Hammonton Town Council for 12 years. Two of those years she served as Deputy Mayor.

David Lester has doctoral degrees from Cambridge University in social and political science and Brandeis University in psychology. He is Distinguished Professor of Psychology at the Richard Stockton College of New Jersey. He has been President of the International Association for Suicide Prevention, and he has published extensively on suicide, murder, and other issues in thanatology. His recent books include *Katie's Diary: Unlocking the Mystery of a Suicide* (2004), *Suicide and the Holocaust* (2005), *Is there Life after Death?* (2005), and *Understanding Suicide: Closing the Exits Revisited* (2009).

Marc Lowenstein earned a PhD in philosophy from the University of Rochester. He was a faculty member in philosophy at Stockton in the late 1970s and since then has held a succession of administrative positions at the college, ranging from Divisional Administrator in General Studies to Dean of Professional Studies. He has published a number of influential papers on academic advising.

William Lubenow is the author of *The Politics of Government Growth* (1971), *Parliamentary Politics and the Home Rule Crisis* (1988), *The Cambridge Apostles, 1820-1914* (1998, paperback edition 2007), and *Liberal Intellectuals and Public Culture* (2010). His forthcoming book is on learned societies and the history of cognition.

James McCarthy graduated in 1976 with a BS degree in Environmental Science from Stockton. While working as a Land Use Planner he became interested in automated spatial analysis, computer cartography and computer programming. In 1981 he completed a bachelors degree in Information and Systems Science and later earned an MS degree in Software Engineering. In 1986 he accepted the position of Director of the Stockton's Computer Services Department. He currently serves as Associate Provost for Computing and Communications.

Michael McGarvey is a Professor of Art at Stockton where he has been teaching graphic design and illustration since 1984. His work from the Port Press has been featured in publications and exhibitions for Wood Engravers Network, Society of Wood Engravers, and the Fine Press Book Association.

Nancy Messina graduated in 1982 with a BA degree in Business Studies from Stockton. She was enrolled in the first Master's Program offered at Stockton and completed an MBS in Management in 1999. She has worked at the College since 1974, and currently serves as Assistant Dean for the School of Arts and Humanities.

Ronald J. Moss is Assistant Dean of Education and Professional Studies Emeritus and Adjunct Professor of History at Central Connecticut State University. He was Director of Teacher Education at Stockton from 1977-1991, where he completely restructured the teacher education program and earned state approval of the new EDUC programs. While at his respective colleges, he acted as an unofficial advisor on difficult certification cases to the New Jersey and Connecticut teacher certification bureaus.

Daniel N. Moury earned his PhD in Biochemistry from Purdue University in 1963. He taught at Bowman Gray School of Medicine, NC and Tusculum College, TN before coming to Stockton. He was Dean of Science and Math (1970-73) and Dean of Academic Development(1973-75). He moved on to become Associate Director of State Colleges for New Jersey (1975-77), before working as a full-time consultant at Elon (1977-81) and Academic V. P. at Pfeiffer College (1981-85). He continued Education Association work in NC until 1996, and he is now a retired Grandpa.

Linda Williamson Nelson joined the Writing Program 1981 and taught courses in writing and African American literature before earning a doctorate in linguistic anthropology. She received the 2009 Candace Achievement Award for "excellence in the area of education," from the NJ Chapter of the National Coalition of 100 Black Women, as well as the Asante award in 2010 from Stockton's Africana Studies Program. Her scholarly work and teaching continue to represent her interests in both language and literature. She has written on linguistic form as cultural trope in the African American novel, along with her major work on dialectal codeswitching in extended oral narrative discourse.

Beth Olsen has worked in grants administration since 1985, involved in every aspect of grant-seeking from writing and editing for external funders to coordinating internal award programs, serving the faculty as a resource and advocate. As constant undercurrent to her mainstream activities, she gives time to service—whether standing among the first members of the New Jersey Higher Education Service-Learning Consortium when it formed in 1990s, assisting service-learning at Stockton since the program began, or serving on national and international professional committees. Along the way, Beth works to contribute to the opportunities that change stuff for the better.

Richard E. Pesqueira, 1969 EdD Honors, Educational Psychology, University of California, Los Angeles; 1961 MEd Educational Administration, University of Arizona; 1959 B. S. Secondary Education. After Stockton: Vice President Student Affairs, New Mexico St. University; President, University of Southern Colorado; Executive Director, College Board Western Regional Office. Also: Commissioner and Evaluator, North Central Accreditation Association of Colleges and Universities; Consultant, U.S. Department of Education on Excellence in Schools; Vice Chairman, U.S. Department of Education Emergency School Aid Act Commission; Member, U.S. Army Science Board; Editor, Southwest Journal of Student Personnel Administration; Chairman, Mathematics, Engineering, Sciences Achievement Program.

Israel Posner – a child of two Holocaust survivors, Izzy grew up in Brooklyn, earned his BA from Brooklyn College and a PhD from Temple University. In 1973 he joined "Stockton State College" as a faculty member in the Psychology Program and has spent the past 40 years as a professor, administrator, author and behavioral science consultant dealing with a large variety of human resource and organizational change issues.

Patricia Reid-Merritt is the Distinguished Professor of Social Work and Africana Studies. She joined the faculty in fall, 1976. Dr. Reid-Merritt received the Doctorate of Social Work in Race, Law and Social Policy from the University of Pennsylvania. She is the author of the national Blackboard best-seller, *Sister Power: How Phenomenal Black Women Are Rising to the Top*; *Sister Wisdom: Seven Pathways to a Satisfying Life for Soulful Black Women*; and *Righteous Self-Determination: The Black Social Work Movement in America*

Joe Rubenstein interviewed at the old Mayflower hotel and began teaching Life Sports along with Anthropology on the Pomona campus in the Division of Experimental Studies in 1972. His first course was called "In Search of the Primitive," and he has been pursuing that goal ever since.

Richard N. Schwartz earned a BA in Political Science, and an MA in Public Administration, from the University of Michigan. His career in higher education began as a Campus Planner and led to several posts as Vice President for Business Affairs, and a two-year period as Acting President. After retiring from higher education, he spent a number of years involved in building and operating facilities for Townsend Capital of Baltimore. Now retired, he and his wife Janet, a member of Stockton's first graduating class, live in the Rio Grande Valley of Texas.

John W. Searight, MSW, came to Stockton in June, 1973. Joining the SFT, he served on the negotiating team for the initial contract between the Council of New Jersey State College Locals (AFT) and the State of New Jersey, and became grievance officer (1974-76), and then president (1974-76) of the SFT. John was Program Coordinator of the Social Work Program (1975-79), Chairperson of the Task Force on Health Services (1978-79), and Moderator of the Faculty Assembly (1983-85). From 1985-92 he was Chair and then Dean of SOBL). He retired as Professor Emeritus of Social Work in June 2000.

William Sensiba was determined to participate in the major events of his lifetime. For him that led to East Africa in the Peace Corps and Mississippi in the civil rights movement and into the new left and counterculture in the 1960's. The following years found him active in various anti-war, pro-choice, and environmental movements and picking coffee in Nicaragua. Today he is busy trying to reform the Democratic Party in Philadelphia and helping to raise two granddaughters.

Franklin Ojeda Smith - son, husband, father, grandfather, friend, professor, actor and most importantly a Child of God.

Len Solo: poet, short story & education writer, painter, education consultant, spouse and father. Currently, Len is an education consultant who supports principals and teacher leaders, especially those with progressive views. Prior work includes teaching kindergarten through the university level, establishing and being Coordinator of the Teacher Development Program at Stockton, being the long-term principal of the famous Graham & Parks Alternative Public School (Cambridge, MA) and the principal of the Cambridge Rindge and Latin High Schools. Len is the author of 3 volumes of poetry and of *Making an Extraordinary School: The Work of Ordinary People*, about Graham & Parks. You can check him out at lensolo.com.

Lew Steiner was born in NY City and raised in Ventnor, NJ where he attended the Ventnor Schools, Atlantic City High and the Charter Class of Stockton, graduating with a Bachelor of Arts Degree. Steiner lives in Northfield with his wife Christine and they have two grown children. At the age of 20 while a Junior at Stockton, Steiner recognized that there was a need for an entertainment and dining newspaper in South Jersey and in the spring of '74, Steiner founded *Whoot Newspaper* which he sold in 2000 and renamed it *Atlantic City Weekly* in 2003. Steiner is now in his 37th year as Publisher of *AC Weekly* and more recently ACWeekly.com.

Joel Sternfeld taught at Stockton from 1971 to 1985. Originally a Mayflower faculty member in the Division of Management Sciences, he transferred to ARHU in 1979 to teach photography and Media Studies in the Visual Arts program. He now teaches photography at Sarah Lawrence College and has works in the permanent collection at the MOMA in New York City and the Getty in Los Angeles. He is noted for both his large-format documentary pictures, and for his contribution to establishing color photography as a respected artistic medium.

Ken Tompkins has been teaching for 46 years. He is one of two surviving Founding Deans of the College having been the first Dean of General Studies. His contributions to the College include General Studies, BASK, computer microlabs, the COMM Program, the MAIT Program and the first College website. He has a strong interest in 3D modeling, pedagogy and technology, and long-distance motorcycle touring.

Joseph A. Tosh – One of the original "Mayflower Students". After graduation in 1974 he taught Mathematics and Computer Programming at Atlantic City High School for thirty-five years. He was President of the Stockton Alumni Association from 1993 to 1996. He is now a technology consultant and an avid sailor.

Hannah Ueno was born in Seattle, WA, and raised in Japan. She received an MFA in Visual Communications from Washington State University, BFA in Visual Communications from Nihon University, Tokyo, Japan. After working in the design industry for seven years, she joined Stockton as a faculty in 1994. Hannah has been teaching graphic design, 3-D computer graphics with Maya, interactive media design with Flash courses. Her personal work has been included in numerous juried exhibitions in the US and Italy, in both corporate and private collections.

Joseph L. Walsh, PhD (Brandeis University, History of Ideas), Emeritus Professor of Philosophy and Religion, founding editor of the *Radical Philosophy Review of Books* (now *Radical Philosophy Review*), a founding Fellow of The Hastings Center for bioethics and public policy, editor of the Newsletter of the Marxist-Christian Dialogue (USA), author of numerous articles and reviews in *Socialism and Democracy*, *The Commonweal*, *Cross Currents* and other publications dealing with the interaction of religion and society.

BJ Ward's most recent book is *Gravedigger's Birthday* (North Atlantic Books/ Random House). His work has been featured on National Public Radio, New Jersey Network, and the website Poetry Daily, as well as in publications such as *Poetry*, *The New York Times*, and *The Pushcart Prize Anthology*. He was graduated from Stockton in 1989 with LITT/LANG Program Distinction.

Patricia Weeks came to Stockton in 1973 as a Graphics Assistant in the college's Graphics Production Office and her roles have evolved since then to match the growing needs of the college. She currently serves as the Director of the Southern Regional Institute and ETTC at Stockton. She has a BA in Studies in the Arts from Stockton and an MA in Educational Technology Leadership from George Washington University.

Wendel White joined the faculty in 1986 and is a Distinguished Professor of Art. He is the current chair of the board of the New Jersey Council for the Humanities and was board chair of the national Society for Photographic Education. His fellowships and awards include the Guggenheim Fellowship, two New Jersey Arts Council Fellowships, an En Foco Fellowship, and a grant from the Graham Foundation for the Advancement of the Fine Arts.

James A. Williams, the first Director of Public Safety and Campus Security, is the Owner of Williams Associates, Law Enforcement and Security Consultants in Cherry Hill, NJ. Upon his retirement as Chief, USDOJ Organized Crime DEA Task Forces, he served as the Director of Player Operations for the New York Yankees Professional Baseball Organization. Dr. Williams is currently on staff at Rowan University, Glassboro, NJ in the Law and Justice Department where he teaches courses in Criminal Justice.

Roger Wood is Professor of Zoology and a "Mayflower" member of Stockton's faculty. He married President Bjork's secretary in 1974. He and his wife had two sons, the younger of whom died at age 17 from brain cancer. He chaired the college's first self-study steering committee, which resulted in accreditation for Stockton from the Middle States Association. He also served as the first president of the Faculty Assembly and has served on and chaired the college's R&PD. For more than a quarter of a century he has been affiliated with the Wetlands Institute, first as President of the Corporation and Chairman of the Board of Trustees and, since 1993, Director of the Institute's Conservation and Research Program. He directs the Institute's Coastal Conservation and Research Program which has involved more than 200 undergraduate students from more than 100 different colleges and universities, as well as 20 participants from Southeast Asia, in summer research activities.

187

20/20 Vision, 159, 162

A

Aaronson, Linda, **89**
AC Press, 16, 33, 100
Academic Affairs, Division of, 23, 35, 55, 59, 79, 129, 168, 170
Academic Development, Office of (ADEV), 27, 40, 119
Academic Working Papers, 91, 119
Accounting (ACCT), 27, 149
Acronyms, 42
Administration and Finance, Division of, 30, 55, 183
Administrative Studies, 148
Administration Working Papers, 57, 62
Admissions, Office of, 44, 55, 132
Advising, Office of, 57, 113, 129-30, 132, 160
Affirmative Action, 53, 70, 79
Affirmative Action Committee, 79
African American/Africana Studies, 95, 97, 124
Ahlsted, David, **endpapers**, 168, **184**
Alexakis, Alex, 169
Allied Health Sciences, 153
Alten, Margot, **162, 171, 184**
Alton, Elizabeth, 1, 15, 16, 17, 19, 23, 33
Alton Auditorium, 161
American Association of State Colleges and Universities (AASCU), 56
American Association of University Professors (AAUP), 40, 57
American College and University Presidents' Climate Commitment (ACUPCC), 138, 140-42
American Council of Learned Societies (ACLS), 95, 117, 170
American Federation of Teachers (AFT), 40, 57, 58, 63
Americorps, 140, 170
Architectural Master Plan, 1971, 145
Arcuri, Alan F., 111, **112-13**, 168, **184**
Area Studies, 83, 91
Argo, The, 49, 62, 159, 179-80
Arndt, Rudy, 145, 169
Arts and Humanities, Division/School of (ARHU), 8, 26, 28-29, 51, 74, 106, 120, 138, 149, 168-70, 180
Arts and Sciences Building, 55, 85
Ashton, Nancy, 76
Assessment, 114-16
Association of Colleges of Teacher Education (AACTE), 104
Association of New Jersey State Colleges and University Faculty (ANJSCUF), 40
Atlantic City, 15, 16, 18, 29, 30, 32, 34, 35, 41, 45, 49, 55, 56, 66, 68, 72, 102
Atlantic City Medical Center, 82
Atlantic County, 1, 16, 30, 56, 135-37, 169, 175, 177
Atlantic County New School, 103
Atlantic White Cedar Regeneration, 135

B

Baccalaureate Child Welfare Education Program (BCWEP), 159, 177-78
Bannan, Marieann, 183
Barlatt, Rogers, 170
Basic Studies (BASK), 9-10, 26, 71, 89, 95, 97, 117, 120
Bass, Henry, 78
Bean, Ralph, 26, 58, 63, 64, 96, 102, 103, 106
Berense, Jack, 80
Bergen County, 16
Berry, Franklin, 17, 19
Berry, Richard C., 152
Bierbrauer, Sandra (Hartzog), 88, 145
Birchler, Christina, 176
Birdwhistell, Anne, 168
Biodiversity Working Group, 140
Bioethics, 88
Biology (BIOL), 37, 38, 40, 86, 106, 107, 138, 150, 152
Biomedical Communications, 152, 153
Bjork, Joan, 20, 183
Bjork, Richard, 1, 5, 15, 16, 17, 18, 19, 20, 22-26, 29-35, 39-40, 43-45, 51-52, 54, 58, 62-63, 70, 80, 81, 87, 108, 119, 148-49, 182
Blake, Allison, 178
Block, Lester, 145
Bogart, Karen, 108, 109
Bond Issue, 1968, 33
Bookstore, 74
Bordentown Prison, 40
Boulding, Kenneth, 97
Bowen, Julie, 183
Boyd, Tom, 34
Boyer, 114
Board of Higher Education, 16, 35, 37, 63
Brann, Eva, 97
Broughton, Shelby, 88, 100
Brown, Bob, 98
Brown, Steve, 146
Burdick, David, 96
Bulletins, 68, 76, 119-20, 122

Bureau of Land Use Regulations (NJDEP), 137
Burke, Ruth, 70
Burlington County College, 41, 137
Burnham, Christopher, 120
Bursar, Office of the, 160, 180
Burton, Royce, 74, 120
Business, School of (BSNS), 51, 55, 82, 109, 138, 148, 150, 152, 156, 168; Program, 106; MBA, 111, 162
Byrne, Brendan, 64

C

Cabot, Josh, 168
Camden County College, 49
Campbell, Joseph, 129
Campus Activities, Director of, 49
Campus Center, 141, 146, 160
Campus Hearing Board, 80
Campus Planning, 30-34, 57
Cantiveros, Mark, 180
Cape May County, 173
CAPP (Curriculum Advising and Program Planning), 130
Carnegie Classification, 56, 157
Carnegie Library, 125, 161, 163
Carpenter, Nikki, 179
Carr, David, 1, **4**, 61, 113, 114, **133**, 155, 161, **163-64**, 169, **184**
Carrier Services, 72
Carrier-oriented education, 5, 6, 11
Carter, Jimmy, 56, 70
Casinos & casino gambling, 82, 173
Catto (Kahoe), MaryAnn,
Center for Economic and Financial Literacy, 163
Cerreto, Frank, 70, 71, 111, **116-18**, 171, 182
Chait, Richard, 19
Chambers, Paul, 180
Chancellor of Higher Education, 16, 18, 19, 30, 86, 87
Chayevsky, Paddy, 88
Civility, Harmony, Education, Environment, Respect (CHEER), 175
Chemistry (CHEM), 37, 38, 41, 88, 92, 107, 136, 138-39
Children's Bureau of the US Department of Health and Human Services, 177-78
Children's Rights Inc. (CRI), 177
Chirenje, Tait, 134, 136, **138-44, 184**
Choice (in the curriculum), 3, 8 23 72, 93
Chronicle of Higher Education, The, 27, 43, 51
Citizens Committee for a State College/University, 16
Citizens Committee for Higher Education in New Jersey, 17
Civil rights movement, 21, 35, 70
Clark, Abraham, 21
Coastal Research Center, 138-39, 169, 171
Colby, Richard, 37, 137, 173, 183
Colijn, Jan, 1, 86, **94-95**, 120, 183, **184**
College of New Jersey (TCNJ), 17
College Council, 57, 58, 60
College Examiner, The, 18
College Walk, 141
Collegewide Personnel Committee (CPC), 112
Collegia, 11, 48, 57, 58, 62, 108
Collegiate Level Assessment (CLA), 114
Commission of Higher Education of the Middle States (report 1975), 58
Committee for Diversity, Equity, and Affirmative Action, 79
Committee of 50, 19
Communication Studies (COMM), 123
Community Colleges (see also, individual colleges), 131
Community Relations, 81
Comprehensive School Reform, 175
Comprehensive Writing Program, 120
Computational Science, 136, 138, 156, 162
Computer Science and Informational Systems (CSIS), 148, 150
Computing & Computer Services, 126-28
Connor, Jack, 145
Constantelos, Demetrios, 16, **31**, **113**, 182
Constanza Construction, 33, 173
Construction, 32-34, 169
Cooke, Oliver, 159, **172-73, 184**
Cool, Michael, 159
Coordinators, 8, 37, 63, 115
Cordero-Román, Arnaldo, **181, 184**
Corpus, Alfonso, 168
Costaris, Michael, 109
Council of Black Faculty and Staff, 71
Council of Graduate Schools, 157
Council of New Jersey State College Locals (CNJSCL), 63, 64
Council of State Colleges Affirmative Action Committee (1973), 79
Creative Writing (LITT program), 123, 165-66
Cresson, Pat Hill, 168
Criminal Justice (CRIM), 27, 70, 108, 136, 156, 157, 163
Cromartie, Jamie, 134-37, **145-46, 184**

Cultural Audit, 79
Cumberland County College, 177
Curriculum, 6-9, 11-13, 37, 41, 43, 53, 58, 72, 86, 87, 89, 91-93, 106, 108-09, 116-18, 122-23, 134, 138, 149; subscripts, 95, 117

D
Dagavarian, Deb, **61**
Daly, William, vii, 2, **5-13**, 16, 18, 54, 82, 89, 96, 108, 112, 182, **184**
D'Augustine, Robert, 173
Davies, Gordon K., **vii-viii**, 1, **18**, 27, 40, 119, **184**
Davis, Nancy, 148, **184**
Davey, James, 178
Day of Scholarship, 171
Deans/Chairpersons, 53, 59
Deininger, Madeline, 183
DeLussa, Bruce, 152
de Man, Paul, 83
Department of Education, Bureau of Certification, 104
Department of Higher Education, 18, 20, 26, 35, 150, 170
Department of Social Relations, Harvard, 83
Dewey, John, 102
Diamond, Stanley, 68
DiGiorgio, Emari, 121
Distinguished Faculty, 182
Distinguished Faculty Fellowship (DFF), 169
Diversity, 53, 70, 77-80
Division of Youth and Family Services (DYFS), 177
Divisional Review Committees, 58, 112
Dixon, Robert, 152
Dobron, Linda, 178
Dollarhide, Kenneth, 74
Don, Alex, 120
Drugs, 45-46, 88
Dugan, Penelope, 76, **96-97**, 111, **119-21**, **184**
Dungan, Ralph, 17-20, 23, 40, 87
Dunn, Stephen, 1, 54, 159, 165-66, **166-67**, 168-69, 182, **184**
Durham, Gina, 179
Dury, Carl, 135

E
Earth Day, 25
Economics (ECON), 70, 108
Education, Division/School of (EDUC), 104, 150, 162, 176
Educational Facilities Authority, 33
Education Policies Committee, 26
Educational Leadership (MAEL), 150, 156, 162
Educational Opportunity Fund (EOF), 56, 71, 78
Educational Services, 128
Educational Technology Training Center (ETTC), 127, 159, 175-76
Elbow, Peter, 97
Elliott, Paul, 119
Elmore, Betty, 70, 71
Emmons, David, 70, 71, 95, 161, 169
Energy House, 41
Energy Studies Certificate Program, 170
Engagement, vii, 162
Enscoe, Gerald, 88, 98, 123
Environment, 33, 134-46
Environmental Protection Agency (EPA), 137
Environmental Studies (ENVL), 37, 38, 40, 86, 88, 106, 107, 134, 135-37, 138-40, 145
Epps-Kearney, Ricky, **105**
Epstein, Claude, 86, 134, **135-37**, 145, 183, **184-85**
Esalen, 108; Summer Institute, 88
Evergreen College, 83, 84, 87
Evidence, 183
Experimental Studies (EXPT), 1, 26, 35, 40, 66, 67, 101

F
Facilities and Plant, 144
Faculty, 8, 76; workload of, 12, 23, 40, 53, 54, 62, 64; tenure and promotion of, 29, 42, 58, 99, 112, 161, 163
Faculty Assembly, 51, 58 61, 65, 76, 79, 89, 116, 120, 140, 161, 171; Task Force on governance, 60
Faculty Review Committee (FRC), 112
Faculty Senate, 60-61
Falk, Candace, 80
Falk, Diane, 159, 169, 171, **177-78**, **185**
Fall Faculty Conference, 76, 113
Fan, Weihong, 136
Farley, Frank "Hap", 17, 33
Farrell, Stewart, 169, 171
Farris, Vera King, 51, 55-56, 78, 79, 114, 116, 150, 153, 155, 169, 170, 183
Federal Aviation Administration Tech Center, 148, 172
Figart, Deborah M., 111, 155, **156-57**, **185**
Filimon, David, **103**, 119
Finance, 148

Financial Aid, 72-73
Fish, Stanley, 83
Florence, Mary Ellen, 76
Foner. Eric, 67
Food & Drug Administration (FDA), 25
Frank, Michael, 115, 161
Franklin Parker Preserve, 135, 136
Free Speech Movement, 35
Free to Be (daycare center), 74
Freshman Seminars, 10, 59, 170
Freshman Year Experience, 164
F-wing Overbuild, 141-42, 160

G
G. Theodore Mitau Award for Innovation and Change in Higher Education, 121
Gajewski, Richard, 15, **30-31**, 33, 45, **185**
Galloway Township, 30, 135, 145, 172
Gambert, Dan, 183
Geddes, Robert, 33
Geddes, Brecher, Qualls, Cunningham (GQBC), 33
Geertz, Clifford, 83
Geller, Michael, 136-37, 145
Gender, Gender Studies (see also, Women's Studies), 2, 83
General Studies, 1, 5, 8, 9, 11-13, 23-24, 26, 28-29, 36-37, 40-41, 53, 58, 62, 68, 71, 74, 76, 80, 86-95, 98, 100, 108 , 120, 123, 130-31, 149, 164
General Studies, Division/School of (GENS), 90-97, 120, 156-57, 168
Geographical Information Systems (GIS), 137-38
Geology (GEOL), 107, 136; Geology Club, 140
Georgetown University, 152
Georgian Court University, 178
Geothermal/HVAC, 55, 135
Gerontology (GERO), 124
Gilmore-Lehne, William, 1, 169, 183
Gitchell, Alice, 135, 137
Glassboro State College (see also, Rowan University), 18, 23, 108-09
Global Perspectives, 162
Goals 2000, 176
Goddard, Malcolm, 108
Gonsalves, Sonia, 111, **114-15**, 162, 170, **185**
Goodman, George J.W., 100
Governance, 11, 23, 51, 53, 57-61
Governor's Office of Employee Relations, 63
Grades and grading, 59, 72, 74, 95, 99
Graduate Studies (GRAD), 56, 106, 155
Grant, Gerald, 1, 87
Grant vs. Sessions, 78
Grants Office, 159, 163, 168-71
Graves, Michael, 56
Gregg, Rob, 1, 15, **20-21**, **22-24**, 51, **52-54**, 74, **80**, 159, **160-61**, **163-64**, **185**
Griffiths, Jonathan, 88, 120
Grissom, Vergil, 21
Grites, Thomas, 111, 129-30, **131-32**, **185**

H
Hadassah, 19
Hadley, Amy, 153
Hagen, Peter, 111, **129-30**, 171, 182, **185**
Hager, Melissa, 183
Hager, Richard, 182
Hammonton Township, 135, 159, 161
Hampshire College, 83-84, 87
Haresign, Tim, 161, 170
Harrison, Kenneth, 70, 71, 96
Hart, John, 21
Hartzog, Sandra (Bierbauer), 88, 145
Harvard University, 95
Hayward, James, 23
Headway, 157
Health Sciences, School of, 138, 150, 152-54, 163
Heerema, Emily, 159, **179-80**, **185**
Heffernon, Thomas, 74
Helsabeck, Robert, 51, **57-61**, 98, 108, 119, 161, 170, **185**
Hendrick, Pamela, 115
Hentoff, Nat, 102
Herlands, Rosalind, 88
Hicks, Nancy, 51, **79-80**, **185**
Higgins, William, 103
Hippies (& hippie culture), 5, 92, 109
Historical Studies (HIST), 91, 115
Holocaust and Genocide Studies (H&G), 55, 56, 71, 124, 176; Masters Program (MAHG), 156, 157, 163
Holocaust Resource Center, 55, 82, 95, 176
Holt, John, 102
Homo Ludens, 67
Honaker, Lisa, 183
Honors Program, 162

Hopkinson, Francis, 21
Horowitz, Leo, 97
Hospitality and Tourism Management Program (HTMS), 82, 150, 162
Hossay, Patrick, 134, **138-44**, **185**
Housing, 44, 55, 72-73
Hoxter, Lee, 120
Hozik, Michael, 163, 183
Hughes, Richard, 19
Huneke, Donna, 179
Huizinga, Johan, 67
Hussong, Lillian, 115
HVAC, 33

I
IDEA, 109, 112, 113, 115
Improving Active Partnerships and Collaboration in Teaching (IMPACT), 176
Improving Teacher Quality Grant (ITQG), 176
Independent Studies, 63, 99
Indiana University, 91, 108
Information Sciences, 148, 149
Ingulli, Elaine, 51, **76**, **185**
Innovation in Energy Efficiency and Renewable Energy, 142
Instant Decision Days, 132
Institute for Faculty Development (IFD), 114, 115, 161, 163
Institute for the Study of College Teaching (ISCT), 114, 163
Institutional Planning, 34
Institutional Research, Office of, 114
Institutional Review Board (IRB), 171
Instructional Technology (MAIT), 56, 157
Interdisciplinarity, 23, 32, 35, 40, 68, 83, 86, 91, 94-95, 117, 124-25, 135, 136, 149
Interdisciplinary Center for Hellenic Studies (ICHS), 56, 115, 164
Interdisciplinary Minors, 124-25
International Association of Chiefs of Police, 46
International Studies, 162
Intervention and Referral Services Technical Assistance Program (I&RS), 172
Internships, 63
Ismail, Amanda, 180
Iyer, Renga, 178

J
Jacobson, Keith, 179
Jaffe, Adrian, 74
Jackson, Brian, 183
Jackson, Rodger, 171, 180, 182
Jacobson, Kristin, 183
James, G. Larry, 51, 68, 69, 180
Jassel, Lucinda, 131
Jaynes, William, 70, 71
Jankiwicz, Paul, 49
Jefferson, Thomas, 6
Jencks, Christopher, 83
Jewish Studies, 97, 124
Johnson, Lyndon, 3, 6
Jones, Martin, 74
Joseph, Janice, 163, 182
Judy, Jim, 21, 33, 126
Junior Faculty Funding, 163, 170
Junior Writing Test, 120

K
Kaden, Lewis, 64
Kairys, David, 80
Kansas State University, 130
Kathrins, Bess, 148, 153, **154**, **185**
Kean, Thomas, 55
Kean University, 178
Keenan, Claudine, **162, 163-64**, 173, **185**
Keefe, Barry, 177
Kennedy, John, 6
Kent State shooting, 27
Kesselman, Harvey, 51, **55-56**, 73, 159, 171, **175-76**, **185**
Kiwanis Club, 16
Kinsella, Thomas, 111, **122-23**, **146**, 169, **185**
Kleinman, Neil, 168, 170
Klukoff, Phil, 25, 26, 28, 29, 120, 123
Kohl, John, 33
Kondracki, Steve, 49
Konrady, Russell, 146
Kozol, Jonathan, 102
Kresge College, 87
Kuhn, Thomas, 83
Kwanzaa, 71

L
Laboratories, 35, 37-39, 106-07
Labor Education Center, Rutgers, 64

Labovitz, Sherman, 70, 71, 108
Lacatena, Marcoantonio, 64
Lacy, Allen, 51, 86, 169
LaFleur, Ingie, 1, 86, 96-97, 183
Lake Fred, 13, 43, 49, 72, 134, 145, 146, 166, 178
Lakeside Residential Center, 55, 161
Lakew, Melaku, 51, **70-71**, **185**
Lalalian, Aida, 120
Language Program (LANG), 119, 122, 123
Language requirements, 95
Lasch, Christopher, 67
Latin American/Caribbean Studies, 124, 162
Lawrence, Joyce, **85**, **186**
Leadership in Energy and Environmental Design (LEED), 141, 143
League of Women Voters, 19
Lechner, David, 171, 182
Leeds Point, 99
Leitner, Lewis, 104
Lenard, G.T., 61
Lepelletier, Lori, 179
Lester, David, **42**, 86, **108-09**, 182, **186**
Leuchter, Ben, 19
Leuchter, Magda, 15, 17, 19
Levine, Marshall, 109
Lewis, Jeanne, 51, **72-73**, **186**
Liberal arts and Liberal Studies (LIBA), 5, 6, 26, 29, 93, 98, 129
Library, 24, 54, 63, 160
Licensed Practical Nursing, 152
Life Center, Philadelphia, 99
Life Sports, 26, 66-68
Literature (LITT), 119, 120, 122-23
Lloyd D. Levenson Institute of Gaming, Hospitality and Tourism, 82, 164
Lopatto, Claire, 61
Lowenstein, Marc, 76, 105, 130, 148, **149-51**, 155, **162**, **186**
Lubenow, William, 18, 51, 80, **83-84**, **186**
Lyons, Paul, 1, 70-71, 95, 96, 169, 171, 182, 183

M
Makepeace Lake, 135
Mall, Joy, 153
Mallory, David, 177
Management Sciences, Division of, 27, 28, 80, 148, 149
Marcus, Larry, 78
Margarita, Mona, 76
Marine Sciences (MARS), 37-38, 40, 88, 106-07, 138, 145; Marine Science Club, 140
Marino, Alex, 125, 163
Marino, Anthony, 64
Marsh, Elizabeth, 26, 135, 136
Marsh, Margaret, 74, 168, 170
Martin, Heather, 1
Martin, Ted, 152
Master of Science in Computational Science, 106
Master Plan, 160
Mathematics (MATH), 37, 40, 70, 106, 116, 126
Mathematics and Science Partnership, 176
Mattlage, Alan, 178
Mayflower Hotel (and faculty), vii, 1, 5-6, 15-16, 18, 24, 30-31, 37-38, 42, 44-45, 47-48, 51, 66, 72, 77, 107, 112, 149, 161, 172, 183
McCabe, Kim, 183
McCarthy, James, 111, **126-28**, **186**
McGahn, Joseph, 168
McGarvey, Michael, **64**, **167**, 182, **186**
McGreevey, James, 177
McIntire, Carl, 16, 81-82
McMahon, Dan, 49
McMahon, Joe, 179
Mench, Fred, **16**, 58, 74, 88
Mercado, Peter, 78
Mercer, Jean, 169, 183
Messina, Dominick, 180
Messina, Nancy, 51, **74-75**, 180, 183, **186**
Messina, Sarah, **180**
Methods of Inquiry (META), 26, 86-87, 95
Mickey Finn Room (Mayflower Hotel), 49
Middle States Association, 56, 162, 163; Report, 1990, 60
Mikulak, Maxim "Mic", 106
Miley, William, 109
Miller, Glenn, 183
Miller, Marty, 18, 51, 67-68
Millikin University, 28-29, 91
Minority Recruitment Committee (1972), 79
Mitchell, Peter, 51-54, 58-59, 70, 148, 152, 183
Modern Languages Association (MLA), 91
Moll, Joy, 170
Monacelli, Katie, 179
Monday Club, 99

Moss, Ronald, 86, **104-05**, **186**
Moury, Dan, 15, **25-27**, 28-29, **35-42**, 106, 135, **186**
Mueller, Ray, 136, 145

N
Nacote Creek, 97, 107
Nader, Ralph, 135
Nanzetta, Phil, 120
Natale, Naomi, 124
National Academic Advising Association (NACADA), 129
National Association of Colleges for Teacher Education (NACTE), 104
National Association of Social Work (NASW), 178
National Collegiate Athletics Association (NCAA), 51, 55, 67-69
National Defense Act, 87
National Endowment for the Humanities (NEH), 120, 176
National Institute of Sciences (NIS), 78
National Science Foundation (NSF), 95, 117, 171, 170, 175
National Survey of Student Engagement (NSSE), 114
Natural Resource Conservation Service/District, 137, 146
Natural Sciences and Mathematics (NAMS), 15, 26, 28, 35-42, 71, 106-07, 126, 135, 138-39, 150, 168-70
Naughton, Neil, 103
Nelson, Linda Williamson, 105, 111, **124-25**, **186**
Nelson Denny Reading Comprehension Test, 120
Nettles, Bill, 77
New Jersey Association of Colleges of Teacher Education (NJACTE), 104
New Jersey Athletics Conference (NJAC), 63
New Jersey Baccalaureate Social Work Education Association, 178
New Jersey Board of Nursing, 153
New Jersey Commission on Higher Education, 156
New Jersey Conservation Foundation, 136
New Jersey Department of Education (NJDOE), 175-76
New Jersey Department of Teacher Education, 101
New Jersey Department of Transportation, 33
New Jersey Educational Association (NJEA), 57, 63
New Jersey Historical Commission, 125
New Jersey Public Interest Research Group, 140
New Jersey's Green College, 138, 144
New Jersey Statewide Systemic Initiative (NJSSI), 175
New Jersey Teacher Education Regulations and Standards, 104
New Jersey Wetlands Commission, 34
New Media Studies, 123
New York Review of Books, 67
New York Times, 173
Nietzsche, Friedrich, 101
No Child Left Behind, 123
Noyes Museum of Art, 161, 164
Nursing, 56, 100, 149, 152, 153, 155, 156, 163
Nutt, Larry, 108

O
Oberlin College, 67
Ocean County College, 137
Occupational Therapy, 156
Office of Children's Services (OCS), 178
Offices, 8, 76
Ogden, Kate, **125**, 180
Ogden, Warren, 171, 182
Oldis, David, 177
Olsen, Beth, 113, 125, 159, 161, 163, **168-71**, **186**
Olsen, Lance, 171, 182
"One Million Bones", 125
Open Houses, 132
Oral History of Stockton College, 88
Occupational Safety & Health Administration (OSHA), 38, 107
Oswego River, 135

P
Papademetriou, Anastasios, 115
Parker, Robert, 120
Pennsylvania State University, 130
Penrose Research Laboratory, 152
Perez, Madeline, 183
Performing Arts Center (PAC), 33, 74, 75, 159, 161, 163, 172
The Perpetual Dream, 1, 87, 96
Personnel Process (see also; faculty), 161-63
Pesqueira, Richard, 15, **43-44**, **186**
PHA Contractors, 33
Phelps, Stephen, 119
Philadelphia sports teams, 70
Philadelphia Zoological Gardens, 152
Philosophy (PHIL), 86
Philosophy of Science, 91
Physical Plant, 138
Physical Therapy, 150, 153, 156; DPT, 150, 155, 157, 163; MPT, 155, 157
Physics (PHYS), 37, 40, 107, 170

Pine Barrens, 135-36
Pinelands Commission, 135-37, 145
Pinto, David, 171, 182
Pitney Tavern, 82, 109
Plage, Peter, 135
Plank, Don, 70, 71, 106, 120
Plant Management, 135, 145
Pleasantville, 29
Pokras, Mark, 106
Pokras, Martha, 106
Police, 15, 45-46
Political Science (POLS), 99, 108, 112, 136, 141, 183
Polsinelli, Phil, 125
Pomeroy, Anne, 171, 182
Pomona & Pomona campus, 14, 15, 18, 30-34, 49, 77, 82, 158, 175
Posner, Israel, 109, **186**
Port Republic, 34, 141
Potter, George, 1
Power Purchase Agreements (PPAs), 141-42
Powers of Mind, 100
Preceptorial advising, 6, 11, 18, 29, 31, 48, 58, 74, 76, 93, 105, 112, 129-30
President, Office of, 140, 141
Princeton, 21, 44
Princeton University, 23, 33, 67
Procedure 6136, 63
Professional Studies, Division of (PROS), 26, 108, 120, 126, 148, 149-51, 154, 163, 169
Professional Science Master's in Environmental Science (PSM), 106, 137, 156, 163
Project SafetyNet, 170
Psychology (PSYC), 40, 93, 106, 108-09; Psychology Club, 109; Psi Chi (Honors Society), 109
Public Health (PUBH), 136, 152, 153
Public Safety and Security, 45-46

Q
Quantitative Reasoning Across the Disciplines (QUAD), vii, 10, 95, 111, 116-118, 170, 171
QUAD Summer Institute, 117
Quinn, John, 171

R
Ramapo College, 1, 83, 84, 87, 178
Reagan, Ronald, 70
Regan, Donald, 74
Registrar, Office of, 160
Reid-Merritt, Patricia, **70-71**, 182, **186**
Research and Professional Development (R&PD), 168
Retention, 55
Reynolds, Charles, 23, 33, 119
Richert, John, 108, 168
Rickert, John, 19, 26, 80, 148, 149
Riesman, David, 1, 83, 87, 96
Rittner, Carol, 182
RMJM Hillier (architects), 160
Rogers, Carl, 98
Rokita, John, 145
Rorty, Richard, 83
Rosner, Lisa, 163
Rowan University, 18, 108, 109
Rubenstein, Joe, **34**, 51, 65, **66-68**, 161, **186**
Rutgers University, 16, 104, 120, 178
Rutgers University—Camden, 49

S
Saatkamp, Herman J., Jr., 1, 2, 3, 79, 155, 159, 160-61, 162, 170, 183
Sabbatical Leave, 168
Safe Schools Safe Communities, 176
St. Andrew's Presbyterian College, 37, 107
St. John's College/University, 91
Sanfilippo, Mark, 180
Santayana, George, 2, 160, 161
(SAT) Student Aptitude Test, 109
SAVE, 137, 140
Schneeman, Liane, 168
Schulman, Sharon, 183
Schwartz, Mimi, 120 169
Schwartz, Richard, 15, **33-34**, **186-87**
Scott House, 26, 28, 29
Scott, Jack, 67
Seabrook, N.H., 100
Searight, John, 51, **62-65**, 70, 71, 169, 171, 177-78, **187**
Seaview Hotel, 62, 68, 142, 159, 161, 163
Senate Bill—S434, 16
Sensiba, Gordon William, 86, 88, **98-100**, **187**
Service Learning, 163, 170
Seton Hall University, 53, 178
Sewerage, 34, 135

Sharon, Yitzhak, 88, 170
Shuttle, 141
Simmons, Margaret, 180
Simsen, Charlotte, 103
Sinton, John, 135, 168, 169
Sites, Ed, 174
Situ, Yingyi, 169
Sixties, The, 5-6, 11, 25, 94
Skills, 6, 9-11; Skills Center, 119; Skills Planning Development Committee, 119
Skinner, B.F., 109
Slate, Dennis, 135
Small Business Development Center, 164
Smith, Franklin Ojeda, 51, **77-78**, **187**
Smith, Meghan, 183
Soccer, 51, 69, 74
Social and Behavioral Sciences, Division/School of (SOBL), 8, 26, 28, 70, 71, 98, 109, 112, 120, 126, 138- 39, 168, 169
Social Work (SOCW), 70, 71, 173; MSW, 162
Sociology/Anthropology (SOAN),
Solar energy, 41, 142
Solar Renewable Energy Credits, 142
Solo, Len, 18, 86, **101-03**, **187**
Sosnowski, Cynthia, 171
South Africa, 71, 124
Southern Regional Institute (SRI), 159, 175-76
South Jersey Energy Company, 142
Speech, Pathology and Adiology (SPAD), 152, 153
Sports Center, 56
Stanton, Jacqueline, 108, 109
Staten Island Community College, 96
State University of New York—Old Westbury, 87
Steinbach, Marcia, 170
Steinberg, Alan, 26, 169
Steiner, Lew, 15, **49**, **187**
Sternfeld, Joel, **50**, **187**
Stevenson-Marshall, Brenda, 153
Stiles, Lynn, 169, 170
Stockton Affiliated Services, Inc., 173
Stockton Center for Successful Aging, 109
Stockton Day Camp, 74, 180
Stockton Faculty Band, 181, 182
Stockton Federation of Teachers (SFT), 24, 51, 53, 54, 58, 62-65, 71, 161, 170
Stockton Idea, The, 5-13, 159, 183
Stockton Institute for Gaming Management (SIGMA), 82
Stockton, Richard (naming of the College), 19, 23
Stockton Text Center, 164
Straub, Peter, 145, 169
Strike, 64
Student Aptitude Tests (SATs), 55, 109
Student Affairs, Division of (Student Services), 15, 23, 43-44, 55, 129, 160, 175
Student Evaluations of Teaching (SETs), 112, 115
Student Non-violent Coordinating Committee (SNCC), 98
Student Senate, 59, 170
Study Abroad, 162, 179
Summer Faculty Writing Institute, 97
Summer Research Fund, 170
Summer Tech Academy, 170
Sussex County Colege, 137
Sustainability, 134-46, 162
Sustainability Committee, 140
Sustainability Living Learning Community, 140
Swarthmore College, 153

T
Tantillo, Chuck , 182
Taylor, David, 15, 17, 19, 23, 33
Taylor, Harold, 65, 170
Teacher Development (TDEV), 29, 86, 101-04
Teacher Training, 86
Teaching, 35-36, 111-115
Teaching American History (grant), 176
Tenure quota, 24, 39, 54, 58, 63, 153, 161, 163
Theatre Program (ARTP), 115
Thomas, Mark, 109
Thrombley, Woodworth, 26, 28, 29, 40, 78, 108, 109, 119
Tilley, Dave, 102
Tilley, Wes, 26, 28, 29, 31, 35, 42, 86-89, 91, 93, 108, 120, 122, 123, 182
Tillstrom, Louise, 173, 183
Tolosa, Juan, 176, 178
Tompkins, Kenneth, 1, 5, 15, **16-21**, 19, 26, **28-29**, **42**, 67, **80**, 86-89, **90-93**, 94, 97, 103, 108, 120, 122, 123, 128, 180, 182, **187**
Tosh, Joseph, 15, **47-48**, **187**
Townsend Residential Life Center, 55
Trail, Mary Ann, 161
Transfers, 131-32; Transfer seminars, 161; Summer Transfer Orientation, 132
Trenton, 30-33, 39, 101

Trenton State College of NJ (see also, TCNJ), 17
Trow, Robert, 153
Trustees, Board of, 1, 19, 20, 25, 30, 33, 44, 51, 57, 59, 63, 64, 68, 78, 79, 97, 135, 156, 168, 171, 173, 176
Tumas, Deanna, 183
Tutorials, 63

U
Ueno, Hannah, **147**, 171, **187**
Underground Thermal Energy Storage (UTES), 169
Understanding 9/11 (course), 95
Unified Sciences Center, 141, 160
Union County College, 137
Unions (see also, AFT, SFT), 51, 62, 78, 159, 161
University of California, Los Angeles, 43
University of California, Riverside, 43
University of California, Santa Cruz, 87
University of Massachusetts, 101
University of Michigan, 152
University of Pennsylvania, 152
Urban Studies, 83, 86
US Corps for National and Community Service, 170
US Department of Energy, 170
US Forest Service, 137
US Geological Survey, 137
US Green Building Council (USGBC), 143

V
van Kuiken, Henry, 94, 159
Vaughn, Beverly, 159, 174, 180
Vassar, Darilyn, 78
Veterans, 38, 44, 49
Vietnam War, 5, 25, 28, 49, 68, 70, 83
Vineland, 19
Vineland Hospital Board, 19
Vineland Times Journal
Visual Arts (ARTV), BFA, 162
Vito, Marilyn, 161, 171

W
Walsh, Joseph, 86, **87-89**, 169, **187**
Ward, B. J., 159, **165-66**, 187
War on Poverty, The, 6
Washington, George, 22
Washington, D.C., 100
Water Watch, 140
Wayman, Lina, 180
Weber, Max, 68, 95
Weeks, Patricia, 159, 171, **175-76**
Werner, Ralph, **107**
Wessler, Betty, 152
West Quad Building, 153
White, Theodore, 83
White, Wendel, **110**, 125, 128, 171, **174**, 180, 182, 183, **187**
Whitman, Christine Todd, 150, 175
Wildfogel, Dennis, 175
William J. Hughes Center for Public Policy, 164
Williams, Claudia, 78
Williams, Faheen, 177
Williams, James, 15, **45-46**, **187**
Williams Plaza, 29, 30, 31, 43
Wimberg, Florence, 152
Wind energy, 41, 141, 142
Wind Turbine Feasibility Study, 142
Wirth, Thomas, 63, 64
Witherspoon, John, 21
Wollock, Len, 120
Women's and Gender and Sexuality Studies, 54, 76; Minor, 111, 124
Women's Liberation, 70
Wood, Roger, 86, 88, **106-07**, 145, 168, **187**
Woody, Alma, 152
WLFR, 49
Writing (writing across the curriculum), vii, 10, 95, 97, 105, 117, 119-21; Writing Minor, 121
Wu, Chai-Lin, 118

Y
Yale University, viii
Yung, Shao, 168

Z
Zechman, Martha, 183
Zennario, Susan, 183
Zimmermann, George, 135, 136, 145